S0-ARO-833

FLUCTUATING
FORTUNES

The Political Power of
Business in America

FLUCTUATING FORTUNES

The Political Power of
Business in America

DAVID VOGEL

BEARDBOOKS
WASHINGTON, DC

Original copyright © 1989 by Basic Books, assigned to
David Vogel, July 13, 1995.

Reprinted 2003 by Beard Books, Washington D.C.

Printed in the United States of America

Library of Congress Cataloging-in-Publication Data

Vogel, David, 1947-
    Fluctuating fortunes: the political power of business in America / David Vogel.
        p.cm.
    Originally published: New York: Basic Books, c1989.
    Includes bibliographical references and index.
    ISBN 1-58798-169-6
        1.Business and politics—United States. 2.United States—Politics and government.
    I.Title.

    JK467.V64 2003
    322'.3'0973—dc21

An earlier version of chapter 9 was originally published in
Business in the Contemporary World 1, No. 1 (Fall 1988).
Reprinted with permission.

For my family,

Virginia, Philip, and Barbara

Contents

Preface

While there is an extensive literature on the politics of business-government relations during both the Progressive Era and the New Deal, there does not yet appear to be a history of the equally significant changes in the relationship between business and government in the United States that have taken place since 1960. This book may represent the first comprehensive effort to provide such an account.

Various aspects of this topic have been covered in other works, which I have drawn upon. Both Michael Pertschuk's *Revolt Against Regulation: The Rise and Pause of the Consumer Movement* and Charles Noble's *Liberalism at Work: The Rise and Fall of OSHA*, as their subtitles indicate, trace changes in the relative political influence of business over the last quarter-century, but each focuses on only one policy area. *The New Politics of Inequality*, by Thomas Edsell, and *Right Turn: The Decline of the Democrats and the Future of American Politics*, by Thomas Ferguson and Joel Rogers, provide a comprehensive discussion of the resurgence of business power since the mid-1970s, but they do not explain how or why it declined in the first place.

All four of these books have a political agenda as well as an intellectual one: their authors consider it unfortunate that the political influence of business has increased, and look forward to its subsequent decline. My book does have an intellectual agenda: I am interested in presenting a new way of thinking about the political power of business. It does not, however, have a political one. I make no judgment about how much political power business ought to have; rather, I am interested in describing and explaining the amount of power it does have. I have tried to make both my narrative and my analysis as objective as possible. Whether or not I have succeeded I leave for the reader to judge.

I have been interested in the changing dynamics of business-government relations in the United States for more than fifteen years. Sections of this book draw upon some of my previous writings on this topic, including "The New Political Science of Corporate Power," published in *The Public Interest*, Spring 1987; "The Political Impact of the Large Corporation: A Legislative History of Federal Clean Air Policy, 1963–1981," which appeared in *The Impact of the Modern Corporation,* edited by Betty Bock, Harvey Goldschmid, Ira Millstein, and F. M. Scherer (New York: Columbia University Press, 1984); "The Power of Business in America: A Re-Appraisal," published in the *British Journal of Political Science,* January 1983; "The Public Interest Movement and the American Reform Tradition," which appeared in the *Political Science Quarterly,* Winter 1980–81; and *Ethics and Profits* (with Leonard Silk), published by Simon and Schuster in 1976.

Authorship is a collegial undertaking. A number of my colleagues have generously put aside their own work to assist me with mine. Their extensive comments and criticisms of earlier versions of the manuscript have significantly improved the quality of the finished product. I am pleased to acknowledge the contributions of Richard Abrams of the University of California at Berkeley's Department of History, Jeffrey Berry of the Department of Political Science at Tufts University, Earl Cheit of the Berkeley Business School, Meinolf Dierkes of the Science Center in Berlin, Martin Shefter of the Department of Government at Cornell University, Dow Votaw of the Berkeley Business School, Barry Weingast of the Hoover Institution, and Aaron Wildavsky of the University of California at Berkeley's Political Science Department. My editor at Basic Books, Martin Kessler, also made a number of extremely helpful suggestions.

I also want to acknowledge another kind of debt to my colleagues in the Business and Public Policy (BPP) Group at the Berkeley Business School. Established more than two decades ago, the BPP Group represents one of the few academic settings where scholars from a variety of disciplines focus their research and teaching on the changing political, social, and legal environment of business. I am pleased to be able to work in such a supportive and intellectually stimulating environment.

The endless inputting and re-inputting of my illegible handwriting and even more indecipherable typing was competently and cheerfully handled in the Center for Research in Management by Patricia Murphy and Josef Chytry under the able supervision of Rota Ince. Sections of the book were also typed by Marcie McGaugh and Serena Joe. The entire manuscript was carefully edited by Timothy Kessler.

Grants from the Program in Business and Public Policy, the Institute for Governmental Studies, and the Committee on Faculty Research, all associated with the University of California at Berkeley, provided funds for typing and research assistance. The latter task was efficiently discharged by Anthony Daley, now on the faculty of the Department of Political Science at Wesleyan University, and Timothy Kessler, an undergraduate political science student at Berkeley. I am deeply indebted to both of them as well as to Karen Schnietz, a doctoral student in Business and Public Policy who helped track down a number of missing footnotes.

As always, my greatest debt is to my wife and best friend, Virginia, whose love and faith sustained me during the time it took to complete this project.

June 1988
Berkeley, California

Fluctuating Fortunes

I

Introduction:
The Power of Business

Introduction

How politically powerful is American business?

Few questions have been the subject of as much political debate and conflict in the United States over the last century. Prior to the Civil War, few Americans worried about the power of business. Firms were relatively small and whatever economic or political power their owners wielded tended to be strictly local. But the emergence of the large, national, industrial corporation during the latter part of the nineteenth century transformed the position of business in American society. Industrial capitalism created potential tension between the nation's central economic institutions and its democratic heritage. This tension has become a recurrent feature of American political life. In America, "money becomes evil not when it is used to buy goods but when it is used to buy power . . . economic inequalities become evil when they are translated into political inequalities."[1]

From the 1880s through the beginning of the First World War, debate over the power of the trusts dominated American national politics. In a book provocatively entitled *Wealth Against Commonwealth,* published in 1894, Henry Demarest Lloyd argued that "liberty produces wealth, and that wealth destroys liberty." Lloyd's history of Standard Oil demonstrated how "government was being used as an active partner by the great business interests."[2] His position was echoed by the Populists, who characterized American politics as "a struggle between the robbers and the robbed."[3] A widely circulated Populist manifesto declared:

> There are but two sides in the conflict that is beginning to be waged in this country today. On one side are the allied hosts of monopolies, the money power, great trusts and railroad corporations, who seek the enactment of laws to benefit them and impoverish the people. On the other are the . . . people who produce wealth and bear the burdens of taxation.[4]

Similarly, the Progressives were "haunted by the specter of a private power far greater than the public power of the state."[5]

While the "dollar decade" of the 1920s temporarily put to rest the nation's fears of the power of business, they were revived by the Great Depression.[6] President Franklin D. Roosevelt, campaigning for reelection in 1936, warned his supporters at a Madison Square Garden rally that "business and financial monopoly, speculation, reckless banking and class antagonism" were seeking to regain their influence, adding that "we now know that Government by organized money is just as dangerous as Government by organized mob." Roosevelt concluded: "I should like to have it said of my first Administration that in it the forces of selfishness and of lust for power met their match. I should like to have it said of my second Administration that in it these forces meet their master."[7]

Since the 1930s, public discussions of business power have lacked the political intensity and moral fervor of the preceding half-century. Unlike the Populists and the Progressives, we no longer view "big business" as a "mysterious mutation, the consequence of some evil tampering with the natural order of things."[8] And, in contrast to the 1930s, we have not confronted the challenge of having to reconstruct the American economic and financial system following its collapse. Nevertheless, criticism of the political power of business has persisted. Those who contend that American democracy is flawed invariably focus on the disproportionate political power enjoyed by "big business." Thus, Charles Lindblom concludes *Politics and Markets,* one of the most influential studies of business-government relations to be published during the last quarter-century, with the statement: "The large private corporation fits oddly into democratic theory and vision. Indeed, it does not fit."[9]

During the 1980s, largely as a result of Ronald Reagan's election to the presidency, the power of business in American politics became subject to increased scrutiny. A number of political commentators, including Thomas Edsell, Michael Pertschuk, Thomas Ferguson, and Joel Rogers, argued that the administration's probusiness policies did not reflect a more conservative or pro-business outlook on the part of the American electorate.[10] Rather, they revealed the vulnerability of the American political system to a highly organized and well-financed campaign by the nation's corporate elite to increase its economic and political power.

The question of how much political power is exercised by business has also been a recurrent source of controversy among scholars. The views of political scientists have fallen into roughly two categories. Pluralists view business primarily as an interest group, actively competing with other organized groups to define the political agenda and influence governmental decisions. In the political marketplace, business does not enjoy any advantages that cannot be matched by other interest groups. Their critics counter that business is not just another interest group but is a kind of private government that enjoys a privileged position in American politics. Its ability to control the terms of public debate and its superior access to government officials is seen as overshadowing that of any other political constituency, thus making a mockery of the principles of interest-group democracy.

The study of American politics was dominated by pluralists from the early 1940s through the late 1960s. The most influential studies of American politics—such as David Truman's *The Governmental Process,* published in 1951, V. O. Key's *Politics, Parties and Pressure Groups,* which went through five editions and more than twenty-five printings between 1942 and 1964, and Robert Dahl's *Who Governs?* published in 1961—argued that the American political system was both fluid and accessible.[11] No single interest group, including business, was able to dominate it. Over the last two decades, however, this pluralist interpretation of American politics has been increasingly challenged.[12] In fact, two of the discipline's most prominent pluralists—Yale political scientists Robert Dahl and Charles Lindblom— have publicly repudiated their earlier position. In 1976 they wrote that: "Businessmen play a distinctive role in polyarchal politics that is . . . much more powerful than an interest group role. . . . [C]ommon interpretations that depict the American or any other market-oriented system as a competition among interest groups are seriously in error for their failure to take account of the distinctive privileged position of businessmen in politics."[13]

In *Politics and Markets,* Lindblom argued that the probusiness slant of public policy is not merely the result of business's superior economic and political resources; rather, corporate leaders enjoy a privileged position in a capitalist system because of their unique relationship to the public welfare. As a result, "In the eyes of the government officials, businessmen do not appear simply as representatives of a special interest, as representatives of interest groups do, they appear as functionaries performing functions that government officials regard as indispensable." Lindblom argues that his analysis of corporate power requires "no conspiracy theory of politics, no theory of common social origins uniting government and business officials, no crude allegation of a power elite established by clandestine forces." Rather, politicians simply understand "that to make the system work, government leadership must often defer to business leadership."[14] As a result, "pluralism at most operates only in an imprisoned zone of policy making."[15]

Lindblom's position has in turn been widely criticized.[16] In a review published in the *Wall Street Journal,* James Q. Wilson stated that *"Politics and Markets* reads like a burlesque of the actual political position of business,"[17] and Irving Kristol contended that it was not large companies whose position in American politics was privileged but rather that of their opponents and critics. Kristol attributed the increase in government controls over business during the 1970s to the ability of a "new class" of middle-class professionals to impose their antibusiness values on both business and ordinary Americans.[18]

The Importance of Time

The purpose of this book is not to continue the debate between those who argue that the political position of business is privileged and those who assert that it is not. It is rather to move us beyond it. I offer a new way of looking at the political power of business in contemporary American politics. My central argument is that both perspectives are flawed because they mistakenly assume that the power of business is relatively stable. The pluralists contend that the political power of business is usually countervailed by other interest groups, while the critics of pluralism assert that it rarely is. Both contentions are incomplete. The political power of business can and does vary. Furthermore, these variations follow a discernible pattern, which can in turn be explained.

The power of business in American national politics has changed substantially since 1960. The political position of business was relatively secure during the first half of the 1960s, declined significantly between the mid-1960s and mid-1970s, increased between the mid-1970s and early 1980s, and has since slightly eroded. These changes are not unprecedented: the political power of significant segments of American business also declined during both the Progressive Era and the New Deal. This book describes and explains the third major set of fluctuations in the political fortunes of business since the turn of the century.

There is no need to choose between the depictions of business power offered by the pluralists and their critics. The accuracy of each perspective depends on the period in which one is interested. In a number of respects, the political position of business in America could be accurately characterized as "privileged" during the 1950s and through the first half of the 1960s. Few issues appeared on the political agenda that threatened business prerogatives, and business exercised virtual power over the resolution of those few issues that did. Correspondingly, American politics between the mid-1960s and mid-1970s more closely resembled the pluralists' description of interest-group competition. The power of business was challenged by both the public-interest movement and organized labor, while public confidence in business dropped dramatically; between 1968 and 1977, the percentage of Americans who believed that "business tries to strike a fair balance between profits and the interests of the public declined from 70 percent to 15 percent.[19]

The pluralists had the misfortune to publish their most important work a decade or two too soon. They failed to appreciate the extent to which the "mobilization of bias" of the 1950s and 1960s limited the number of interests that enjoyed political representation.[20] Ironically, just as American politics was in fact becoming more pluralist, the influence of pluralists began to decline. By 1977, when *Politics and Markets* was published, business had been on the political and intellectual defensive for more than a decade; indeed, the years immediately prior to the publication of Lindblom's book mark the nadir of business political influence in the postwar period. On the other hand, Lindblom's analysis does help us understand the resurgence of business power that took place in the years following his book's appearance.

It is possible to interpret the ten-year period during which business found itself on the political and ideological defensive as a brief interlude in a political system normally characterized by business dominance. Similarly, the relative resurgence of the influence of business during the next fifteen years, rather than representing a return to the status quo, could instead be viewed as a temporary phenomenon—one shortly to be followed by a backlash from nonbusiness constituencies. My position is that neither period constitutes the norm. While it is true that during this century the years when business has been relatively powerful have been more numerous than those when it has not, it does not necessarily follow that the former state of affairs is the normal one. Rather, as in the case of the business cycle, each "phase" is temporary. Which state of affairs is prefera-ble I leave to the readers' judgment.

Political Power and Economic Conditions

Because both the pluralists and their critics tend to ignore the extent to which the political influence of business changes over time, they have also overlooked the relationship between political developments and changing economic conditions. In neither *Who Governs?* nor *Politics and Markets* is the political significance of changes in growth rates or the position of the United States in the global economy discussed. These omissions are crucial. The political influence of business has been significantly affected by the long-term performance of the American economy. Over the last three decades, the two have been inversely related. Paradoxically, business has tended to lose political influence when the economy was performing rela-tively well and has become more influential when the performance of the economy deteriorated.

The relative political power of business is *not* a function of the business cycle. Otherwise, the political power of business would be more unstable than it actually has been. Rather, what *is* critical is the public's perception of the long-term strength of the American economy. The unprecedented increases in both government regulation of corporate social performance and in social-welfare expenditures from the mid-1960s through the early 1970s was made possible by the equally unprecedented economic growth rates of the 1960s. The economy grew at an average rate of 4.5 percent between 1961 and 1968, and between 1965 and 1969 the after-tax rate of return of nonfinancial corporations averaged 9 percent—its highest level since the Second World War. As a result, significant segments of the American middle class began to take both their own prosperity and the success of business for granted. They believed that business could afford to rebuild the inner cities, hire the chronically unemployed, make safer products, clean up air and water pollution, provide all Americans with a healthy and safe working environment and, at the same time, still further improve their own living standards. Politicians from both parties competed with each other to propose policies based on this assumption.

However, during the second half of the 1970s, the American public's perception of the American economy and the continued profitability of the business corporation began to change. The recession of 1974–75 was not simply another downturn in the business cycle. It marked a major discontinuity in the postwar development of American capitalism: rates of economic growth, investment, growth in productivity, and growth in wages and family incomes were all significantly lower in the decade after 1973 than they had been during the preceding one. Between 1975 and 1978, corporate profit rates averaged 5.9 percent, their lowest level since the Second World War. Persistent double-digit inflation, declining real wages and stagnant family income, increased dependence on imported oil, and a dramatic growth in imports in highly visible sectors of the American economy all made the American business corporation, and consequently America itself, suddenly appear economically vulnerable. General Motors, the epitome of arrogant and omnipotent big business during the 1960s, now found itself pleading for government to protect it from Japanese imports; Chrysler, the nation's ninth largest corporation, was on the verge of bankruptcy.

Consequently, the political and social climate became transformed. College students in elite universities, who during the second half of the 1960s were so reluctant to go to work for large companies that business executives publicly worried about the long-term survival of the business system, began to enroll in business schools in record numbers. "Baby boomers," who had played a critical role in organizing and supporting the public-interest movement during the first half of the 1970s, discovered "bracket creep" and became preoccupied with finding well-paying jobs in the private sector or in starting their own companies. The "new class" of college-educated professionals, now worried about their own economic prospects, became more sympathetic to the demands of business to reduce taxes, to slow down the growth of government spending and regulation, and to weaken the power of unions. As a result, the political pendulum shifted. The political position of business once again became relatively privileged: the second half of the 1970s and the early 1980s witnessed a substantial increase in the ability of business to define the terms of political debate and affect governmental decisions.

The economy performed relatively well after 1982. And this in part explains why the political influence of business did not continue to increase throughout the decade: the Reagan administration was unable to deliver on its promises to provide business with significant regulatory relief, and corporate taxes were increased in both 1982 and 1986. But both the rate at which new regulations have been imposed on business and the growth in social-welfare expenditures were far less during the 1980s than they were during the 1960s. Politicians from both parties were also more willing to support increased government assistance to industry than they were fifteen years earlier. And these developments in turn can be attributed to the public's continued concern about the apparent ability of American industry to compete successfully in the global economy—particularly vis-à-vis Japanese firms. A poll taken in January 1987 reported that "88 percent of all Americans say that they are concerned that this country is losing its competitive edge and cannot remain the world's preeminent economic power."[21] The globalization of the American economy may have created severe economic difficulties for substantial segments of American business, but politically it has been something of a boon.

Business and the Political System

Both pluralists and their critics have also paid insufficient attention to the relationship between the political influence and strategies of business and the changing structure of American politics. Between the mid-1960s and mid-1970s, the American political system changed substantially. One reason why business suffered so many political defeats during this period is that business lobbyists failed to appreciate the extent to which public policy was no longer being made in private negotiations between Washington insiders and a handful of strategically placed representatives and senators. Power within Congress had become more decentralized, the number of interest groups represented in Washington had increased, the role of the media in defining the political agenda and the terms of political debate had expanded, the importance of political parties had declined, and the courts had begun to play a much more active role in making regulatory policy. In a remarkably short period of time, consumer and environmental organizations were able to take advantage of these changes to move from a peripheral position in American politics to become active and effective participants in the making of public policies in the nation's capital.

It took business about seven years to rediscover how to win in Washington. Significantly, when business did become more politically active, it did so in ways that recognized how fundamentally the American political system had changed: it proceeded to imitate the political strategies that had previously been responsible for so many of its defeats. The sponsorship of research studies to influence elite opinion, the attention to the media as a way of changing public attitudes, the development of techniques of grass-roots organizing to mobilize supporters in congressional districts, and the use of ad hoc coalitions to maximize political influence had all been successfully employed, and in some cases even developed, by the public-interest movement. Campaign finance reform, by legalizing the formation of political action committees (PACs), opened another path for business participation in politics. Just as the decentralization of power within Congress during the second half of the 1960s and early 1970s helped reduce the political influence of business, the dramatic growth of business PACs during the second half of the 1970s helped increase it.

In contrast to both the Progressive Era and the New Deal, the role played by the presidency in changes in the relative political power of business since 1960 have been relatively modest. Theodore Roosevelt and Woodrow Wilson were key figures during the Progressive Era, and the New Deal was defined by Franklin Roosevelt. By contrast, Congress has played a much more crucial role in shaping public policies toward business over the last quarter-century. Presidents Kennedy, Johnson, and Nixon only marginally influenced the increases in government regulation that took place during their administrations; most were initiated by Congress. Presidents Ford and Carter were both more interested in domestic economic and regulatory policies, but their impact on the legislative process was relatively modest because neither was able to work effectively with Congress. Ironically, the most dramatic increases in the scope of government regulation over corporate social conduct took place during the presidency of Richard Nixon, and the resurgence of the political power of business actually began during the Carter administration. President Reagan had a more substantial impact on public policies toward business, but the political pendulum had begun to shift in business's favor before he took office.

The relative political influence of business has been only marginally affected by the relative strengths of the Democratic and Republican parties in Congress. It is true that with the exception of a brief period during the middle of the 1960s, large corporations have identified their interests more closely with the Republican than the Democratic party. But while Democrats in Congress have been consistently more supportive of government regulation of business than have Republicans, only issues involving labor-management relations have been fought primarily along partisan lines. The partisan composition of Congress hardly changed at all between 1968 and 1974 or between 1976 and 1980. And yet the former period witnessed a dramatic decline in the political effectiveness of business and, after 1976, the political influence of business increased substantially. The changing political fortunes of business have had less to do with changes in the relative electoral strengths of the two parties than with shifts in the priorities and preferences of Democratic senators and representatives.

My Approach

Most studies of the political power of business have tended to identify "business" with large corporations, or, more specifically, the Fortune 500. This reflects in part the nation's Populist heritage as well as the tendency of Americans to equate the size of firms with their political influence. However, an exclusive focus on large firms leads to a very distorted understanding of the dynamics of business activity and influence. Large corporations did become much more politically active during the 1970s. But among the most significant political developments of the last two decades has been the dramatic increase in the political activity of smaller companies. There are approximately fifteen million businesses in the United States and nearly a quarter have joined some kind of business, professional, or trade association. Businesspeople and their families constitute a significant part of the American electorate. Owners of small businesses frequently enjoy better access to their representatives and senators than do lobbyists for larger companies, and have often been more influential. Many of the business community's most important political successes after 1976 were made possible by the fact that many small companies chose to cooperate with organizations such as the Business Roundtable, which represent only large companies.

The interests of business are not monolithic: firms can use politics either to compete with each other or advance their collective interests. Among the most important factors affecting the relative political influence of business since the early 1960s has been the extent to which firms of different sizes and in different industries have been able to work together politically. When business has been unified, its political power has often been extremely impressive. But the degree of business unity also varies over time. With the exception of a relatively brief period between 1977 and 1981, business tended to function as a "community" in name only. Particularly during the 1980s, American business lacked effective leadership. And this, in turn, enabled both politicians and nonbusiness constituencies to play off different segments of business against each other.

This book assumes that it is legitimate to generalize about the political fortunes of business. Admittedly, just as the profit rates of all firms or industries are not affected equally by variations in the business cycle, the political influence of all firms does not vary uniformly. At any given time, some firms or industries have more influence over the decisions of government than others. Nevertheless, the efforts of particular industries and firms to achieve their political objectives do not take place in isolation; they are affected by and in turn affect changes in the relative political influence of other segments of the business community. Thus, the passage of the National Traffic and Motor Vehicle Safety Act in 1966 was not simply a political defeat for the automobile industry: by revealing the political ineptness and the vulnerability of the nation's largest industrial corporation, as well as the political popularity of consumerism, it opened the floodgates for the enactment of scores of additional regulatory statutes over the next decade. Similarly, the defeat of legislation legalizing common situs picketing by the House of Representatives in 1977 was not simply an unexpected political victory for the construction industry and a demoralizing defeat for the building-trade unions: by exposing the political vulnerability of organized labor and the responsiveness of a Congress dominated by liberal Democrats to intensive and sophisticated business lobbying, it encouraged business to become much more politically aggressive.

Momentum is important in politics. Many of the business community's most important political setbacks and gains over the last two decades have come in waves. From 1969 through 1972, Congress enacted the most progressive tax bill in the postwar period, reduced the oil-depletion allowance, imposed price controls on oil, transferred the primary authority for the regulation of both pollution and occupational health and safety from the states to the federal government, established the Consumer Product Safety Commission, and banned the advertising of cigarettes from radio and television. In a comparable span of four years—1978 through 1981—Congress defeated labor-law reform, voted against the establishment of a Consumer Protection Agency, restricted the power of the Federal Trade Commission, deregulated oil prices, delayed the imposition of automobile-emission standards, reduced price controls on natural gas, and enacted two tax bills, the first of which primarily benefited the wealthy and a second which reduced corporate taxes to their lowest level since the Second World War.

It is also characteristic of periods when business finds itself on the defensive that an unusually large proportion of public policies affects relatively large segments of the business community, though not necessarily in an identical manner. Among the most distinctive features of the regulatory statutes enacted during the first half of the 1970s was precisely that they were not directed toward specific industries. Rather, they sought to change the behavior of companies in a wide variety of different industries. This made many business executives much more conscious of their common or class interests, which in turn led to both the formation and revival of political organizations that represented firms in many different industries, such as the Business Roundtable, the United States

Chamber of Commerce, and the National Federation of Independent Business.

The history of government intervention is also replete with examples of industry's inability to recognize its self-interest. It is now clear that the business community seriously underestimated the economic consequences of both the Occupational Safety and Health Act and the National Environmental Policy Act. And, in retrospect, the enormous resources the energy industry devoted to the phasing out of federal price controls was ill-advised, since the subsequent decline in the price of oil would have made them obsolete in any event. A similar analysis can be made of the political strategies of other interest groups. The Campaign Reform Act of 1971, which was initiated by organized labor, legalized the use of political action committees—which in turn enhanced the ability of business to participate in the electoral process. In addition, many of the regulatory statutes and rules for which public-interest groups fought so strongly have failed to accomplish their objectives. Indeed, some appear to have made the constituencies in whose name they were enacted actually worse off. This, however, does not detract from the political significance of their enactment; it merely suggests that the particular regulatory approaches favored by activists were ill-advised. In short, I am not primarily interested in whether particular policies were really in the best interests of the various political factions that fought for or against them. Rather, I am prepared to accept at face value their own definition of where their self-interest lies— as revealed by their actual efforts to influence the terms of political debate and policy—and to use this as a standard by which to measure their political influence. While the rhetoric of business need not always be taken seriously, the decision of businesses to commit their political resources to support or oppose particular policies should be.

To suggest that the political power of business varies still leaves unanswered an important question. How powerful is business when it is dominant, and how weak is it when it is on the political defensive?

Many students of American politics have argued that the range of political debate about the relationship between industry and government is narrower, and thus more conservative, in the United States than in other capitalist nations. This is not true. The debate over public policies toward business is more biased toward the needs of industry in Japan than in the United States. In recent decades, the political agenda of business-government relations in the United States has been much different than in Western Europe. But it is incorrect to equate "different" with "narrower." The intensity of public debate in the United States over corporate social conduct in areas ranging from the control of toxic substances to equal employment has been far greater in the United States than in Western Europe.[22] Regulations to protect the consumer and the environment in the United States tend to be stricter than in other capitalist nations, and consumer and environmental organizations in the United States have been far more influential than their counterparts in Europe and Japan. The United States was also the only capitalist nation to impose price controls on energy after 1973. The political defeats experienced by American business have not concerned only secondary political issues. Nationalization and worker representation on corporate boards are not a greater challenge to managerial prerogatives than the establishment of the Occupational Safety and Health Administration, significant changes in corporate tax rates, or price controls on energy.

My analysis of contemporary business-government relations is selective rather than exhaustive. I have chosen to trace changes in the relative political influence of business in the United States at the federal level in the last three decades by focusing primarily on four sets of issues: the regulation of corporate social conduct (especially in the areas of health, safety, and the environment), tax policy, labor-management relations, and energy policy. These certainly do not encompass all aspects of business-government relations in the United States. But by any conceivable index, they are extremely important. Public policy in each of these areas changed substantially between the early 1960s and the late 1980s and these policy changes had far-reaching political and economic consequences. In many respects, they were comparable in importance to those that took place during the Progressive Era and the New Deal.

II

The Privileged
Position of Business,
1960 to 1966

John F. Kennedy and Business

Of the four individuals who occupied the White House between 1960 and 1976, only John F. Kennedy had the reputation of being "antibusiness." Yet business fared better politically under his administration than under his three successors, each of whom was far more popular with business. Only one major law opposed by significant segments of the business community was enacted between 1961 and 1963: the 1961 legislation raising the minimum wage from $1 to $1.25 per hour and extending coverage to 3.6 million additional workers. On the other hand, the Food and Drug Amendments of 1962 were significantly weakened as a result of pressure from the pharmaceutical industry, and the tax legislation enacted in October 1962 included virtually none of the reforms originally proposed by the administration. There were a number of highly publicized squabbles between the administration and the business community, the most notable associated with the increase in the price of steel in April 1962. But in marked contrast to his two Democratic predecessors, Franklin Roosevelt and Harry Truman, Kennedy reacted defensively to criticism from business: he continually sought to reassure business executives that he shared their objectives and appreciated their contribution to the nation's well-being.

While most businessmen did not support Kennedy's election in 1960, his victory did not raise any concern within the business community. Indeed, much of the rhetoric of his campaign, particularly his emphasis on the need to accelerate economic growth and increase spending for space exploration and defense, was welcomed by the private sector. Many executives were confident that the narrowness of his victory over Richard Nixon would effectively curb whatever liberal tendencies the president might have. *Business Week* reported the prevailing attitude to be, "Sure, I voted for Nixon, but I don't believe Kennedy's administration can bring us any real harm."[1] The *Wall Street Journal* did express some concern about the liberalism of some of Kennedy's campaign advisers, such as John Kenneth Galbraith and Chester Bowles, but it was reassured by the president's appointments to the Cabinet, which included Republican businessmen Douglas Dillon as secretary of the treasury and Robert McNamara as secretary of defense.

The first conflict between the Kennedy administration and the business community involved the relationship between the federal government and the Business Advisory Council (BAC). The BAC was an organization of 150 senior corporate executives that had been established in 1933 by Franklin Roosevelt as a quasi-official vehicle to enable business to advise and assist government. Shortly after becoming secretary of commerce, Luther Hodges, a former textile manufacturer from North Carolina, moved to redefine the BAC's relationship with his department. He disliked the fact that the membership of the BAC was dominated by representatives of big business and urged an expansion of its membership to include executives from smaller firms. He was also upset by the fact that the BAC's chairman, Ralph Cordiner, was also chairman of the board of General Electric, because shortly before Kennedy took office, a dozen corporate managers, including some from GE, had been sent to prison for violating the Sherman Antitrust Act. According to Hodges, "Privileged discussions of federal policy with such a person as Cordiner . . . was equivalent to electing a murderer county sheriff."[2] Hodges demanded that Cordiner be immediately replaced as the BAC's chairman. He also requested the right to approve all corporate executives tapped for membership in the BAC, as well as control over both the dates and agendas of council meetings. In addition, the secretary proposed that BAC meetings be open to the press. In a series of meetings held with council leaders during the first two months of the Kennedy administration, Hodges threatened to abolish the council unless his demands were met.

Initially, the council responded favorably to most of Hodges's requests. In March, Cordiner resigned and was replaced by Roger Blough, the chief executive officer of U.S. Steel. However, at the council's semi-annual meeting in May 1961, there was considerable tension between the assembled members and the administration. In a conspicuous break with precedent, Hodges was the only administration official to attend: he insisted on paying his own bill and left after forty-eight hours. The meeting itself was dominated by criticism of both the secretary of commerce and the Kennedy administration for attempting to interfere with the BAC's established procedures and customs. The next month, the council's executive committee visited the White House and announced that it planned to sever all official ties with the government. On July 10, the council voted to become independent; its name was changed to the Business Council.

Although he initially supported Hodges's efforts to reform the council, Kennedy then proceeded to undermine his secretary of commerce. Faced with international problems in Berlin, Laos, Vietnam, and Cuba (the abortive Bay of Pigs invasion had taken place in July) as well as an increasing federal deficit and a deterioration in the nation's balance of payments, Kennedy had no desire to antagonize business. The president "feared that the Business Council–Commerce Department divorce might lend credence to the charge that the Democrats were anti-business. Kennedy had enough difficulties without a whispering campaign aimed at him emanating from corporate boardrooms."[3] As a result, the council's fall meeting was attended by a number of senior administration officials. In addition, the administration sent two of its aides on a goodwill tour of corporate America and a series of private meetings was arranged between council members and government officials. In September, at a White House party for forty council members, Special Presidential Assistant McGeorge Bundy stated:

> The whole notion of drawing a line between anything as varied as the business community of the United States, and anything as complex and multifarious in its machinery as the Government of the United States is foolishness. You know that it's foolishness—we know that it's foolishness. . . . It is important that we give up the easy contests between the business interest and the wicked Administration which have been part of our folklore before.[4]

Nevertheless, mistrust between the business community and the Kennedy administration persisted. "By mid-September [1961] there was hardly a Washington business column or tipsheet that was not retailing evidence of Kennedy hostility toward business. It was close to a crisis in confidence." The president responded by attempting to break decisively with "the anti-business attitudes of his Democratic predecessors" and "became the first Democratic President since Woodrow Wilson to launch an ardent campaign to woo business." Members of the administration volunteered to speak at business gatherings throughout the United States and Kennedy himself was the first president since McKinley to address the annual convention of the National Association of Manufacturers. The administration's message was a simple one. In the words of Attorney General Robert Kennedy, "The U.S. must have a strong and rapidly expanding economy to survive and this Administration and any Administration has no choice but to be pro-business."[5]

These initiatives, however, were overshadowed, first by the downturn in the economy in the winter of 1961–62, and second by the administration's confrontation with the steel industry in April 1962. As part of its program to reduce inflation, the administration had strongly encouraged the steel industry not to raise prices in the fall of 1961. It hoped that if prices were kept stable, the United Steel Workers of America would agree to moderate its wage demands when its contract was renegotiated the following spring. When a contract was signed in March 1962 that increased wage costs by only 4.5 percent, the president telephoned his congratulations to both labor and management leaders. A month later, however, Roger Blough visited the White House to inform the president that the United States Steel Corporation was increasing its prices by six dollars a ton. Within twenty-four hours, almost all other steel producers announced similar increases. The stage was thus set for the most dramatic confrontation between business and government since the seizure of the steel mills by President Truman fifteen years earlier.

The president was furious. Blough's decision threatened not only the administration's entire anti-inflation program, but its relationship with organized labor. During a nationally televised press conference the day after Blough's visit, the president stated:

The simultaneous and identical actions of the United States Steel and other leading steel corporations . . . constitute a wholly unjustifiable and irresponsible defiance of the public interest. In this serious hour in our Nation's history . . . the American people will find it hard, as I do, to accept a situation in which a tiny handful of steel executives, whose pursuit of private power exceeds their sense of public responsibility, can show such utter contempt for the interests of 185 million Americans.[6]

The secretary of defense announced that his department would redirect its purchases of steel to those manufacturers that had not raised prices. The Justice Department subpoenaed documents relating to the pricing decision and ordered an immediate grand-jury investigation. A few steel companies declined to follow U.S. Steel's lead, and two days later, on April 12, the nation's largest steel firm announced that its increase would be rescinded. The rest of the industry followed immediately thereafter.

While Kennedy had won, the price of his victory was high: "The administration's swift coercion of the steel firms frightened the business community and severely strained relations between private enterprise and the president." A survey of executives by *Business Week* concluded that "the damage is irreparable."[7] The business community appeared to be particularly upset by Kennedy's use of "media diplomacy"[8] to challenge corporate pricing decisions. As one executive put it, this "brutal exercise" of presidential power was "a pretty hairy, scary performance in a nation which presumably operated a relatively free enterprise system."[9]

Tension between Kennedy and the business community was further exacerbated by rumors that the president had privately described all businessmen as "sons of bitches." Kennedy had in fact been misquoted. His unflattering reference had been confined to "steel men," a point he sought to clarify at a press conference held in early May.[10] However, the original misquotation continued to haunt the administration. Buttons with the letters "S.O.B." began to appear on Wall Street. "Business cards, bumper stickers, and sly jokes combined wit and sarcasm to attack the president, the administration, his advisors, and his family."[11] And to make things still worse, on May 28, 1962, stock prices fell more than on any single day since October 29, 1929.

Although the president's action had received strong public support, he declined to use his triumph to challenge politically the business community. Instead, at a press conference on April 18, 1962, he stated that his administration harbored "no ill will against any individual, industry, corporation, or segment of the American economy,"[12] and pledged that there would be "no public recriminations" now that the industry's "mistake had been retracted."[13] On April 30, the president assured the annual meeting of the United States Chamber of Commerce that his administration was well aware that the federal government depended heavily on business earnings for its revenues.

During the remainder of his administration, Kennedy went out of his way to assure the business community that he indeed both respected and appreciated it. A number of advisory groups were formed to deal with the problems facing certain industries, particularly in the area of trade policy. The administration worked closely with business in designing the Communications Satellite Act, which established a private commercial communications satellite corporation governed by representatives of both business and government, legislation that was criticized by liberals in Congress for being too generous to AT&T. It also cooperated with business to negotiate a wide range of tariff reductions in 1962. In addition, the administration began to rely on the Business Council as a source of both policy suggestions and personnel. In December 1962, sixty active members of the council were invited to the White House for an off-the-record meeting with the president, during which he briefed them on the foreign policy challenges confronting the administration. The highlight of the meeting was a personal exchange of toasts between the president and head of the Business Council, Roger Blough. In April 1963, the president gave his tacit approval to selective increases in the price of steel.

Kennedy's eagerness to cooperate with business became apparent in the course of the negotiations that led to the Revenue Act of 1962. Shortly after assuming office in 1961, the president had proposed a series of tax cuts for business, designed to stimulate capital investment; they were to be accompanied by a series of tax reforms designed to recapture some of the resulting loss in revenue. The president's proposal consisted of two main parts. The first called for a complex sliding scale of investment tax credits intended to benefit specifically those firms which increased their purchases of machinery and equipment. The administration also proposed four tax reforms: business executives would no longer be able to deduct the cost of entertainment from their taxable income; corporations and banks would be required to deduct 20 percent of the interest and dividends they paid out; companies would no longer be able to defer paying taxes on the earnings of their overseas subsidiaries; and the special tax privileges given to income from dividends instituted by the Eisenhower administration would be abolished.

Much to the astonishment of the administration, the business community was divided on the advisability of the proposed investment tax credit. While trade associations representing retailers, wholesalers, and other parts of the service sector supported the president's plan, manufacturers strongly opposed it. They viewed it as too "gimmick-ridden" and indicated their preference for a straightforward, across-the-board acceleration of depreciation allowances. There was, however, little disagreement within the business community on the president's four tax reforms. More than seventy witnesses representing business testified against the proposal to change the tax status of foreign earnings, and the savings and loan industry launched an extensive grass-roots campaign designed to convince Congress that the administration's withholding plan constituted a tax increase that would harm the poor and elderly. Opposition to the proposal to tighten expense account allowances was led by the restaurant industry, but virtually the entire business community opposed this change as well. One executive criticized the administration for its preoccupation "with the Hollywood image of business, complete with champagne, yachts, and luxury suites."[14]

"[W]hen the dust settled eighteen months later, the President had approved a potpourri of tax changes that resembled his original plan about as much as canned fish chowder tastes like Coison's bouillabaisse."[15] Business lobbyists had succeeded in persuading Congress to alter virtually every one of the president's reform proposals, and even the tax reduction plan itself was extensively modified. The tax legislation signed by the president did not include a sliding-scale investment credit; rather it provided a simple tax credit for any new investment, regardless of whether it represented a change from the company's previous practices. (Earlier, by executive order, the president had permitted businesses to deduct larger amounts for the wear and tear on their machinery, a measure originally prompted by the plight of the textile industry, but which resulted in a tax reduction of approximately $1.5 billion for all corporations.) It did limit company gifts and require stricter record keeping, but these changes did little more than curb cheating and particularly lavish spending. The withholding provision was eliminated and the dividend loophole was left open. The 1962 Revenue Act did make the evasion of taxes by corporations that had created paper companies overseas more difficult, but did not change the rules regarding overseas earnings. In sum, the 1962 legislation was a major political triumph for business. Correspondingly, the president's unwillingness to fight for his initial proposal as it was repeatedly changed in Congress disappointed many of his liberal supporters. However, Kennedy had clearly concluded that tax reduction was more important than tax reform.

On June 7, 1962, President Kennedy announced that he would ask Congress for additional tax legislation. On January 24, 1963, in a special message to Congress, he stated: "The largest single barrier to full employment of our manpower and resources and to a higher rate of economic growth is the unrealistically heavy drag of Federal income taxes on private purchasing power, initiative, and incentive." He therefore called for tax cuts of $13.5 billion in the next two years. Shortly after the president's message, a Business and Finance Committee for the reduction of taxes was formed. It quickly grew to include nearly three thousand members, including four hundred major corporations. At hearings held by the Senate Finance Committee, "almost without exception . . . business spokesmen endorsed the tax cut as vital to the nation's economic health."[16] However, once again, the price for business support was the scuttling of virtually all the tax reforms that were a part of the administration's original proposal.

The course of each of these issues—the role of the Business Advisory Council, the steel price rise, and tax policy—had a similar pattern. Each time, the administration initiated a policy change of which many business-people disapproved. Twice, Kennedy backed down relatively quickly: he did everything possible to placate the Business Council in the first instance and, in the second, signed a tax law that embodied virtually none of the reforms he had earlier proposed. The administration did force the steel companies to roll back their price increases, but the president's action was motivated less by a desire to challenge industry than to keep the lid on wages; it was thus directed more against labor than management. More-over, the White House carefully refrained from any further interference in corporate pricing decisions and made no effort to capitalize politically on the unpopularity of the steel industry. Kennedy's second tax proposal was a challenge to orthodox economists in that it mandated major tax reduc-tions during a period when there already was a budget deficit. But if the president had embraced a form of Keynesianism, it was its most conserva-tive variant: the administration specifically chose to stimulate the economy not by increasing spending, as many liberals had advocated, but by reduc-ing taxes. *Fortune* concluded, in February 1963:

> The New Frontiersmen can make out quite a case to support their complaint that business is growling at a helpful hand. No general legislation extending government interference with business has been passed. Some tax relief has already been given to business, and President Kennedy's position on tax reduction, as expressed in his 1963 State of the Union address and elsewhere, can hardly be distinguished from that of spokesmen for the business commu-nity.[17]

Business and the Great Society

The growing sense of rapport between business and the White House that characterized the last year of the Kennedy presidency increased sig-nificantly following Lyndon Johnson's accession to the Oval Office. Writ-ing in *Fortune* magazine on "LBJ's Romance with Business," Harold Meyers noted that, "Certainly no President has worked more energetically to establish a rapport with business, meeting with the Business Council and other management groups, wining and dining businessmen at the White House and dancing with their wives, consulting with businessmen by telephone as well as in person." He added: "No businessman of stature can be certain when he picks up his telephone these days that a voice won't say, 'The President is calling. One moment please.'"[18] A survey of a cross-section of business executives conducted by the *Harvard Business Review* in 1964 reported:

> A large majority of the responding businessmen believe that the influence of business on political affairs in general and on elected officials in particular has *increased* since 1960. In fact, more of today's executives believe that the political influence of business has increased since 1960 than did their counterparts of five years ago in responding to a similar question on the trend in the political influence of business from 1950 to 1959.[19]

While most small-business owners voted for Republican Barry Goldwater for president in 1964, Johnson did receive more support from corporate executives than any other Democratic presidential candidate since the 1930s. David Bazelon concluded that "the greatest political event of 1964 . . . has been the inclusion of a glittering section of the national corporate community within the Democratic Party."[20] The National Independent Committee for President Johnson and Senator Humphrey counted among its members a considerable portion of the nation's corporate elite, including Henry Ford II, a number of New York investment bankers, and senior executives at Kaiser, Curtis-Wright, Inland Steel, American Electric Power, Burroughs, American Can, Western Pacific Railroad, and Texaco.

Some of this rapport between business and the Democratic party was due to Johnson's personal style: while businessmen often felt looked down upon by the Kennedy White House, many felt that Johnson both understood and respected them. But, business attitudes toward government itself also appeared to be changing. During the Johnson administration's third year in office, Theodore Levitt wrote in the *Harvard Business Review:*

> It may seem the height of grandiloquence to say so, but there is abundant evidence that the American business community has finally and with unexpected suddenness actively embraced the idea of the interventionist state. . . . [I]mportant elements of American business have now come to the clear conclusion that the federal government can and probably should be an active agent of social and economic betterment—not just that big government is here to stay.[21]

In a similar vein, *Fortune* observed that in order to rebuild America's cities, "what is needed most of all is a new form of partnership between government and private enterprise."[22] Significantly, none of the major social initiatives of Johnson's Great Society, including the War on Poverty, Federal Aid to Education, and Medicare, was opposed by the executives of large companies. On the contrary, on October 9, 1966, when Johnson's proposal to establish "demonstration cities" was in difficulty in Congress, twenty-two corporate chief executives issued the following statement: "Our cities are being submerged by a rising tide of confluent forces— disease and despair, joblessness and hopelessness, excessive dependence on welfare payments, and the grim threats of crime, disorder and delinquency. America needs the demonstration cities act."[23] Nor did the nation's business community—outside the South—oppose the 1964 Civil Rights Act, even though it represented an unprecedented increase in the scope of federal controls over corporate personnel policies. In an article entitled "The New Partnership: Big Government and Big Business," Richard Barber concluded:

> A new breed of corporate executive is on the scene, professionally trained and more oriented to the science of management than to the perpetuation of an ideology which looks upon government as intrinsically evil. The modern company officer accepts government (much like he accepts the labor union) and works actively with it.[24]

With steadily increasing profits and a booming stock market, the business community had little reason to regard either the spending or the regulatory programs of the Great Society as threatening. In May 1965, a member of the Business Council told *Newsweek*, "What the hell, business is making money. We've solved every damned problem except unemployment. We've got a President who listens to us, and one of our own men is Secretary of Commerce. It's no wonder you see people smiling."[25]

The social programs of Lyndon Johnson's Great Society—in sharp contrast to those of FDR's New Deal—neither expanded the authority of government over industry nor acted to empower political constituencies that threatened corporate interests. Instead, as Max Ways noted in an influential article published in *Fortune* in January 1966, the Great Society appeared to embrace the principle of "creative federalism." He wrote: "As the range of conscious choice widens, it is possible to think of vast increases of federal government power that do not encroach upon or diminish any other power. Simultaneously, the power of private organizations, including businesses, will increase; and the power of individuals will increase."[26] Nor did the public find this objectionable. When asked, in 1966, if "government and business are learning to work together for the well-being of the country," 85 percent of those polled answered yes.[27]

Perhaps the clearest expression of the change in the attitudes of many business executives toward government was their support for the Kennedy-Johnson tax cut of 1964. For the first time, substantial segments of the business community abandoned their historical commitment to a balanced budget. While Johnson did agree to hold federal spending to $100 billion in 1965, it was obvious that the 1964 Revenue Act would increase the federal deficit—at least in the short run. Yet the primary political force behind the substantial tax cut that was approved in 1964 was the business community, significant segments of which had at last come to accept the principles of Keynesian economics. And, in fact, their confidence was not misplaced: the 1964 tax cuts were followed by the longest sustained expansion of the economy since the end of the Second World War.

Social Regulation, 1960–1965

The politics of government regulation of corporate social conduct provide another indication of the relative political strength of business during the first half of the 1960s. A number of important regulatory statutes in the areas of consumer and environmental protection were enacted, including the Food and Drug Act Amendments (1962), the Wilderness Act (1963), the Clean Air Act (1963), the Water Quality Act (1965), the Motor Vehicle Air Pollution Control Act (1965), and the Cigarette Labeling and Advertising Act (1965). The passage of these statutes indicated the beginning of a shift in the political agenda; none of these laws was initiated by the firms or industries affected by them. Yet they also reveal the continued influence of business over the substance of public policy. Both the drug amendments and the cigarette labeling act were significantly weakened as a result of political pressures from industry, while the four environmental statutes represented relatively uncontroversial, modest expansions of federal regulatory authority.

THE FOOD AND DRUG ACT AMENDMENTS

In January 1957, Senator Estes Kefauver (Democrat-Tennessee) became chair of the Anti-trust and Monopoly Subcommittee of the Senate Judiciary Committee. He decided to investigate administered prices, whose pervasiveness in a large number of industries had been described in *The Corporate Revolution in America,* published a few years earlier.[28] After initially focusing on the steel and automobile industries, the committee, at the suggestion of one of its staff members, began to focus on the drug industry. It subsequently held a series of hearings. Labor unions, health insurance representatives, hospital officials, and some consumer groups testified in favor of additional federal regulation, while both the Pharmaceutical Manufacturers Association (PMA) and the American Medical Association indicated their preference for the status quo. While the main emphasis of the hearing was on the excessive costs of drugs, safety was raised as an issue in connection with the industry's advertising and promotion. The subcommittee's report concluded that drug prices were "generally unreasonable and excessive," and proposed legislation to provide the public with "relief from a monopolistic industry by infusing therein the force of price competition."[29]

The subcommittee's recommendations were strongly opposed by Republican senators Roman Hruska of Nebraska and Everett Dirkson of Illinois, who contended that the public interest was well served by the industry's current research and marketing practices. Kefauver's bill was subsequently referred to another subcommittee, one dealing with patents, trademarks, and copyrights. This subcommittee immediately voted to gut Kefauver's proposal to amend the patent sections of the Sherman Antitrust Act by restricting the granting of exclusive rights to drug patents to three years. (The original subcommittee's report had noted that the United States was the only major country to grant unlimited patents for drugs.) This was the provision to which the drug industry most strongly objected and which Kefauver regarded as the heart of his bill.

Initially, the Kennedy administration took no position on this legislation. On March 15, 1962, the president delivered a message to Congress in which he outlined a Consumer Bill of Rights which encompassed "the right to safety, to be informed, to choose, and to be heard."[30] In spite of the urging of Senator Kefauver, the president made no reference to the drug legislation then pending before Congress. Subsequently, the administration, increasingly concerned about the sluggish progress of its legislative program and under growing criticism from the AFL-CIO for its indifference to Kefauver's bill, decided to become involved. Two officials from the Department of Health, Education and Welfare (HEW), along with staff members representing Senator James Eastland (Democrat-Mississippi), the Judiciary Committee's conservative chairman, and two representatives from the Pharmaceutical Manufacturers Association, held a day-long meeting to mark up the legislation. Kefauver was not invited.

The law drafted at this session bore little resemblance to the legislation approved by Kefauver's subcommittee. The bill completely eliminated the section on patent protection and weakened its provisions requiring the proof of efficacy of all new and existing drugs and establishing licensing standards for the manufacture of pharmaceuticals. The industry did make one compromise—it supported a proof-of-efficacy provision on the condition that only "substantial evidence of effectiveness" would be required. Although this concession subsequently came to haunt the industry, "it seems doubtful that the PMA representative appreciated the power he was handing over to the FDA to demand large and vigorously designed studies to substantiate a drug's efficacy."[31] On balance, with the help of its supporters on the Senate Judiciary Committee and some assistance from the administration, the industry appears to have successfully defused Kefauver's challenge.

However, "like the cavalry coming to the rescue in the nick of time," on July 15, three days after the bill had been reported out by the Judiciary Committee, Morton Mintz, a reporter for the *Washington Post*, published an article that revealed that the sedative Thalidomide could cause deformity in fetuses and that only the persistent efforts of Dr. Frances Kelsey, an FDA medical officer, had kept it off the American market. The timing of the *Post*'s story was not coincidental. A committee staff member, John Blair, had earlier begun compiling information on the drug, and two months before Mintz's article appeared Emmanuel Celler's House Judiciary Committee had heard testimony describing Thalidomide's harmful effects. Celler's committee, however, had not alerted the press to cover the hearings and Blair sought to keep the story under wraps. As Blair put it: "It's too early to spring this kind of story. All the various bills are far from reaching the floor of either house, and it's clear that the Thalidomide story, or something like it, is just what we need to ram through some legislation." He added, "In a situation like this, timing is vital." Once the weakened bill had left the Judiciary Committee, Blair alerted the *Washington Post* and the *Washington Star;* the former ran the story on the front page of its Sunday edition and it instantly became national news.[32]

Two weeks later, in response to the resulting public furor, the president declared that the Judiciary Committee's bill was inadequate and indicated his support for legislation introduced into the House of Representatives by Oren Harris. The Senate Judiciary Committee then amended its bill to bring it closer to Kefauver's original version. On October 10, approximately three months after Mintz's story was published in the *Washington Post,* the Kefauver-Harris drug amendments of 1962 were signed into law by President Kennedy. This legislation did not address Kefauver's original concern, namely, the excessive costs of drugs, and ironically it would not even have prevented the Thalidomide tragedy, since that drug would not have been approved by the FDA in any event. Nonetheless, the amendments made a substantial change in the regulation of the pharmaceutical industry. Their most important provision required the manufacturer to provide "substantial evidence" that it was "effective" in achieving its stated purpose, a requirement that was also applied retroactively to previously approved drugs. The bill also required the approval of the FDA before a new drug could be tested.

The passage of the Food and Drug Act Amendments of 1962 demonstrated the vulnerability of industry to adverse publicity as well as the extent of public support for additional consumer protection legislation. At the same time, it revealed the political weakness of the consumer movement. There was no active consumer lobby to countervail the influence of the drug industry: only the AFL-CIO pressed the president to support more effective drug legislation. And were it not for the scandal surrounding Thalidomide, no legislation of any consequence would have been enacted. Moreover, the drug industry, while it clearly would have preferred the weaker administration bill, was only marginally disappointed with the legislation that was enacted. The 1962 amendments did not require federal licensing of drug makers nor did they include Kefauver's original proposal to reduce the period of exclusive patent ownership—a provision that directly threatened the profitability of the industry. In fact, "the president of a major pharmaceutical manufacturing company" subsequently described the law "as good legislation in the public interest."[33]

CIGARETTES

The politics of the regulation of cigarettes during this period reveals a similar pattern. In the early 1960s, a number of private health organizations, led by the American Cancer Society, began urging the federal government to take a position on the relationship between smoking and disease. In 1962, a panel of ten scientists was formed; both health groups and the cigarette industry were given veto power over its membership. Fourteen months later, in January 1964, the panel released its report: it unanimously concluded that smoking was related to lung cancer, chronic bronchitis, emphysema, heart disease, and cancer of the larynx. The Federal Trade Commission (FTC) immediately announced that it would hold hearings to establish new regulations for labeling and advertising cigarettes. In June, the FTC issued a regulation requiring all cigarette packages and advertisements to carry labels warning the public of the health hazards of smoking.

The tobacco industry decided upon a two-pronged response. First, in order to give the impression of reasonableness, the industry indicated that it would accept the package labeling requirement in exchange for protection against other advertising requirements and state regulation. Second, the industry decided to challenge the FTC's decision by appealing to Congress—instead of the courts. To accomplish this strategy, a committee of lawyers drawn from a number of major Washington law firms and each of the six major tobacco companies was formed. Its members included Abe Fortas, a close personal friend of President Johnson and his subsequent nominee to the Supreme Court. This committee met almost daily for the next eighteen months and played a crucial role in presenting the industry's position at both FTC and congressional hearings.

In its effort to persuade Congress to limit the regulatory authority of the FTC, the industry began with two important advantages. First, because the tobacco industry was so important to the economies of a number of southern states, the entire southern congressional delegation could be expected to join ranks to defend it. Second, because the issue involved an expansion of government regulation of business, the industry could also count on the support of most Republicans. The position of the tobacco manufacturers was also supported by the National Association of Broadcasters, which feared that the FTC's efforts to restrict cigarette advertising would reduce its revenues. Arrayed on the other side was the Public Health Service and a number of private and public health organizations, including the American Cancer Society and the American Heart Association. However, while public opinion surveys taken between 1964 and 1966 showed strong support for tighter restrictions on tobacco products, the antitobacco forces were neither well organized nor politically sophisticated. And they faced a powerful coalition. As one member of congress commented, "Let's face it. . . . When you combine the money and power of the tobacco and liquor interests with advertising agencies, newspapers, radio and television . . . there is too much political muscle involved to expect much accomplishment."[34]

The tobacco industry scored its first success when the House Interstate and Foreign Commerce Committee convinced the FTC to delay imposing its regulations in order to give Congress additional time to act. Since the majority of the members of the House committee were either southerners or conservatives, the principal battleground then switched to the Senate Commerce Committee, only one of whose Democratic members, Ross Bass of Tennessee, came from a tobacco-producing state. At hearings before the Senate committee, Bowman Gray, chair of the board of R. J. Reynolds, stated that the tobacco companies were "profoundly conscious" of the health questions concerning cigarette smoking, but did not believe that there was sufficient evidence proving that "smoking causes lung cancer or any other disease." He added that even if Congress did decide to require a warning label in packaging, it should do nothing to interfere with "the right to advertise—an essential commercial right."[35]

The Senate Commerce Committee approved a bill requiring a warning on cigarette packages beginning in January 1966, but suspending any restriction of advertising for five years. The bill was approved overwhelmingly by the full Senate. "As the time for the voting approached, a number of senators honestly believed that all they were about to do was to join the Commerce Committee in taking the heroic step of warning the public about the health dangers in smoking." Yet, in fact, the 1965 legislation was a clear victory for the tobacco industry. All the law required was a label warning of the health hazards of cigarette smoking to "appear in conspicuous and legible type" on each package of cigarettes. Most important, the FTC was forbidden from restricting cigarette advertising for five years. Furthermore, in a relatively unusual exercise of federal power, Congress explicitly prohibited both state and local governments from enacting any regulations affecting either cigarette labeling or advertising. As Elizabeth Drew put it, the industry had "found the best filter yet—Congress."[36]

CLEAN AIR

The federal role in the control of air pollution dates from the 1950s, when Congress approved a request from the Eisenhower administration that the Public Health Service be given additional funds to study the problem of air pollution and recommend more effective means of controlling it. Three years later, a bill was introduced by Representative Paul Schneck (Republican-Illinois) directing the surgeon general to publish "standards as to the amount of unburned hydrocarbons which is safe, from the standpoint of human health . . . for a motor vehicle to discharge into the atmosphere."[37] It further provided that motor vehicles exceeding this standard be prohibited from use in interstate commerce. This legislation was strongly opposed by the Automobile Manufacturers Association, which contended that there was insufficient information to determine appropriate automobile-emissions standards. As a result, Congress enacted legislation in 1960 that merely instructed the surgeon general to study the effect on health of motor-vehicle emissions and report its findings within two years.

The Clean Air Act of 1963 included a provision that directed the surgeon general to "encourage the continued efforts on the part of the automobile and fuel industries to develop devices and fuels to prevent pollution from being discharged." This provision aroused no controversy, and the automobile industry did not even bother to send representatives to any of the hearings held on the act. However, a subcommittee of the Senate Public Works Committee, chaired by Edmund Muskie of Maine, subsequently held a series of hearings around the country on national air pollution problems. On the basis of these hearings, the committee issued a report that concluded that "automobile exhaust . . . is . . . the most important and critical source of air pollution and it is, beyond question, increasing in seriousness."[38] It recommended that the federal government establish national standards for automotive exhausts. The committee's recommendation was opposed not only by the automobile manufacturers—which contended that they were working as hard as they could to upgrade their abatement technology—but also by the Kennedy administration, which urged that emissions standards for automobiles be delayed until more information was available. The Motor Vehicle Air Pollution Control Act of 1965 was a compromise: the Secretary of HEW was given the authority to prescribe emissions standards, but was not required to do so.

With the exception of the automobile industry, which was finding itself under increasing pressure from both the federal government and the State of California to reduce auto emissions, the increase in public interest in pollution control through 1966 did not appear threatening to business. On the contrary, a number of observers argued that controlling emissions presented business with the opportunity both to demonstrate its social responsibility and increase its profitability and efficiency. An article published in the *Harvard Business Review* in the fall of 1966 stated:

> Private enterprise has the opportunity to participate in a ready-made market that will total at least $275 billion over the next 34 years and, at the same time, to ensure the availability of two essential resources—namely, clean air and clean water. Moreover, to add to the attractiveness of the opportunity for providing solutions to the nation's air and water pollution problems, industry can gain the goodwill and wholehearted support of the public on a scale never before enjoyed.[39]

The authors concluded that improving air and water quality was well within both the financial and technological capacity of the private sector and confidently predicted that through continued improvements in abatement technologies, the nation's pollution problems could be substantially ameliorated—particularly as more companies came to recognize the economic opportunities that lay in the design and manufacture of improved pollution-control equipment. In short, business viewed the public's increased interest in reducing pollution in much the same terms that it regarded the social programs of the Great Society: both represented opportunities for business to grow—and at the same time help improve the quality of American society.

Business and Politics

Through the middle of the 1960s, the political position of business certainly appeared to be a privileged one. Richard Hofstadter wrote in 1964: "The existence and the workings of the corporations are largely accepted, and in the main they are assumed to be fundamentally benign."[40] Public approval of business steadily increased during the first half of the 1960s. According to the Opinion Research Corporation (ORC), the percentage of Americans who registered "high approval" of large companies increased from 15 percent in 1961 to 20 percent in 1965 while those who indicated "low approval" declined from 55 to 47 percent.[41] Similarly, the percentage of Americans agreeing with the statement that "large companies are essential for the nation's growth and expansion" increased from 83 percent in 1961 to 88 percent in 1965, while the proportion of those agreeing that "there's too much power concentrated in the hands of a few large companies for the good of the nation" declined from 57 to 52 percent during the first half of the 1960s. In 1966, public approval of American business reached its postwar high: 55 percent of the American public expressed "a great deal of confidence" in the leaders of major corporations.[42] A survey conducted by Louis Harris that same year reported that 96 percent believed that "free enterprise has made this country great," while more than three-quarters agreed that "most businessmen are genuinely interested in [the] well being of the country."[43] Thus the mid-1960s marked a high point not only of business confidence in government but also of public confidence in business. The interests of business, government, and the public appeared to have become remarkably congruent.

The lack of effective political challenges to business in Washington through the first half of the 1960s meant that business needed to devote relatively modest resources to influencing public policy. In 1961, only 130 corporations were represented by registered lobbyists, and only 50 of these firms had staff with Washington addresses. The activity of these "Washington representatives" was primarily directed at increasing the sale of company products or services to the government. A Brookings study reported: "representation [in Washington] appears to be a direct function of volume of sales to the federal government."[44] Not surprisingly, the defense industry was the most politically active, although a number of oil companies, because of their sensitivity to decisions made by government, also had Washington representatives. In 1964, Bauer, Pool, and Dexter published a major study of business lobbying, based on the efforts of business to influence trade legislation in 1962. They found that most business lobbyists were poorly informed, had few resources, and were on the whole ineffective. Of the 166 large firms they surveyed, only 37 had had any communication with Congress in the previous two years. They concluded: "When we look at a typical lobby we find that its opportunities to maneuver are sharply limited, its staff mediocre, and its typical problem not the influencing of Congressional votes but finding the clients and contributors to enable it to survive at all."[45] The former director of public relations at DuPont added, "generally speaking, business has less contact with people in government than does any major section of our society."[46]

To the extent that firms were politically represented in Washington in the early 1960s, it was largely either through trade associations or general business interest groups. The former, however, were frequently understaffed, relatively unsophisticated, and were held in little regard by either the companies that belonged to them or the legislators whose views they were supposed to influence. Both the National Association of Manufacturers and the United States Chambers of Commerce did have large Washington offices, but neither was well respected or influential. Aside from being opposed to labor unions, higher taxes, and welfare, they had no practical political orientation. Rather, their interests were primarily ideological: in the early 1960s, among the Chamber of Commerce's major activities was the sponsorship of a series of courses for executives on the topic, "Freedom versus Communism."[47]

However, in part as a response to Kennedy's election, there were some signs of increased business interest in the political process. In 1962, former President Eisenhower publicly urged business executives to become more politically active by getting more involved in the Republican party. He stated, "Businessmen now have to do a little waking up. Businessmen can no longer be sure that there are well designed and well observed limits beyond which government will not go. If businessmen do not realize the need, they are not going to have a prosperous business in the long run."[48] The following year, a group of executives formed the Business Industry Political Action Committee to solicit campaign contributions from business and thereby offset the influence of the AFL-CIO's Committee on Political Education (COPE). However, neither of these initiatives met with much response. An extensive survey of the political activity of business-people conducted by the *Harvard Business Review* in 1964 concluded that "while the trend is in the direction of greater involvement, the absolute level of such participation is still relatively low." Nevertheless, in contrast to a similar survey in 1959 which had reported that many executives were unsure as to "why" they should be more active in politics, 72 percent of those questioned in 1964 believed that the political activity of business should increase.[49]

Conclusion

For all the political influence and public approval that business enjoyed between 1960 and 1965, the first half of the 1960s helped set the stage for the erosion of the political influence of business that began in the second half of that decade. The passage of the Food and Drug Act Amendments of 1962 revealed the enormous potential power of the media in affecting public policy toward business; without the press coverage of the Thalidomide scandal, no significant legislation would have been approved. Likewise, the controversy over the regulation of cigarette advertising signaled the beginning of an increase in public concern about the health hazards created by industry. Cigarettes became the first in a long list of products whose use or misuse would come to be perceived as hazardous to the health of the American public—and thus prompt demands for additional government control. Similarly, the debate about automobile-emission standards marked the beginning of an increase in public pressure for laws designed to safeguard and improve the quality of the environment.

Most important, the Great Society, while not directly affecting business, did mark an important change in the dynamics of public policy formation: it introduced "an unprecedented wave of policy innovation" on the part of Congress.[50] Prior to the mid-1960s, the nation's legislature was a relatively conservative institution whose principal role was to prevent the enactment of any major new policy initiatives. From the late forties through the mid-1960s, a loose alliance of southern Democrats and conservative Republicans had effectively defeated the entire liberal Democratic policy agenda, including federal aid to education, civil rights legislation, and medical care for the elderly. But the 1964 election provided liberal northern Democrats with control of both houses of Congress for the first time since the Second World War. The result was to undermine the congressional blocs that had previously checkmated liberal policy initiatives. In this sense, congressional enactment of the programs of the Great Society foreshadowed the unprecedented increase in regulatory legislation that began in 1966. The Democratic party landslide of 1964 was certainly not a mandate to reduce the autonomy or power of business. Indeed, not since before the New Deal had so many executives from large corporations supported the Democratic party's presidential candidate. But, ironically, that proved to be one of its most important results.

The Great Society also affected the future of business-government relations in another way: it transformed the prevailing political consensus on the appropriate role of government in general, and the federal government in particular, in American society. Prior to the mid-1960s, this consensus emphasized the value of limited government: the burden of proof was on those who favored government intervention. And, if government was to intervene, then there was a strong preference that the intervention take place at the local level. This consensus had greatly contributed to the political strength of American business in the two decades following the Second World War; the strength of the principles "limited government" and "states' rights" enabled business to effectively oppose numerous proposals to expand government regulation of the private sector on the grounds that they constituted an inappropriate exercise of public authority, particularly at the federal level. However, congressional enactment of the legislative programs of the Great Society signaled an erosion of this "legitimacy barrier" to increased federal intervention. There were no longer any national problems—whether the cost of medical illness for the aged or the educational deficiencies of inner-city schools—that the federal government was not now responsible for addressing. The "solutions" initially offered by the Great Society primarily involved the expenditure of federal monies. Beginning in 1966, the liberal agenda would come to focus increasingly on expanding the authority of government over business.

III

The Rise of
Consumerism,
1966 to 1969

Introduction

The decline in the relative political influence of business in the postwar American period dates from 1966. In that year, Congress enacted four important pieces of consumer-protection legislation, the most important of which, the National Traffic and Motor Vehicle Safety Act, constituted the first major political defeat for one of the nation's most visible and powerful industries. These laws marked the beginning of an upsurge in federal legislation regulating corporate social conduct that would continue uninterrupted for more than a decade. By 1967, the promise of "creative federalism"—of a simultaneous increase in the power of both business and government—had begun to fade. It became increasingly challenged both by business—which was concerned about increased government regulation and spending—and various liberal critics who began to perceive business-government cooperation as signifying less the fulfillment of American liberalism than its betrayal. In 1967, John Kenneth Galbraith articulated the latter position in *The New Industrial State*, a book whose popularity both reflected and reinforced a more hostile attitude toward business on the part of the American public.[1] A year later, Theodore Levitt admitted that "history will show that business's current association with Great Society activities has been largely episodic. It is an incident in time, not an element of a trend."[2] In short, "corporate liberalism" had begun to unravel.

The Politics of Consumerism: 1966–68

In the space of only three years Congress enacted the National Traffic and Motor Vehicle Act, the Fair Packaging and Labeling Act, the Federal Hazardous Substances Act, the Federal Meat Inspection Act, the National Gas Pipeline Safety Act, the Truth in Lending Act, the Flammable Fabrics Act, and the Child Protection Act. Such an outpouring of consumer legislation by the federal government was unprecedented in the history of business-government relations in the United States. What was unusual was not only the sheer volume of legislative activity, but its substance: in contrast to the consumer laws enacted during the first half of the 1960s, these laws were often strengthened, rather than weakened, as they worked their way through the Congress. What accounted for the sudden willingness of Congress to challenge the prerogatives of such a broad range of industries, a willingness conspicuously lacking in the earlier cases of the Food and Drug Amendments (1962) and the Cigarette Labeling Act (1965)?

Consumer legislation is virtually a textbook case of a public policy in which the costs are concentrated and the benefits diffused.[3] Accordingly, producers enjoy an inherent advantage: the companies in a particular industry each have a clear and direct stake in opposing additional restrictions by government. Moreover, their publicity and organizational costs are relatively low, since they are usually already organized into a trade association—one of whose functions is to represent their political interests. By contrast, the stake of any individual consumer in consumer protection legislation is extremely small. This is particularly true of health and safety regulations: the chance of any individual suffering harm from the use of any particular product is relatively remote. Moreover, while producers enjoy the advantage of being able to confine their political efforts to public policies that affect only their particular industry, the individual consumer enjoys no such luxury. Finally, consumers are far more difficult to organize than producers for the simple reason that there are so many more of them.

This analysis explains why citizens in their role as consumers tend to be less well organized than in their role as producers.[4] In fact, this imbalance persisted throughout the 1960s: the emergence of a relatively well organized consumer movement followed rather than preceded the outpouring of consumer-protection legislation. The Consumer Federation of America—a broad coalition of 140 organizations, including state consumer organizations, consumer cooperatives, and a number of unions—was not established until November 1967. It had a small Washington office and left lobbying to its member organizations. Not until the early 1970s did it become a significant political presence in Washington. The National Consumer Union, while keeping its 1.3 million members informed of political issues through its magazine *Consumer Reports,* did not establish a Washington office until September 1969. Similarly, only in 1969 did Ralph Nader establish an organization with a year-round political presence in Washington. Throughout the 1960s the only organized political supporter of strong consumer protection was the AFL-CIO, but consumer issues constituted only a small part of its legislative agenda.

During the second half of the 1960s, the relative responsiveness of officials in both the executive and legislative branch to consumerism was thus not due to the power of the "consumer lobby." Rather, it reflected the emergence of what James Q. Wilson has characterized as "entrepreneurial politics." He writes:

> It may seem astonishing that regulatory legislation . . . is ever passed. It is, and with growing frequency in recent years—but it requires the efforts of a skilled entrepreneur who can mobilize latent public sentiment (by revealing a scandal or capitalizing on a crisis), put the opponents of the plan publicly on the defensive (by accusing them of deforming babies and killing motorists), and associate the legislation with safety. The entrepreneur serves as the vicarious representative of groups not directly part of the legislative process.[5]

In the case of consumerism, these entrepreneurs were primarily northern Democratic senators aided by their staff. Senator Abraham Ribicoff of Connecticut was the major initiator of automobile safety legislation, Senator Paul Douglas of Illinois of truth in lending legislation, Senator Philip Hart of Michigan of truth in packaging legislation, and Senator Warren Magnuson of Washington of flammable fabrics legislation. For these senators, the sponsorship of consumer legislation was a way to increase their national visibility and help ensure their reelection. At the same time, the ability of individual senators to initiate new legislation was enhanced by four changes within the structure of the Senate itself. The first was an increase in the influence of junior members, who no longer had to serve a lengthy apprenticeship before they were allowed to sponsor legislation. The second was an increase in the size of congressional staffs and the number of subcommittees. In addition, "these tendencies toward a more decentralized, activist legislative system were further encouraged by the shift in the leadership of the majority party from the centralized, closely held power of Lyndon Johnson to the more consensual leadership style of Mike Mansfield" (Democrat-Montana).[6] Finally, thanks to the Democratic landslide of 1964, the Senate itself had become more liberal and younger, with power shifting away from older conservative southern Democrats to younger liberal senators from the northern industrial states. It was these later individuals who played a crucial role in initiating both new legislation in general and consumer laws in particular.

This does not by itself explain why so many politicians suddenly became so eager to embrace the cause of consumer protection. After all, Senator Estes Kefauver was also a political entrepreneur, and yet the result of his efforts to strengthen controls over the pharmaceutical industry in 1962 were rather modest. There is certainly nothing intrinsically liberal or left-of-center about entrepreneurial politics. Nor, as we shall subsequently see, is there anything inherently liberal about a more decentralized style of congressional decision making. Why, then, in the fall of 1964, did Warren Magnuson, the chair of the powerful Senate Commerce Committee, hire Michael Pertschuk as the committee's consumer counsel and instruct him to build a "consumer record" on which he could campaign for reelection in 1968? And why did other senators and representatives actively compete with him to have their names identified with as many pieces of consumer legislation as possible? In short, why were so many politicians not only no longer afraid of offending particular industries, but in many cases eager to "keep the big boys honest"?[7]

In brief, consumerism was a beneficiary of rising public expectations about the capacity of government to improve the quality of life in American society. As Michael Pertschuk recalled in 1982, "Though barely more than a decade ago, it now seems strange to us that Lyndon Johnson and other lawmakers sought to measure their effectiveness—and be measured—by the number of new laws proposed and enacted under their sponsorship." Consumerism was an intrinsic part of the liberal agenda of the second half of the 1960s; not only did it flow out of the same political and social vision as the War on Poverty and other social-welfare programs of the Great Society, but it represented a substitute for them. By 1966, much of the broad liberal agenda left over from the Kennedy administration had been enacted. At the same time, the budgetary problems created by the Vietnam War had made it more difficult to secure congressional approval for costly governmental programs. But "consumer issues, which entailed little direct budgetary cost, appealed increasingly to the president's agenda setters, such as Joseph Califano, domestic counsel in the

White House."[8] They were a vehicle by which liberal politicians could continue to increase the responsibilities of government without increasing federal spending, since regulatory statutes conveniently passed on the costs of reform to the private sector.

Underlying the willingness of the public to place additional financial burdens on industry—even if many would ultimately be borne by consumers themselves—was the extraordinary health of the national economy. As Daniel Yankelovitch observed:

> Virtually all of us presupposed that our economy would continue to function automatically and successfully, as surely as the sun would rise each morning without effort on our part. . . . Americans had grown used to the idea that the giant corporations, the government and other economic institutions, would simply and eternally be there—to support the aged, build the infrastructure, create jobs, turn out wealth and do the country's work, as much a part of nature as trees and rainfall from heaven.[9]

A survey taken in 1966 reported that 60 percent of those polled believed that American living standards would be higher in 1978, and 62 percent expressed the opinion that the United States would "always have the [world's] highest living standards."[10] Michael Pertschuk writes:

> For though we might question the good faith of corporate commitment to the consumer and the environment, we never thought to question the capacity of business to meet any standards imposed efficiently and at minimal cost. Indeed, we believed that if business turned to the task of assuring product or worker safety or environmental wholesomeness with good will, those ends could be accomplished at negligible cost.
>
> . . . This faith, too, was not without substance, for it had more often than not proved true that when industry predicted that dire economic consequences would flow from proposed regulation, it nonetheless demonstrated innovativeness and efficiency in responding.[11]

Significantly, the outpouring of consumer legislation between 1966 and 1969 was paralleled by a revival of interest in corporate social responsibility. Beginning around 1967, a number of major companies attempted to employ their skills and resources in order to respond to what was viewed as the nation's major domestic problem: the deterioration of its inner cities and the exclusion of poor urban blacks from the economic mainstream. By the end of the decade, the notion that the responsibilities of business were not exhausted by competing successfully in the marketplace had become widely accepted within the business community. Corporate annual reports featured descriptions of companies' efforts to "improve society" and executive speeches stressed the links between corporate social performance and corporate survival. The minority employment program of the National Alliance of Businessmen gained the participation of 27,500 companies, and a nationwide survey of 247 companies made in 1969 and 1970 reported that 201 had established urban affairs programs since 1965.[12] In a special issue devoted to the "urban crisis" published in January 1968, *Fortune* noted with pride that government was increasingly looking to business for help in revitalizing the nation's cities. *Newsweek* observed: "The rare corporation now is one that doesn't have some active social program. The list is endless, running the gamut from minority training and housing rehabilitation to day-care centers, medical services and experiments in education."[13] For its part, the public, although remaining skeptical of the effectiveness of these corporate social initiatives, strongly supported them. More than 80 percent of those polled in the early 1970s believed that business "should provide special leadership" in "rebuilding our cities," "eliminating racial discrimination," and "wiping out poverty."[14]

There was nothing contradictory about an expansion of government regulation on one hand and a renewed interest in corporate responsibility on the other. Both reflected the same increase in expectations of business performance: each assumed that there was no tension between making safer products and providing jobs and housing for inner-city residents, on one hand, and continued corporate profitability on the other. In fact, the parallels between the two developments are even more precise. Both the reemergence of the doctrine of corporate social responsibility and the expansion of government regulation flowed from essentially the same political and social currents. Both initiatives—one public, the other private—were welcomed by the Johnson administration as devices for sustaining the momentum of the Great Society in the face of budgetary constraints caused by expenditures for the Vietnam War.

Nonetheless, while the public's increased expectation of corporate performance may have been flattering to business, it also undermined its political influence. Ironically, the strong performance of the economy—between 1961 and 1968, economic growth rates averaged 4.5 percent and real disposable income per person grew by an average rate of 3.1 percent—heightened the political vulnerability of business. Business's economic achievements also made it more difficult for companies to oppose additional regulations on the grounds that they could not afford them, since they clearly could: corporate profit rates reached a postwar peak between 1965 and 1969.

Automobile Safety

The legislation whose passage signaled a significant decline in business's influence over regulatory policy was the National Traffic and Motor Vehicle Safety Act of 1966. After declining almost every year since 1945, traffic deaths began to increase significantly after 1960. They rose sharply in four out of the next five years, the longest and greatest increase since the government had begun to keep records, reaching a record 53,041 in 1966. Yet this increase in traffic fatalities went largely unreported and there was little pressure on the federal government to address this problem. Rather, automotive safety was placed on the political agenda by the initiatives of three political entrepreneurs: Senators Warren Magnuson, Robert Kennedy, and Abraham Ribicoff. Public interest in the issue followed rather than preceded their efforts.

In 1965, Senator Ribicoff became chair of the Senate Governmental Relations Operations Committee's Subcommittee on Executive Reorganization. Known as "Mr. Safety" because of his efforts to crack down on speeders when he was governor of Connecticut, Ribicoff decided to examine the role of the federal government in automobile safety. In February 1965, he held hearings to investigate the "fantastic carnage" on the nation's highways.[15] They were highlighted by the appearance of the top executives of the nation's four major automobile companies. Under persistent questioning by Senator Kennedy of New York, Frederick Donner, chairman of the board of General Motors, admitted that, while GM had made a profit of approximately $1.7 billion the previous year, it had spent only $1.25 million on automobile safety. Although the company subsequently revised its estimate of expenditures on automobile-safety research to $193 million, the later figure was suspect and the industry appeared to have severely damaged its credibility with both the public and the committee. Thanks to the extensive publicity the hearings had received by July 1965, the public now viewed traffic safety as one of the nation's six or seven major national problems.[16]

Toward the end of 1965, Ralph Nader published *Unsafe at Any Speed*, subtitled *The Designed-in Dangers in the American Automobile*. Nader contended that the automobile injuries were caused not so much by the collision of the car with another object, but rather the subsequent collision of the automobile's passenger with the interior of the automobile itself—the so-called second collision. He argued that while automobile accidents were inevitable, the significant number of injuries they caused were not.[17] Although the book initially sold few copies, it was the subject of a front page story in the *New York Times,* and received numerous favorable reviews. Nader's book helped shift the public's perception of responsibility for automobile injuries from the driver to the manufacturer. *Unsafe at Any Speed,* with its specific examples of individuals needlessly injured by automobile accidents and its extensive discussion of the "designed-in" defects of the Corvair, effectively personalized the issue of automobile safety.

In his 1966 State of the Union Address, President Johnson told Congress that he intended to propose a Highway Safety Act. The administration drafted a bill that permitted the secretary of commerce to set federal standards after two years if the industry failed to improve automotive safety. However, by the time the details of this legislation were leaked to the press, public interest in safety regulation had substantially increased. Nader criticized the administration's proposal as a "no-law law,"[18] and Senator Ribicoff complained on the floor of the Senate that the bill permitted too much delay. In March, Senator Magnuson, who had become jealous of Ribicoff's identification with the issue of automobile safety, directed the Senate Commerce Committee to hold hearings on the administration's bill.

In their testimony before the Senate Commerce Committee, industry spokespersons demonstrated "a profound misunderstanding of the climate in Washington." Their suggestion that state governments play a larger role in setting safety standards and that the antitrust laws be relaxed was greeted with general disbelief. No one, not even the Republican members of the Commerce Committee, supported the industry's position. How had the industry managed to so completely misjudge the mood of Congress? One executive admitted, "One of the serious problems in our industry is provinciality. The auto industry is a giant, with a fantastic impact on the economy. But the sun rises in Detroit and sets in Dearborn. Besides, our laissez-faire attitude had worked so far." Moreover, the industry's trade association, the Automobile Manufacturers Association (AMA), was a weak, Detroit-based organization. While GM, Ford, and Chrysler did have Washington offices to monitor political trends, in general they served as little more than "outposts." "The people who man them haven't spent a lifetime in the corporation, and they aren't slated for a rise in the corporation. It's very hard for them to make themselves heard back in Detroit."[19] David Halberstam writes, "In 1966 the American auto industry was at the absolute height of its powers, so rich and mighty that its arrogance, its certainty that it *was* America was almost unconscious."[20]

Before the administration released its bill, Senator Ribicoff reopened his hearings on auto safety and Ralph Nader made his debut as a congressional witness. His initial appearance attracted little attention. However, in early

March, news stories began to report that Ralph Nader was being followed and that private detectives were asking his relatives and friends about his political and sexual preferences. On March 9, shortly before midnight, GM issued a press release admitting that it had "initiated a routine investigation . . . to determine whether Ralph Nader was acting on behalf of litigants or their attorneys in Corvair design cases pending against General Motors."[21] Shortly after this announcement, Ribicoff convened a hearing to determine whether Nader had been "harrassed." Before a national television audience, GM's president, James Roche, apologized to Nader and stated that while he had known nothing of the investigation, he was "fully responsible" for it. Subsequent questioning of both GM's general counsel and the head of the private detective agency hired by GM revealed that the company's "routine inquiry" had gone far beyond Nader's efforts to assist Corvair's litigants. The private investigator hired by GM had been told that GM wanted "to get something, somewhere, on this guy to get him out of their hair and to shut him up."[22]

While the enactment of some automobile safety standards was likely in any event, GM's investigation of Ralph Nader made their adoption a certainty. The company's actions caused it to be seen as the epitome of a self-serving giant corporation that was attempting to crush attempts by citizens to protect their legitimate interests. One senator remarked: "Everybody was so outraged that a great corporation was out to clobber a guy because he wrote critically about them." Another noted, "When they started looking in Ralph Nader's bedroom, we all figured that they must really be nervous. We began to believe that Nader must be right."[23] The industry's executives, in turn, were "visibly shaken by the exceptionally critical onslaught which they faced."[24] An automotive executive from another company told *Fortune:* "I get mad every time I think about that stunt. They made the entire industry look bad, and we're all going to suffer for it." *Fortune* observed, "Many strong supporters of auto-safety legislation agree that GM's conduct . . . was the most important single factor in establishing a congressional climate conducive to passage of a tough safety bill."[25] A one-day hearing convened by Senator Ribicoff to investigate GM's investigation of Nader took on "all the fascination of a public whipping."[26] Virtually overnight, Nader became a celebrity and his book a best-seller.

In mid-April 1966, the AMA hired Lloyd Cutler, a prominent Washington attorney who had previously represented the pharmaceutical industry, to attempt to make whatever federal standards were adopted as palatable as possible. Cutler, along with the Washington representatives of the four major automobile companies, met with a number of members of Congress, and lobbyists from each of the four major domestic manufacturers visited representatives in whose districts they had manufacturing facilities. Had the manufacturers been able to mobilize the support of their dealers, suppliers, and employees, they might have constituted a powerful political force. However, the United Automobile Workers Union was uninterested in cooperating with its employers, while the dealers and suppliers were primarily interested in protecting their own interests—which were not necessarily the same as those of the manufacturers. The National Automotive Dealers Association did provide some modest help to the industry, but for the most part the manufacturers were on their own. Aside from the representatives from Michigan, no other members appeared particularly interested in the industry's problems. One automobile executive noted: "That left us with emphasizing the potential damaging economic impact of the proposals: that was our only real political muscle."[27]

The National Traffic and Motor Vehicle Safety Act, signed into law by President Johnson on September 9, 1966, was an important political milestone. Congress had passed regulatory legislation whose enactment no one would have predicted even six months earlier. In contrast to the 1962 Food and Drug Act Amendments, Congress did not simply expand the scope of an existing regulation of a specific industry: it established legal standards for a product which formerly had not been regulated at all by the federal government. Elizabeth Drew described it as "a radical departure from the government's traditional, respectful, hands-off approach to the automobile industry, an industry which politicians . . . had long considered sacrosanct." In short, "the giant, fearsome, incredibly wealthy automobile industry . . . when it reluctantly lumbered into the unfamiliar political arena, turned out to be a paper hippopotamus."[28] Unlike previous regulatory laws, the bill had been strengthened rather than weakened as it worked its way through the legislative process, indicating "a congressional perception of a more militant consumer protection demanded by the public."[29] Moreover, "as a result of this controversy, a majority coalition was discovered in the Senate for an unprecedented expansion of the federal government's efforts to ensure the safety of its citizens. Both proponents and opponents of reform immediately were put on notice that new political opportunities existed in this policy area."[30] Mark Nadel noted: "The impossible had been done . . . consumer legislation was [seen] to be a popular issue with good publicity value. Future bills would be easier."[31]

The Deluge

Only a month after the automobile safety bill was approved, President Johnson signed the Fair Packaging and Labeling Act of 1966. Hearings on this legislation had been held each year since 1961. The terms of the debate had remained the same. Consumer advocates contended that "the eight thousand different items" displayed in a typical large supermarket made it impossible for even the most educated consumer to make rational choices, while industry representatives countered that the large number of different goods available to consumers testified to "the great strides that industry had made in providing an increasing array of goods from which consumers could choose."[32] The provisions of the law finally enacted by Congress were substantially weaker than its proponents had hoped, in part because the issue of deceptive packaging was incapable of generating the degree of public interest aroused by automobile safety. While the version passed by the Senate permitted the government to establish standards governing the weights and quantities in which products would be marketed, this provision was dropped by the conference committee in order to overcome industrial opposition to the bill's passage: a broad coalition of companies and trade associations successfully argued that "mandatory standards would result in greatly increased cost to the consumer and would stifle packaging innovations."[33]

However, the legislation for which Senator Philip Hart had been crusading since 1961, and which had become an important priority of a number of consumer organizations, did require manufacturers to provide consumers with specific information about a product's contents, as well as a separate and accurate statement of the net quantity in a uniform location on the principal display panel of the label.[34] *Consumer Reports* noted that while the law "fell short of what it should be," it was "something of a legislative miracle" that it passed at all.[35] *Fortune* concluded:

> The consumer goods industry is going to have to face up to the fact that "consumerism" has become politically popular. As industry learned when it tried to kill truth in packaging, "consumerism" cannot be killed. It is part of the Democrats' legislative program; it is strongly supported by organized labor and other groups; and consumers themselves have become more aggressive and articulate.[36]

A year later, another politically powerful industry suffered an important legislative defeat when Congress approved the Flammable Fabrics Act.

Unlike automobile safety, in which the federal government had played no regulatory role prior to 1966, legislation had been enacted in 1953 establishing flammability standards for clothing. These standards were relatively lax and they did not cover potentially flammable blankets, bedding, drapes, upholstery, and other common household products. Moreover, there was little the administration could do to strengthen the legislation, since Congress had specifically prohibited the secretary of commerce from issuing stricter standards or regulating the flammability of products other than clothing.

The initiative for amending the 1953 legislation came from Senator Warren Magnuson. In order to overcome the opposition of the textile industry—whose lobbyists had vowed that "blood would run in the halls of Congress" before his bill passed—the staff of the Senate Commerce Committee set about orchestrating the hearing process. Pertschuk recalled: "Our objective was simple: to gain access to the media, to evoke public concern and reaction to the pain and suffering caused by child burnings, and to demonstrate that failure of the industry to make any effort in good faith to raise the inadequate voluntary standards of flammability."[37] The committee's first witness was the president's new special assistant for consumer affairs, Betty Furness. Since this was also her first appearance before a congressional committee, her testimony attracted considerable press coverage. She was followed by Peter Hackes, a prominent CBS news commentator whose eleven-year-old daughter had recently suffered serious burns when her cotton blouse—which met all current federal standards—caught on fire when a match dropped on it. The second day of hearings featured representatives of the Cotton Textile Council, who testified that the Flammable Fabrics Act had produced "admirable" results and that no further legislation was required. They stated that the industry was already working, through its voluntary standards review committee, to promulgate standards as high as existing technology made economically feasible. However, it turned out that the standards committee had met only once in the previous decade. The Senate committee subsequently issued a report stating that "burns from ignition of clothing and other household fabrics clearly constitute an extremely serious health problem in the United States."[38]

On July 25 the commerce committee unanimously voted to substantially strengthen and expand the 1953 legislation. Its bill granted the secretary of commerce the power to establish flammability standards for fabrics in order "to protect the public against unreasonable risk of injury, death or property loss."[39] It included hats, gloves, and footwear under the definition of "wearing apparel" and expanded the scope of federal regulation to encompass all fabrics used in the home. The bill was passed by the Senate without debate and approved four months later by the House of Representatives with only minor changes. It was signed into law on December 14, 1967, by President Johnson.

The following day, President Johnson signed legislation significantly extending the scope of federal regulation over yet another industry, meat packing. As in the case of drugs, the federal role in meat inspection dated from the Progressive Era when, prompted by both the descriptions of grotesque conditions in meat-packing plants in Upton Sinclair's *The Jungle* and the exclusion of American-produced beef from a number of European markets, Congress had enacted the Meat Inspection Law of 1907. However, this law covered only meat produced for sale in interstate commerce, thus excluding 15,000 of the nation's 17,000 slaughter and packing plants from federal regulation.

Early in 1966, the Johnson administration proposed legislation that amounted to little more than a routine updating of federal standards for meat sold in interstate commerce. But, as in the case of automobile safety, both congressional and public pressure forced the administration to revise its legislative agenda. Indeed, "revelations in the press and during committee hearings about slaughter and packing practices at some state plants made meat inspection the most emotional consumer issue of 1967."[40] There was relatively little controversy about the need to strengthen federal standards for the inspection of animals. The real issue was the extent to which the federal government should attempt to supplement—or even supersede—the states' own inspection systems.

On October 1, 1967, the House of Representatives narrowly defeated an amendment offered by Neal Smith of Iowa and Thomas Foley of Washington that provided for federal inspection of all plants doing more than $250,000 of business in intrastate commerce each year. However, instead of resolving this issue, the defeat of the amendment polarized both congressional and industry opinion. The AFL-CIO attacked the House's bill as "a snare, a delusion and a hoax on the American people," and Ralph Nader accused the Agriculture Department of "behaving in this meat controversy in a manner that suggests an untoward submission to powerful state agricultural departments and meat industry pressures." Senator Walter Mondale of Minnesota informed a Senate subcommittee that meat products not inspected by the federal government were being sold in such major chain stores as A&P and Safeway. President Johnson subsequently indicated that he wanted legislation stronger than that passed by the House. He stated on November 20 that "we need the strongest possible meat inspection bill."[41] A month later the Senate approved legislation

requiring states to establish inspection systems at least equal to those of
the federal government and granting the secretary of agriculture the power
to assume the inspection of intrastate plants if a state failed to establish
such a program within two years. The House subsequently accepted the
Senate's version with only minor changes and, on December 15, President
Johnson, with Upton Sinclair at his side, signed into law the Wholesale
Meat Act of 1967—the first legislative change in meat inspection in more
than half a century.

A year later Congress approved a Truth in Lending Law, described as
"one of the toughest and most far-reaching consumer bills enacted . . . in
many years."[42] The idea behind this legislation had originated with Senator Paul Douglas of Illinois, who had unsuccessfully campaigned since
1959 for a law that would require consumers to be provided with information about the cost of credit. While his proposal was endorsed by President
Kennedy, it was repeatedly defeated by the Senate Banking and Currency
Committee. Ironically, it was Senator Douglas's defeat in 1966 that helped
make its enactment possible, for it was his insistence that a simple annual
interest rate be disclosed to all creditors that had made any compromise
impossible. In addition, Senator Willis Robertson (Democrat-Virginia),
who as chair of the Senate Banking and Currency Committee had played
a critical role in blocking any truth in lending legislation, was defeated for
reelection that same year.

While credit unions and mutual savings banks supported the enactment
of truth in lending legislation, the bill was strongly opposed by other
financial institutions and retail merchants. The merchants argued that
requiring interest changes to be stated on an annual rather than a monthly
basis would "create an undesirable psychological effect on the American
consumer's buying habits, resulting in a serious business lag."[43] A compromise was subsequently worked out by Senator William Proxmire (Demo-
crat-Wisconsin). It essentially exempted revolving charge accounts and
contracts calling for less than ten dollars in finance charges from the bill's
rate disclosure requirements. This served to eliminate the opposition of
both large department stores and small retail merchants. The bill was
unanimously reported out of committee and approved by the full Senate,
but the House approved two amendments that significantly strengthened
it. The House eliminated both the revolving charge account amendment
and the ten-dollar minimum provisions. The Senate accepted the stronger
House version, and a bill roughly similar to that originally proposed by
Senator Paul Douglas was signed into law by President Johnson on May
29, 1968.

Coal Mine Safety

While consumer issues dominated the politics of government regulation during the second half of the 1960s, at the end of that decade the regulatory agenda began to broaden. In 1969, Congress, after an extremely bitter legislative battle, approved legislation expanding government protection for coal miners. Like automotive safety, this issue emerged in response to a real problem: cars killed more consumers than any other product, and more workers were killed and injured in coal mines than in any other sector of the economy. Yet, prior to 1969, the coal industry had succeeded in keeping federal and state regulatory and enforcement powers at bay. A widely publicized incident transformed the political climate: in November 1968, seventy-eight miners died in an explosion in mine number 9 of the Consolidated Coal Company in Farmington, West Virginia. Congress responded by enacting the Federal Coal Mine Health and Safety Act of 1969.

A distinctive aspect of the 1969 legislation was its linkage of health and safety issues, and it is conceivable that even *without* the Farmington disaster, legislation would have passed to protect miners from black-lung disease. A number of associations organized outside the auspices of the United Mine Workers (UMW) had been created in the Appalachian coal region to defend black-lung victims. Preliminary research by the U.S. Public Health Service from 1963 to 1965 documented the extent to which black-lung disease was a serious health hazard to coal miners. The surgeon general reported in 1968 that over 125,000 retired and active miners suffered from the disease. Three states—Alabama, Pennsylvania, and Virginia—had already authorized benefits under statewide workmen's compensation programs, thus recognizing that the disease was occupationally related. Thus rank-and-file miners (the UMW and its head, W. A. "Tony" Boyle, were silent) and the medical profession were lobbying actively for federal legislation well before the Farmington disaster.

Nonetheless, that tragic incident forged the critical link between mine safety and the high incidence of black-lung disease. The disaster was in the headlines for a week as rescuers tried unsuccessfully to remove miners or their corpses from the burned-out mine. While the cause of the explosion remained uncertain, numerous reports indicated that mine number 9 had been cited as unsafe by the Bureau of Mines for the previous two years. Moreover, the technical problems of improving health and safety were not unrelated. The major cause of mine explosions was the build-up of methane, which was then ignited by sparks from electrical equipment or improper explosives. Accumulations of coal dust increased the volatility of the methane, which was also the main cause of black-lung disease. Reduction of coal-dust levels within the mines would thus lower both the threat of explosion and the incidence of black-lung disease. As Nixon's secretary of the interior, Walter Hickel, subsequently put it: "The health and safety of the coal miners are so closely interwoven that it is inappropriate to even contemplate their consideration as separate issues. Miners are dying from accidents in the mines and from occupationally caused disease. In our opinion, those who oppose health legislation are the same people who oppose safety legislation."[44]

The Johnson administration hurriedly wrote a bill on coal mine health and safety before it left office in January 1969. The new Nixon administration also produced a bill with remarkable speed and submitted it to Congress in early March. (At the same time, the Bureau of Mines ordered its inspectors to stop giving notice of impending inspections; thus, the mines could not be "cleaned" for the inspector's eye.) The Nixon bill was somewhat stronger and more inclusive than its predecessor. It authorized hefty fines for operators who mined when dust levels exceeded specified limits and granted the secretary of the interior the power to regulate the type of equipment and building materials used in the mines. It also gave black-lung victims the right to be assigned to posts with cleaner air.

The coal industry publicly supported the legislation, although expressing reservations about its permissible dust levels. The U.S. Public Health Service (USPHS), using British data, had recommended in 1968 a standard of 3.0 milligrams of dust per cubic meter of air. The original Nixon bill recommended a 4.5-milligram level six months after enactment, later to be reduced to 3.0. Apparently, the Nixon proposal was a compromise between the USPHS and the industry. Privately, the industry backed the 4.5-milligram standard, probably in the belief that it was the best it could attain. As legislation moved through Congress in the summer and fall of 1969, its fears seemed justified. The House passed a bill requiring a 4.5-milligram standard, but the Senate set the level at 3.0 milligrams. Both versions provided for a future standard of 2.0 milligrams.

The coal operators had trouble arguing against standards more stringent than the 4.5-milligram level because of the industry's economic health. By the late 1960s, the soft-coal industry was booming. Mechanization in the early 1950s had led to a 300 percent increase in labor productivity and the worldwide boom in the steel industry had significantly increased the demand for U.S. coal. Production in the late 1960s exceeded the previous highs of the 1940s; consequently, the industry could argue against stringent dust level standards only on the basis of inadequate existing technology.[45] It found support from the Bureau of Mines, which claimed that a 4.5-milligram, but not a 3.0-milligram, level could be immediately attained.[46] Along with the technical argument, the coal operators downplayed the incidence of black-lung disease and stressed the effect of human error on the workers' health and safety. Nonetheless, Congress mandated levels of 3.0 milligrams within six months and 2.0 milligrams after three years. A 4.5-milligram standard was permissible only after approval by a federal panel. *Business Week* explained that the industry had too often cried "foul" in the past.[47]

Implications

The significant increase in the volume of regulatory legislation between 1966 and 1969 indicated that the relative political influence of business had begun to erode. Politicians, much to their surprise, had discovered that the public was willing to support a "get-tough" attitude toward particular industries. Companies, for their part, could no longer assume that the political process was either irrelevant or benign: the scope of government intervention in the economy, after remaining relatively stable for nearly a generation, had again begun to increase. Historically, consumer protection legislation had been primarily initiated by companies or industries as a way of strengthening their competitive position. But this was not true of the statutes enacted during the latter half of the 1960s. While their interests were far from identical, most companies preferred the status quo to the enactment of any new regulatory legislation at all.

At the same time, the actual significance of these laws was rather modest. With the exception of the Flammable Fabrics Act, which was adamantly opposed by the textiles manufacturers, the final form of each of these laws represented a political compromise. While the concessions industry was able to exact varied—they were greatest in the Fair Packaging and Labeling Act and somewhat less in the other three laws—the final version of each of the regulatory statutes enacted during the mid-1960s was one with which the affected industries could clearly live.

Two of the laws—truth in lending and truth in packaging—were unlikely to have any significant economic impact, and the meat inspection legislation affected only the relatively small portion (15 percent) of the nation's processed meat that was sold intrastate. The automobile safety legislation, the coal mine safety legislation, and the Flammable Fabrics Act did impose real costs upon the three industries affected by them, but these costs appeared unlikely to affect their profitability adversely since they could readily be passed on to consumers. Besides, all three industries were relatively prosperous. With the exception of the Federal Coal Mine Health and Safety Act, none of the regulatory laws enacted during the 1960s was technology-forcing; each established requirements which were well within industry's ability to achieve. Moreover, since each regulatory statute affected only one industry, their overall effect on the economy was rather small. Thus, through 1969, most industries in the United States had not experienced any increase in federal controls over their activities in the areas of health, safety, or environmental protection.

But while the actual political losses experienced by business may have been relatively modest through 1969, the increased popularity of government regulation of business needs to be placed in a broader context. Not only had new issues emerged on the political agenda, issues with which business was unaccustomed to dealing, but public support for business declined steadily and rapidly after 1966: between 1968 and 1970 the percentage of Americans agreeing with the statement, "business tries to strike a fair balance between profits and the interest of the public" fell from 70 percent to 33 percent. The percentage of Americans expressing a "great deal of confidence in the leaders of major companies," dropped from 55 percent in 1966 to 47 percent in 1967 and then to 27 percent in 1971. ORC survey data also reveal a steady increase in antibusiness sentiment after 1967. "Not a single industry out of twenty-five and not a single firm out of fifty actually improved its public reputation between the late 1960s and the 1970s."[48]

The mid-1960s also witnessed the beginning of a shift in cultural and social attitudes toward business. An important expression of this development was a growth in the disenchantment of students with business. A widely quoted 1966 *Newsweek* survey of a cross-section of 800 college seniors reported that only 31 percent were seriously considering a career in business and that only 12 percent considered business their first choice.[49] Of the students surveyed, 74 percent felt that the business world was accurately described by the phrase "dog eat dog" and 64 percent agreed that "business cares too little about the individual." A survey conducted by *Moderation* magazine in 1967 revealed that 61 percent of its respondents found "their fellow students to be indifferent or hostile toward working in industry,"[50] and a poll of 19,000 college seniors by the College Placement Council reported that only half "regarded business as either a likely or an alternative employer."[51] During the second half of the

1960s, enrollment in business schools increased only one-third as fast as total college enrollment.

Many business commentators were particularly troubled by both the hostility and indifference to business among students at elite universities. In general, the more prestigious the institution the students attended and the higher their academic standing within that institution, the less likely they were to be interested in working in the private sector. Businesses had no lack of eager applicants, but compared to five years earlier, they were less likely to include the nation's "best and brightest." Of the students who graduated from the nation's top-ranking colleges in June 1966, more than two-thirds went on to graduate school. Only 3.4 percent of the 1966 freshman class at Berkeley indicated an interest in pursuing careers in business and a survey of all undergraduates at Stanford reported that only 15 to 18 percent were aiming for a career in business. Of the 1,091 individuals in Harvard College's class of 1966, only 63 went to work in the profit sector after graduation, though an additional 130 indicated that they "definitely . . . intended to end up in business."[52] Only 10 percent of those who were graduated from Columbia College in 1967 expressed an interest in business as a career. At Princeton, the percentage of seniors planning immediate employment in business declined from 13 percent in 1961 to 7 percent in 1966. Only 152 of the 761 men who graduated from Princeton in 1966 indicated that they planned a career in business. *Fortune* concluded that "the prejudice against business is undeniable, and permeates the country's highest-ranking colleges."[53]

What did students have against business? An informal discussion with students at nine universities conducted by *Fortune* revealed that "the idea of making money appealed to very few young men and women with whom the question was discussed."[54] The most frequent criticism of business was that it placed too much pressure on conformity and failed to provide significant opportunity for personal fulfillment. One nineteen-year-old told an interviewer for Young & Rubicam: "The field of business is a great wasteland, inhabited by men of narrow horizons and personal interest, where anti-creativity and anti-idealism is the rule and not the exception."[55] Some young people also believed that working in the private sector meant they could not make a positive contribution to the nation's pressing social problems. A poll of young adults, published in *Fortune* in June 1969, reported that 94 percent of the students interviewed and 92 percent of the others were "convinced that business was too profit-blinded and not concerned with public welfare."[56] *Business Week* quoted a student at the Harvard Graduate School of Business: "If people are really interested in tackling social problems, they will have nothing to do with the Fortune 500 or business."[57] A student intern at Bankers Trust complained to *Business Week* that "there seemed to be a conformity in ideas. There were no intellectual conversations, no discussions of the war in Vietnam. It was all business, and it got boring after a while."[58]

An article in the *Financial Executive* in March 1968 reported that "businessmen are very concerned these days about the reluctance of college students to go into the business world. You hear this concern expressed everywhere."[59] A vice president of General Electric told a college audience: "I am concerned that the future effectiveness of business will suffer if we cannot attract into managerial ranks the kind of idealism, sense of purpose, and just plain talent of a whole wave of young people who all too often look on business as a dull drab world of 'organization men.' "[60]

In fact this discontent appeared to extend far deeper than a simple change in the career preferences of a small portion of the nation's students. The second half of the 1960s also marked the emergence of the "counterculture"—a social phenomenon whose political significance extended far beyond those who "tuned in and dropped out." This subculture represented the popularization of the impulses of modernism that had previously been confined to an elite avant-garde. It explicitly challenged the values of Protestant work ethic—with its emphasis on rationality, restraint, self-discipline, and prosperity—that had traditionally provided the cultural foundation of capitalism. In *The Making of a Counterculture,* published in 1969, Theodore Roszak wrote: "The bourgeoisie is obsessed by greed; its sex life is insipid and prudish; its family patterns are debased; . . . its mercenary routinization of existence is intolerable."[61] Other works, most notably *The Greening of America,* attacked the "consumer culture" of American society, accusing it of being dehumanizing and manipulative.[62] These sentiments were widely echoed in the nation's popular culture—in movies like *The Graduate,* novels like *Catch-22,* and the songs of Bob Dylan—leading one marketing professor to conclude that "the discomfort of American culture with the businessman may be growing at an alarming rate."[63]

At about the same time, the New Left and the antiwar movement began to direct more of their political energies against business. Between 1966 and 1968, Dow Chemical, which manufactured napalm for the Defense Department, was the object of 183 major campus demonstrations to bar its recruiters from campus; in the fall of 1967, over one-third of all campus demonstrations were directed against Dow. As a Dow public-relations director noted: "In frequency and consistency of attack this is a record unmatched over the past two years even by recruiters for the U.S. armed forces." In November 1969, in the radical magazine the *Guardian*, activist Staughton Lynd asked:

> Why . . . do we continue to demonstrate in Washington as if the core of the problem lay there? The small group of activists who have burnt . . . corporate records have pointed to the proper targets. . . . We need to find ways to lay siege to corporations. . . . We need to invent anti-corporate actions which involve masses of people, not just a dedicated few.[64]

Lynd proceeded to list the annual meeting dates of twenty-one of the largest defense-related corporations. He predicted, "Our inevitable enemy in the coming year is the corporation."[65] During 1970, scores of corporate annual meetings were the focus of demonstrations by antiwar activists. Thirty-nine branches of the Bank of America were physically damaged and one, near the University of California at Santa Barbara, was burnt to the ground.

In a confidential memo (subsequently leaked) to the U.S. Chamber of Commerce entitled "Attack on American Free Enterprise System," Supreme Court Associate Justice Lewis F. Powell observed that "no thoughtful person can question that the American economic system is under broad attack." After visiting his alma mater, columnist Stewart Alsop concluded, "Yale, like every every other major college, is graduating scores of bright young men who despise the American political and economic system."[66] Daniel Yankelovich observed:

> This massive withdrawal of public confidence has created a severe problem business is going to have to deal with. For some of the demands arising directly or indirectly out of the student revolution include a desire to regulate business more closely, to curb its power and influence, to restrict its overseas investments, and to prevent it from growing through increased use of technology.[67]

Reporting on "Our Future Business Environment," researchers for the General Electric Corporation (GE) concluded that there had been a "relative decline of industry as a prime motive force in our society." They predicted that the "key problem for the next decade for business would be environmental adjustment."[68]

The interest on the part of many business executives in the notion of corporate social responsibility can be seen, in part, as a way for companies to improve their image among the nation's highly educated and socially concerned youth—often their own children. The expansion of corporate programs designed to address the plight of the nation's urban poor that took place in the late 1960s enabled many companies to demonstrate that business need not be "socially irrelevant." Yet these efforts did nothing to improve the image of business and, for a variety of reasons, many were cut back during the early 1970s. Whether or not corporations actually began to behave more responsibly in the mid- and late 1960s, the gap between the public's expectation of business and its perception of its performance continued to widen. By 1970, the corporation—its size, social role, political impact, and public accountability—would move from a peripheral to a central position on the nation's domestic political agenda. And the undergraduates who had once picketed companies on campuses would begin to lobby against them in the halls of Congress and sue them in federal courts.

IV

Business on the Defensive, 1969 to 1972

Introduction

During the second half of the 1960s, the political defeats experienced by business were confined to individual industries. But from 1969 through 1972, virtually the entire American business community experienced a series of political setbacks without parallel in the postwar period. In the space of only four years, Congress enacted a significant tax-reform bill, four major environmental laws, an occupational safety and health act, and a series of additional consumer-protection statutes. The government also created a number of important new regulatory agencies, including the Environmental Protection Administration (EPA), the Occupational Safety and Health Administration (OSHA), and the Consumer Product Safety Commission (CPSC), investing them with broad powers over a wide range of business decisions. In contrast to the 1960s, many of the regulatory laws enacted during the early 1970s were broader in scope and more ambitious in their objectives. In this sense, they represented a kind of Great Society for the private economy. The result was a fundamental transformation of both the politics and administration of government regulation of corporate social conduct.

Notwithstanding the considerable degree of public support for legislation to protect the consumer during the 1960s, the consumer laws of that decade were enacted without the effective political support of a consumer movement. Members of Congress had responded more to their perception of changing public attitudes toward business than to the specific demands of consumer organizations. The only organized political constituency that supported consumer protection was the AFL-CIO. But at the end of the 1960s, a number of new interest groups began to lobby for additional government controls over the private sector. Common Cause, Friends of the Earth, the Natural Resources Defense Council, Ralph Nader's Public Citizen, Environmental Action, the Center for Law and Social Policy, and the Consumer Federation of America were all established between 1969 and 1970, and the National Consumer Union opened a Washington office in 1969. By 1971, almost seventy national conservation and environmental organizations had offices in Washington.

In the 1960s, the consumer movement had operated in labor's shadow; indeed, labor's "political resource[s] . . . dwarfed the efforts of all other consumer advocates combined."[1] But in the 1970s, the consumer and environmental movements emerged as a political force in their own right. They became active and sophisticated participants in the policy process, able to hire lobbyists, work effectively with the press, and mobilize their supporters in the grass roots. Their leadership also became more outspoken, and as a result the relationship between liberal legislators and activists became less symbiotic and more adversarial. For example, in 1970, Ralph Nader and his associates played a critical role in pressuring Senator Edmund Muskie to support much stricter air-pollution standards than he had initially favored.

The contrast between the politics of business-government relations before and after 1968 is striking. The most obvious example is in the area of tax policy. Both the 1962 and 1964 tax bills, while approved during the administrations of two liberal Democratic presidents, were extremely favorable to investors and corporations. Yet in the space of only five years, "the basic emphasis in tax reform had completely shifted." The Tax Revenue Act of 1969, approved during the presidency of Richard Nixon, significantly increased the tax burden on business; virtually all the relief it provided went to middle-income individuals. The "most liberal peacetime tax bill ever enacted," it represented a response to the "perceived mood of the nation as antiwar, antibusiness, and liberal in domestic policy."[2]

An even more dramatic change took place in environmental policy. Explaining the lack of public interest in the debate over the 1967 Clean Air Act Amendments, two journalists concluded: "Pollution and environmental concerns, despite their recent vogue, simply do not impress most Americans as a problem of major concern to themselves or their country."[3]

Yet only three years later, Congress passed, and President Nixon signed into law, the most far-reaching set of pollution-control requirements ever imposed upon American industry. Since 1966, Congress had been considering a change in water-pollution control policy. Because, in large measure, of the opposition of both the oil and utility industries, no legislation was enacted. However, in 1972, Congress approved a radical change in water-pollution policy. For nearly a decade, it had dutifully appropriated funds for the construction of a supersonic transport. In part because of concerns about the SST's effects on the environment, all federal support for the development of the aircraft was terminated in 1971.

Throughout the 1960s, the oil and gas industries had been able to prevent the enactment of additional federal controls over oil spills. In 1970, Congress made the industry strictly liable for any accidental discharges. In the same period, despite growing public concern about the use of pesticides, prompted by Rachel Carson's best-seller, *Silent Spring*, the manufacturers and users of pesticides had successfully opposed any further government regulation of their products. But in 1969 the chemical industry suffered a major setback. President Nixon transferred the responsibility for controlling the use of pesticides from the Department of Agriculture to the newly established Environmental Protection Agency. And three years later, Congress significantly expanded EPA's controls over the use of pesticides.

Although Johnson's administration had urged Congress to enact federal occupational health and safety standards, business had succeeded in preventing any broad expansion of the federal government's regulatory authority in this area. In 1970, Congress approved a sweeping change of occupational health and safety regulation that effectively transferred the locus of regulatory responsibility from the states to the federal government. Finally, five years after the tobacco and broadcasting industry had persuaded Congress to prevent the Federal Trade Commission (FTC) from restricting cigarette advertising, Congress completely banned the advertising of this product from both radio and television.

The Tax Reform Act of 1969

The Tax Reform Act of 1969 was the first important piece of domestic legislation enacted during Nixon's presidency. The cause of tax reform had received a major impetus in the closing days of President Johnson's administration, when retiring Secretary of the Treasury Joseph Barr warned of a "taxpayer's revolt" if tax inequities were not alleviated.[4] According to Barr, middle-income taxpayers were bearing the brunt of taxes while numerous millionaires paid nothing because of tax shelters. Hearings by the House Ways and Means Committee began less than a month after Johnson left office. The committee had received the outgoing president's proposals on January 30 and used them as a basis for its deliberations. Johnson had proposed tightening loopholes for upper-income groups, thus gaining roughly $3.4 billion and passing this savings on to lower-income individuals. The hearings were exhaustive, covering foundations, banks, depletion allowances, capital gains, investment credits, real-estate depreciation, tax treatment of state and municipal bonds—even Social Security benefits. Barr had clearly struck a responsive chord: over the following year Congress received more mail about the injustices of the tax system than any other issue, including the Vietnam War.

From the very beginning, Representative Wilbur Mills, chair of the House Ways and Means Committee, had made clear that equity would be first on his agenda, and he coordinated the attack on existing loopholes. The committee voted to tax interest on state and municipal bonds assets that were used as tax shelters for the very wealthy. (Cities and states would be compensated by federal subsidy.) Mills also successfully opposed the Nixon administration's recommendations that tax schedules remain unchanged. While the administration had argued that such changes would result in too great a loss of revenue, Mills pushed through an average reduction of 5 percent in most income categories. And when the tax bill came before the Rules Committee and it was discovered that it had provided no tax relief for middle-income wage earners, Mills called a lunch break and added rate cuts totaling $2.4 billion.

The spirit of tax reform also reached into the administration. In general, the conflicts between Nixon and the Congress were not over individual items but their potential effects on revenue. The administration opposed certain changes favored by Mills, such as cutting the oil-depletion allowance to 20 percent and taxing state and municipal bonds. But in general, the thrust of the administration's proposals were not far removed from those of the House and Senate. For instance, the administration endorsed a plan to create a "low-income allowance" which effectively removed two million taxpayers from the tax rolls. And, of utmost interest to the business community, Nixon proposed the repeal of the tax credit for investments enacted in President Kennedy's administration, which would increase corporate taxes by nearly $3 billion. Nixon argued that "the repeal of the investment tax credit will permit relief to every taxpayer."[5] His administration also endorsed an increase in the capital-gains tax and limitations on the use of tax shelters. A writer in *The New Republic* commented: "What can be said without any fear of contradiction, is that it [the set of Nixon proposals] is far and away the most 'anti-rich' tax reform proposal *ever* proposed by a Republican President in the 56 years of the existence of the income tax."[6]

As they made their way through Congress, the amendments to the tax bill that affected business consisted almost entirely of revenue-gaining proposals. The proposals that did provide additional tax breaks for business did so in a very selective way and in response to important issues on the nation's social agenda. For example, pollution-control equipment was allowed to be amortized over a five-year period. (This was a House provision accepted by the Senate with an important proviso that the equipment be in service before 1975.) Five-year amortization was also provided for coal-mine safety equipment as mandated by the 1969 Coal Mine Health and Safety Act. Four- to five-year amortization was passed for railroad rolling stock. Finally, accelerated depreciation was also granted for renovations of rental property. Thus, the concessions to business responded to central features of the liberal agenda: commitment to pollution control, mine safety, mass transportation, and housing. The remainder of the provisions that affected the corporate community were either revenue-neutral or increased their tax bite.

The Ways and Means Committee, under Wilbur Mills's leadership, worked with such diligence that a number of business lobbies were caught off guard. According to committee member Al Ullman (Democrat-Oregon), the opportunities for logrolling were minimal: "for once, we are not trading on each other's loopholes."[7] A "closed" rule imposed by the Rules Committee allowed amendments on the House floor only by members of the Ways and Means Committee. Thus, the bill passed the House with only two amendments: the provision of $2.4 billion in relief to middle-income taxpayers and the extension of oil-depletion allowances to extraction from oil shale. When the bill came to the floor of the Senate, Tennessee's Albert Gore argued that the 5 percent average reductions in tax rates provided insufficient tax relief to those who needed it the most. He proposed eliminating the reductions but increasing the level of personal exemptions from $600 to $800 by 1971. This change won acceptance on the floor and was only slightly modified later by the House-Senate conference committee. The Senate also agreed to establish a maximum tax rate of 50 percent on earned income, and up to 70 percent on unearned income. Most important, by a vote of 62 to 30, the Senate defeated an amendment to restore the oil-depletion allowance to 27.5 percent; as a result, it was reduced to 22 percent, giving liberal critics of the oil industry a victory for which they had been campaigning since 1918. Senator William Proxmire had described the depletion allowance as "a symbol of privilege and inequity in our tax laws" and informed his colleagues that unless it was reduced, "the bill would be considered a mockery, a hypocritical, meaningless mockery by most Americans."[8]

The final version of the bill, signed by President Nixon on December 30, 1969, increased the maximum tax on capital gains, limited real-estate depreciation schedules, eliminated the tax credit for investments, and reduced the depletion allowance for a number of natural substances, including oil and gas. At the same time, it provided a modest degree of tax relief for the middle class and the poor. The single most important factor underlying the 1969 legislation was the "liberal atmosphere in the country." John Witte wrote:

> The Great Society programs in education, income support, health care, civil rights, and job programs preceded this legislation, and the large regulatory reforms in environmental protection and occupational health and safety lay ahead. This spate of liberal legislation lasted less than a decade, but the Tax Reform Act of 1969 fell right in the middle of that remarkable period.[9]

Business Week observed that:

> When tax reform was the pet of far-out liberals, it was relatively easy to beat back. But now it appears almost to have become part of the revolt of the solid middle-class citizens against the swinging tendencies of American life. The new cries against "millionaires with loopholes" apparently spring from the same wells of resentment that produce feeling against "hippies" and "freeloaders on the welfare rolls."[10]

The National Environmental Protection Act

If consumerism was the cutting edge of the political challenge to business prerogatives during the second half of the 1960s, then environmental protection held a similar status at the beginning of the 1970s. The political impact of environmentalism was both rapid and dramatic: virtually overnight, environmental policy became the primary focus of public concern with the power and performance of the business corporation. A review of public-opinion surveys conducted in 1969 and 1970 reported that "alarm about the environment sprang from nowhere to major proportions in a few short years."[11] While only 1 percent of those polled in May 1969 regarded "pollution/ecology as an important national problem," one-quarter of those questioned listed it as such a year later. Gallup reported that public concern over air and water pollution had jumped from tenth place in the summer of 1969 to fifth place a year later. When asked to identify the three national issues to which government should give the most attention, "reducing air and water pollution ranked ninth in 1965 and second in 1970." A Louis Harris survey taken in December 1970 revealed that Americans considered pollution to be "the most serious problem" facing their communities. On April 22, 1970, an estimated twenty million Americans participated in Earth Day—a series of rallies, teach-ins, and other events organized to express concern with the condition of the nation's physical environment. Five new important environmental organizations were organized between 1967 and 1971: the Environmental Defense Fund, Friends of the Earth, the Natural Resources Defense Council, Environmental Action, and the Union of Concerned Scientists. Between 1967 and 1971, enrollment in the Sierra Club increased from 48,000 to 130,000, and in 1970 the membership of the National Audubon Society more than doubled, rising to 150,000. All told, membership in the nation's five largest environmental organizations increased by 30 percent between 1970 and 1971.[12]

Environmentalism had become more than an important political issue. For a brief period—roughly from the middle of 1969 to about 1972—it virtually acquired, in words used by *Time* magazine, the status of a "national obsession."[13] Obviously, the quality of the nation's environment did not suddenly deteriorate between 1967—when Congress handed the coal and utility industries a major political victory by limiting HEW's authority to establish emission standards for sulphur oxide—and 1970, when it amended the Clean Air Act to require EPA to establish national air-quality standards. Yet a sense of urgency—even crisis—suddenly pervaded public discussion of environmental issues. The press was filled with stories of environmental trauma, such as the actual burning of the Cuyahoga River in Ohio and an air-pollution alert in New York City. Only eight days after President Nixon took office, crude oil from a Union Oil Company well in the Santa Barbara channel began to leak onto the shore: the television evening news programs filled American living rooms with pictures of thousands of dead or dying seabirds trapped in the oozing gooey blackness. This incident, according to John Whitaker, "was comparable to tossing a match into a gasoline tank: it exploded into the environmental revolution, and the press fanned the flames to keep the issue burning brightly."[14] Author Paul Ehrlich and activist David Brower predicted "eco-catastrophe" by the end of the decade unless major changes were made in the nation's modes of production and consumption. Democratic Senator Gaylord Nelson of Wisconsin expressed the hope that "Earth Day . . . may be the birth date of a new American ethic that rejects the frontier philosophy that the continent was put here for our plunder, and accepts the idea that even urbanized, affluent, mobile societies are interdependent with the fragile, life-sustaining systems of the air, the water, the land."[15]

To some extent this obsession reflected the crisis orientation of this period: the nation had previously gone through the "urban crisis" and within a few years it would undergo the trauma of the "energy crisis." Environmentalism also emerged in the political agenda at a particular point in the nation's economic development: it appeared at the tail end of a quarter-century of extremely rapid economic growth as well as the longest peacetime expansion of the economy in the postwar period to date. The longevity and magnitude of this growth had severely strained the quality of the nation's physical environment: both air and water pollution had become serious problems in a number of areas, and urban and industrial development was beginning to encroach on the nation's undeveloped land. While advocates of zero growth remained a distinctive—and somewhat eccentric—minority, for a few years in the early 1970s it did appear that many Americans had become much more skeptical of the benefits of material abundance, rapid economic growth, and technological progress. In this sense, environmentalism can be seen as a kind of middle-class embrace of the values of the counterculture. The proportion of Americans willing to give business high marks for "bringing better quality products to people" declined from 75 percent in 1960 to 42 percent in 1973, leading pollster Louis Harris to conclude: "People have come to be skeptical about American 'know-how,' worried that it might pollute, contaminate, poison or even kill them."[16]

At the same time, the widespread sense of public confidence in the continued capacity of the American economy to generate additional wealth had persuaded many Americans that the nation did have the resources to improve rapidly the quality of the environment; all that was required was the political commitment. In this sense, the environmental movement, notwithstanding the apocalyptic tone of some of its supporters, reflected the optimism of the 1960s. The federal government began that decade by committing itself to place a man on the moon by 1970. It then promised an end to racial injustice and shortly thereafter declared war on poverty. It now was about to make another sweeping commitment: it would make the nation's air and water clean again. Prior to 1970, government regulatory policy had been focused on ameliorating specific hazards, such as those associated with the use of drugs, automobiles, meat, and cigarettes; beginning around 1970, the government began to assume responsibility for eliminating virtually all of them.

The first concrete political expression of this escalation of public expectations was Congress's unanimous passage of the National Environmental Protection Act (NEPA) in December 1969. Signed into law by President Nixon the following month, this legislation declared improvement of the quality of the environment to be a major national priority, required all federal agencies to consider the impact of their decisions on the environment, and established a Council on Environmental Quality in the Executive Office of the President to monitor the nation's environmental policies.

> NEPA was enacted when public interest in the quality of the environment was rising. Clearly a gesture of congressional concern was in order. For many legislators, undoubtedly, a vote for NEPA was symbolic—akin to a vote for motherhood and apple pie. . . . Little did they realize, however, that in voting to enact NEPA, they were placing a potent weapon in the hands of citizen activists.[17]

That weapon was section 102(2)c, which mandated the preparation of a "detailed environmental statement to accompany proposals for legislation and other major federal actions significantly affecting the quality of the human environment."[18] It was included at the suggestion of Lyton Caldwell, a political scientist who had persuaded Senator Henry Jackson (Democrat-Washington) and his staff of the need for an "action forcing" mechanism to make sure that federal agencies did not ignore Congress's statement of broad policy goals. This provision was deemed crucial in view of the likely indifference of the administration to the work of the Council on Environmental Quality; however, at the time, few appreciated its significance. The legislative history of the NEPA, while placing "much of the blame for environmental deterioration on the unresponsiveness of governmental institutions,"[19] contained no hint that the courts would come to play an important role in remedying this situation. This lack of foresight is not surprising: in 1969 there was as yet no real history of environmental litigation. As a result, section 102(2)c attracted little public attention and neither environmental organizations nor trade associations expressed much interest in it.

Six months later, the Nixon administration accepted the recommendation of the President's Advisory Council on Executive Organization and created a separate pollution control agency. The establishment of the EPA was also relatively uncontroversial. While a representative of the National Association of Manufacturers (NAM) stated that "many businessmen are wary of the idea of a super-environmental office," the *National Journal* reported that "there are indications that some corporate interests would welcome a centralization of environmental programs in the Federal government."[20] In any event, the only active opposition came from agricultural interests, which opposed the removal of pesticide registration from the Department of Agriculture to the EPA on the grounds that the EPA would be likely to treat agricultural chemicals as pollutants rather than aids to production.

The EPA brought together six thousand employees, working on fifteen different programs located in three departments, into one administrative body. Its organization was significant in two respects. First, it was given responsibility for regulating an aspect of the behavior of all industries, rather than the behavior of a particular industry or set of industries. Second, it was headed by a single administrator directly responsible to the president, rather than by a commission whose members had staggered terms. The first of these innovations was dictated by the nature of the problem the agency was established to address. In the president's words, the EPA was to deal with the environment "as a single interrelated system."[21] The second reflected a growing dissatisfaction with the performance of independent regulatory agencies that extended across the political spectrum. With the exception of the Equal Employment Opportunity Commission, Congress had not created a new independent regulatory agency since 1938. The fact that the EPA's structure was based on the recommendations of the President's Advisory Council on Executive Organization, headed by Roy Ash, a former Litton executive, suggests that its formation was not intended to weaken the ability of business to shape the direction of federal regulation. If anything, making it accountable to the president enhanced rather than reduced the ability of business to influence its decisions. However, like section 102 of the NEPA, the EPA would come to assume a political significance that few appreciated at the time of its creation.

Why did the business community fail to appreciate the political significance of either the NEPA or the establishment of the EPA? In part, because neither expanded the scope of government controls over the private sector: they both represented an effort to shift priorities within the government— not to change the balance of power between the private and public sectors. Moreover, given an administration which was widely regarded as sympathetic to business, the private sector had no reason to expect an unwelcome shift in public policy in this area. Indeed, much of the business community

appeared to welcome the public's sudden interest in environmental quality, in part because they viewed it as a way of reducing the growing
polarization of American society: unlike Black Power or the Vietnam War,
environmentalism appeared to emphasize what Americans had in common
rather than what divided them. Even though many of the activities of
Earth Day had a distinctly antibusiness flavor, many companies actively
participated in them: they sponsored programs and sent speakers to teach-
ins and radio and television shows to describe the extent of their companies' efforts to reduce pollution.

Moreover, many executives appeared to share the public's concern with
the need for stronger government regulation in this area. A survey of 270
chief executives conducted for *Fortune* in late 1969 reported that 60 percent
believed that the environment was a problem of "the highest priority" and
that environmental quality was deteriorating. Almost as many, 57 percent,
stated that the "federal government should step up its regulatory activities
while 53 percent supported the establishment of a single water pollution
plan." When asked if "the protection of the environment [should] be taken
into consideration even if it means inhibiting the introduction of new
products," 88 percent responded in the affirmative.[22]

Amendments to the Clean Air Act

Within a few months, this consensus had been shattered. The source of
the conflict was the Clean Air Act Amendments of 1970—one of the
strictest, most controversial, and bitterly fought pieces of regulatory legislation enacted by the federal government. The Clean Air Act Amendments
were an important departure in two respects. First, unlike virtually all
previous regulatory statutes, they included specific timetables and deadlines: for example, states were given one year to adopt plans prescribing
emission limitations that would enable their air quality to meet national
health standards by 1975. In the case of pollution from motor vehicles,
Congress not only provided a timetable for compliance, but went a step
further by specifying what pollutants had to be reduced and by what
percentage. At the same time, in order to increase the likelihood that these
timetables and standards would actually be implemented, the legislation
included a provision authorizing citizens to file suits in the federal courts
to force compliance by the EPA.

Second, the goals specified in the statute were meant to be met regardless of economic or technical considerations. Thus the EPA was explicitly enjoined from considering costs in establishing national ambient-air standards designed to protect public health (primary standards). Senator Edmund Muskie admitted on the floor of the Senate that he had no idea whether the automobile manufacturers were likely to develop the necessary pollution-control technology in time to meet the deadline specified in the statute. He told Republican Senator Robert Griffin of Michigan: "The deadline is based not, I repeat, on economic and technical feasibility, but on considerations of public health . . . this is a necessary and reasonable standard to impose upon the industry."[23]

What accounts for this political shift? Why did business, which had been relatively successful throughout the 1960s in resisting pressures for stricter environmental standards, suffer such a major political setback? On the surface, what happened was that industry in general and the automobile industry in particular found itself caught between the efforts of President Nixon and Senator Muskie to each cast himself as the more ardent defender of the environment in anticipation of the 1972 presidential election. But what gave these politicians reason to believe the public wanted such a sudden and significant expansion of government controls over industry—one without precedent in the postwar period?

Part of the explanation has to do with the intensity and scope of public interest in this issue. But this explanation is insufficient. Increased public concern about the quality of the environment need not necessarily have led to such a major escalation of government demands on industry. The public could have, with equal logic, chosen to support increased government subsidies for purchases of pollution-control equipment or laws mandating changes in individual and household patterns of consumption. A roughly similar increase in public interest in environmental protection took place in almost every industrialized nation at about this same time: yet, while America's actual environmental problems were no more serious than those of other nations—indeed considerably less than Japan's—only the United States chose to impose such strict controls on the private sector.[24]

But unlike the Europeans and Japanese, the American public did not simply become more worried about pollution; it also chose to blame industry for the nation's environmental problems. When asked in 1965 to identify "the most important causes of air pollution here in this part of the country," 34 percent of those polled cited "factories and plants." Two years later, the percentage of those choosing this response had increased to 53 percent; by 1970 it had increased to 64 percent.[25] Gladwin Hill reported that the public perceived pollution to be primarily caused by the "economic giants of the steel industry, the power industry, the petroleum industry, the chemical industry, the pulp and paper industry, and many lesser enterprises." After observing that nearly two-thirds of the nation's air pollution came from motor vehicles, he concluded, "growing public awareness of the automobile's big part in smog has tended to put the auto industry in the same uncomfortable position as if the effluvia were coming out of the smokestacks in Detroit."[26] Significantly, while critics of the air-pollution law enacted in 1963 tended to focus on the need for a more aggressive federal stance vis-à-vis the states, the tone of public criticism of the effectiveness of the 1967 Air Quality Act was primarily directed at the intransigence of industry and its ability to dominate regulatory enforcement.

Senator Muskie informed the Senate that the "country was facing an air pollution crisis [with] . . . the costs of air pollution . . . counted in death and disease and disability," and proposed a comprehensive air-pollution control statute. In an effort to prevent the cause of pollution control from becoming identified with the Democratic party in general and with Senator Muskie—then a front-runner for the 1972 Democratic presidential nomination—in particular, President Nixon's 1970 State of the Union address emphasized the importance of a prompt national response to the issue of environmental protection. According to the president, "Clean air, clean water, open spaces—these should once again be the birthright of every American. If we act now—they can be."[27] Reacting to substantial public criticism of the administration's record on pollution control, Nixon revealed his intention of proposing to Congress "the most comprehensive and costly program in this field in the nation's history."[28]

The president's legislative proposals, submitted to Congress on February 10, 1970, involved a substantial escalation of the federal government's role in controlling air pollution. They also went considerably beyond those proposed by Senator Muskie a few months earlier, thus enabling the president to emerge as the stronger champion of pollution control. The administration's bill contained three important provisions: the first gave the secretary of Health, Education and Welfare (HEW) the power to establish national standards of air quality and to supervise their administration by the states. Second, Nixon, as had Johnson before him, proposed that the federal government be authorized to establish and enforce national standards for emissions from stationary sources that substantially threaten the public health or welfare. Third, the administration recommended that HEW be given the power to establish emission standards for new vehicles and engines to regulate fuel and fuel additives and to set standards for fuel composition. Bills either identical, or substantially similar, to the administration's were immediately introduced in the House and were cosponsored by nearly 130 representatives from both parties.

The business community's political response to the 1970 Clean Air Act Amendments was neither uniform nor vigorous. Even the automobile industry, which President Nixon had earlier singled out as the major source of air pollution, did not actively lobby the House of Representatives. There were several reasons for the lack of intensive industry opposition to the administration's proposals. Some corporations were responding to the change in the climate of public opinion that had occurred since 1967. As an official of one large industry association told a reporter, industry is "tired of being cast in the role of the heavy."[29] More important, many industries were finding themselves under intense political pressure at the state level; particularly with a Republican in the White House, they now preferred a more active federal role. One administration official stated that industry's opposition was less than in the past because business strategists had "come around to thinking that it's cheaper and better for us to have national emission standards than to fight all these battles locally."[30] According to the *National Journal*, "Several industry spokesmen, reversing the time-honored opposition of the private sector to federal controls of any kind, have said national air quality standards for stationary pollution sources would be easier to live with than the varying and increasingly tough standards being adopted at state levels."[31]

Also, business did not view the congressional arena as particularly critical. None of the bills debated by the House of Representatives included specific standards; these would be established at some future date by administrators. Those industries that would potentially be affected by the standards for ambient air or emissions felt confident that they would enjoy substantial input in setting these requirements, particularly since the Nixon administration had recently established a National Industrial Pollution Control Council. This council, formally attached to the Department of Commerce, consisted of the chief executives of a number of major industries and trade associations, and its existence appeared to assure the business community that its concerns would be carefully considered before specific regulations were promulgated.

The bill that was reported out of committee and subsequently approved by the House with relatively little debate included a provision authorizing the secretary of HEW to establish standards for stationary-source emissions. It was thus an important legislative defeat for a substantial segment of the American industrial community—including the steel, chemical, utilities, coal, oil-refining, and mining industries—which would have preferred that the federal government confine its role to the setting of air-quality standards. Nonetheless, while the bill was stronger than that fa-vored by any company or trade association, most indicated that they could "live with it."

Meanwhile the Senate Public Works Subcommittee on Air and Water Pollution, chaired by Senator Muskie, had begun hearings. Seven citizens' action and professional groups, along with the AFL-CIO, testified in favor of strengthening the bill approved by the House. It was following the formal hearings by Muskie's subcommittee, however, that the real drama of the 1970 Clean Air Act Amendments began to unfold. With the passage of the House bill, the Nixon administration had firmly established a pre-eminent position in the field of environmental protection. It had initiated a significant strengthening and broadening of the federal government's regulatory authority over what was literally the most visible dimension of pollution control. But at about the same time that the Nixon administra-tion had succeeded in identifying itself with the cause of environmental protection, Senator Muskie, the Democratic party's leading presidential contender, found himself challenged from another direction. In May 1970, Ralph Nader's study group's report on air pollution, entitled *Vanishing Air*, was released.[32] Along with a detailed description of industry's role in effectively preventing any serious effort to address the problem of air pollution, the report included a pointed attack on Senator Muskie's role in the shaping of federal pollution control policies:

> The Task Force . . . believes that Senator Muskie has failed the nation in the field of air pollution control legislation. . . . Muskie is . . . the chief architect of the disastrous Air Quality Act of 1967. That fact alone would warrant his being stripped of his title as "Mr. Pollution Control." But the senator's passiv-ity since 1967 in the face of an ever worsening air pollution crisis compounds his earlier failure. . . . Perhaps the senator should consider resigning his chairmanship of the subcommittee and leave the post to someone who can devote more time and energy to the task.

The task force's criticisms of Muskie received widespread press coverage. While Muskie accused its authors of "distort[ing] the story of air pollution control legislation and my role in drafting it," there is no question that it had its intended effect: Muskie was put "in the position of having to do something extraordinary in order to recapture his leadership."[33]

Meeting in executive session, Muskie persuaded the other members of his subcommittee to endorse a bill significantly stronger than that ap-proved by the House of Representatives. The subcommittee's bill substan-tially reduced the amount of discretion available to the executive branch to enforce clean-air requirements. It also included strict legislative deadlines for pollution abatement as well as for meeting stationary-source emission standards. Its most controversial provision, however, focused on automotive emissions: the bill required vehicular emissions of hydrocarbons and carbon monoxide to be reduced by 90 percent by 1975, with a similar reduction in nitrogen oxide to take place a year later.

The subcommittee's report came as a total surprise to the business community. Neither the House nor the Senate hearings had indicated that such a significant escalation of the federal government's regulatory role was actually on the political agenda. An intense lobbying effort was immediately launched to weaken the bill before it was reported out by the full Senate Public Works Committee. A number of trade associations, including the National Lead Association, the American Petroleum Institute, the Manufacturing Chemists Association, the Automobile Manufacturers Association, and the Coal Policy Conference, along with individual corporations including Standard Oil of Indiana, the Sun Oil Company, the National Steel Corporation, and the Union Carbide Corporation, either attempted to meet with members of the committee and subcommittee staffs or testified before the full committee.

Not surprisingly, the four individual automobile manufacturers were the most active. Between August 21 and September 17, General Motors, Ford, Chrysler, and American Motors launched a highly coordinated and intensive effort aimed at convincing the Senate Public Works Committee that, in the words of GM President Cole, "[we do] not have the technological capability to make 1975 production vehicles that would achieve emission levels the legislation requires."[34] The presidents of the three largest manufacturers, along with the vice president of American Motors, met with Senator Muskie on August 25, while each of the other fourteen members of the committee were "assigned" to one of the four companies in the industry. In addition, frequent strategy sessions were held among the companies' Washington representatives.

Yet the industry's lobbying efforts were ineffective. One Michigan representative observed, in 1970:

> GM probably has the worst lobby on Capitol Hill. It ranks at the bottom in terms of effectiveness. Its Washington operation is the most inept and ineffectual I've seen here.
> It's not the fault of the guys in the Washington office. It's just that management has this disdain for relations in Washington. . . . GM is constantly getting hit in the back of the head because they don't pay enough attention to Washington. They get more bad surprises than any other major firm in the nation.

Another added: "They send a guy up here to talk to a committee chairman or a Member, thinking that is the best way to do it. It isn't. A call from the district from someone you know who will be affected by a bill is far more effective." A congressional staff member echoed this observation: "GM's lobbying effort in 1970 was among the most inept I have ever seen. They had no idea how to relate to Congress."[35]

Not surprisingly, the Senate Public Works Committee made no substantive changes in the subcommittee's stationary-source requirements and only two changes in its rules affecting automotive emissions. By 10-to-3 vote, the full committee gave the EPA the right to grant the auto industry a single one-year extension of the 1975 and 1976 deadlines. It also included a provision providing for judicial review of the secretary's decisions on extensions. The bill was then unanimously approved by the full committee.

The debate on the floor of the Senate focused primarily on the deadline for the reduction of automobile emissions. Muskie, the bill's floor manager, told his fellow senators, "Detroit has told the nation that Americans cannot live without the automobile. This legislation would tell Detroit that if this is the case, then they must make an automobile with which Americans can live." Muskie publicly conceded that no hearings had been held on the issue of whether or not the automobile industry actually had the ability to meet the deadlines contained in the committee bill. He insisted that "the deadline is based not . . . on economic and technological feasibility, but on considerations of public health." Senator Robert Griffin, after noting the importance of the automobile industry to the nation's economy, replied, "This bill holds a gun at the head of the American automobile industry in a very dangerous game of economic roulette." One of GM's lobbyists told the *National Journal* that "the atmosphere [in the Senate] was such that offering amendments seemed hopeless." He added, "We did nothing about the bill in the full Senate. I wouldn't think of asking anybody to vote against that bill."[36] The Senate approved the bill by vote of 73 to 2.

The legislation that emerged from the Senate had clearly taken business by surprise. The *National Journal* reported: "Senate action on the complex, one hundred-page bill was so swift that corporate interests had little opportunity to react before it was passed." The director of air-pollution control for the National Coal Association remarked, "The bill that came out of the Senate was not the bill that anybody had testified to."[37] When various staff members of Muskie's subcommittee met with automobile industry representatives on August 21 to inform them that the committee

intended to report a bill requiring 90 percent reduction of various emissions by 1975, the meeting became "a little tense."[38] Industry lobbyists
reported it was their first inkling that the 1970 amendments might contain
the 90 percent provision.

Both business and the administration did actively lobby in favor of the
House version when the bill came before the House-Senate conference
committee. After extremely lengthy negotiations, agreement was finally
reached on December 16. The bill that emerged made relatively few
concessions to either industry or the administration. The auto manufacturers were granted an extra year in which to apply for an extension of the
1975 deadline and automobile antipollution requirements were limited to
five years, or fifty thousand miles, whichever came first, rather than to the
life of the vehicle. The conference committee also agreed to some modification of provisions governing warranties that were strongly desired by
independent manufacturers of auto parts.

The conference committee, however, ignored the requests of the oil
industry and the manufacturers of lead additives to modify the regulations
affecting fuel composition: the government was granted the power to
"control or prohibit fuels or fuel additives which harm public health or
welfare or impair a device or system to control emissions." The bill also
required that the EPA promulgate national ambient-air quality standards
"for each air pollutant for which air quality criteria had been issued" based
on "such criteria and allowing an adequate margin of safety . . . requisite
to protect public health."[39] The cumulative effect of various other provisions effectively established the preeminence of federal authority in air-
pollution control. The conference report was adopted by voice vote by
both houses the next day and signed into law by President Nixon a few
days later.

The automobile industry had been caught off guard. Like virtually the
entire business community, it had failed to appreciate the extent to which
business-government relations had become transformed. New issues,
along with new interest groups, were emerging: business neither an-
ticipated these political changes nor understood how to respond to them.
Equally important, each segment of the business community continued to
view Washington politics through the lens of its trade associations; each
industry remained preoccupied with its own immediate concerns. As a
result, the divide-and-conquer strategy of proregulation constituencies
and politicians proved extremely effective. By making sure that a disproportionate amount of the burden of pollution abatement fell on one particular industry, they effectively isolated the automobile manufacturers from

the rest of the business community. Detroit lost, in part, because it was forced to fight the Clean Air Act Amendments all by itself.

The Defeat of the Supersonic Aircraft

The following year, another traditionally powerful industry experienced a significant political defeat when Congress voted to halt further federal support of Boeing's effort to develop a supersonic transport plane (SST). Federal support for this project had begun in 1963 when President Kennedy responded to a joint British-French program to develop the Concorde by announcing federal support to help American industry develop a comparable aircraft. He committed the federal government to pay 75 percent of the plane's development costs, then estimated at one billion dollars.

During the program's first five years, it attracted little public attention: the only political constituencies interested in the plane's development were those that supported it, namely the aerospace industry, various government agencies, and their congressional allies. They viewed the plane "as a logical development in the aerospace field." However, by 1970, the controversy over the aircraft's development had broadened in scope: "it had changed from an internal and rather technical debate into an all-out societal war. Ultimately the SST became to environmentalists a symbol of all that was wrong with technology and to SST proponents a symbol of technological progress and technology's benefits to humanity." In this sense, "The SST [became] significant as a barometer and as a catalyst for larger societal changes that occurred during the 1960s."[40] Most important, the controversy it created appeared to reflect an important shift in American attitudes toward technology: no longer was technological innovation automatically viewed as socially beneficial.

The first sign of a broader public interest in the aircraft took place in 1967 when Harvard physicist William A. Shurcliff established the Citizens League Against the Sonic Boom. Although small, the league was able to raise sufficient funds to place advertisements opposing the SST in a number of newspapers and magazines. Within a year it had grown to about two thousand members. In the fall of 1967, Shurcliff persuaded the Sierra Club to become involved. At its September board of directors' meeting, the environmental organization declared itself "opposed to the operation of civil aircraft under conditions that produce sonic booms audible on the surface of the earth."[41] Although articles began to appear discussing the detriments of the sonic boom the plane's opponents contended the SST would create, public interest in the issue was still minimal.

President Nixon's decision in September 1969 to continue government funding of the plane was the catalyst for the transformation of "a simmering but fragmented discontent into a widespread effort to make the SST a key target of the merging environmental movement."[42] The environmental movement became actively involved. The Natural Resources Council and the Environmental Defense Fund announced their opposition to the aircraft's development, the recently established Friends of the Earth stated that opposing the SST would be one of its major political priorities, and the Sierra Club became even more interested in the issue. On Earth Day, April 22, 1970, the SST was a major target of protests in many parts of the country. Speaking at the University of Minnesota, Senator Walter Mondale of Minnesota angrily compared the $200 million allocated to "feed hungry children" with the $290 million SST appropriation requested by the administration for fiscal 1971. In May 1970, an ad hoc Coalition Against the SST was formed: it included fourteen organizations, the majority of them environmental groups. The latter argued that the plane would create an annoying and dangerous sonic boom, increase pollution in the upper atmosphere, and adversely affect the nation's weather patterns.

During the fall of 1970, as Congress neared a vote on future government funding, the coalition substantially increased its lobbying efforts: various legislators were deluged with thousands of cards and letters opposing the plane, and a number of environmental activists paid personal visits to their representatives. A Seattle housewife collected a quarter-million signatures opposed to the plane which she then presented to the Washington State congressional delegation. The coalition also circulated a map of the United States showing the nation crisscrossed by fifty-mile sonic boom zones and claimed that the only ones who would benefit from the aircraft's operation would be "rich people in a hurry."[43]

Although the House of Representatives voted to continue funding the plane, opponents regarded the closeness of the vote as a major turning point in their campaign: an amendment to delete SST funding from the fiscal 1971 budget was defeated by only seven votes, indicating that a number of previous supporters of the plane had switched their position. In September 1970, the opponents of the aircraft received two major boosts. First, the prestigious Federation of American Scientists came out against the SST. Even more important, a group of prominent economists, including Milton Friedman, John Kenneth Galbraith, Paul Samuelson, and

Walter Heller, signed an open letter expressing their reservations about government funding for the aircraft. Their statement attracted considerable publicity. The *New York Times* commented, "Now that most leading economists agree that the plane makes no economic sense for the nation, surely it is time for the Administration to wheel it back to the hangar and turn its attention to more important transportation problems."[44] The Nixon administration countered by redoubling its lobbying efforts, but on December 3, 1970, the Senate voted 52 to 41 to deny further SST funding.

The aerospace industry blamed its loss on its own ineptness. *Aviation Week and Space Technology* wrote, "There was considerable ineptness and apathy by both the Nixon Administration and the Aerospace industry. Boeing might be located on another planet for all the support it provided. The highly paid functionaries of the Aerospace Industries Association daintily avoided the strife until the disastrous vote was recorded." However, the SST's defeat appeared to be primarily due to the close identification of its opponents with the cause of environmentalism—an issue that was at the peak of its popular appeal precisely when the vote on the 1971 appropriations took place. Senator Proxmire, the plane's principal opponent, attributed its defeat in the Senate to "heightened awareness of the SST's potential environmental hazards."[45]

However, the SST had not yet been finally defeated, since the House had voted to appropriate funds for it. A Senate-House conference committee agreed to continue the program's funding for another year, after which it would be completely eliminated unless both houses subsequently voted their support. The aerospace industry, which had previously relied upon the administration to carry the burden of its lobbying efforts, now belatedly began to mobilize. It established two committees—the National Committee for the SST and the National Committee for an American SST. Supporters of the plane argued that the government's failure to support the SST would impair the balance of payments, cost considerable tax revenue, and eliminate fifty thousand jobs. They further contended that the plane's critics had exaggerated the amount of noise and air pollution that it would produce. The two organizations were funded by contributions from forty-one companies, including the plane's two prime contractors, Boeing and General Electric, as well as from a number of unions whose members stood to benefit from the plane's development. A letter-writing campaign was organized and pro-SST ads were placed in a number of newspapers. The industry's efforts were strongly supported by the administration and by the congressional delegations of the states where the plane would be produced.

The vote on SST funding in 1971 was extremely close: the House denied further funding by a vote of 215 to 204 and the vote in the Senate was 52 to 41. A decisive factor affecting the outcome appeared to be the economic arguments against the plane's construction: the plane's critics argued that no market existed for the aircraft and that its only beneficiaries would be wealthy travelers. They also contended that the federal government should direct its resources toward more "socially useful activities." However, the environmentalists were the main political force against the SST and they claimed much of the credit for its defeat.

Other Environmental Legislation

A year later, Congress approved two major changes in the direction and scope of federal environmental policy: the Federal Environmental Pesticide Control Act of 1972 and the Federal Water Pollution Control Act Amendments of 1972. While both were passed in a form weaker than many environmentalists preferred, their enactment demonstrated the movement's continued political strength.

In 1971, President Nixon delivered an environmental message to Congress that included a number of proposals for strengthening the federal role in controlling water pollution. He asked Congress to increase federal subsidies for the construction of waste treatment plans, require industrial users to pay for the treatment of their effluent, establish limitations on both industrial and municipal effluents, and authorize the EPA to establish and revise water quality standards. The president's proposals were generally supported by the business community, which had become reconciled to an expanded federal regulatory role. However, they were immediately criticized by both environmentalists and a number of Democratic members of Congress as being too weak.

Under the leadership of Senator Muskie, the Senate, by a vote of 86 to 0, approved a bill that went significantly beyond the administration's. It represented "a major change in the enforcement mechanism of the federal water pollution control program, from water quality standards to effluent limits." The latter were regarded as easier to enforce, since they allowed the EPA to tailor its pollution-control requirements to particular industrial technologies, rather than having to establish the links between a particular emission and water quality. Declaring that "no one has the right to pollute," the statute established the goals of making the nation's waters suitable for swimming and fish propagation by 1981 and eliminating all pollutant discharges by 1985. Muskie informed his fellow senators that such strong legislation was necessary because "the quality of our environment was deteriorating at an alarming rate." He added, "It is imperative that we attempt to stop pollution."[46] This bill, however, after being passed by the Senate, was not acted upon by the House.

The following year, the House did approve a water-pollution control bill, although it was somewhat weaker than the version passed earlier by the Senate. The bill, reported out of conference committee on September 14, 1972, more closely reflected the House version. For example, it changed the 1981 and 1985 deadlines from "goals" to "policies" and made their elimination contingent upon another vote to be taken by the Congress in two years. In addition, while the Senate had made the initiation of criminal or civil suits by the EPA against violators of the statute mandatory, the bill approved by the conference committee left the decision to prosecute up to the EPA. Also, while the Senate version had permitted any citizen to sue violators of the mandatory provisions of the legislation, the committee bill allowed such suits only if the citizen or group had an interest that was adversely affected. (This was consistent with the April 1972 Supreme Court decision in *Sierra Club v. Morton*, to be discussed in the following chapter.) On the other hand, the conference committee's bill did include the limitations on effluents that constituted the heart of the Senate version. All industries were required to employ the "best practicable" abatement technology for any discharges into U.S. waters by July 1, 1977, and the "best available" equipment by July 1, 1983. The bill was then approved by both houses with only 11 dissenting votes.

The Federal Water Pollution Control Act of 1972 represented one of "the most sweeping environmental statutes ever considered by Congress." It declared the government's intent to respect and maintain the "natural chemical, physical and biological integrity of the nation's waters."[47] Major waterways were required to be fishable and swimmable by 1983 and totally free of polluting discharges by 1985. In contrast to the relatively uncontroversial Water Quality Act of 1965, the 1972 legislation provided for the development of nationally uniform, technology-based effluent limits that would have to be met before emitters could obtain discharge permits. And, like the Clean Air Act Amendments of 1970, it also established detailed timetables for enforcing its various provisions.

As in 1970, the Nixon administration, while initially having supported a bill more responsive to the concerns of industry, appeared prepared to go along with the much tougher version finally approved by the Congress. The president, however, objected to the level of the bill's budgetary authorizations, which were triple those of his original 1971 proposal. Claiming that the legislation threatened to wreck his budget (in fact, the bill did not appropriate any funds, it only authorized them over a three-year period), he vetoed it. The next day, both houses overrode his veto—the Senate by a vote of 52 to 12 and the House by a vote of 247 to 23—thus giving the EPA a second, new sweeping piece of environmental legislation to enforce.

Public attention to the issue of pesticides dates from the 1962 publication of Rachel Carson's best-seller, *Silent Spring,* which argued that since many pesticides had an unknown and cumulative effect on plants, animals, and people, their use should be curtailed. She also strongly criticized the lack of effective monitoring of pesticides by the Department of Agriculture.[48] Public awareness of this problem resurfaced in the spring of 1968, when the Food and Drug Administration seized several interstate shipments of Lake Michigan salmon which contained abnormally high residues of DDT.

Throughout the 1960s, environmental groups had repeatedly urged restrictions on the use of pesticides. Linda Billings of the Sierra Club contended, "There's got to be a profound and complete overhaul in the way this country deals with pesticides." By the end of the decade, the debate over pesticide use had begun to shift from its impact on nature to its effects on human health. In the fall of 1968, a General Accounting Office study reported that the Department of Agriculture had made little effort to enforce the regulation and labeling provisions of a 1947 federal regulatory statute. It also revealed that while 25 percent of the 2,751 pesticides tested in 1966 were in violation of this statute, the Department of Agriculture had acted to remove pesticides from the market on only 106 occasions, and that many of these removals were strictly local in nature. Several congressional committees also issued reports highly critical of the Department of Agriculture's record in protecting public health and safety. In 1969, HEW Secretary Robert Finch appointed a commission to study the health effects of DDT and other pesticides, and the National Academy of Sciences released a report recommending more careful use of pesticides such as DDT. The following year, a report commissioned by HEW concluded that "there is a wide range of potential for acute toxicity of man" and recommended that many pesticides be restricted to specific essential uses.[49]

On June 6, 1970, President Nixon, responding to growing public concern over both the effects on health of pesticides and the performance of the Department of Agriculture, announced that the department's authority over pesticide use would be transferred to the newly created Environmental Protection Agency. According to Russell Train, the chairman of the President's Environmental Quality Council, "It just doesn't make any sense to have an environmental protection agency and not include pesticides." This decision was an important victory for the environmental movement and a clear defeat for both the chemical industry and the American Farm Bureau Federation. The federation viewed the shift with considerable "alarm," fearing that "the economic consequences for farmers and the pesticide industry might be overlooked by a new agency."[50]

The Federal Environmental Pesticide Control Act, approved by both houses of Congress in October 1972, was a compromise between those who advocated stricter controls over pesticide use and the firms involved in their manufacture and use. It followed the president's recommendations by significantly expanding the scope of federal controls over pesticide use. But, while providing for judicial review of most of the EPA's decisions, it did not allow for citizen suits against the EPA administrator. On the most controversial issue, it favored the manufacturers of pesticides, allowing for them to be compensated in cases of immediate hazard—provided they did not know in advance that their product was illegal under the act. This legislation was signed into law by President Nixon on October 21, 1972. Although weaker than the environmental movement preferred, its approval signaled another political setback—one with significant long-term economic and social consequences—for an important segment of the American economy.

Occupational Health and Safety

The Occupational Safety and Health (OSH) Act of 1970 emerged from the same social and political currents as the Clean Air Act Amendments of 1970. Both laws reflected a growing public awareness of the adverse effects of industrial production on public health and safety—stimulated in part by increased media coverage of health hazards. While the original impetus for expanding the regulatory role of the federal government came from the Johnson administration, congressional inertia, as well as business opposition, had prevented the passage of any important legislation during the 1960s. The only important piece of occupational health and safety legislation approved during that decade was the Coal Mine Safety Act of 1969. It affected workers in only one industry—albeit among the most hazardous—and its passage was due to a relatively unique set of circumstances.

In 1968, President Johnson had asked Congress for legislation placing the authority for setting standards, for inspection, and for enforcement of occupational health and safety regulations in the Department of Labor. This law would have given the federal government, for the first time, a major role in the regulation of working conditions. Testifying on behalf of the legislation, Labor Secretary Willard Wurtz stated that "the clear central issue . . . is simply whether the Congress is going to act to stop a carnage which continues . . . because the people in this country . . . can't see the blood on the food they eat, on things they buy, and on the services they get."[51] The administration's proposal met with very strong opposition from a number of business organizations, most notably the NAM and the U.S. Chamber of Commerce, which feared giving the Department of Labor, regarded by them as sympathetic to organized labor, any additional authority over industry. Thanks both to business opposition and the lack of interest on the part of the trade-union movement, the administration's bill was not reported out of committees in either house during Johnson's presidency.

However, the climate of public and political opinion changed substantially within a remarkably brief period of time. Like the NEPA and the Clean Air and Water Act Amendments, the OSH Act was enacted out of a widespread sense of crisis—in this case "what was perceived as a mounting toll of industrial injuries."[52] Hearings held by Congress in 1968 documented both the seriousness of the problem of occupational safety and the inability of the states to deal with it. Led in part by the Oil, Chemical and Atomic Workers Union, whose members were particularly vulnerable to health hazards, the trade-union movement began to lobby actively for federal regulation. Moreover, in the course of enacting the Coal Mine Health and Safety Act of 1969, many legislators had become much more aware of the hazards that faced workers in other industries. The increase in public awareness of the health hazards caused by pollution after 1969 also had a spillover effect into this issue area. Finally, political momentum played an important role. Jack Walker wrote:

> Passage within only three years of both the auto safety and coal-mine safety bills was a political earthquake that provided enormous momentum for the safety movement. . . . Once the opposition of the powerful automobile and coal-mining industries had been brushed aside, it became difficult for senators to resist appeals to complete the job by ensuring the safety of all the rest of the workers and products in the economy.[53]

Shortly after President Nixon took office, Democrats in both houses had proposed legislation similar to that introduced the previous year by President Johnson. President Nixon, anxious to enlist blue-collar workers as part of the new Republican majority and to demonstrate its "commitment to the public interest and nascent environmental movements,"[54] responded by calling for proposals to help "guarantee the health and safety of workers" in a message to Congress on April 14, 1969. However, the legislation submitted to Congress four months later by the administration differed from the Democratic proposal in one important respect: it placed the authority for setting and enforcing health and safety standards not in the Department of Labor but in a newly created National Occupational Safety and Health Board, whose members would be appointed by the president.

The fight for the Democratic version of the occupational safety and health bill was spearheaded by a coalition of more than one hundred labor, consumer, religious, and environmental groups. The role of the last was of particular importance. Not only did they enjoy greater public support than organized labor, but they helped rebut industry's claim that the issue of occupational health and safety was simply designed to advance the special interests of unions. Environmental Action issued a letter signed by a number of distinguished scientists stating that "the in-plant environment [was] merely a concentrated microcosm of the outside environment. The environmental health hazards that workers face affect the entire population." For its part, the business community was divided. Most business firms reacted defensively, denying the need for any government action and instead urging continued reliance on voluntary action on the part of employees. Others, however, reflecting the "general support among many corporate leaders for social reform in this period," indicated their support for the principle of federal health and safety legislation.[55]

The debate over occupational health and safety legislation was an emotionally charged one: Congress was being asked to legislate on what had become identified as a matter of life and death. As in the case of environmental policy, advocates of additional controls over industry had extremely high expectations: they wanted the government to require the private sector to do everything possible to eliminate workplace injuries—regardless of cost. Thus when Senator Peter Dominick (Republican-Colorado) argued that "absolute safety is an impossibility and it will only create confusion in the administration of this act for Congress to set impossible goals," Senator Ralph Yarborough (Democrat-Texas) asked rhetorically, "what about the man . . . tied to a wheelchair or a hospital bed for the rest of his working life? . . . We are talking about people's lives, not the indifference of some cost accountant."[56]

By 1970, virtually the entire business community had become reconciled to some form of federal regulation. The safety director of the NAM conceded that "all the activity on the legislation in the past year has alerted the public to problems . . . that must be handled."[57] The legislative director of the Chamber of Commerce observed that the business community was now convinced "that a safety bill would be passed." He added that their challenge was now "to work for one they could live with."[58] Accordingly, most business firms and organizations decided to support the administration's bill, since it granted the least amount of power to the secretary of labor. The U.S. Chamber of Commerce, reversing its previous opposition to any federal legislation, described the administration's bill as "a responsible attempt to better our industrial safety and health record."[59] However, the trade-union movement urged the enactment of the Democratic version on the grounds that an independent board would hopelessly fragment any federal safety and health program. As one union lobbyist put it, "[we] can get to the Labor Department but not to a commission, and all protections are no good without standards." Thus the OSH Act became one of the only pieces of regulatory legislation in which opinion was largely divided along partisan lines. With the exception of a few Republican senators from northern cities, Republican legislators represented the point of view of the business community, while Democratic representatives and senators—with the exception of those from the South—supported organized labor.

After almost two years of complex political maneuvering, Congress finally completed action on comprehensive health and safety legislation designed to protect the fifty-five million industrial, agricultural, and construction workers employed by firms engaged in interstate commerce. The final version, passed by both houses in December 1970, was a compromise. On the other hand, it met an important union objective by giving to the secretary of labor, rather than to an independent board, the power to set health and safety standards. At the same time, it reflected the influence of industry by establishing a separate three-person commission to enforce the regulations promulgated by the secretary. In addition, the conference committee bowed to pressure from industry and deleted a provision from the Senate version that granted the secretary of labor the right to close a plant if an imminent danger threatened the lives of workers. Instead, the committee accepted the stipulation contained in the House version that a court order was necessary before a plant could be closed. The final version was endorsed with varying degrees of enthusiasm by both business and organized labor, passed by both houses by wide margins, and signed into law by President Nixon on December 29, 1970.

Nonetheless, on balance, the OSH Act constituted a political defeat for the business community, even though its provisions did not affect all firms equally. Like the Clean Air Act Amendments, it was written so as to maximize the likelihood that it would be enforced in ways that would be relatively unpalatable to industry. Most obviously, its goals were expressed in language that sought to place as high a priority as possible on protecting the health and safety of workers. In addition, the Occupational Safety and Health Administration (OSHA) was instructed that "if, upon inspection or investigation, the Secretary or his authorized representative believes that an employer has violated a requirement of . . . this Act he shall with reasonable promptness issue a citation to the employer."[60] Graham Wilson concludes: "It would be hard for OSHA to present itself to employers as a friend and guide when Congress had instructed inspectors to send a formal notice of guilt to employers every time a breach of regulations was noticed, and to commence consideration of a fine. Congress had made it as difficult as possible for regulator and regulated to be friends."[61] Not surprisingly, OSHA would be the first of the new social regulatory agencies to experience a backlash from business.

The Politics of Consumer Protection

After a brief hiatus in 1969, the pace of new consumer-protection legislation increased again in 1970. In that year, Congress approved both the Poison Prevention Packaging Act, designed to prevent the accidental misuse of hazardous products by children, and the Consumer Product Safety Act, which established the Consumer Product Safety Commission in order to protect consumers from "unreasonable" product hazards. The following year, both the Federal Boat Safety Act and the Lead-based Paint Elimination Act became law. However, the most important consumer legislation of the early 1970s was the Cigarette Advertising Act of 1970.

In 1965, Congress, in a major victory for the tobacco industry, had prohibited the federal, as well as any state or local, government from requiring health warnings in cigarette advertising for a period of five years. In 1968, with this statutory restriction soon to expire, two federal regulatory agencies announced their intention of imposing major restrictions on cigarette advertising. The Federal Trade Commission, apparently reacting to an extensive industrial public-relations campaign that sought to discredit all the government's efforts to establish a connection between smoking and health, issued a report to Congress that went a step beyond what it had proposed during the mid-1960s: it recommended that tobacco companies be forbidden to advertise cigarettes on radio or television. This report was adopted with only one dissenting vote.

About the same time, the Federal Communications Commission (FCC) agreed to apply the fairness doctrine to commercial advertisements for cigarettes. The FCC required television and radio stations to provide "a significant amount of time for the other [anti-smoking] viewpoint." The commission's decision came as a complete surprise. The National Association of Broadcasters (NAB) described it as an "unwarranted dangerous intrusion into American business,"[62] and the tobacco industry promptly challenged it in the U.S. Court of Appeals for the District of Columbia. The court ruled in favor of the commission on November 21, 1968. As a result, a significant number of antismoking ads began to appear in the nation's broadcast media in the eight months following the FCC's decision. The American Cancer Society alone distributed more than five thousand commercials.

In February 1969, the FCC announced that on July 1, 1969—the expiration date of the Cigarette Labeling Act of 1965—it would propose a rule banning all cigarette advertising from radio and television. This decision placed the antismoking forces in Congress in an extremely favorable position: all they had to do to triumph was to prevent Congress from acting. As Democratic Senator Frank Moss of Utah informed his colleagues, "for the first time, the legislative advantage lies with the public. It is the cigarette industry which has the burden of getting Congress to act. If there is no new legislation extending the ban on agency regulation, then the agencies will again be free to act on July 1."[63] However, the tobacco industry was well prepared for the act's expiration. In spite of the increase in public concern with health issues, its strength in the House of Representatives remained formidable: ten of the thirty-six members of the House Interstate and Foreign Commerce Committee came from tobacco-growing districts or districts closely allied with them. As one observer put it, "there [was] a feeling among the industry's Washington strategists that they['d] done it before and they [could] do it again."[64] The bill subsequently reported out of the committee and approved by the House "was a nightmare for the health interests."[65] It prohibited the states permanently, and federal agencies for six more years, from regulating cigarette advertising.

But this time the industry appeared to have overplayed its hand. In contrast to 1965, thanks both to the antismoking ads the networks were forced to run under the fairness doctrine and the increased public concern with health hazards, there was considerably more public awareness of the dangers of cigarette smoking. The California State Senate voted to ban all cigarette advertising and the New York Times announced that it would no longer carry cigarette advertising without health warnings. Moreover, antismoking forces were far better organized: unlike in 1965, consumer groups now had an effective Washington presence.

However, what really undermined the position of the cigarette industry was the desertion of the broadcasters. By February 1969, the nation's broadcasters estimated that they had lost more than $75 million in revenue by being required to run antismoking ads. Before the bill came before the Senate, the National Association of Broadcasters volunteered to phase out all cigarette advertising within three years. This announcement came as a shock to the tobacco companies, which felt that they had been betrayed and, as a result, the industry was forced to retreat. The Tobacco Institute offered to discontinue the broadcasting of cigarette advertising by September 1970, provided Congress granted the companies antitrust immunity when all its major contracts expired. The industry's stance appears to be due to two factors. First, it was bowing to the inevitable: in the political climate of the late 1960s, it appeared highly unlikely that it would be able to repeat its political victory of 1965. There was absolutely no chance that the Senate would approve legislation prohibiting both the FTC and the FCC from restricting cigarette advertising. More important, since the broadcasters had begun giving "equal time" to the opponents of cigarette smoking, cigarette sales had actually declined for the first time since the surgeon general's report (see chapter 2). By removing its own ads, the industry would be depriving its critics of one of their most effective forums.

The Senate subsequently voted to ban cigarette commercials from radio and television by January 1, 1971, but to prohibit the FTC from requiring health warnings on other forms of advertising until eighteen months after the broadcast ban went into effect, unless it determined that cigarette advertising practices constituted a "gross abuse." Congress took no further action in 1969, but in 1970 the House of Representatives approved legislation essentially similar to that previously adopted by the Senate. The bill finally approved by both houses of Congress banned all radio and television commercials as of January 2, 1971 (the later date was adopted in order to permit cigarette advertisements during the telecasts of the football bowl games on New Year's Day, 1971) and prohibited the FTC from regulating cigarette advertising until July 1, 1971. Senator Magnuson, the bill's floor manager in the Senate, stated that the legislation represented a "landmark legislation in the health field," achieved despite the "great economic forces aligned against it," while Senator Moss observed that "thanks to this bill, Marlboro Country will fade into television history after next January."[66]

Conclusion

Ironically, the period of industry's greatest political vulnerability—at least in the areas of social regulation and tax policy—coincided with the presidency of Republican Richard Nixon. Just as it took the presidency of Lyndon Johnson to enact the legislative agenda of John Kennedy's New Frontier, so were many of the most important regulatory initiatives of Johnson's Great Society approved during the presidency of Richard Nixon.

The primary impetus for increased governmental intervention in the economy came not from the executive branch but from Congress. The White House did play an important role in drafting particular pieces of regulatory legislation, but its efforts were primarily a response to pressures from Congress. On no occasion did President Nixon urge the Congress to enact stricter or more extensive controls over corporate social conduct than the nation's legislators had originally preferred. On the contrary, in virtually every instance, Congress was less responsive to the interests of business than the White House. But while the White House was able to weaken the provisions of specific legislation, the Nixon administration was unable to prevent the passage of a new single regulatory law itself. Only one important regulatory statute was vetoed by Richard Nixon, and his veto was promptly overridden. Seen from this perspective, the increases in government regulation of business during this period coincided with—and to an extent were made possible by—a relatively weak presidency and a relatively activist and powerful Congress.

Yet this analysis is incomplete. It is true that Nixon, like Kennedy, was unable to develop an effective working relationship with Congress. But in other policy areas, the White House showed considerable initiative. The imposition of wage-price controls, the removal of the U.S. dollar from the gold standard, the impounding of congressional appropriations, the conduct of the war in Indochina, the opening of relations with the People's Republic of China—to say nothing of the events surrounding Watergate—reveal an administration with a firm sense of its own priorities and a willingness to do all it could to achieve its objectives, sometimes to the point of violating the law.

In fact, the president was largely indifferent to the substantial changes in government-business relations that occurred while he was in office. Government regulation of business was simply not an important issue to the White House. The Republican platforms of 1968 and 1972 had ignored it: the 1968 campaign had been dominated by the issues of foreign policy and race relations, and the 1972 campaign by the Vietnam War and priorities for domestic spending. Like President Kennedy, Richard Nixon was primarily interested in foreign policy: world affairs commanded his personal attention and he spent virtually all of his limited political capital on them. Lacking any strong convictions about domestic policies in general and government regulation in particular, the Nixon White House was prepared to react passively to whatever shifts took place in public and congressional opinion. In this sense, Nixon was similar to Kennedy: neither was particularly interested in business-government relations. The substantial differences in federal regulatory policy between their two administrations had more to do with shifts in public opinion and the emergence of public-interest lobbies than with differences in the ideologies of the two men.

As a result, business did not have a committed ally in the White House between 1969 and 1973. Faced with a choice between his personal political interests and those of business, the president invariably chose the former. In 1970, the White House proved more than willing to support far more ambitious federal regulation of air pollution than business preferred, when doing so appeared to be of value to Nixon in weakening the electoral appeal of Senator Muskie. Likewise, that same year, the president endorsed a stronger occupational safety and health bill than business wanted in order to strengthen his electoral support among blue-collar workers. Watergate reveals a similar pattern: the president's fund raisers took advantage of the increased scope of government regulation in order to pressure companies into providing increased funds for Nixon's reelection. Ironically, one of the tactics that the Committee to Re-elect the President used to pressure companies into making illegal contributions to the 1972 campaign was to threaten them with the strict enforcement of environmental regulations.

Significantly, the only important regulatory statute that President Nixon vetoed, the Clean Water Act Amendments of 1972, was opposed by the White House not because of its burden on the private sector but because of its effect on the administration's budget. (In October 1972, Nixon vetoed two minor environmental statutes, the Mining and Minerals Policy Act and the National Environmental Data Act, for the same reason.) In fact, the White House appeared to have no philosophical difficulty with expanding federal controls over corporate social conduct. On no occasion did the White House argue that a particular regulatory measure should be left to the states rather than the federal government or suggest that it constituted an inappropriate or excessively costly intrusion of government into the affairs of the private sector. The administration was extremely responsive to the American Bar Association's suggestions for revitalizing the Federal Trade Commission and it appointed officials to administer newly created social regulatory agencies such as the OSHA and the EPA, which generally supported the latter's objectives. And Congress's penchant for establishing new regulatory agencies that reported directly to the White House rather than functioning as independent commissions was fully in accordance with the president's preference for a more centralized governmental bureaucracy.

What of the role of Congress in increasing the scope of government regulation of business? The change in the composition of Congress certainly accounts for at least some of the changes in regulatory policy between the first and second half of the 1960s. The 1964 election significantly strengthened the influence of liberal Democrats and removed much of the "veto power" of southern Democrats and Republicans over new government initiatives. But the willingness of Congress to support increased regulatory controls of business after 1968 was clearly *not* a response to a change in its partisan or ideological composition; neither the 1968 nor 1970 elections significantly affected the balance of power between the Democrats and Republicans. The Republicans gained a total of five seats in the House of Representatives and six in the Senate in 1968, and in 1970 the Democrats gained twelve seats in the House of Representatives and lost two in the Senate. These relatively modest changes cannot account for such a significant decline in the ability of business to influence Congress. It is true that Democrats were consistently more likely to support increased regulation of corporate social conduct than Republicans.[67] But then why did the Democrats in Congress become so much *more* willing to oppose business than they had been in the past?

The answer has to do with an important change in the preference of an influential segment of the electorate. For Democrats, and indeed for Republicans as well, the single best predictor of their position on regulatory statutes and amendments was the socioeconomic characteristic of their districts: "the indicator with the greatest explanatory power . . . was median school years completed." Thus, the more middle-class the constituency of a senator or representative, the more he or she was willing to vote for legislation that challenged corporate prerogatives. Kathleen Kemp concludes: "This finding gives some support to those who have argued that many, if not most, of the reforms of this period can be attributed to a 'new class' of the highly educated middle class."[68] The political mobilization of this constituency is the subject of the next chapter.

V

The Public-Interest Movement

Introduction

Each of the three major political waves of challenge to business that has taken place in the United States in this century has been accompanied by the mobilization of a new political constituency. At the turn of the century, this constituency consisted primarily of municipal-reform groups, and in the 1930s, the trade-union movement emerged as a major force in American politics and a key component of the New Deal coalition. The most characteristic and distinctive feature of business-government relations in the 1970s was the emergence and institutionalization of the public-interest movement.* Senator Ribicoff observed in 1976: "instead of the big lobbies of the major corporations dominating the hearings process, you have had practically every committee in Congress according 'equal time' to public interest people." Representative Abner Mikva (Democrat-Illinois) noted that the emergence of public-interest groups represented "the biggest change I've seen in Congress since I first came here. . . . Instead of anti-establishment groups handing out leaflets on a street corner we have people working very effectively in the halls of Congress."[1] Jeffrey Berry writes that public-interest groups helped change "the overall environment within which government officials formulate public policy. . . . The opinion they can arouse, the bad publicity they can generate, the lawsuits they can file,

*My use of the term "public interest" does not imply that the objectives of these organizations are identical with the public interest. I use the term because that is how these groups are commonly designated.

are all factors that are relevant to the deliberations of those who must make policy decisions."[2]

According to a 1977 study of eighty-three public-interest organizations with offices in Washington, D.C., fifty-two, or nearly two-thirds, had been established since 1960 and thirty-nine, or nearly half, had been founded since 1968.[3] Of the thirteen consumer organizations that were politically active in the early 1970s, all but two had been founded since 1965. Although the nation's three largest environmental organizations—the Sierra Club, the National Audubon Society, and the National Wildlife Federation—had each been formed much earlier, their membership increased by 33 percent, or 400,000, between 1970 and 1971. In addition, five new important environmental organizations were organized between 1967 and 1971: the Environmental Defense Fund, Friends of the Earth, the Natural Resources Defense Council, Environmental Action, and the Union of Concerned Scientists. Ralph Nader established the Center for Responsive Law in 1969 and John Gardner organized Common Cause in 1970. By 1976 there were eighty-six public law firms, collectively employing approximately 575 lawyers and 450 other professionals. Only 16 percent of these firms existed in 1968; two-thirds had been formed between 1969 and 1973.[4] The nation's first major gathering of public-interest activists in 1976 included representatives of 165 organizations, of which approximately two-thirds had offices in Washington, D.C., and nearly all of which were less than a decade old.[5]

Not all left-of-center political constituencies organized in the late 1960s and early 1970s were primarily, or even especially, interested in business. Their attention was engaged by a variety of issues, including American defense and foreign policy, the rights and status of women and blacks, hunger and poverty, and ethics in government. All of these issues competed for attention with business-government relations, but a major portion of the efforts of citizen activists focused on the governance, power, and social performance of the large business corporation. Their interests both reflected and reinforced a growing public preoccupation with the role of big business in American society. In 1971, Mintz and Cohen's *America Inc.*, with its wide-ranging critique of "concentrated economic power," reached the best-seller lists.[6] That same year, *Newsweek* ran a cover story entitled "The American Corporation Under Fire," which described the multiplicity of pressures under which corporations were now finding themselves: they were being simultaneously pressured to ameliorate the plight of poor urban blacks, to make safer products, to end their investments in Angola and South Africa, to employ more women and minorities, to cease the manufacture of war materiel, and to improve the quality of the environment.[7]

The concept of "corporate social responsibility," which had stressed the voluntary nature of corporate social commitments, was challenged by the notion of "corporate accountability," which contended that managers ought to be made politically accountable to all those affected by their decisions, not just their stockholders.[8] In 1970, for the first time, stockholders' meetings, traditionally an occasion for the chief executive officer to demonstrate commitment to the financial well-being of stockholders, became the setting for a wide-ranging and often heated debate over management's responsibility to all the firm's "stakeholders." The proxy proposal, formerly focused exclusively on various matters affecting stockholders' pecuniary interests, became a vehicle for politically oriented shareholders to challenge management's commitment to the "public interest."[9]

Causes of Citizen Activism

What accounts for the emergence of the public-interest movement? How were these organizations able to overcome the obstacle to political mobilization described in Mancur Olson's *The Logic of Collective Action,* namely, that it is irrational for any individual to devote political resources for the achievement of collective goals?[10] As Andrew McFarland asks: "Why do 275,000 persons send $15 to $20 a year to Common Cause, when they receive nothing in return but thank-you letters and an eight-page monthly newsletter? The 100,000 persons who send an average of $11 a year to Nader's Public Citizen, Inc., get a five-page progress report and a pamphlet, but no thank-you letter (to save money)."[11]

Part of the explanation is that the United States has long had a tradition of civic activism. Compared to their counterparts in other capitalist democracies, Americans are more likely to believe that they have both the ability and the opportunity to affect government decisions. The penchant of Americans for organizing and supporting voluntary organizations—a number of which take on a political or quasi-political character—was noted by Alexis de Tocqueville one hundred and fifty years ago. During the first half of the nineteenth century, the United States witnessed an active Prohibition movement, a number of antislavery organizations, and the formation of groups that sought to reform education and improve the status of women. Arthur Schlesinger wrote in 1950: "So thoroughly did those [Jacksonian] crusaders work out the pattern of reform organization and propaganda a hundred years ago, that later generations have found little to add beyond taking advantage of new communication devices such as the movies and the radio."[12]

To this cultural explanation must be added an institutional one: compared to other capitalist democracies, political parties in America have been weak and nonideological. As a result, those interested in advancing various collective or quasi-public goods in American society have frequently formed their own organizations rather than becoming primarily active in a national political party. Significantly, voting declined steadily between 1960 and 1980—with the greatest drop occurring between 1968 and 1972, precisely the period when public-interest organizations experienced their greatest growth.[13] Party identification also fell. Between 1964 and 1972, the percentage of Americans identifying themselves as either "strong Democrats" or "strong Republicans" decreased from 38 to 25 percent of the electorate, while the number identifying themselves as "independent" increased from 8 to 13 percent. Strikingly, during the late 1960s and early 1970s, nearly half of those New Age cohorts entering the electorate refused to identify themselves with either major party. Straight ticket voting also declined during this period: it stood at 43 percent in 1964, 34 percent in 1968, and 33 percent in 1972.[14]

But what specifically contributed to an upsurge of citizen activism during the late 1960s and early 1970s? One important reason was the performance of the economy. Economic growth was particularly strong during the second part of the 1960s and early 1970s, averaging 4.75 percent between 1964 and 1969 and 5 percent between 1965 and 1969. While there was a slight downturn in 1970, the nation's GNP grew by 6.1 percent in 1972 and 5.9 percent in 1973. In the quarter-century after 1947, median real income in the United States doubled: "the average family gained more purchasing power than in all preceding periods of American history combined."[15]

This prosperity laid the groundwork for civil activism in a number of ways. Most importantly, it encouraged the American public to take for granted economic growth in general and corporate profitability in particular. During the second half of the 1960s, many Americans, influenced by books such as Galbraith's *New Industrial State*[16] and the evident success of Keynesian economics, assumed that the fundamental problems of the American economy had, in an important sense, been solved. Large numbers of relatively affluent citizens believed that the private sector could now afford to allocate additional resources to objectives they now considered important, without in any way compromising its economic viability. They regarded the large business corporation as a powerful economic institution, one whose managers were no longer constrained by market forces; indeed, corporations appeared to make money almost automatically. The frequent depiction of the corporation as a "private government" or a "sovereign state" reflected a perception not only of its size and political power but also of its economic strength and stability.

While neither growth nor unemployment rates changed significantly in the years immediately preceding and following the emergence of the public-interest movement, in one other dimension the performance of the economy did deteriorate: there was a measurable, though modest, increase in inflation. After remaining below 3 percent between 1960 and 1967, prices increased at an average annual rate of 4.64 percent between 1968 and 1972. This inflation deepened the anxiety of middle-class consumers about their economic and social status and increased their mistrust of large firms. The increase in prices between 1968 and 1972 was large enough to make individual consumers appear impotent vis-à-vis large corporations, but not so large as actually to affect the standard of living of the average American, which continued to increase steadily through 1973. Inflation thus aggravated the public's mistrust of business, without undermining its faith in the essential strength of the American economy.

There were also significant demographic and educational changes in American society. Between 1960 and 1970, a dramatic change took place in the age distribution of the American population. The portion of young men between fifteen and twenty-nine in the total male population increased from 19.5 percent in 1960 to 24.4 percent in 1970: "The absolute increase—13.8 million—in the youthful population (ages 14 to 24) during the 1960s was greater than the total increase in the youthful population—12.5 million—during the 70 years prior to 1960."[17] Not only did the population become younger, it also became more educated. The percentage of American adults aged twenty-one or older having some college education increased from 16.5 percent in 1960 to 21.2 percent in 1970, and then to 25.2 percent in 1974. This development was particularly significant because college-educated citizens are more likely to share an issue-orientation to politics. "Since environmentalist, consumer, and good-government groups with large memberships appear to rely primarily on the college educated for support, increases in the numbers of those with higher education are a predisposing factor to the appearance and maintenance of such groups."[18] During the early 1970s, nearly 100,000 households in the United States contributed at least $70 a year to three or more of the following: Common Cause, Public Citizen, ACLU, public television and public radio, and environmental lobbying groups.

The increase in antibusiness attitudes between 1967 and 1977 was particularly great among the college-educated and the young. "By 1977 business had lost most support among young, high-status and well-educated Americans."[19] Likewise, support for environmentalism was greatest among the young and relatively well-educated.[20] In brief, the typical supporter of an organization like Common Cause, Public Citizen, or the Sierra Club was a middle-class, college-educated professional, a member of what Irving Kristol and others have characterized as a "new class." Kristol writes:

> This "new class" is not easily defined but may be vaguely described. It consists of a goodly proportion of those college-educated people whose skills and vocations proliferate in a "post-industrial society" (to use Daniel Bell's convenient term). We are talking about scientists, teachers and educational administrators, journalists and others in the communication industries, psychologists, social workers, those lawyers and doctors who make their careers in the expanding public sector, city planners, the staffs of the larger foundations, the upper levels of the government bureaucracy, and so on. It is, by now, a quite numerous class; it is an indispensable class for our kind of society; it is a disproportionately powerful class.[21]

Paul Weaver adds: "The New Regulation . . . is the social policy of the new class—that rapidly growing and increasingly influential part of the upper-middle-class that feels itself to be in more or less adversary posture vis-à-vis American society and that tends to make its vocation in the public and not-for-profit sectors."[22]

Kristol and Weaver attributed this "class's" dislike of business to their jealousy of the latter's power and privileges. However, individuals who supported public-interest organizations were no more—or less—likely to be employed in the profit than the nonprofit sector. Everett Ladd reports:

> The data tend to question theories about the sources of the new class that emphasize occupation, sources of income, the profit versus nonprofit sector, and the like. The traditional differences separating the basic occupational categories—professional, managerial, white-collar, blue-collar—are more modest than the differences produced by education alone. The most applicable and narrowly defined occupational categories, such as "word workers," indicate about the same support for the new liberalism as does the simple indicator of postgraduate education. . . . The distinction between the "profit" and "nonprofit" sectors yields almost nothing.[23]

Moreover, to attribute the increase in civic activism to the hostility of middle-class professionals to business overlooks the fact that business was only one of a number of institutions whose authority was questioned by the "new class." More generally, public confidence in the leadership of virtually all the nation's major institutions, including the military, organized religion, organized labor, political parties, the executive branch, and Congress, declined significantly between the mid-1960s and the mid-1970s.[24]

Nevertheless, both Weaver and Kristol are essentially correct in their identification of the kinds of people who constituted the base of support for political opposition to business between the mid-1960s and mid-1970s. In sharp contrast to the liberalism of the 1930s, support for the "new liberalism" of the 1970s was highly correlated with education—and thus income. In the 1972 presidential election, "for the first time in modern electoral history . . . college-educated Americans voted more Democratic than their fellow citizens with a high-school or grade school education."[25] In sum, during the first half of the 1970s, "the upper-middle class in the United States . . . shed much of its identification with the business world. Increasingly, large segments of the broad, new upper-middle classes . . . think of themselves primarily as professionals—business administrators, engineers, accountants, lawyers, and so on—all responding to intellectual values and orientations rather than those traditionally associated with business."[26]

Political challenges to business during the 1960s and 1970s were also facilitated by a significant increase in the power, and change in the practices, of the media. For the first time, television news became a major political force, particularly after the increase in the length of the network evening news from fifteen to thirty minutes in 1963. A national press also emerged, composed of newsmagazines such as *Time* and *Newsweek* and newspapers such as the *Washington Post* and the *New York Times.* Moreover, reporting became more investigative and sophisticated. During the 1960s, the income and educational level of journalists increased significantly. Many individual television and print journalists were sympathetic to the goals and values of public-interest activists, and the latter, in turn, later came to depend on them for favorable and extensive press coverage. As one public-interest magazine put it, "Without extensive media coverage, many citizen group lobbying campaigns would be stillborn."[27] Significantly, the media was the only major American institution in whose leaders public confidence actually *increased* between 1966 and 1976.

The emergence of the public-interest movement during the 1960s and

1970s was closely connected to the two political movements that both preceded and accompanied it, namely, the civil rights and antiwar movements. The former played a particularly significant role. It resulted in the first mass mobilization of citizens in the United States since the trade-union organizing drives of the 1930s. For literally millions of Americans, support for the civil rights movement was among their first acts of political participation other than voting. The significance of the civil rights movement was not only its success in achieving its basic objective, namely, the ending of legalized discrimination in the United States, it was also the way this result was achieved. It succeeded not so much through the ballot box or the electoral arena but via civic activism, that is, boycotts, picketing, demonstrations, petitions, letter writing, and the forming of new organizations. By its emphasis on the importance of new forms of political participation as crucial to political and social change, the civil rights movement created a model for the public-interest movement. The civil rights movement also pioneered the use of what became one of the most important political strategies of the public-interest movement, the filing of lawsuits. In this sense, the NAACP Legal Defense Fund, which filed the lawsuit that led to *Brown v. Board of Education,* was the forerunner of public-interest law. And the importance of media coverage to its success also became a model for public-interest activists.

Not coincidentally, many public-interest activists had earlier been active in the struggle for civil rights, including the challenges to corporations such as Woolworth's and Eastman Kodak over their consumer and employment policies. It was the civil rights movement that inspired Campaign GM, an effort by a small group of lawyers to use the filing of proxy resolutions as a means of pressuring management to improve its social performance. They defined the corporation as a "private government," equivalent to the "official" government in terms of its size and social impact but differing from it in its lack of accountability to those affected by its decisions. To remedy this imbalance, they sought to require the world's largest industrial corporation to include a worker, an environmentalist, and a black on its board of directors. As one of Campaign GM's founders asked rhetorically: "If blacks could get the vote in the South, why shouldn't the constituency of General Motors be enfranchised?" Another wrote: "Corporate reform today is a natural, appropriate extension of the social and political movement of the 1960s—now the movement of the sixties is redirecting its energies from institutions of government to institutions of private power."[28]

Public-Interest Organizations

Interest groups, however, do not form spontaneously: they require leadership and resources. During the 1960s, the initiatives for new government controls over business came primarily from politicians. But during the late 1960s and early 1970s, the leadership of political challenges to business came primarily from private citizens. A number of individuals played a prominent role in organizing middle-class opposition to business, including John Gardner, the founder of Common Cause, and David Brower, who established Friends of the Earth. However, the most important "public-interest entrepreneur" was undoubtedly Ralph Nader. A lawyer from Connecticut, Nader first became nationally prominent in 1966 during the controversy over automobile safety regulation. His book *Unsafe at Any Speed* helped focus public attention on this issue,[29] while GM's subsequent admission that it had hired private detectives to spy on him assured the passage of the first important piece of consumer legislation enacted during the 1960s. Three years later, in an effort to build upon this personal triumph, Nader established the Center for the Study of Responsive Law. With a small, full-time staff and relying heavily on the work of student summer volunteers—dubbed "Nader's Raiders" (who grew from five in 1967 to two hundred in 1971)—the center produced a score of popular books documenting the failure of federal regulatory agencies to protect the public and arguing the case for a more adversarial relationship between business and government. These books, along with Nader's own steady stream of articles, interviews, and media appearances, helped popularize the "capture" theory of government regulation of business.

By the mid-1970s, Nader had established a series of interrelated organizations.[30] In addition to the Center for Responsive Law, they included Congress Watch, a lobbying operation; the Public Citizen Litigation Group, which engaged in public-interest litigation; the Health Research Group, which specialized in the monitoring of the Food and Drug Administration; the Corporate Accountability Project, which focused primarily on corporate governance; the Tax Reform Research Group, which lobbied for changes in tax policy; the Center for Auto Safety, which monitored the NHTSC; and the Airline Consumer Action Project, which challenged the policies of both the Federal Aeronautics Administration (FAA) and the Civil Aeronautics Board (CAB). By the mid-1970s, Nader's "public interest conglomerate" employed approximately seventy-five full-time lawyers, lobbyists, and researchers and had an annual budget of over a million dollars. It was funded primarily by two sources: Nader's speaking fees and book royalties, including a cash settlement of $270,000 from General Motors, and direct-mail fund raising. The latter effort, organized under the rubric of "Public Citizen," received contributions from more than 175,000 individuals in the mid-1970s.

The impact of Ralph Nader, and the organizations he helped establish or fund, was considerable. The center's research reports played a critical role in revitalizing two of the nation's oldest social regulatory agencies, the Federal Trade Commission and the Food and Drug Administration. *The Chemical Feast* helped lead to the banning of cyclamates from soft drinks and the ending of the inclusion of monosodium glutamate in baby food.[31] Nader himself was instrumental in the passage of a number of regulatory laws, including the Natural Gas Pipeline Safety Act (1968) and the Radiation Control for Health and Safety Act and the Wholesome Meat Act (1967), and his efforts and those of his associates contributed to the passage of the Coal Mine Health and Safety Act (1969) and the Comprehensive Occupational Safety and Health Act (1979) and to the strengthening of the Clean Air Act Amendments of 1970.

An important key to the effectiveness of many of Nader's organizations and operations was their ability to develop considerable expertise in a large number of policy areas, mostly in consumer protection. The decentralized structure of Nader's operation enabled small, but highly resourceful, groups of people to specialize in a particular regulatory agency or policy area and thus, in time, develop a degree of expertise equivalent to, and in some cases surpassing, that of corporate lobbyists and government officials. These individuals constituted what the most prominent raider, Mark Green, described as a "government in exile," waging "a crusade against official malfeasance, consumer fraud and environmental devastation."[32] The *New York Times Magazine* observed: "Raiders have shown again and again what one man can do in Washington if he spends full-time on a single issue or bird-dogging one agency."[33]

Nader also proved extremely adept at influencing public opinion. He contributed a torrent of articles to newspapers and magazines, made frequent appearances on television, and lectured widely throughout the United States, particularly on college campuses. Nader was particularly effective with the press.

More than an investigator and scholar, drawing upon, but transcending, his lawyer's skills, he was an advocate skilled at seizing the symbols of debate—not a traditional advocate but one finely attuned to the uses and the needs of the media: the beats, the deadlines, the need for fresh "copy," for conflict, for heroism if available, but certainly for villainy, and, above all, for clarity and simplicity. ("Ralph Nader speaks in perfect bites!" said a TV consumer reporter, with professional respect.)[34]

He was also able to develop an effective network of informants within the government, who kept him abreast of developments affecting policies in which he was interested.

Nader affected public thinking about business, and the relationship between business and government, not simply by his relentless exposés of various acts of private and public malfeasance, but by the tone of moral outrage and indignation in which those indictments were expressed. In a sense, Nader was like a contemporary Old Testament prophet, criticizing the irresponsibility of those who had abused their power and authority and calling upon the public to demand that they be held responsible and made accountable. More than any other single individual, he effectively politicized the role of the consumer, articulating and giving political content to the frustration and anger of ordinary citizens. Most important, he became an inspiration to thousands of college graduates by providing them with a role model and an alternative vocation, namely, public-interest lawyer and advocate. The annual survey of American leaders conducted by *U.S. News and World Report* in 1974 found Nader to be the fourth most influential American, a ranking never before or since achieved by any business executive.[35]

The efforts of political entrepreneurs like Nader were in turn greatly facilitated by two developments. The first was the willingness of a relatively large number of extremely competent, well-educated, and highly motivated people to work for activist organizations for relatively modest salaries or, sometimes, for no salary at all. During the early 1970s, the blocks surrounding DuPont Circle in Washington, D.C., were filled with scores of extremely modestly furnished offices, from which hundreds of people were engaged, either directly or indirectly, in attempting to counterbalance the political influence of business. They wrote reports and studies, issued press releases, solicited funds, filed lawsuits and petitions, testified at congressional and administrative hearings, and lobbied in the halls of Congress. The commitment of these individuals was crucial to the formation and effectiveness of public-interest lobbying and public-interest law. A major portion of the Yale Law School class of 1969 went into the practice of public-interest law.

A second development was the emergence of new technologies that significantly lowered the costs of access to the political process. "Although satellite television links and survey research are important tools, the technology of direct mail has had by far the greatest impact on interest group politics."[36] Computer-based direct mailing made possible the targeting of individuals who were likely to provide financial support. Common Cause, for example, sent out more than 6.5 million pieces of mail in its first year and signed up 230,000 members. Between 1970 and 1983, the organization mailed a total of 82 million solicitations. Direct-mail solicitations proved to be an effective source of fund raising. Indeed, 30 percent of the public-interest groups studied by Berry in the mid-1970s had no individual members at all, only contributors. In addition, the reduction in the cost of long-distance telephone service, most notably through the introduction of the WATS line, significantly lowered the costs of communicating with supporters throughout the United States.

Several of the largest and most prominent public-interest organizations, including Common Cause, the Sierra Club, Friends of the Earth, Public Citizen, the Wilderness Society, and the Consumer Federation of America, were funded almost entirely by private contributions or dues, solicited primarily through the mails. Yet the increased willingness of citizens to contribute to citizen movements was not by itself sufficient to provide the resources necessary for the formation and maintenance of citizen groups. According to one study, "only 22 percent of the citizen groups receive as much as 70 percent of their budget from dues."[37]

From where did the others receive financial support? Foundations were another important source of funds. Of the eighty-three public-interest organizations examined by Berry in his 1977 study, one-fifth received more than half their funds from private foundations.[38] The role of the Ford Foundation was particularly crucial. Between 1970 and 1975, it made grants totaling nearly $31.9 million to several public-interest law firms, including the Environmental Defense Fund and the Natural Resources Defense Council. The Carnegie, Field, Stern, and Rockefeller foundations also provided substantal support for public-interest organizations. In addition, more than two-thirds of the citizen groups formed between 1946 and 1980 relied upon individual gifts as an important source of funding. In 1980, according to one study, these gifts provided 17 percent of the revenue of the citizen groups.[39]

A final source of financial support for citizen groups was the government itself. Under section 501(c)(3) of the Internal Revenue Code, charitable and educational organizations are eligible for special tax treatment. While they cannot devote a "substantial" amount of their activities to lobbying, they may advocate positions before administrative agencies, initiate litigation, and communicate to Congress in an "educational" capacity. Organizations qualifying under this section receive a number of public subsidies. All contributions to the organization are tax deductible, thus significantly lowering the effective cost of donations for relatively well-to-do individuals. In addition, the organization becomes eligible to receive financial support from private foundations, which, according to Internal Revenue Service rules, cannot contribute to "political or propagandistic activity." Section 501(c)(3) status also allows an organization to be granted a "special third class" bulk-mailing permit, which allows mass mailings of printed literature at approximately one-third the normal cost.

Public-interest organizations also received more direct forms of government support. Under the private attorney-general concept, courts were allowed to award attorney's fees to prevailing plaintiffs if the litigants had conferred a substantial public benefit by enforcing a federal statute. This provided an important supplemental source of income to a number of public-interest law firms, helping to make many of them virtually self-supporting. In 1975, the Supreme Court restricted the authorization of attorneys' fees to suits brought to enforce those statutes that specifically authorized such compensation (as of 1976, forty-six federal laws fell into this category). This decision was partially reversed by the Civil Rights Attorneys' Fees Act of 1976, which provided for attorneys' fees for successful plaintiffs in a number of additional cases. Class-action suits were another form of indirect subsidy of public-interest litigation, since they allowed citizen groups to combine a large number of relatively small individual complaints against a particular company into one suit. Following a change in federal court rules in 1966, thousands of class-action suits were brought, many of which resulted in substantial pretrial settlements. In 1973 and 1974, however, the Supreme Court made the filing of class-action suits much more difficult by requiring that each individual's claim amount to more than $10,000 and ordering plaintiffs to pay the full cost of notifying each member of the class before litigation could proceed. (In 1974, Congress modified these restrictions for consumers seeking damages for unfilled warranties.)

In addition, some public-interest groups were able to secure a federal subsidy for their participation in administrative proceedings. The legislation establishing both the Consumer Product Safety Commission and the Federal Trade Commission Improvement Act of 1974 specifically authorized financial support for the "attorney fees and expert witness costs and other expenses of participation by parties otherwise unable to represent their interest in rule-making proceedings." Between 1975 and 1979, the FTC made a total of $1.5 million in grants to various consumer groups. A similar provision was included in the Toxic Substances Control Act of 1976, which offered refunds even for petitioners. In 1977, the FDA announced that it would help defray the costs of participation in its deliberations on the grounds that "legal rights to participation are meaningless without positive official support."[40] Notwithstanding the controversy that these "subsidies" created, their actual monetary significance was modest: on average, public-interest groups received less than 10 percent of their revenues from agency participation or subsidies, court-awarded legal fees, or other forms of government assistance.

The Role of the Courts

Public-interest activists took the capture theory of government regulation of business for granted; they began with the assumption that the history of the efforts to control corporate social conduct was a history of failure. As Simon Lazarus put it, "Regulation of industry would have to be regarded as one of the least successful enterprises ever undertaken by American democracy."[41] This perspective owed much to the writings of political scientists such as Marver Bernstein, Theodore Lowi, and Grant McConnell, whose books were widely read by college students during the latter part of the 1960s. Bernstein's *Regulating Business by Independent Commission* contended that regulatory agencies go through a life cycle: they begin highly committed to the fulfillment of the objectives for which they were established, but in time come to identify increasingly with the companies whose conduct they are responsible for supervising. McConnell's *Private Power and American Democracy* offered a critique of Progressivism, and Lowi's *The End of Liberalism* questioned the legacy of the New Deal. Both reached a similar conclusion: attempts to control private power had failed because reformers had not created structures of public authority powerful enough to challenge the autonomy and authority of the private sector.[42]

What public-interest activists learned from their analysis of the failures of both Progressivism and the New Deal was that enacting new regulatory laws or establishing new regulatory agencies was not by itself sufficient to restrict corporate prerogatives. As two public-interest lawyers wrote, "Left to their own resources, the public bureaucracies possess neither the motivation nor the strength needed to fulfill their tasks; they, too, like the corporations, can function for the public benefit only when the public itself is given greater participation in their processes."[43] Rather, a way had to be found to make certain that regulatory officials actually carried out the intent of Congress. How could this be done? How could the public-interest movement increase the likelihood that the defeats experienced by business in Congress would be duplicated in the executive branch of government as well?

Their solution involved two basic elements. The first, which reflected Lowi's influence, was to reduce the discretion of regulators by making regulatory statutes as specific as possible. Both the Coal Mine Safety Act and the Clean Air Act Amendments of 1970 included specific numerical standards, and both the Clean Water and Clean Air amendments enacted in the early 1970s contained relatively clear goals as well as strict time-tables for achieving them. The last specifically listed the six pollutants for which the Environmental Protection Agency (EPA) was required to issue health quality standards. Between 1970 and 1980, Congress included more than three hundred deadlines in the fifteen environmental laws it enacted. The Occupational Health and Safety Act of 1970 mandated the imposition of fines and other penalties for noncompliance. The provision of the National Environmental Policy Act requiring all federal agencies to include an analysis of the environmental impact of their proposals was a similar "action-forcing mechanism." These provisions marked a decisive break with the traditions of both New Deal and Progressive reform legislation, which had established broad policy goals and then left it up to administrators to determine how best to enforce them.

The second element involved expanding the judicial oversight of agency decisions. This likewise marked a decisive break with the past because historically the judicial branch of government had been the one least sympathetic to nonbusiness interests. The courts had overturned scores of regulatory statutes passed by state governments in the late nineteenth and early twentieth centuries and, in the 1930s, had declared significant portions of the New Deal unconstitutional. The Administrative Procedures Act of 1946, which provided a statutory framework for judicial review of agency rule making, was a key part of the corporate backlash against the New Deal; it enabled business to use the courts to curb abuses of authority by the executive branch of government.

One way of increasing the likelihood of judicial review was to mandate it within the regulatory statutes themselves. Provisions governing judicial review of regulatory enforcement were the subject of considerable debate in Congress during the early 1970s, and much of the regulatory legislation enacted during this period did authorize "public" challenges of agency decisions in the courts. This meant that public-interest groups would no longer have to rely upon the good faith of regulatory officials to enforce the intent of Congress: they could, in effect, directly participate in its enforcement. As Ralph Nader put it:

We're interested in the development of initiatory democracy, and this is more fundamental than participatory or representative democracy. . . . We need a fundamental change in our structure so that people can initiate actions to make sure public officials are acting responsibly. I'm talking about rights plus remedies plus legal responsibilities so it can be a citizen versus the ICC or the FDA. A civil servant should be forced to make the law work, and if he won't do it he should be censured or expelled from the Government.[44]

Public-interest activists made litigation a key component of their political strategy. They were inspired to do so, in part, by the critical role the judiciary had played in the civil rights movement, and by the general liberal thrust of judicial decisions throughout the 1960s. Moreover many public-interest activists—most notably Ralph Nader himself—were lawyers by training; engaging in litigation was thus a way for them to employ their professional skills in the pursuit of their political objectives. Judicial reasoning, with its emphasis on rights, also appealed to the ideology of the public-interest movement. Just as the courts had defined and enforced civil "rights," so now they could be used to extend to the public the "right" to clean air and water, a safe workplace, and food free from dangerous chemicals. Public-interest lobbies did not possess the political resources that could enable them to countervail business influence over the executive branch of government, and they confronted the considerable resources of business lobbyists in the legislature. But the federal courts were an arena of policy making in which they could, at least in principle, compete with business on an equal basis.

The ability of the public-interest movement to use the courts to affect regulatory policy was in turn made possible by three important changes in administrative law. The first was a significant expansion of the doctrine of standing—the grounds upon which an aggrieved party could demand the right to have its grievances heard in the federal courts.[45] The second was the increased willingness of the courts to broaden the grounds on which they were willing to overturn agency decisions. The third involved the legal recognition of the right of private citizens to participate in the decisions of administrative agencies. Summarizing the expansion of judicial oversight of agency decisions that had occurred during the second half of the 1960s and the first half of the 1970s, Richard Stewart concluded that administrative law in the United States had been "transformed." He wrote in 1975:

In the space of a few years the Supreme Court has largely eliminated the doctrine of standing as a barrier to challenging agency action in court, and judges have accorded a wide variety of affected interests the right not only to participate in, but to force the initiation of, formal proceedings before the agency. Indeed, this process has gone beyond the mere extension of participation and standing rights. . . . Increasingly, the function of administrative law is not the protection of private autonomy but the provision of a surrogate political process to ensure the fair representation of a wide range of affected interests in the process of administrative decision.[46]

In effect, the federal judiciary had endorsed the public-interest movement's two central arguments, namely, that federal regulatory agencies—regardless of whatever statutes Congress enacted—could not, by themselves, be trusted to represent the public interest; and second, that, consequently, the public interest could be protected only if organizations representing the interests of citizens were allowed the same rights and opportunities to participate in the regulatory process that business had historically enjoyed.

In deciding for the plaintiff in *Environmental Defense Fund, Inc. v. Ruckelshaus*, Chief Justice Bazelon of the D.C. Circuit predicted:

We stand on the threshold of a new era in the history of the long and fruitful collaboration of administrative agencies and reviewing courts. . . . Courts are increasingly asked to review administrative action that touches on fundamental personal interests in life, health, and liberty. These interests have always had a special claim to judicial protection, in comparison with the economic interests at stake in a ratemaking or licensing proceeding.[47]

As Bazelon's remarks suggest, in no area of federal regulatory policy was the judiciary as solicitous of the interests and values of citizen groups as in the area of environmental policy. The courts have been at least as responsible as the Congress for the erosion of the ability of business interests to affect environmental policy that began in the late 1960s and continued throughout the 1970s; indeed, the judicial reverses suffered by business in this policy area preceded its defeats in Congress.

Even before the National Environmental Policy Act (NEPA) was enacted, a number of environmentalist plaintiffs had succeeded in persuading federal judges that environmentally protective language could be found in highway and forestry statutes, and that they therefore were entitled to challenge actions taken in connection with these laws. However, following NEPA, the grounds for filing lawsuits by environmental groups significantly expanded. The most common kind of lawsuit file by environmental law groups was under section 102(2)(c) of NEPA, which required all federal agencies to prepare environmental impact statements for all major federal actions significantly affecting the quality of the human environment. It was the success of environmental law firms in two cases decided in the spring of 1970—the Alaska pipeline case and DDT litigation—that effectively established the credibility and impact of public-interest litigation and made possible its subsequent foundation support. NEPA has been described as "the Magna Carta of the environmental movement, not only because it established a broad national environmental policy, but because it is a great equalizer in the hands of skilled litigants."[48]

Environmental law firms began to make extensive use of NEPA as a means of challenging federal policies with which they disagreed following the decision of the D.C. Circuit in *Calvert Cliffs' Coordinating Committee v. Atomic Energy Commission* (AEC) in July 1971.[49] This decision, which found that the AEC's regulations for enforcing NEPA had violated the act's requirements, convinced environmental groups that the judiciary planned to take NEPA seriously. During the next decade, approximately a thousand lawsuits alleging violations of the NEPA by federal agencies were filed—about two-thirds by citizens' or environmental groups.[50] The suits filed by environmentalists under the NEPA played an important role in preventing a number of projects, including the Cross-Florida Barge Canal, which was canceled by President Nixon following litigation by the Environmental Defense Fund, and a plan by the Walt Disney company to develop a ski resort at Mineral King Valley. These were unusual results, however; the more common outcome was to delay or modify projects that were eventually approved. The most important impact of environmental litigation was more indirect: it led to the preparation of more than ten thousand environmental-impact statements in the decade following the enactment of the NEPA.

The lawsuits filed by environmentalists under the Clean Air Act had a more measurable impact on the nation's environmental policy, since they challenged rules and regulations rather than specific projects.[51] Suits filed by the Natural Resources Defense Council against the EPA resulted in decisions that prohibited the agency from approving variances granted by the states to be extended beyond 1975, required the agency to promulgate regulations for asbestos, beryllium, and mercury, and ordered the agency to set air quality standards for airborne lead. In 1972, the District of Columbia circuit ordered the EPA to disapprove state plans for implementing the Clean Air Act Amendments of 1970 that did not prevent the deterioration of air quality in those parts of the nation that already met the EPA's national ambient air requirements. The effect of this decision, which was subsequently reaffirmed by Congress in 1977, was to prevent industries from complying with federal emissions and air quality standards by moving from the industrialized northeast to the relatively underdeveloped and "cleaner" southwest.

The increased willingness of the courts to overrule the decisions of administrative agencies on the grounds that they had violated the intent of Congress or had not followed proper administrative procedures constituted an important constraint on agency rule making—one to which they had not been previously subject. It forced regulatory agencies to take the views of public-interest groups seriously. As the director of the Center for Law and Social Policy put it, "In the early days, we had to sue because no one would listen to us. We lacked clout. Once we succeeded in some cases, the threat to sue automatically gives us more weight and gives the agencies more incentive to bring us in at an earlier stage."[52] As a result, unlike in the past when judicial oversight was employed exclusively by business to challenge rules that it found objectionable, beginning in the late 1960s, it became a tool that was equally available to interest groups that wanted to strengthen federal controls over business.

Conclusion

During the 1960s, many students of American public politics argued that the locus of control over public policy was "vested in an informal but enduring series of 'iron triangles' linking executive bureaucracies, congressional committees and interest group clienteles with a stake in particular programs."[53] The governmental process was effectively balkanized, overt and visible policy conflict occurred relatively infrequently; as a result, policies tended to be both stable and predictable. Consequently, the main role of Congress, or of the Executive Office of the President, was essentially to ratify the decisions made by various relatively autonomous "subsystems or subgovernments." As one political scientist put it, "Interest groups in a mature subgovernment enjoy[ed] an intimate cooperative relationship with government, and . . . seldom [were] directly challenged by groups fundamentally hostile to their interests."[54]

The public-interest movement undermined the system of iron triangles in a number of ways. Most obviously, their very existence meant a significant increase in the number of interest groups represented in the nation's capital and an expansion in the scope of political conflict. Many of the issues that the public-interest movement helped place on the political agenda could not be accommodated within the existing system of subgovernments: issues such as environmental and consumer protection and occupational health and safety cut across the previously existing divisions of authority among subgovernments and directly challenged their priorities 'and prerogatives. Bureaucracies such as the Army Corp of Engineers or the Department of Agriculture found themselves, for the first time in a generation, challenged to make decisions that reflected interests other than those that favored additional construction or farm subsidies. (This of course was the purpose of requiring environmental-impact assessments.)

At the same time, the mandates of newly established agencies such as EEOC, EPA, and OSHA did not lend themselves to stable accommodations with any particular interest group. Too broad in scope to be dominated by a particular industry, too visible to ignore the purposes for which they were established, and too important to business to be captured by a public-interest group, they found themselves immediately caught in a crossfire between segments of the business community and public-interest lobbies. They also found themselves confronted by a judiciary that was not willing to accord their decisions the same deference it had extended in the past; by a Congress, many of whose members were highly responsive to the demands of public-interest groups; and by a press that was interested in and capable of closely scrutinizing their decisions. In short, the public-interest movement transformed both the nature of the political agenda and the way in which administrative decisions affecting business were made. For the first time since the 1930s, business found its political influence seriously challenged by a new set of interest groups.

V I

The Politics of Economic Stagnation, 1973 to 1976

Introduction

The years between 1973 and 1976 were a transitional period, in terms of both the development of the American economy and the dynamics of business-government relations. The OPEC price increase and the recession that followed did more than simply plunge the nation into its worst economic crisis since the Second World War. They also signaled an end to the postwar economic boom: the performance of the economy after 1973 was significantly inferior to what it had been in the previous decade. While real growth in the Gross National Product (GNP) of the United States averaged 3.5 percent between 1966 and 1973, the annual growth of the GNP averaged only 2.2 percent between 1974 and 1981. Per capita GNP—the wealth produced per citizen—grew approximately 3 percent each year between 1966 and 1973; between 1974 and 1981, it averaged just under 1 percent. Inflation, which had averaged 4.8 percent between 1966 and 1973, increased at an average annual rate of 9.3 percent between 1974 and 1981. Real hourly wages, after increasing steadily throughout the 1950s and 1960s, peaked in 1972 and actually declined during the next decade. Equally important, overall productivity, which had grown by an average rate of 3 percent between 1947 and 1973, grew by only 1 percent after 1973.[1]

Around 1978, this long-term decline in the nation's relative economic performance began to transform the political agenda and, in doing so, significantly increased the power of business in American politics. However, through 1976, business continued to find itself on the defensive. The energy crisis, Watergate, the scandals surrounding overseas payments, and the continued disarray of the economy all exacerbated the public's disapproval of business. The percentage of Americans expressing "a great deal of confidence" in the leaders of big business, after declining from 51 percent in 1967 to 27 percent in 1971, remained between 27 and 30 percent for the next three years. In August 1974, it declined to 22 percent and the next month fell to 16 percent.[2] In 1973, only 18 percent of the population believed that "business tries to strike a fair balance between profits and the interest of the public."[3] A 1976 poll reported that 82 percent of Americans believed that big business had "too much power"—making big business the least trusted of the twenty-four groups about which the public was questioned.[4]

In part as a result of the substantial Democratic gains in the 1974 congressional elections, the public-interest and trade-union movements were able to maintain much of their political strength. In spite of a determined effort on the part of the utility and coal industries following the 1973–74 energy crisis, Congress refused to make any enacted major modifications in the 1970 Clean Air Act Amendments; in 1976, it enacted a statute regulating toxic substances. The trade-union movement was successful in securing federal controls over private pensions, and the consumer movement scored a major political triumph when Congress strengthened the powers of the Federal Trade Commission (FTC). Price controls were also maintained on energy.

However, these years also marked the beginning of a backlash against increasing government controls over business. In 1973, amid fears of a growing shortage of energy, Congress voted approval of the construction of the Alaska pipeline, and a year later it passed legislation forbidding the National Highway Traffic Safety Administration (NHTSA) from requiring the installation of interlock systems on automobiles. In 1975, owing to fears of unemployment, the environmental movement was unable to secure the approval of legislation regulating the strip-mining of coal. Business was also successful in weakening the power of OSHA and in defeating the consumer movement's efforts to establish a consumer protection agency. The energy industry was also able to resist successfully the efforts of a number of Democratic senators and to break up the integrated oil companies. Finally, while the 1974–75 recession spawned a number of left-liberal policy proposals aimed at involving the federal government more actively in the management of the economy, these initiatives remained stillborn.

The Nixon Presidency and Corporate Campaign Contributions

Most of the drama surrounding Watergate focused on the role of the president and his senior advisers in seeking to cover up the break-in at the Democratic party's headquarters on May 28, 1972. However, investigations into the conduct of the president's 1972 reelection campaign also revealed that a number of American corporations had violated the federal law prohibiting them from contributing to campaigns for federal offices. The break-in and the illegal campaign contributions were, in fact, closely connected: it was company funds—many dispersed in cash—that financed many of the unethical and illegal activities associated with the president's 1972 reelection campaign. At the same time, the paper trail left by these contributions helped bring to light many of the revelations that ultimately forced the president's resignation in the summer of 1974.

Controversy surrounding the efforts of business to influence the policies of the Nixon administration actually preceded the emergence of the Watergate scandal. A suit brought by Ralph Nader and three consumer groups in federal court on January 24, 1972, charged that the government had granted increased price supports for dairy products in return for "promises and expectations of campaign contributions for the reelection campaign of the incumbent President."[5] It was subsequently revealed that in 1971 the Associated Milk Producers (AMP) had donated $197,500 to the Nixon campaign through the establishment of 150 secret fund-raising committees. The AMP, along with two other major dairy groups, contributed an additional $422,500 to the president's reelection the following year. In addition, the Lehigh Valley Cooperative Farmers, a dairy group from Pennsylvania, made two secret contributions of $25,000 in $100 bills to the Nixon campaign. The former general manager of the AMP testified that he had personally met with President Nixon before the White House decision on price supports was announced, and that the decision to increase milk price supports was made by the White House, not by officials of the Department of Agriculture.

Shortly before his ouster, Watergate's Special Prosecutor Archibald Cox obtained a copy of a letter to the president from a representative of the AMP suggesting that if the administration imposed import quotas on certain dairy products, the president could expect up to two million dollars in campaign contributions. Fifteen days after the White House received the letter, the president imposed quotas on four specific dairy products, though at a level lower than that desired by the industry. In addition, Cox's investigation established a connection between a secret $5,000 campaign contribution by AMP and the break-in at the office of the psychiatrist who had treated Daniel Ellsberg.

The staff of the Senate Watergate Committee subsequently concluded that campaign pledges made by the major dairy cooperatives, totaling two million dollars, were "apparently directly linked to a favorable milk price support decision by the President worth hundreds of millions of dollars to the industry—and costing the same amount to the government and consumers." The report accused Nixon of ignoring "the opinion of every agricultural expert in his Administration" in making his decision. On January 8, 1974, President Nixon issued a report that defended as "totally proper" his decision to reverse an Agricultural Department ruling and allow an increase in the federal price support for milk.[6] He did, however, acknowledge that at the time he had been aware that the dairy industry had pledged to contribute at least two million dollars to his reelection campaign.

A month later, syndicated columnist Jack Anderson disclosed a confidential memo from the International Telephone and Telegraph Corporation (ITT) that linked the settlement of a government antitrust action against ITT with a pledge to underwrite a large part of the funds needed to hold the Republican National Convention in San Diego. The memo was from ITT lobbyist Dita Beard to a vice president of the corporation. In it, she specifically linked ITT's willingness to pay a major share of the cost of holding the Republican Convention in San Diego to a favorable settlement of an antitrust suit then pending against the corporation. On March 19, 1973, the House Interstate and Foreign Commerce Committee's special subcommittee on investigations released a report prepared by the Securities and Exchange Commission (SEC). This report, along with a series of leaked memos to the press, provided a detailed description of ITT's lobbying efforts.

Between 1969 and early 1971, ITT's president, Harold Geneen, had met with seventeen cabinet secretaries and members of the White House staff to discuss the government's antitrust policy. "The officers of ITT had numerous opportunities to lobby the highest officials of the Administration and enjoyed access to decision makers not exceeded by any other Washington lobby."[7] However, there does not appear to have been any direct relationship between the company's willingness to subsidize the costs of holding the Republican Convention in San Diego (in any event it was held in Miami Beach) and the Justice Department's decision to negotiate a settlement with ITT rather than take its antitrust suit to the Supreme Court. Special Prosecutor Leon Jaworski, who succeeded Cox, stated that he had uncovered no evidence that ITT officials had committed a criminal offense, though former Attorney General Kleindienst did plead guilty to not testifying "accurately and fully" before a congressional committee that was investigating the administration's handling of the controversial antitrust settlement.[8] But the extended investigations of ITT's lobbying activities, along with the disclosure that the company had sought to enlist the cooperation of the State Department in order to prevent the inauguration of socialist Salvador Allende as president of Chile, made the conglomerate multinational the most widely criticized corporation in the United States during the mid-1970s—a status previously held by General Motors.

In the fall of 1973, the public was exposed to a series of additional revelations about corporate political activity. Herbert Alexander writes that "although there had been sporadic federal prosecutions of corporate political practices in past elections, the picture that unfolded from 1973 to 1975 suggested illegal corporate giving on a scale unlike anything previously imagined. . . . What was particularly startling about the roster of illegal corporate contributions in 1972 was its 'blue chip' quality and the amounts involved."[9] A number of firms, in order to conceal the source of their contributions to the Nixon campaign, had "laundered" them either by channeling monies through their overseas subsidiaries or by inventing fictitious bonus schemes for their employees.

The Watergate special prosecutor filed suit in U.S. District Court in the District of Columbia against American Airlines, Goodyear Tire and Rubber Co., and Minnesota Mining and Manufacturing Co. alleging violations of federal laws prohibiting campaign contributions by corporations for candidates for federal office. Between November 13 and 15, 1973, the Senate Watergate Committee heard testimony from six corporate executives who admitted making or authorizing contributions to the president's 1972 reelection campaign. In all, twenty-one companies pleaded guilty to having violated the federal campaign laws. However, "business sources have estimated that . . . at least one third of the top Fortune 500 . . . made systematic, but illegal, campaign contributions."[10] Yankelovitch reported that 70 percent of Americans believed that Watergate revealed the way that big business controlled government through illegal contributions.[11]

Paradoxically, the revelations about illegal corporate campaign contributions revealed not so much the political strength of business during the Nixon administration as its weakness. Nixon repeatedly placed his own political interests ahead of those of business. Indeed, most of the companies that contributed so generously to the president's reelection had not sought any particular favors. Rather, they contributed primarily in order to insure goodwill or access—presumably something that business had every reason to expect from a Republican president in any event. As Orin Atkins, chairman of Ashland Oil, testified: "I can see no way we were benefited . . . its intention was to give us a means of access to present our point of view to the executive branch of the Government." Claude C. Wild, Jr., vice president of governmental affairs for Gulf Oil, told Senator Sam Ervin (Democrat-North Carolina) that he decided to contribute to the Nixon reelection campaign in order to make sure that "we were going to be treated in an equal way," adding, "I would just like [someone] to answer my telephone calls once in a while."[12] While some companies did volunteer funds, many others contributed out of a fear that unless they did so, their firm would suffer. George Spater of American Airlines testified that his company had contributed in response to a personal request by Herbert Kalmbach: "I knew Mr. Kalmbach to be both the President's personal counsel and counsel for our major competitor. I concluded that a substantial response was called for." He added that "most contributions from the business community are not volunteered to seek competitive advantage but are made in response to pressure for fear of competitive disadvantage."[13]

A year before the 1972 election, Congress had enacted the first major change in federal campaign finance regulations since the turn of the century. The Federal Election Campaign Act of 1971 set a ceiling on the amount federal candidates could spend on media advertising and required the full disclosure of all campaign contributions and expenditures. It also allowed corporations to establish a "separate segregated fund" or political action committee (PAC) for the purpose of making campaign contributions. These funds could be financed by contributions from corporate shareholders and executives. While companies could not contribute their own funds, they were permitted to defray the costs of establishing and administering a corporate PAC. However, the significance of this provision—which eventually revolutionized the financing of election campaigns—was not widely appreciated at the time and there was "no substantive impact in shaping the legislation from the business community."[14] Ironically, this legislation was actually enacted at the initiative of organized labor, which feared that a recent Supreme Court decision would prevent it from soliciting campaign contributions from its membership.[15] However, the disclosure provisions of this statute, which also attracted little attention at the time, played a major role in breaking open the Watergate scandal.

Pressure for additional federal regulation increased following the revelations of the Watergate Committee. A Gallup poll of September 1973 found 65 percent of those surveyed in favor of public financing and a ban on private contributions, a significant increase over previous years. In addition, "Many members of Congress also took up the cry for reform, particularly in the wake of a January 1974 Harris survey that showed Congress ranking even lower than the president in public esteem."[16] The result was the 1974 Federal Election Campaign Act, which placed strict monetary limits on what both PACs and individuals could contribute to campaigns for federal office. It also imposed spending limits on campaigns for federal offices and provided for the public funding of presidential general elections. A Federal Election Commission (FEC) was established to enforce it.

The business community welcomed this legislation since, by reaffirming the provisions of the 1971 statute allowing companies to form PACs, it provided them, for the first time since the dawn of the Progressive Era, with a legal way to contribute to campaigns for federal offices. At the same time, it made corporations less vulnerable to blackmail from politicians for illegal contributions. Two subsequent rulings by the FEC facilitated the use of PACs by corporations. In an advisory opinion requested by Sun Oil Company (SUN), corporate PACs were permitted to solicit contributions from employees as well as shareholders. In addition, the FEC allowed corporations to establish more than one PAC, even though each PAC could contribute only $5,000 to any one campaign. This provision effectively removed any limitations on the amount a company's executives and shareholders could contribute through the PAC mechanism, since corporations could establish as many PACs as they could fund.

Following the Supreme Court decision in *Buckley v. Valeo,* which struck down the provisions of the 1974 legislation limiting individual contributions but reaffirmed the FEC's SUN-PAC ruling, Congress reconsidered the issue of campaign finance reform. The drive for revising the 1974 legislation was initiated by organized labor, which feared that the rapid proliferation of corporate PACs, nearly three hundred of which had been established between 1971 and 1976, would dilute its own campaign spending. As a result of the 1974 election, the Republicans lacked sufficient strength in Congress to defeat the efforts of the Democrats to restrict the use of PACs by corporations. They were, however, still capable of sustaining a filibuster or a presidential veto.

A compromise was subsequently reached, which on balance favored organized labor more than business. Companies were restricted to seeking contributions from their stockholders, executives, and administrative personnel and their families. Union PACs were restricted to soliciting contributions from union members and their families, but unions could collect funds through payroll deduction plans if the company also employed that method of collecting funds from its stockholders or executive and administrative personnel. A number of corporate lobbyists were very unhappy with this legislation and urged President Ford to veto it. Although he was uneasy with a number of its provisions, Ford reluctantly signed the legislation in order "to maintain the integrity of our election process" for the 1976 election.[17]

Overseas Payments

No sooner had the public become aware of the magnitude of illegal corporate contributions to politicians in the United States than a major scandal erupted concerning the disbursement of corporate funds in other countries. In the course of investigating the financing of the 1972 campaign, the Watergate special prosecutor had uncovered a number of corporate slush funds that were concealed from regular corporate accounting controls. Contending that the existence of these funds undermined the accountability of management to the firms' stockholders, the Securities and Exchange Commission (SEC) began its own investigation. It soon found evidence that a number of these slush funds had been used to bribe foreign officials. The SEC's chair, Ray Garrett, Jr., stated that his commission had uncovered "bribery, influence-peddling and corruption on a scale I had never dreamed existed . . . none of us dreamed there were the millions, the tens of millions, the hundreds of million that we found." The SEC's chief of enforcement, Stanley Sporkin, remarked: "Until two or three years ago, I genuinely thought the conduct of business . . . was generally rising. But what can you say after the revelations of the last couple or three years?"[18]

The Senate Subcommittee on Multinational Corporations, chaired by Frank Church of Idaho, subsequently began its own investigation, as did both the Internal Revenue Service and a special presidential task force on questionable corporate payments abroad, headed by Secretary of Commerce Elliot Richardson. A number of stockholders' suits were also filed by public-interest groups. In the next three years, more than four hundred

American corporations admitted making illegal or questionable payments to foreign officials, primarily for the purpose of securing sales. In a number of cases, companies had used the same accounting mechanisms both to conceal illegal payments in the United States and make "questionable" payments overseas.

By the time the scandal had run its course, it had led to one suicide, the resignation of a number of senior corporate executives, and the toppling of several foreign governments. The Ad Hoc Committee on Foreign Payments noted that "no single issue of corporate behavior has engendered in recent times as much discussion in the United States." One commentator concluded that "the leadership of American big business has never been held in such low regard since perhaps the days of the Great Depression," adding that "big business is now close to the bottom rung in measures of public trust and confidence." *Time* and *Newsweek* both printed special cover stories on the payoff scandal, and the *Washington Post* editorialized that American confidence in business institutions was in a "process of disintegration" and that the country was in the midst of a "national crisis."[19]

A committee headed by John J. McCloy subsequently revealed that the Gulf Oil Company and its subsidiaries had spent more than twelve million dollars in the United States and abroad on "political contributions and payments."[20] Following a dramatic and lengthy meeting of Gulf's board of directors, three of its senior managers, including the chairman of the board, Robert Dorsey, were removed.[21] In February 1975, Eli Black, the chairman of United Brands, jumped to his death from his office on the forty-fourth floor of the Pan Am building in New York City. While Black's suicide was originally attributed to the pressures of his job, a subsequent investigation by the SEC revealed that Black had previously authorized a bribe of $1,150,000 to officials of the Honduran government to reduce the company's taxes. The sum of $750,000 had also been dispersed to officials in Italy in order to prevent restrictions on United Brand's exports to that country.[22] Early in 1976, it was revealed that Lockheed, the nation's largest defense contractor, had dispersed more than twenty-four million dollars to promote its planes outside the United States. Among the recipients of Lockheed's largess were Prince Bernhard of the Netherlands, politicians in Italy's ruling Christian Democratic party, and high-ranking officials in the Japanese government and the ruling Liberal Democratic party. On February 13, the company's two senior executives resigned. Following the disclosure that Northrop had paid more than thirty million dollars in commissions and bribes to government officials and agents in Holland, Iran, France, West Germany, Saudi Arabia, Brazil, Malaysia, and Taiwan, its president was pressured into resigning.

In 1976, Congress began to consider legislation designed to restrict the payment of bribes to government officials outside the United States. There was little dispute about the need for such a policy: the disclosures had not only proven highly embarrassing for American corporations, but had severely strained relations between the United States and a number of its allies. The White House and Congress, however, differed as to the form it should take. Senators Proxmire and Church wanted strict standards to be applied to the conduct of American corporations abroad, while the Ford administration was uncomfortable with the idea of Americans attempting to police the conduct of their own overseas firms with foreign officials. The result was a stalemate: Congress adjourned in 1976 without taking any action.

The Energy Crisis

The industry that found itself under the most intense public scrutiny—and criticism—between 1973 and 1976 was the energy industry. The oil industry was among the major targets of reformers during the Progressive Era, one result of which was the breaking up of the Standard Oil Trust in 1911. But during the next half-century its political fortunes improved considerably. Indeed, until the late 1960s, the political power of the oil industry seemed virtually unassailable. The concentration of production in a few states meant a concentration of political power among a handful of elected officials closely identified with their welfare, including such powerful members of Congress as Senate Majority Leader Lyndon Johnson and Speaker of the House Sam Rayburn, both from Texas. Given the stability of Democratic party politics in the South, the party traditionally nominated young and capable men who could grow old in Washington. While less than 30 percent of all senators came from oil-producing states, over 40 percent of the members of the Senate Finance Committee came from such states during the 1950s and 1960s.[23]

Prior to the early 1970s, the oil industry had suffered only two political setbacks in the postwar period: President Eisenhower's veto of a bill deregulating the price of natural gas in 1956 and a reduction in the size of the depletion allowance from 27.5 percent to 22 percent, which was part of the Tax Reform Act of 1969. However, the industry was adversely affected by the environmental legislation approved in the late 1960s and early 1970s; it rivaled the automobile industry in being blamed for the nation's environmental problems, particularly after the accidental discharge of oil onto the beach at Santa Barbara in 1969.

In the winter of 1973, many parts of the United States experienced shortages of fuel oil. Schools were closed in Denver and factories shut down in Des Moines. In the spring and summer of 1973, gasoline shortages began to inconvenience and worry American drivers. Several of the larger integrated firms responded by restricting their allocation of fuel to their own distributors, thus squeezing out independent oil marketers—a number of whom were forced to close down their discount outlets. These shortages hurt the integrated oil companies politically: they were accused of intentionally causing them in order to drive out the independents, whose market share had recently been increasing. *Time* noted that the independent marketers "suspect the major oil companies have contrived the shortages to force them out of business," and *Newsweek* reported: "With the gasoline shortage becoming worse each day, growing numbers of . . . officials are asking: 'Is the shortage . . . due to a conspiracy by oil-industry giants to drive competitors out of business, boost their own profits and win major concessions'?" In the summer of 1973, the FTC filed an antitrust complaint against the nation's eight largest oil companies, requesting vertical divestiture of the industry as a remedy for their "interdependent behavior."[24]

In an effort to control inflation, President Nixon had frozen all wages and prices, including oil prices, in August 1971. With the subsequent imposition of voluntary price guidelines in phase 3 of the president's stabilization program, the industry sought to have these controls removed. However, in view of the highly publicized shortage of energy, the administration decided to deny the industry's request. In March 1973, the Cost of Living Council issued regulations that reimposed control of prices of crude oil products charged by the twenty-four largest companies, which accounted for 95 percent of the market. Nonetheless, gasoline prices increased 30 percent because the independent refiners and distributors were not affected by federal price controls. Shortages persisted as the major producers, in order to prevent the independents from increasing their market share, hesitated to share their limited reserves with them. In August 1973, the Cost of Living Council removed price controls from all products save oil. A two-tier pricing structure was established for domestic production: "new" oil was decontrolled but controls were retained on "old" reserves. These phase 4 controls satisfied no one, but the industry's response was divided because they affected each firm differently. In any event, they were due to expire in April 1974.

In October 1973, the Arabian exporters of crude oil declared an embargo on their sales to the United States in retaliation for American backing of Israel in the Yom Kippur War. At the same time, OPEC announced a major increase in oil prices. The Arab boycott exacerbated an already extremely tight supply of oil and gas, but tankers full of Arabian oil were already en route to the United States and the effect was not felt until December. However, panic ensued immediately. Widespread hoarding and forecasts of a major depression became commonplace. Panic buying drove oil prices even higher: within three months they had increased three to five times. Lines developed at gas stations throughout the United States, and many motorists waited two to three hours to purchase a half-tank of gas—if they were fortunate enough to be served before the station's daily allocation was exhausted. A national speed limit of 55 miles per hour was decreed, homeowners were ordered to cut their heating temperature to 68 degrees, and gas stations were required to close on Sundays.

Almost immediately, at the request of President Nixon, Congress enacted the Emergency Petroleum Allocation Act. This legislation transferred the allocation of the nation's limited energy supplies from the marketplace to the government. It established a Federal Energy Agency with responsibility for allocating all petroleum products to all end users throughout the United States. It also extended phase 4 price controls for another year, in order to prevent windfall profits and price gouging. It also restored the market share of each sector of the oil industry to what it had been in 1972 and declared the federal government's commitment to preserving "the competitive viability of independent refiners, small refiners, non-branded independent marketers, and branded independent marketers."[25]

The agency got off to a rocky start, owing both to the inexperience of its staff and the complexity of the allocation rules. Spot shortages developed everywhere and hundreds of state and local officials, along with representatives of the oil companies themselves, descended upon Washington to plead for increases in their allocations. Thanks in part to a relatively mild winter, the oil-supply crisis ended by the summer of 1974, though gasoline prices were considerably higher than they had been the year before. In the first quarter of 1974, the nation's real GNP fell 7 percent, largely because of cutbacks in energy-related industries. However, overall unemployment rose only slightly, as the rest of the economy continued its inflationary boom.

Energy prices increased dramatically in every capitalist nation in 1973 and 1974. Yet only one industrialized nation—the United States—chose not to pass on the full increase in world market prices to the public. It did this by continuing price controls on domestic oil discovered before 1972.

And it accompanied these controls by establishing an elaborate system for allocating oil among different segments of the industry. The explanation of this policy became clear in the months following the Arab oil embargo and OPEC price increases, as the nation attempted to understand why it had suddenly been faced with an "energy crisis."

From the very beginning of the shortages in the winter of 1972, the public blamed them on the oil industry. A survey conducted by Louis Harris in April 1973 found that most people blamed the shortages of energy on "a conspiracy among utility and fuel companies." A rumor circulated that scores of oil tankers were being kept a few miles from the nation's coasts, waiting until prices rose still further before delivering their cargo. Richard Vietor wrote: "The conspiracy interpretation of the oil crisis stemmed from a historic conviction that the oil industry was an oligopoly, which controlled government policy as well as world oil markets. . . . Circumstantial evidence suggested that the oil industry was manipulating data, withholding supplies, squeezing independents, cooperating with OPEC, bribing the White House, and using the crisis as an excuse for eliminating environmental legislation."[26] By 1975, only 5 percent of the American public had a "great deal of confidence" in the oil industry.

The large oil companies found themselves challenged from three directions: from consumers upset about increased prices, from independents worried about being driven out of business, and from environmentalists who believed that the industry was using the energy crisis as a way of scaling back the nation's pollution controls. Whatever initial suspicions of the oil industry any of these constituencies may have had were significantly exacerbated by press coverage of the energy crisis. The media "largely ignored available evidence relevant to evaluating oil monopoly charges" and relied extensively on industry critics as sources, "giving their charges overwhelming weight and coverage in comparison to explanations by industry or academic spokesmen."[27] Media coverage of the energy crisis also emphasized the industry's long history of special tax advantages and its insensitivity toward the public.

Early in 1974, the industry reported a dramatic increase in its first-quarter earnings. Exxon's profits were up 59 percent from the previous year; with total sales of $28 billion, it now surpassed General Motors as the world's largest industrial corporation. Texaco's profits were up 70 percent and Mobil's had increased by 68 percent. A number of oil companies increased their dividends and provided additional salaries and bonuses to their top managers. These developments received extensive media coverage and further reinforced the public's perception that the industry was benefiting at its expense. *Time* reported that "the industry's profits amid scarcity have reduced the public image of the oil company to a new low."[28]

Industry representatives claimed that it needed increased earnings to finance the search for new energy. However, the credibility of this claim was undermined in June 1974, when Mobil announced that it was bidding five hundred million dollars to purchase Marcor, Inc., a holding company whose major asset was Montgomery Ward. The oil industry mounted an extensive public-relations campaign to explain its increased profitability and persuade the public that the energy shortage was indeed genuine. However, this effort did little to allay public suspicion of the industry, particularly after the press reported that oil and gas inventories had remained at normal levels throughout the winter and spring of 1974.

In February 1974, the Senate's Permanent Subcommittee on Investigations, chaired by Henry Jackson, held a series of hearings on the energy crisis. Their tone was set by his opening remarks:

> The American people want to know if there is an oil shortage.
> The American people want to know whether oil tankers are anchored offshore waiting for a price increase or available storage before they unload.
> The American people want to know whether major oil companies are sitting on shut-in wells and hoarding production in hidden tanks and at abandoned service stations.
> The American people want to know why oil companies are making soaring profits.
> The American people want to know if this so-called energy crisis is only a pretext, a cover to eliminate the major source of price competition—the independents—to raise prices, to repeal environmental laws, and to force adoption of new tax subsidies.[29]

The highest-ranking executives of the nation's seven largest oil companies were subpoenaed by the committee, and Jackson promised that he would get them to answer his questions "one way or another." Senator Abraham Ribicoff told the executives assembled in front of him and the TV cameras that they were now "reaping the whirlwind of 30 years of arrogance"[30] and accused the companies of engaging in a "conspiracy" to create a "panic situation" in the United States. For several days the executives were subjected to hostile questioning and were required to provide extensive documentation on a few hours' notice. Gulf's president subsequently remarked, "They made me feel I was at a criminal trial."[31] The chairman of Mobil complained, "For God's sake, we're being treated like criminals."[32]

The nationally televised hearings provided no useful additional information about the energy crisis, and Jackson himself conceded that they had "not turned up any hard evidence that the major oil companies deliberately created the crisis."[33] Nonetheless, congressional challenges to the energy industry increased. They were spearheaded by Democratic senators and representatives from oil-consuming states who sought to protect the economic interests of their constituents and make energy policy into a partisan issue. Between 1973 and 1975, fifteen of the thirty-nine permanent committees of the U.S. Congress conducted investigations into the energy crisis. "In the course of these hearings, the motives and practices of business executives were scrutinized and castigated more harshly than at any time since World War II."[34]

In 1975, two bills were introduced in Congress to break up the integrated oil companies. The Petroleum Industry Competition Act of 1975, cosponsored by senators Birch Bayh of Indiana and Philip Hart of Michigan, required the eighteen largest oil companies to separate their production, pipeline, refining, and marketing operations within five years. The Interfuel Competition Act of 1975, cosponsored by Senator Edward Kennedy of Massachusetts and Representative Morris Udall of Arizona, prohibited any firm engaged in either the production or refining of petroleum or natural gas from acquiring interests in other energy sources, such as coal, oil shale, or solar. Going a step further, Senator Adlai Stevenson of Illinois proposed that the government establish its own energy corporation to serve as a yardstick for measuring the industry's performance.

Both antitrust proposals, which paralleled the recommendations of the FTC report issued a few months before the Arab oil embargo, were predicated on the assumption that the energy crisis had been exacerbated—if not caused—by the lack of adequate competition, particularly from alternative forms of energy. Senator James Abourezk of South Dakota contended, "It doesn't take much brilliance to figure out that if an oil company can make high profits on oil during a shortage period, its managers will not be enthusiastic about developing a lower cost competitor."[35] However, the root of the case for divestiture was not so much economic as political: it reflected a mistrust of concentrated economic power, particularly over a product as vital as energy. Senator John Durkin of New Hampshire dramatically informed his colleagues: "We must act before this petroleum octopus violates and subverts any more of what is good, decent, and fair in our political system."[36]

At the 1975 annual meeting of the American Petroleum Institute, Charles Spahr, chairman of Standard Oil of Ohio, stated that the threat of divestiture was the most important political challenge confronting the industry. He warned that "if divestiture takes place, the industry will have chaos for all time," and called for a concerted lobbying effort aimed at making the oil industry's views "visible and credible."[37] This effort was successful. When the Bayh-Hart legislation came to the floor of the Senate, it was defeated by a vote of 54 to 45. This vote, which took place on October 8, 1975, marked the nadir of the industry's political fortunes. Although the issue of divestiture remained on the political agenda for the next two years, no similar proposal ever again made it to the floor of either house. Nor, for all the enthusiasm that divestiture elicited from a number of senators, was it supported by a majority of the American public.[38] With the return of relative price stability in 1977, the interest of politicians in the issue temporarily faded.

However, the oil-depletion allowance became a major target of liberal Democrats in both houses of Congress. In December 1973, Arco's president Thornton Bradshaw publicly broke ranks with the other integrated oil companies and announced his support for the elimination of the depletion allowance, contending that it had become an "albatross" around the industry's neck. Following Bradshaw's statement, the independent oil producers abandoned the majors and struck a deal with Senator Russell Long (Democrat-Louisiana) to eliminate the allowance for the major integrated firms, although retaining it at a rate of 15 percent for themselves. In 1974 a bill to phase out the depletion allowance was tabled by the House Rules Committee, but in 1975 the Democratic caucus managed to get a proposal for its abolition passed as a floor amendment to the Tax Reduction Act of 1975. After Russell Long obtained an exemption for small producers in the House-Senate conference committee, Congress approved the abolition of the allowance as part of the 1975 tax bill, thus reversing a half-century of federal energy policy.

However, the most important political setback experienced by the integrated oil companies during the first half of the 1970s was the retention of price controls. In 1975, President Ford proposed a compromise: price controls would be phased out over a period of thirty months, but a tax on windfall profits would be imposed on the industry. This proposal pleased no one. The integrated and independent producers opposed the tax on windfall profits, and independent refiners, distributors, and retailers favored price controls in order to protect their allocations. Liberal Democrats in Congress, whose numbers had increased considerably in 1974, were against the proposal because it would increase energy prices. Representative John Dingell of Michigan stated that "sudden decontrol of domestic oil prices would be nothing short of disastrous for the U.S. economy," and Representative Richard Ottinger of New York described the president's proposal as "cruel and unfair, designed to sock the poor, the working man, and the middle-income people by leaving allocation of the hardship entirely to the marketplace." Ralph Nader attacked Gerald Ford as "a sales agent for Exxon and the OPEC cartel."[39]

A few weeks after it abolished the depletion allowance, the House of Representatives voted to extend the Petroleum Allocation Act. "The atmosphere was one of reprisal and reprobation. Every compromise was cast as a plum for 'Big Oil.' "[40] Finally, in the fall of 1975, Congress approved the Energy Policy and Conservation Act. While the legislation did enact a number of other aspects of the president's energy policy, it actually reduced the price of domestic oil, extended controls for a minimum of forty months, and preserved the entitlements program for the nonintegrated oil firms. Although the president disliked the bill's price controls as much as the oil producers, he was reluctant to face the voters in the New Hampshire presidential primary without any energy legislation, and reluctantly signed it into law.

Environmental Policy

The energy crisis and the recession that followed it posed the first major challenge to the environmental movement and the laws it had helped enact between 1969 and 1972. The first environmental policy affected by the energy crisis was the construction of the Alaskan oil pipeline. Between 1970 and 1972, environmentalists filed a series of lawsuits that effectively delayed the construction of a pipeline designed to transport oil from the North Slope of Alaska to the West Coast. In 1972, the seven oil companies involved in the pipeline's construction began to press for legislation to expedite its construction. In response, more than thirty organizations, the majority of them environmental groups, formed the Alaska Public Interest Coalition. Having recently defeated a powerful coalition of aerospace firms and labor unions over the development of supersonic transport (SST), the environmental movement was confident that it would win the ensuing congressional battle. As George Alderson, the legislative director of the Friends of the Earth, and the coalition's coordinator, put it: "This is the type of issue the conservation movement has been accustomed to dealing with. The movement has rallied time and again to oppose such a thing as this move. We have an excellent coalition of forces."[41]

The lobbying and public-relations effort to expedite approval of the Alaska pipeline was primarily led and funded by the oil and natural-gas industry. Their position was supported by the State of Alaska, which hired the Washington law firm of Covington and Burling as its lobbyists, and the Ford administration. Oil firms placed a large number of ads in newspapers in major cities stating the industry's case. Testifying before Congress on March 27, Arco's president, Thornton Bradshaw, whose company owned 28 percent of the pipeline as well as a major share of North Slope exploration rights, stated that the country "can no longer afford continuing delay in bringing Alaska oil to the people that need it." He told Congress that "every day we delay costs us, in terms of the 1980 trade deficit, another $10 million." Bradshaw promised that, if construction began at once, Alaskan oil could be delivered to the continental United States by 1977. He did concede that the pipeline was now "better and safer . . . than it would have been without the intervention of the environmentalists," but added, "we thank the environmentalists, but we think they are overdoing it now."[42]

The Sierra Club countered that "the Alaska route would be an environmental disaster" and urged that other routes, including one through Canada, be studied. The organization furthermore contended that there was "an almost total lack of information on the justification for haste."[43] However, in July 1973, the Senate voted to bar further court challenges to the pipeline's construction on environmental grounds and directed the secretary of the interior to issue the necessary authorization for the pipeline's construction. Four months later, final action on this legislation was completed by Congress.

The environmentalists attributed their defeat to the power of the oil industry and its allies. Alderson said: "This is the greatest accumulation of power that ever confronted the environmentalists in a legislative fight." However, they had defeated another powerful coalition two years earlier when Congress had refused to appropriate funds to construct a SST. What made the difference? The answer is a simple one: while it had proved difficult for the advocates of the SST to convince the average citizen of how he or she would benefit from the construction of an expensive aircraft, the nation's dwindling gasoline supplies directly affected the individual motorist. One environmentalist observed, "the oil companies put across a wide range of pressure to convince Americans that Alaska oil would be put into their gas tanks."[44] Faced with a choice between potential ecological damage to a remote wilderness area and a continued shortage of gasoline, the American public chose the former.

Following the energy shortage of 1973, the utility and coal industries began lobbying Congress to relax the Clean Air Act of 1970. They wanted to be allowed to burn more coal, an energy source whose use the 1970 legislation had severely restricted. Their effort to weaken the 1970 amendments was joined by both the steel industry, which wanted a three-year delay in clean-air deadlines, and the automobile industry, which desired a delay in the effective date of standards for automobile emissions.

Most of the conflict over the 1974 Clean Air Act Amendments focused on the burning of coal. Representatives of a number of utility companies informed Congress that the shortage of clean, that is, low-sulphur, fuels was a major stumbling block to their effort to meet clean-air deadlines. Since most eastern coal was relatively high in sulphur, they were forced to purchase their coal from western states, thus incurring a considerably greater transportation cost. Moreover, these supplies were insufficient. One major southern utility was forced to import low-sulphur coal from Australia and South Africa.

The standards established by the 1970 statute did not require utilities to burn low-sulphur coal; they could also meet the act's clean-air requirements by installing scrubbers. However, the utility industry was strongly opposed to the use of this particular abatement technology. Their representatives argued that scrubbers were expensive, unreliable, consumed considerable energy themselves, and created waste sludge whose disposal then presented an environmental problem. Donald Cook, the chairman of American Electric Power, launched a $3.1 million advertising campaign to mobilize public opinion against scrubbers, contending that they "at best were in a primitive state of development."[45] The chairman of the board of the Tennessee Valley Authority (TVA) complained that scrubbers frequently broke down and operated only sporadically under peak loads.[46] Representatives of the utility industry also argued that stringent pollution control measures were not necessary for utilities located in rural or isolated areas. Aubrey Wagner of the TVA urged that such plants be allowed to use intermittent controls to curb pollution—a strategy prohibited under the Clean Air Act. (Intermittent controls involve a combination of tall stacks, monitoring equipment, and only the occasional use of scrubbers or low-sulphur fuels.)

The environmental movement's lobbyists urged Congress to reject each of the utility industry's demands. They argued that the utilities had only themselves to blame for waiting until the last minute to attempt to meet air-pollution control deadlines. Richard Ayres, an attorney for the Natural Resources Defense Council, stated that "the Clean Air Act Amendments of 1970 gave the coal burning utilities . . . ample notice more than three years ago that they have five, or if they need it, seven years to equip their plants with control equipment."[47] Ayres contended that intermittent controls were neither reliable nor enforceable and that scrubbers were both efficient and effective, while Senator Edmund Muskie accused the utility companies of making impossible demands upon the manufacturers of scrubber equipment.

The Clean Air Act Amendments approved by Congress in June 1974 did allow utilities to convert from natural gas and oil to coal, but only if they could do so without violating primary standards for clean air. They also permitted the suspension of air-pollution standards through June 30, 1975, but only if clean fuels were unavailable. Both these provisions were designed to increase the use of coal. However, by keeping the air-pollution control standards established by Congress in 1970 virtually intact, the legislation was actually a defeat for both the coal and utility industries. Moreover, the bill allowed the Environmental Protection Agency (EPA) to ban or even reverse coal conversions if it determined that sulfate particulate emissions had reached dangerous levels. An official of the Sierra Club concluded: "The coal industry, the utilities, everybody who just wanted to be exempted from the Clean Air Act have lost." The president of the National Coal Association agreed with this assessment. He stated, "It's a substantial retreat from the commitment to coal we thought we could get last winter. I'm afraid the coal industry is again becoming the ambulance rather than the cornerstone of national energy policy."[48]

The amendments were also a political defeat of the automobile industry. The House of Representatives rejected an amendment by Representative Louis Wyman (Republican-New Hampshire) that would have postponed the enforcement of automobile-emissions controls until September 30, 1977, for cars registered in the 90 percent of the nation's land area that did not have significant pollution from automobile emissions. The amendment was supported by the automobile industry and representatives from rural areas but strongly opposed by the EPA, the National Clean Air Coalition, and several real-estate companies and developers. The last were concerned that relaxation of automobile-emissions standards would require local governments to meet federal standards for exhaust air quality by restricting additional construction. Congress did delay the enforcement of the emissions standards it had approved in 1970, but for only one year.

In 1975, with the authorization of the Clean Air Act Amendments of 1970 about to expire, a number of different industries began a campaign to have them modified. The drive for reform was led by the utility industry, which wanted to be able to employ tall stacks and intermittent controls in place of scrubbers, and with the automobile industry, which wanted a five-year limit on emissions standards for automobiles produced in 1977. In addition, as a result of a 1975 Supreme Court decision that interpreted the Clean Air Act Amendments as prohibiting industry from meeting pollution control standards by relocating to less polluted regions of the country, much of the nation's industry now found itself confronted with what amounted to a system of national land-use controls. They too joined the effort to have the 1970 legislation amended. *Business Week* observed: "At first glance, the time seems ripe for major concessions to business. The costs of compliance—at least $130 billion by 1982 . . . —are biting just when the nation is reeling from the worst economic crunch since the Depression. And the still-unresolved energy crisis strengthens the hand of some industries . . . that are seeking relaxed emission rules."[49]

However, during 1975 and 1976, Congress refused to weaken or even modify any of the goals or standards of the 1970 amendments. The legislators' lack of responsiveness to industry appears to have been due to a number of factors. Most important, the law's requirements had become closely identified with the protection of public health. Notwithstanding the significant gap between the goals that Congress had mandated in 1970 and what industry had actually been able to achieve, discernible progress had in fact been made: since 1970, sulphur-oxide emissions had been reduced 25 percent, and particulate emissions had declined 14 percent. Few in Congress appeared willing to take responsibility for reversing this improvement. Moreover, the credibility of business among those legislators and their staffs responsible for drafting air-pollution legislation remained very low. Leon Billings, chief of staff of the Senate subcommittee and a close ally of Senator Muskie, compared industry's complaints to the "boy who cried wolf." One industry lobbyist told *Business Week:* "One time we gave Billings some ideas we had typed on a piece of paper, and during our talk he made a paper airplane out of it."[50]

However, while the energy crisis did not succeed in tempering the nation's commitment to improved air quality, the 1974–75 recession that followed it did have an important impact on another aspect of environmental policy: federal regulation of strip-mining. In December 1974, Congress approved legislation establishing minimal environmental standards to be followed by the states in controlling strip-mining: all land stripped in the future had to be returned to its original contours unless a better use for it could be established. The legislation had been bitterly opposed by the mining industry, which contended that it would inhibit additional production of coal and raise the cost of electricity. Although several of the bill's requirements had been modified to meet the objections of the coal industry, President Ford vetoed it on the grounds that it would cause undue hardship for the industry at a time when coal was becoming increasingly important to the nation's energy needs.

Six months later, Congress passed similar legislation, and again it was vetoed by President Ford on the grounds that "it would cost more in lost jobs, lost coal production, and higher electricity bills than the American economy could stand." By a margin of only three votes, the president's veto was sustained by the House of Representatives. The House's decision was a surprising one, since the bill had been passed only three months earlier by a 333 to 86 vote, a margin well above the two-thirds required to override a presidential veto. (The Senate had passed the bill by 84 to 13.) This change in the bill's fortunes was a result of an "extraordinary lobbying campaign in which coal and utility lobbyists worked on vulnerable Democrats, and Ford used his own personal goodwill to keep Republicans in line."[51] While their lobbying effort in 1974 had emphasized the potential shortage of energy, the coal companies now argued that 40,000 jobs would disappear if the president's veto was overridden. The coal industry's position was also backed by the utility industry, which sought to appeal to the interests of consumers by contending that federal strip-mining regulation would force utilities to raise their rates. The lobbying of the utilities was crucial, as they were able to persuade a number of representatives with whom the coal lobbyists had no influence. But the key to sustaining the veto was the strong shift among several members of Congress toward concern over the economy and away from the environment.

The same year that President Ford vetoed the strip-mining bill, Congress enacted, and the president signed, the Toxic Substance Control Act, though, unlike the major environmental laws passed earlier in the decade, its provisions were significantly weakened as a result of intense business opposition. Congress had been debating the need for new legislation in this area since 1971, when the Council on Environmental Quality had urged Congress to plug the gap in existing regulations that allowed hundreds of new chemicals to be marketed each year without adequate testing and that provided no way for the government to test the safety of chemicals already in use. Just as public concern about the effect on health of DDT had played an important role in the passage of the Federal Pesticides Control Act in 1972, so did the discovery of high levels of PCBs (a compound used as an insulator in electric transformers and capacitors) in a number of lakes and rivers help persuade Congress to enact the Toxic Substances Control Act four years later.

Business Week noted that "the chemical industry's long term nightmare— a stiff Toxic Substances Control Act—has finally come true." Yet at the same time, it observed that "strangely, the prevalent reaction within the industry is one of relief that the long fight is finally over and that the result was not worse than it is." The chairman of a committee of the Manufacturing Chemists Association, which had lobbied extensively on the issue, stated: "It's not perfect, but it represents a balanced view that came out of extensive negotiations." However, a number of other industry representatives expressed concern that the costs of compliance would be much more difficult for small companies and thus lead to increased industry concentration. The EPA, however, hastened to assure the industry that its enforcement would be "as palatable as possible":[52] the agency stated that it intended to test no more than two hundred of the approximately one thousand chemicals marketed each year. In any event, the final version of the legislation was supported by the chemical manufacturers as well as the environmental, labor, and consumer groups which had originally pressed for a stronger law.

The Politics of Consumer Protection

While the visibility of consumer issues diminished after 1970, in 1974 the consumer movement was able to secure the passage of one additional piece of consumer-protection legislation, the Magnuson-Moss Consumer Warrantee Act. In 1970, the Senate had approved legislation establishing minimum federal standards for warranties on consumer products valued at fifty dollars or more. The bill was supported by the Consumers Union and the Consumer Federation of America and opposed by automobile and appliance manufacturers as well as the American Retail Federation. The warranty bill was not acted upon by the House, and a year later the Senate passed it again, this time combining it with legislation strengthening the consumer-protection powers of the Federal Trade Commission (FTC). The House again failed to act, and the Senate in turn approved the law for the third time in 1973. Finally, in June 1974, the House Interstate and Foreign Commerce Committee reported the bill out of committee. It was subsequently approved by both houses of Congress and signed into law by President Ford in January 1975. Jeffrey Joseph, chief lobbyist for the U.S. Chamber of Commerce, recalled:

> Magnuson-Moss was done with a business community mostly unaware. We started getting calls from major businesses around the country saying, we just heard that this bill passed, what is it? Although it had been going through discussion in the Congress for four or five years, business didn't even want to try to fight against something with a consumerist handle on it. They weren't that sophisticated, they weren't well organized.[53]

While it was the popularity of the bill's warranty provisions that made
its passage possible, the statute's real significance lay in another direction.
Magnuson-Moss significantly expanded the regulatory authority of the
FTC: it gave it the power to spell out the standards to be met by written
warranties given by manufacturers or retailers, to file suits seeking consumer redress from unfair or deceptive business practices, and to seek civil
penalties for knowing violations of FTC orders against such practices. The
bill also allowed consumers to file suit in state or federal courts for damages
stemming from the failure of companies to honor their warranties and
allowed class-action suits by consumers seeking damages for unfilled warranties—provided the total sought was at least fifty dollars. At the same
time, the legislation, at the insistence of the House, also included a provision designed to protect companies from arbitrary action by the commission by requiring the regulatory agency to follow a series of detailed
procedures before issuing rules or policy statements on "unfair or deceptive acts or practices."[54] More important, for the first time in its history,
the commission was given the power to issue rules governing the competitive practices of entire industries, not just individual firms.

The Politics of Organized Labor

The deterioration of the American economy in 1974 and 1975 was unprecedented in the postwar period. Real GNP fell by a calamitous 7.5
percent in the fourth quarter of 1974, bringing the total annual output of
the economy 1.8 percent below the level of the previous year. The unemployment rate was 5.2 percent in January 1974; by December it had increased to 7.2 percent. While nominal wages increased 8.7 percent, the
inflation rate was more than 12 percent. Consequently, real compensation
actually declined—the first decline since the Bureau of Labor Statistics
began compiling such data in 1947. This pattern of stagflation continued
through 1975. The GNP declined an additional 2 percent. Unemployment
rose to nearly 9 percent, averaging 8 percent for the entire year. While
inflation did slow to 7 percent in 1976 because of the magnitude of
the economic downturn, food and energy prices continued to increase substantially: "talk of dollar-a-loaf bread matched talk of dollar-a-gallon
gasoline."[55]

The steady and largely uninterrupted growth of the American economy
since the end of the Second World War appeared to have come to an end.

The immediate political impact of this development was to reinvigorate the political effort of organized labor. In the three decades following the New Deal, trade unions had represented the most important organized political opposition to business; they had also played a critical role in the enactment of consumer-protection legislation during the 1960s. However, in the early 1970s, their political role and influence became overshadowed by the public-interest movement. Although organized labor lobbied for the Occupational Safety and Health Act of 1970, and individual unions actively campaigned for federal funding of the SST, for the most part unions played only a marginal role in the major changes in business-government relations described in chapter 4. This situation changed after the 1974 recession. During the mid-1970s labor was very involved in a number of extremely important and hard-fought legislative battles with business, including pension reform, common situs picketing, labor-law reform, occupational health and safety regulation, and the Humphrey-Hawkins full employment bill.

In 1974, although labor was unable to prevent the passage of a bill granting the president broad powers to negotiate trade agreements (it favored the imposition of mandatory quotas on imports), it did succeed in having two of its most important legislative priorities enacted. These were an increase in the minimum wage from $1.60 to $2.30 an hour and federal regulation of private pension plans. The pension law, for which labor had been campaigning for more than seventeen years, established minimum federal standards for private pension plans covering more than twenty-three million workers. It was enacted in response to the experience of a number of workers who had lost their pensions owing to bankruptcies, mergers, and unscrupulous employers. The Employee Retirement Income Security Act of 1974 (ERISA) did not require companies to establish a pension plan, nor did it dictate the size of benefits if they chose to do so. Rather, it sought to ensure that employees who were covered were provided with permanent pension rights after a reasonable period of time.

The approval of ERISA was a major defeat for the business community. In 1972 an Ad Hoc Corporate Pension Fund Committee had been established to lobby on behalf of its forty large corporate members, and both the Chamber of Commerce and the National Association of Manufacturers (NAM) subsequently invested considerable resources to prevent its passage. But the business community's lobbying was poorly coordinated, and its credibility was undermined by its unwillingness to offer an alternative solution to what was commonly recognized as a serious problem. As an internal NAM memorandum admitted: "Outright and total opposition to all [broad reform] places us in an inflexible and tenuous position similar to the one NAM experienced during the legislative battle on occupational safety and health [in 1970]. . . . There is every indication that legislation on private pension plans is imminent. The only question that remains is what kind of legislation."[56] Business lobbyists were able to extract some concessions from Congress that reduced the financial burden of the legislation but, in the end, the political strength of the trade-union movement, as well as the legislation's evident popularity, proved decisive. It was approved by overwhelming votes in both houses of Congress and signed into law by President Ford.

Seeking to take advantage of the Watergate scandal, the AFL-CIO's Committee on Political Education (COPE), the National Committee for an Effective Congress, the United Mine Workers, and the United Auto Workers (UAW) decided to become actively involved in the 1974 mid-term election. The candidates they supported did extremely well: 70 percent of the candidates supported by COPE and the UAW were elected. What made this outcome particularly impressive was that nearly half of the candidates endorsed by the two organizations were not incumbents: the candidates supported by the unions clearly benefited from the political backlash against ex-President Nixon and the Republican party. As a result, the 1974 elections resulted in a partisan and ideological shift in the composition of Congress comparable to that of 1964. The Democrats gained forty-nine seats in the House and four seats in the Senate.

In 1975, organized labor decided to take advantage of the presence of large prolabor majorities in both houses to press for the enactment of legislation legalizing common situs picketing. This legislation would allow unions to picket an entire construction site in a dispute with any individual contractor working at the site—a practice outlawed by the Supreme Court in 1951. As a result of that decision, many unionized general contractors had farmed out much of their work to nonunion subcontractors. The construction unions were prohibited from striking against these contractors because the contractors and the subcontractors were legally considered separate business. George Meany, president of the AFL-CIO, argued that the Supreme Court decision required construction workers to disregard their common interests and break each other's strikes, while the president of the United Steelworkers contended that "there is so much mutuality of interest on the same building site that picketing is essentially primary rather than secondary in its intent, purpose and result in regard to all of the employers on the premises."[57]

The conflict over this bill was a "classic lobbying battle,"[58] pitting labor against business in the kind of confrontation that had not been seen in Congress since the battle over the Taft-Hartley Act during the Truman administration. The union effort was led by the Building and Construction Trades Department of the AFL-CIO and its seventeen-member unions and endorsed by the entire AFL-CIO as well as the Teamsters Union. Opposition to the bill was spearheaded by the two trade associations representing contractors, plus the National Right to Work Committee, the Chamber of Commerce, the National Association of Manufacturers, and a number of individual corporations. An ad hoc organization, the National Action Committee on Secondary Boycotts, was established in June 1975 to coordinate the efforts of the forty different business interest groups opposed to the bill. Both sides used similar lobbying strategies, relying heavily on massive letter-writing campaigns. The National Right to Work Committee spent a total of $750,000 on its letter-writing campaign and the placing of full-page advertisements in fifty newspapers in seventeen states. Organized labor, in turn, informed all of the senators and representatives to whose campaigns it had contributed of the importance it attached to their vote on this bill.

The conflict in Congress was extremely bitter and heated. The chief lobbyists for the AFL-CIO building trades department accused the National Right to Work Committee of trying to smear the unions by referring to "bombings and thugs" in their advertisements. A congressional supporter of the bill stated that "at times in recent discussions I have found it . . . distorted and twisted virtually all out of recognition by its opponents and detractors." Opponents of the bill described it as a "union power grab" and contended that its real purpose was "to see every job in America a union job." The executive director of the Associated General Contractors of America characterized the legislation as "nothing more than a two-fold, well-calculated attempt by the building trades unions to force management to its knees and the construction workers who do not belong to a union off the job site." Representative Robert Bauman (Republican-Maryland) declared that "only ignorance of the issue or a passion for economic self-flagellation would induce this Congress to vote for a measure which would all but guarantee major work stoppages in the construction industry at a time when our ailing economy has hopes of rising from its sick bed."[59]

Legislation legalizing common situs picketing, slightly modified to include some safeguards demanded by President Ford as a condition for signing it, passed the House of Representatives by a large margin. Opponents of the bill, primarily conservative Republicans, then mounted a strong attack in the Senate, but its supporters overcame two filibusters and in late December it was sent to the White House. Organized labor appeared to have scored a major political triumph. However, the business opponents of the bill now pressured President Ford to veto it: the White House received more than 750,000 pieces of mail opposing the bill. On December 22, 1975, President Ford announced that he would veto the legislation on the grounds that it had created too much contention within the construction industry. His decision appears to have been primarily motivated by presidential politics: his chief challenger for the Republican nomination, Ronald Reagan, opposed the bill, and a number of influential Republicans threatened to switch their support to the former California governor if Ford signed the legislation.

That same year, organized labor suffered another important defeat when legislation restricting the power of OSHA was approved. Almost as soon as OSHA was established, Congress was deluged with thousands of angry letters, mostly from small businesspeople, complaining that they were being "treated like criminals" and "harassed" by overzealous officials who were both "judge and jury." Between 1973 and 1976, various congressional committees held more than one hundred oversight hearings. At one of these hearings a business executive stated, "A few years ago this type of harassment by the mobsters was considered illegal. Today the U.S. government does it, and it is legal."[60]

One reason for the anxiety of many businesspeople was the expense of complying with the agency's safety regulations. The NAM estimated the average expense of compliance by a company with more than five thousand employees at $7.1 million, and a survey published by *Safety Management* projected a cost of up to $300 per employee in some plants. In the short run, a number of companies would be required to spend considerable sums purchasing protective equipment and replacing ladders, scaffolding, machinery guards, and ventilating equipment that did not meet the standards of the agency. And in the long term, the principal effect of OSHA's safety regulations would be to force companies to allocate more resources to the maintenance and inspection of equipment.

However, what made OSHA—virtually from the day it was established—the regulatory agency that the business community most resented was not so much the costs of compliance as the regulations themselves. Faced with the overwhelming administrative task of formulating safety rules for thousands of different industries, OSHA simply adopted wholesale the advisory standards of the American National Standards Institute. Many of these standards turned out to be arbitrary, outdated, and trivial. Some of them, such as the standards covering the design of toilet seats and the definition of a ladder, became objects of popular derision. In addition, the regulations were voluminous—they came to more than three hundred pages—and many were incomprehensible. This made it particularly difficult for the owners and managers of smaller firms to know what was required of them. In addition, the law's prohibition against consultative visits by OSHA officials considerably heightened the adversarial nature of each inspection. Particularly during its first year, "overzealous" inspectors frequently issued citations for relatively unimportant violations, thus making many of the agency's regulations appear even more unreasonable and arbitrary than they in fact were.

As a result, a legislative backlash against federal regulation of occupational health and safety began almost immediately. Both the NAM and the U.S. Chamber of Commerce urged Congress to eliminate mandatory first-instance citations and sanctions as well to remove the law's prohibition of advance notice of inspections. During the 92nd Congress (1970–72), more than a hundred bills to amend or repeal the Occupational Safety and Health Act were introduced, and eighty bills were introduced during the following legislative session. In 1972, the House of Representatives approved an amendment to the Department of Labor's appropriations bill removing firms with fewer than fifteen employees from the agency's coverage, but it did not pass the Senate. A year later, Congress approved a similar amendment, but the bill to which it was attached was vetoed by President Nixon for unrelated reasons. In 1974, the House approved an amendment exempting firms with fewer than twenty-five employees from the agency's jurisdiction, but once again it was rejected by the Senate. Finally, in 1976, following the national furor created by an OSHA pamphlet designed to warn farmworkers of the hazards of farming that was written in language that managed to offend nearly everyone, OSHA finally suffered its first congressional defeat. Congress approved a rider to the agency's appropriation bill that prohibited it from covering farms with fewer than ten employees and from issuing fines for minor violations if there were fewer than ten such violations in a citation.

However, for all the intensity of the battles over pension reform, the legalization of common situs picketing, and OSHA, labor's most important legislative priority during the mid-1970s was job creation. In 1974, a National Committee for Full Employment was created: it called on Congress to create a million public-service jobs. That same year, Congressman Augustus Hawkins (Democrat-California) and Senator Hubert Humphrey introduced legislation amending the Employment Act of 1946. The Humphrey-Hawkins amendments required the government to bring the unemployment rate down to 3 percent within eighteen months. Congress did not act on their proposal, and the following year they introduced it again. Extensive hearings were held around the country but the bill attracted relatively little interest or support.

In 1976, the bill moved to the forefront of labor's legislative and political agenda. This was due in part to the continued stagnation of the economy. The real growth of the GNP was 9.2 percent in the first quarter of 1976, but then it declined steadily: the economy grew by only 4.5 percent in the second quarter, and by 3.8 percent in the third. Inflation did decline—it averaged only 3 percent in the first nine months of 1976—but unemployment remained above 7.5 percent during the entire year, a decline of only 1.5 percent from the trough of the recession. In addition, 1976 was an election year, and the Democrats viewed the issue of unemployment as one to which the Republican party was vulnerable.

The Full Employment Act and Balanced Growth Act of 1976 was publicly introduced at a national two-day Full Employment Conference held in Washington in March. Popularly known as "Humphrey-Hawkins," it established "the right of all Americans able, willing, and seeking work to opportunities for useful paid employment at fair rates of compensation."[61] However, unlike the Employment Act of 1946, which contained a similar commitment, the Humphrey-Hawkins bill established both a specific policy goal—namely, the achievement of 3 percent unemployment of adults within four years—and a mechanism for achieving it. It also required the federal government to formulate an annual "full employment and balanced growth plan" and to act as an employer of last resort if fiscal and monetary policy proved unable to achieve the specified employment goal.

In the spring of 1976, a broad coalition was mobilized to support this legislation. It included the AFL-CIO, the UAW, the Congressional Black Caucus, the Americans for Democratic Action, the Environmentalists for Full Employment, and a number of liberal church groups. This coalition effectively united both the old and new political wings of the Democratic party, bringing together minorities, trade unions, and the environmental movement, three constituencies which had had rather disparate—and at times conflicting—political priorities. Stephan Schlossberg, an official of the UAW stated, in July 1976, "It seems to be that the possibilities are limitless." He suggested that this "revitalized coalition . . . could result in an outpouring of labor-supported economic legislation similar to the civil-rights laws that stemmed from the Democratic victories in 1964." The AFL-CIO's legislative director added: "Full employment is the basic fight we hope will start the whole thing. Every other damn thing really focuses around full employment."[62]

The bill was endorsed by every Democratic presidential candidate and was included in the 1976 Democratic party platform. Following extensive hearings and intense partisan wrangling, it was adopted by the House Education and Labor Committee by a vote of 25 to 10: with only two exceptions, every Democrat voted for it and every Republican opposed it.

While there appeared to be no doubt that the bill would have been easily approved by the heavily Democratic Congress—*Dun's* reported that the "bill has caught on like wildfire"[63]—its supporters believed that they lacked sufficient strength to overcome its expected veto by President Ford.

Accordingly, the coalition behind the bill decided to wait until the following year when the Democrats hoped they would have recaptured the White House. An aide to House Majority Leader Thomas O'Neill noted: "Right now we need a two-thirds majority to do anything. Next year it will only take one more than half, and that's a tremendous difference."[64] The importance that labor attached to the 1976 presidential election was further reinforced by President Ford's veto of an emergency jobs appropriation bill that provided $5.3 billion to create more than a million jobs: the vote in the House to override the veto fell short of the necessary two-thirds majority by only five votes.

The Humphrey-Hawkins bill also reflected a revival of interest in the idea of national economic planning. In October 1975 an Initiative Committee for National Economic Planning was formed. Headed by Nobel Prize–winning economist Wassily Leontief, its members included Leonard Woodcock, John Kenneth Galbraith, Robert Lekachman, and Robert Heilbroner. In its first public statement, the committee noted that "few American are satisfied with the way in which the economy is now operating." It attributed this to the fact that "no reliable mechanism in the modern economy relates needs to available manpower, plant and materials." As a result, the United States was currently experiencing "shortages of housing, medical care, municipal services, transportation, energy and numerous other requirements of pressing importance."[65] The committee recommended the establishment of an office of National Economic Planning in the White House. It would be responsible for accumulating and analyzing economic data from a wide range of sources, examining major economic trends, and formulating detailed plans to help the economy realize its long-range objectives.

The committee's proposals were subsequently supported by a handful of business executives including Irwin Miller, president of Cummins Engine Company; Stanley Marcus of Neiman-Marcus; John R. Bunting, Jr., chairman of First Pennsylvania Corporation; and Robert Rossa, an investment banker. Miller stated: "There is no coordination among the various branches of government that do the managing. We need a planning agency to put it all together."[66] A number of other executives, including Henry Ford II and Thornton Bradshaw, endorsed the idea of some form of national planning, though not this particular proposal. A modified version of the committee's blueprint was subsequently introduced by senators

Hubert Humphrey and Jacob Javits (Republican-New York). The Balanced Growth and Planning Act was subsequently endorsed by three Democratic presidential candidates: Senator Birch Bayh of Indiana, Senator Henry Jackson of Washington, and Sargent Shriver.

Like proposals for an American industrial policy that surfaced nearly a decade later, the idea of national economic planning was bitterly opposed by virtually the entire business community. General Motors chairman Thomas Murphy suggested that the government get its own house in order before it began telling business how to manage, and Walter Wriston, chairman of Citicorp, described planning as the first step toward an "economic police state . . . [that] would destroy both our personal liberty and our productive power."[67] The business press was filled with articles, columns, and editorials denouncing the idea. *Business Week* editorialized: "In an economy as big and as complex as the United States, national planning would be national frustration,"[68] and *Fortune* stated that "the Humphrey-Javits bill or anything like it would lead to deep erosion of freedom and economic efficiency."[69] It was also criticized by a number of liberal economists, including Charles Schultze, Arthur Okun, and James Tobin. There was never any possibility that national economic planning would be adopted, for the simple reason that no political constituency supported it. And by 1976, the Humphrey-Javits bill had become overshadowed by the Humphrey-Hawkins bill. Nonetheless, both sets of legislative initiatives contributed to the growing unease of many business executives over the broad direction of American business-government relations.

Conclusion

Through the mid-1970s, business continued to find itself on the defensive. The scandals surrounding Watergate and overseas payments severely damaged the public image of a large number of large American corporations, and the energy crisis resulted in unprecedented public antipathy to the nation's oil companies. For several months the oil companies appeared in danger of being required to divest themselves of a significant portion of their assets. The oil-depletion allowance was eliminated and price controls were maintained. Although Congress approved the construction of the Alaskan pipeline and sustained President Ford's veto of the strip-mining bill, the federal government refused to weaken the Clean Air Act Amendments. In 1976 it expanded the authority of the EPA over another segment of the American economy by enacting the Toxic Substance Control Act. The Moss-Magnuson Act significantly strengthened the enforcement powers of the FTC, and the Employee Retirement Income Security Act created yet another regulatory agency with broad powers over many segments of American business.

Not surprisingly, not since the New Deal had the American business community felt so politically vulnerable. A survey of 1,844 *Harvard Business Review* readers conducted in 1975 revealed that nearly three-quarters were extremely pessimistic about the ability of the American commitment to private property and limited government to survive the next decade.[70] In a survey of Fortune 500 CEO's conducted by *Fortune* in 1976, 28 percent responded that "government" was the most serious problem faced by their companies and 35 percent stated that "government" was the most serious problem faced by business in general.[71] At a series of private conferences of corporate chief executive officers sponsored by the Conference Board in 1974 and 1975, the vast majority indicated that they thought the future of the American free enterprise system was extremely problematic. As one executive put it: "At this rate business can soon expect support from the environmentalists. We can get them to put the corporation on the endangered species list." Another suggested that "the American capitalist system is confronting its darkest hour."[72]

True, the business community as a whole had suffered more substantial political setbacks between 1969 and 1972. But these defeats had taken place during a period of relatively strong economic growth, and thus they were not as threatening or damaging. Indeed, anxious to be seen as "socially responsible," business organized no opposition to NEPA, and many business lobbyists did not vigorously oppose the establishment of OSHA. By contrast, the political battles over public policy between 1973 and 1976 were accompanied by a significant deterioration in the economic strength of the private sector. Corporate profits declined by more than one-third between the mid-1960s and the mid-1970s. Not only were the stakes much higher, but business faced two distinctive, though obviously not unrelated, challenges: stagflation and the political initiatives of a liberal Democratic Congress.

In 1973, a number of prominent business executives founded the American Council for Capital Formation. Their goal was to secure lower corporate taxes in order to stimulate investment. In the fall of 1975, Reginald H. Jones, the CEO of the General Electric Corporation, wrote in the *Harvard Business Review* that "business must convince an indifferent public and skeptical Congress that this country is facing a severe capital gap." He added:

It is obvious to every businessman who has worried over his balance sheet and cut back on his planned investments that corporate tax reform is needed. But it is not obvious to the public and to a Congress that reflects several decades of anti-profits politics. The business community has a selling job to do. The problem of capital formation, and the consequences of inaction, must be set forth in compelling, job-and-pocketbook terms that voters can understand and that politicians will respect.[73]

President Ford's secretary of the treasury, William Simon, also repeatedly emphasized the need to provide business with "adequate incentives for capital formation." He noted in 1975 that "the amount of capital invested in the United States since 1960 has been the lowest of any major industrialized country in the free world."[74] However, while a number of members of Congress were becoming increasingly concerned about the nation's slow rate of capital formation, there was still little public support for lowering corporate taxes.

Moreover, at about the same time that inflation and higher taxes appeared to be reducing the nation's rate of investment, business had begun to experience the cumulative economic impact of the legislative defeats that it had suffered during the preceding decade. Between 1966 and 1974, Congress had enacted more than twenty major pieces of government regulation. Between 1970 and 1975, expenditures by federal social regulatory agencies increased from $1.5 to $4.3 billion, and the number of pages in the *Federal Register* rose from 20,000 to 60,000. The enforcement of government regulation was uneven, but the cost of compliance was nonetheless substantial. Between 1970 and 1974, industry spending on air pollution increased 151 percent in constant dollars. In 1974, business spent $7.4 billion on air- and water-pollution controls and $3 billion on occupational safety equipment. This amounted to 10.8 percent of all capital spending by manufacturing firms, up from 4 percent in 1969. In some industries, this sum exceeded 20 percent.[75] Environmental and workers' health and safety programs cut conventionally measured productivity by 1.4 percent between 1967 and 1975.[76]

Nor was the burden simply an economic one. As one of *Fortune*'s editors put it in that magazine's special bicentennial issue: "Through streams of legislation, spreading and minutely detailed regulation . . . the government is now present—either in person, or somewhat like Banquo's ghost, in disturbing spirit—at every major business meeting. . . . If the government continues to infringe on more and more business decisions, the market system may soon be finished."[77] Surveying America's third century, Norman Macrae, the deputy editor of the *Economist,* concluded: "The bad news for the world's teeming masses this bicentennial is that in America the whole concept of thrustful business is in danger of becoming unloved. The intellectuals have joined in the sneering against it, making it fashionable to believe that stagnation is not only wise but clever. . . . This is exactly how it was when Britain's post-1876 decline began. . . . The United States has joined the Fabian Society of about 1903."[78]

There was another reason why business had little to celebrate during the nation's bicentennial year. Following the 1974 elections, all that stood between a highly reenergized liberal political coalition and the statute book was one person, namely, President Ford. The Watergate scandal had significantly weakened the political power of business in one very important respect: it resulted in a substantial increase in Democratic representation in both houses of Congress in 1974. Not since 1964 had so many liberals been either elected or reelected to the Congress. But, if Watergate moved Congress to the left, it had another, though less widely noticed, political impact: it moved the White House to the right. For in sharp contrast to Richard Nixon, Gerald Ford had strong views on domestic policies that were important to business. A conservative Republican from the Midwest, Ford was personally close to a number of business executives and shared their political and economic philosophy. Unlike Richard Nixon, who never once used his veto power to defend the political interests of business, Ford employed the veto extensively for this purpose. Although he signed some legislation that business opposed—most notably the 1976 Campaign Finance Amendments and the 1975 energy bill—he vetoed a major public-works bill, common situs picketing, and strip-mining legislation. In all, Ford vetoed a total of sixty-four bills, while the threat of his veto prevented the establishment of an agency for consumer protection as well as passage of the Humphrey-Hawkins bill. And it was White House opposition that prevented the approval of legislation prohibiting overseas payments by American corporations. As a result, the actual political consequence of the Democrats' sweep of the 1974 congressional elections proved more modest than business had initially feared.

But if the Democrats were to succeed in recapturing the presidency in 1976, business might well experience a series of political setbacks analogous to those that occurred during the Second New Deal. For although the eventual Democratic presidential nominee was among the more conservative of those who had sought the nomination, his election was strongly supported by both organized labor and the public-interest movement. Business therefore approached the 1976 presidential election with considerable trepidation.

VII

Business Turns the Tide, 1977 to 1980

Introduction

Both the public-interest movement and organized labor had every reason to be optimistic following the results of the 1976 election. Not only did the Democrats retain their large majorities in both houses of Congress but, most important, their party recaptured the White House. Jimmy Carter was not the preferred Democratic nominee of either the public-interest or trade-union movement; the former had been closest to either Congressman Morris Udall of Arizona or Senator Fred Harris of Oklahoma, and the latter had strongly supported the candidacy of Senator Henry Jackson. Yet both strongly backed Carter in the general election. In the course of his campaign, Carter had endorsed a number of the legislative priorities of both constituencies, including the Humphrey-Hawkins bill, labor-law reform, the legalization of common situs picketing, and the creation of an agency for consumer advocacy.

Following his election, President Carter made a number of appointments that affirmed the political influence and status of the public-interest movement. More than sixty public-interest activists were given positions in his administration—many at the same agencies whose policies they had previously challenged. Gustave Speth, formerly of the Natural Resources Defense Council (NRDC), was appointed to the Council on Environmental

Quality; Joan Claybrook, who had directed Ralph Nader's Congress Watch, was named head of the National Highway Traffic Safety Administration; Michael Pertschuk, who had played an important role in shaping consumer legislation as a staff member of the Senate Commerce Committee, was appointed chair of the Federal Trade Commission (FTC); David Hawkins of the NRDC, a prominent environmental law firm, was made an assistant administrator at EPA. *Fortune* commented: "Now public-interest organizations have the kind of access to the departments and the White House once enjoyed only by national labor unions and large corporations working through highly paid Washington lobbyists." The president of Common Cause, David Cohen, predicted that now "we can raise the ante—push for new policy initiatives that have been blocked off in recent years."[1]

The president's first year in office appeared to confirm these expectations. In 1977, President Carter signed into law two regulatory statutes whose approval had been prevented by President Ford: the Surface Mining Control and Reclamation Act and the Foreign Corrupt Practices Act. In addition, the enforcement of existing regulatory statutes became more vigorous. The number of automobiles recalled by the National Highway Traffic Safety Commission in 1977 was more than four times the previous year's total, while OSHA issued more health standards than it had during the previous seven years combined.

Yet, by 1978 it was apparent that business had regained the political initiative. Ironically, just as the election of a Republican president widely regarded as sympathetic to business in 1968 had coincided with a decline in the relative political influence of business, so did the election of a Democratic president supported by anticorporate political forces four years later mark its resurgence. Both times, the key to this shift was Congress. Although there was virtually no change in the partisan corporation of Congress as a result of the 1976 elections, the rapidity of the change in congressional voting patterns after 1976 is striking. For example, while the House of Representatives had overwhelmingly approved legislation legalizing common situs picketing in both 1975 and 1976, on March 23, 1977, in what *Congressional Quarterly* described as a "stunning upset,"[2] it defeated this legislation by a vote of 205 to 217. And after having approved legislation establishing a federal consumer protection agency on three separate occasions between 1972 and 1976, the House voted down this proposal in 1978 by a wide margin. In 1974, Congress had significantly expanded the power of the Federal Trade Commission (FTC); six years later it approved legislation restricting it. In 1978, nine years after approving the most reform-oriented tax bill since the Second World War, Congress enacted a bill that provided significant relief for investors. Congress had responded to the first energy crisis by retaining strict price controls on domestic oil; it responded to the second by approving the phasing out of price controls—though it did add a tax on windfall profits at the insistence of President Carter. In 1974, Congress had resisted pressure from the automobile manufacturers to weaken the requirements of the 1970 Clean Air Act Amendments; three years later, it yielded to most of Detroit's demands.

The increased political effectiveness of business was paralleled by a shift in both the political agenda and the terms of political debate. The relative decline in the performance of the economy after 1973 had initially led to an expansion in the role of government. These policies ranged from price controls on energy to expanding employment in the public sector. During the latter 1970s, however, government intervention began to be perceived less as the solution to the nation's economic difficulties and more as their cause, hence, the tax revolt and the deregulation of oil prices. A similar change took place in the area of government regulation: whereas public attention had focused almost exclusively on the inadequacies of business performance during the first two-thirds of the 1970s, by the end of the decade the public had become responsive to many of the complaints of industry about regulatory excesses. The symbol of the FTC as the "national nanny" had replaced the image of automobiles that were "unsafe at any speed." Instead of debating new legislative proposals to restrict the autonomy of managers, Congress began to discuss strategies for curbing the power of regulatory officials.

This chapter describes the changes in government-business relations between 1976 and 1980. The next chapter explains them.

Organized Labor

Like the public-interest movement, organized labor approached 1977 with high expectations: Carter's election appeared to have removed the one remaining obstacle to the success of its legislative program. Union leaders decided to place the common situs picketing bill at the top of their legislative agenda; they reasoned that its rapid passage would create momentum for both labor-law reform and the Humphrey-Hawkins bill. For precisely the same reason, the business community decided to mobilize its resources to defeat this legislation. Immediately following President Ford's veto of common situs picketing in 1976, Richard Creighton of the Associated General Contractors, who had chaired the National Action Committee on Secondary Boycotts, arranged for weekly meetings of a group of forty construction employer associations. As a result, "the employers were well prepared for labor's early initiative." In 1977, the action committee was expanded to include seventy more business organizations and launched a media campaign to persuade the general public that the "proposed situs picketing bill was the creation of grasping union bosses."[3] Its efforts were eventually backed by more than one hundred trade associations and corporations, as well as the Business Roundtable and the National Federation of Independent Business.

Although the liberal House Education and Labor Committee had reported out—by a party-line vote—a common situs bill stronger than the one Ford had vetoed, the bill's supporters soon realized they did not have sufficient votes to secure its passage on the floor. As a result, the Democratic members of the House Education and Labor Committee agreed to a compromise version offered by Representative Ronald A. Sarasin (Republican-Connecticut). The Sarasin compromise exempted residential construction sites from the bill and prohibited common situs picketing in connection with union jurisdiction disputes and product boycotts. When the bill reached the floor of the House, its backers suffered their first defeat: by a margin of only three votes, the House adopted an amendment which permitted common situs picketing only of construction firms. Although union lobbyists were distressed by the vote, they supported the amended bill. As the legislative director of the building-trades department of the AFL-CIO put it, "It's the best we think we can get."[4]

However, another amendment weakening the bill was subsequently approved by an even wider margin. By a vote of 252 to 167, the House prohibited common situs picketing against any builder of residences of three stories or less. It also approved an amendment exempting all construction already begun or under contract as of the date of enactment of the bill. The Sarasin substitute, along with these additional amendments, was then approved by a wide margin: many of the bill's opponents voted for the substitute bill, reasoning that the final choice would be between a weakened bill or no bill at all. However, that same day the House of Representatives rejected the entire bill by a vote of 205 to 217, an outcome that stunned both the bill's opponents and supporters. One opponent had predicted that his side would lose about thirty votes after the bill's dilution and Representative Frank Thompson, Jr. (Democrat-New Jersey), one of the bill's original sponsors, expressed surprise that the Sarasin compromise, along with the other amendments, had not increased support for the bill. He added: "we couldn't give away much more."[5]

Why did organized labor suffer such an unexpected defeat? To begin with, compared to the other lobbying efforts of business during the previous decade, this one was more intensive and better organized. Choosing what they described as a "rifle" rather than a "shotgun" strategy, business lobbyists carefully targeted those members of Congress whose votes they thought they could influence. They decided to concentrate their efforts on the sixty-eight new House members, reasoning that they would be less likely to have developed a firm position on this issue. As a result of a grass-roots campaign in their districts, each of them received literally hundreds of letters and postcards opposing the legislation. These efforts bore fruit: thirty-seven out of the sixty-eight new members of Congress voted against the bill, including thirteen who had been supported in their 1976 campaign by the AFL-CIO. "Spokesmen for the offices of several freshmen supported by COPE [Committee on Political Education] confirmed that the flow of mail and the personal lobbying had been the most intensive yet seen by the new members and that it had played a role in determining their vote." House Speaker Thomas P. O'Neill, Jr., subsequently remarked that he had "never seen an organization function like the Associated General Contractors, the home builders, and the other" groups opposed to the picketing bill.[6]

By contrast, organized labor appeared to have committed considerably few resources to the support of the bill. One new Democrat received 248 pieces of mail opposing the bill and only a single letter supporting it. O'Neill subsequently criticized organized labor for letting things slide until the last minute, suggesting that "when you get careless, the train goes off the track."[7] In fact, the House Democratic leadership, fearing defeat, had wanted to postpone a vote, but organized labor insisted that it had sufficient votes to prevail.

Like the passage of automotive safety regulation in 1966, the outcome of this legislative battle had a significance that far transcended the particular issue. Two ingredients had been crucial to business's victory: an unusual display of unity and the intensity and sophistication of its grass-roots lobbying. As a result, the business community believed that it had finally figured out a formula for successfully defeating its political opponents in Congress. This "battle was important to the business community because it showed what it could do against great odds when its lobbyists worked together. The employers' victory gave them a tremendous psychological boost because it reversed a string of business defeats in the early

1970s.''[8] Both these strategies would shortly be put to the test as Congress began to debate another piece of legislation initiated by organized labor, but one with far greater economic and legal consequences, namely the reform of the nation's labor laws.

The drive to reform the nation's labor laws was a response to the increasing difficulties of trade unions in organizing American workers. The percentage of workers belonging to unions had been steadily declining since the mid-1950s; by 1976 it stood at slightly more than 23 percent—the lowest point in forty years. Union organizing drives had also become less effective: during the mid-1960s, unions had won 60 percent of representation elections, but a decade later they were winning only 46 percent. The leadership of the trade-union movement attributed these setbacks primarily to more aggressive anti-union tactics on the part of management. Between 1967 and 1977, the number of complaints alleging unfair labor practices filed by unions with the National Labor Relations Board (NLRB) more than doubled. Of the charges filed in fiscal 1977, 69 percent alleged violations by employers, and 83 percent of the complaints issued by the NLRB were against employees. In addition, during the mid-1970s, the AFL-CIO had become involved in an extremely bitter and prolonged confrontation with J. P. Stevens, a major textile manufacturer based in the South which had been repeatedly found guilty of violating the nation's labor laws. A nationwide boycott of Stevens's products had focused considerable public attention on this dispute and further dramatized the need for reforming the nation's labor laws.

A month after Carter's inauguration, the AFL-CIO's Executive Council authorized a special dues assessment of $800,000—subsequently increased to $2.5 million—to conduct a public campaign in support of labor-law reform. Having learned from the common situs picketing battle the importance of not being seen as a "special interest," the unions emphasized "the social justice dimension of the issue rather than their institutional stake in it."[9] The AFL-CIO closely coordinated its lobbying and public-education efforts with the consumers' boycott of Stevens's products organized by the Amalgamated Clothing and Textile Workers. They also formed alliances with religious groups and civil rights organizations. Following extensive negotiations between the AFL-CIO and President Carter, the administration sent a message to Congress recommending a number of changes in federal labor law. These included expediting the process by which the NLRB adjudicated disputes over unfair labor practices and increasing the penalties for noncompliance with the board's rulings.

The administration's bill was quickly approved by the House by a vote of 257 to 163. Its rapid passage was a testimony to the political skills of organized labor: not wanting to repeat their experience with common situs picketing, the unions pressured the House to act before business could mobilize. As a result, the representatives who voted for the bill regarded it as relatively uncontroversial. At this point the lobbyists representing the employers' associations offered labor a compromise. But confident they had sufficient votes to win in the Senate, union representatives turned them down. The battle then shifted to the upper chamber. Since the bill was supported by a majority of this body as well, the employers realized that their only hope of preventing its passage was to make sure it did not come to a vote.

Throughout 1977, business had been mobilizing its political resources to defeat the bill when it came before the Senate. In June 1977, a new organization, the National Action Committee for Labor Law Reform, was formed; it was co-chaired by Richard Creighton, who had masterminded the fight against common situs picketing, and staffed by officials from both the National Association of Manufacturers (NAM) and the Chamber of Commerce. The campaign against the bill was spearheaded by three large business organizations: the United States Chamber of Commerce, the NAM, and the National Federation of Independent Business—all of which represented large numbers of small firms. "The decision by N.A.M. and the Chamber . . . to cooperate in opposition to the . . . bill probably marked a high point in the awareness and density of small business organization since the New Deal."[10] The National Right to Work Committee, which had previously lobbied successfully against the repeal of Section 14(b)— the right-to-work provision of the Taft-Hartley Act—as well as the Associated General Contractors, which had played a crucial role in the defeat of common situs picketing, also joined the opposition to the bill.

The position of these associations and organizations was predictable: a major share of their energies had historically been devoted to combating trade unions. What was particularly significant, however, was the decision of the Business Roundtable to oppose the legislation as well. The Policy Committee of the Roundtable was divided. High-technology firms with comparatively low labor costs, such as IBM and AT&T, as well as companies that were already unionized, such as General Motors, General Electric (GE) and Du Pont, saw no reason to oppose labor-law reform, since the legislation would not affect them. However, other Roundtable members, including Sears Roebuck, which relied heavily on unskilled labor, and the major tire and steel companies, whose profit margins were being reduced by foreign competition, pressed the Roundtable to join the opposition. In August 1977, the Policy Committee of the Roundtable voted 19 to 8 to oppose the bill. Subsequently, even those corporations that had favored neutrality lobbied actively against the bill. GE, perhaps the strongest supporter of neutrality, sent its plant managers to Washington to lobby their representatives. The Roundtable also financed the public-relations work of Edie Fraser Associates, which commissioned public-opinion polls and distributed editorials opposing the bill. They also funded a study to document its inflationary consequences. The decision of the Roundtable to oppose the AFL-CIO lifted the battle to "historic significance. . . . For the first time in decades, the largest American corporations allied with the small business community had committed major resources for a blitz against labor."[11]

While the campaign against labor-law reform was heavily financed by large corporations, its effectiveness was primarily due to the mobilization of the owners of small businesses. More than five hundred state and local chapters of the National Federation of Independent Business, the National Small Business Association, the American Retail Federation, and the National Restaurant Association actively lobbied their representatives. A coordinator was appointed for each targeted state. When Florida's Democratic senator Lawton Chiles casually mentioned to a group of corporate executives that he had heard only from big-business leaders, "as if by magic" a steady stream of small Florida entrepreneurs began visiting his office, traveling to Washington on corporate jets provided by Florida's big businesses. One of his aides remarked: "I can't remember when we last experienced a lobbying effort like this. It's so well-structured and well organized. I don't think they missed a single possible opponent of that bill in our state."[12] An aide to an uncommitted senator observed: "It's a different type of lobbying. I'm seeing people on the bill I wouldn't ordinarily see."[13]

The purpose of this grass-roots strategy was to shatter the appearance of a broad consensus behind labor-law reform. A confidential NAM memorandum stated:

> We should try to make [labor-law reform] an issue that would be "too hot to handle." We should emphasize that the proposed legislation has already aroused the wrath of the entire business community, and that any showdown on the bill will be far more than anything Congress has seen in a long while. In this vein, individual member companies should be encouraged to contact their Representatives early and vent their horror.[14]

The computerized membership and mailing lists of the National Right to Work Committee, the Associated General Contractors, and the Chamber of Commerce were also employed in opposition to the bill. More than fifty million printed postcards were distributed attacking the bill—six million of which were mailed back to Washington. By the end of spring, nearly every postcard maker in the East was sold out. This tactic proved extremely effective since representatives tend to be far more responsive to constituents who own their own companies than to those who work for larger firms.

> Business succeeded in capturing the political center by portraying the issue as a union power grab and the union movement as greedy. In particular, the elevation of the small businessman to the exalted position of potential victim of big labor—even though the bill's impact on small business would have been minimal—was a skillful exploitation of a key American value. Supporting small business plays well in every state and congressional district.[15]

Moreover, in its effort to portray labor-law reform as a "power grab," business was able to tap into popular attitudes: every public-opinion survey taken during the second half of the 1970s reported that the majority of respondents believed that "unions are too powerful in our economy."[16]

Had the bill been sent to the Senate floor when it first was reported out of committee in January 1978, it probably would have passed: labor and its supporters counted sixty-two votes for the bill, two more than necessary to break a filibuster. However, Senate action was delayed until mid-May as a result of the Carter administration's decision to press first for ratification of the Panama Canal treaty. This delay gave the bill's opponents time to organize their campaign: between January and May, senators received more than eight million pieces of mail and were visited by thousands of their constituents. The Senate's debate of the bill lasted nineteen days during May and June. It was heated. Senator Jacob Javits criticized business's "campaign of blatant misrepresentation," while Republican Senator Orrin Hatch of Utah described the bill as a "blatant union power grab." There were six attempts to invoke cloture—two of which were supported by as many as fifty-eight senators. But "the lobbying efforts of the small business owners were crucial in preventing several wavering Senators from voting for cloture."[17] The bill was eventually sent back to committee, thus handing the unions a "stinging humiliation."[18]

Conservative politicians were elated. Senator Hatch characterized the battle over labor-law reform as the beginning of a new era of business assertiveness in Washington. He noted, "When I first arrived, the business community was headed by a bunch of gutless workers." But the labor-law dispute "created a liaison and understanding between business and

Congress. Now some of the so-called intellectuals are re-thinking their antibusiness thinking."[19]

Labor's defeat on an issue of direct importance to its members was hardly unprecedented. In fact, unions had been fighting unsuccessfully for more than two decades to repeal the right-to-work provision of the Taft-Hartley Act. But this political setback was unusual. This time, not only had the unions expected to win, but they regarded their bill's provisions as rather modest and aimed exclusively at rogue companies that had intentionally violated the law. They were particularly upset by the opposition of large corporations—many of whose workers had been unionized for more than a generation—to labor-law reform. Labor leaders accused business of conducting "a shrill and unfair campaign," and of attempting to "destroy the labor movement." One labor official stated, "Business is convinced we're on the run. Each success breeds hope that they can ruin us. They've become completely ideological." The defeat of labor-law reform also strained relations between the trade-union movement and the Carter administration. Douglas Fraser, the president of the United Auto Workers (UAW), withdrew from a government advisory committee formed to promote labor-management cooperation and derided the administration as "ineffective . . . unable to come to grips with the problems of the nation," and George Meany, president of the AFL-CIO, directly attributed labor's political setbacks to the president's "weakness and inexperience in dealing with Congress."[20]

The political weakness of organized labor became even more apparent in the fall of 1978 when Congress finally approved the Humphrey-Hawkins Full Employment Bill. That this legislation was enacted at all did represent an accomplishment of sorts. As Congress neared adjournment, its passage appeared unlikely owing to the strong opposition of Senator Hatch. However, a last-minute compromise was arranged that satisfied the bill's supporters and mollified at least some of its critics. But the final version of the bill bore little resemblance to the massive legislation for federal jobs and economic planning introduced by Humphrey and Hawkins in the depths of the mid-1970s recession. It did retain the goal of reducing unemployment to 4 percent by 1983, but it no longer required the government to provide jobs as a "last resort" for the unemployed. More important, it called for the reduction of the inflation rate to 3 percent by 1983 and zero by 1988—a provision that obviously conflicted with the goal of reducing unemployment. Coretta Scott King described it "as a major victory and an important first step in the struggle for full employment." However, so great was Hatch's role in weakening the bill that, according to the *Congressional Quarterly,* "By the end, some were calling it the Humphrey-Hawkins-Hatch bill."[21]

The decline in labor's political influence during the Carter administration was also reflected in the politics surrounding OSHA. Claiming that workers faced a "national environmental tragedy on the job," Dr. Eula Bingham, a public-health professor and political activist appointed by Carter as director, came into office determined to form OSHA into an advocate of worker rights to health and safety.[22] Economic and technical feasibility were deemphasized; unless compelling evidence to the contrary was presented, the agency would now simply assume that industries possessed the technology needed to safeguard the health and safety of their employees. Bingham also strongly opposed the use of risk-benefit or cost-benefit tests for workers' health standards. In January 1978, the agency issued six major health standards, and in four of them the PEL (permissible exposure level) was set at the "lowest feasible level."

While the agency did reduce the number of inspections and citations, this reflected its decision to deemphasize trivial violations and devote more resources to important ones. As a result, average penalties per violation increased and the percentage of inspections that uncovered serious violations quadrupled. The portion of inspections showing repeat violations increased nearly three times and follow-up inspections rose 25 percent. The agency also devoted more of its enforcement resources to violations of health regulations and promulgated two rules designed to make it easier for workers to participate in health and safety decisions in the workplace.

Bingham's tenure at OSHA provoked a counter-reaction from business. "By the late 1970s opposition to OSHA fines and inspections was intense," and the percentage of contested inspections had more than doubled.[23] A coalition of Democratic and Republican members of the Senate Labor Committee, many of whom had been the agency's original supporters, proposed a major statutory revision of the OSH Act. While they argued that these measures were necessary to save the agency, they actually addressed virtually all of business's complaints: nearly 90 percent of the nation's workplaces were to be exempted from the agency's enforcement machinery. Thanks to intensive labor lobbying and the intervention of President Carter, no additional restrictions on OSHA were enacted in either 1977 or 1978. However, in response to pressure from the White House, OSHA did significantly modify its setting of standards. Indeed, after January 1978—only a year after Carter's inauguration—the agency issued no new health standards. Moreover, two of its original six standards were revised in response to pressure from industry and a White House increasingly concerned about inflation. While OSHA, backed by Secretary of Labor Ray Marshall, did succeed in persuading President Carter to overrule Council on Economic Advisors' Chairman Charles Schultz's efforts to block the cotton-dust rule, the rule itself was modified in a way that reduced the cost of compliance to the textile industry by 75 percent. In a second case—acrylonitrile—the agency chose an industry-supported PEL that was the least stringent of three alternatives.

Although there was no change in the agency's enforcement strategy, in 1978, in response to congressional pressure, OSHA repealed about a thousand pages of regulations deemed unrelated to safety. These changes did little, however, to mollify the agency's critics in Congress and, in 1979, Congress approved an amendment sponsored by Senator Richard Schweiker (Republican-Pennsylvania) that exempted employers with ten or fewer workers in "safe" firms from regularly scheduled OSHA safety inspections and prohibited the imposition of penalties for first infractions. The amendment was bitterly opposed by organized labor—the UAW called it "a license to maim and kill."[24] But it was strongly supported by the Chamber of Commerce, which argued that the bill was needed because workplaces had actually become *more* dangerous since OSHA had been established. In addition, Congress approved an amendment to the Labor–Health, Education and Welfare appropriations bill prohibiting OSHA from inspecting businesses that had been inspected by a state safety and health agency during the preceding ten months. The statutes containing both these amendments were reluctantly signed into law by President Carter.

The Politics of Consumer Protection

INTRODUCTION

Consumerism represented the cutting edge of the political challenge to business during the second half of the 1960s; indeed, for a period of about five years, consumer protection was the only policy area in which business was politically vulnerable. However, beginning around 1970, consumer issues became overshadowed, first by environmental concerns, and subsequently by the politics of energy and economic recovery. In 1978, they reemerged: between 1978 and 1980, the issue of consumer protection became as politically salient as it had been between 1966 and 1969. There was, however, an important difference. During the 1960s, business had found itself on the political and ideological defensive; now it was the consumer movement that found its power and legitimacy threatened by a politically resurgent business community. Business not only once again defeated the consumer movement's major political priority, namely, the establishment of an agency for consumer advocacy, but its lobbyists successfully challenged the authority of one of the most controversial and aggressive regulatory agencies, namely, the FTC. Only in airline deregulation did a segment of industry suffer a political setback, but this was made possible by a unique set of circumstances.

CONSUMER PROTECTION AGENCY

In the course of his election campaign, President Carter had endorsed the establishment of an agency for consumer advocacy, a government agency for which consumer organizations had been campaigning since 1969. He stated that if legislation creating the agency was not enacted by the time President Ford left office, he should like it to be "one of the first bills passed during the next Administration." Different versions of the consumer agency bill had been approved by both houses in 1975 but the Senate-House conferences saw little point in resolving their differences, since the bill's supporters did not have sufficient votes to overturn an expected veto by President Ford. The consumer movement had every reason to be confident of victory in 1977: not only were President Carter and senior members of his administration committed to lobbying for the bill, but the Democratic leadership in both houses also agreed to work for its passage. The *National Journal* wrote, in January 1977, "If all goes as planned, a bill could end up on Carter's desk by April or May. And if, as expected, Carter signs it, the consumer lobby will have won the victory that eluded it under two successive Republican Administrations."[25]

However, during 1977, the Democratic leaders of the House delayed bringing the bill to a vote, since they did not think that they had sufficient strength to secure its passage. Finally, on February 8, 1978, legislation to establish a consumer protection agency was voted on and defeated by a vote of 189 to 227. This was a major defeat for the consumer movement since nearly identical legislation had been passed by the House three times since 1971—albeit by steadily declining margins. Following this vote, the proposal to establish a consumer protection agency disappeared from the political agenda. While the consumer movement remained active, it would now spend the next decade trying—with limited success—to halt the erosion of its previous gains.

The bill's defeat was, in part, due to the sophistication and intensity of business's lobbying against it. Most businesses had opposed the bill from the outset. As early as 1969, a Consumer Issues Working Group had been established in order to coordinate and direct corporate lobbying. While varying from year to year, at one point between three hundred and four hundred trade associations and individual firms had participated. The group's efforts dramatically intensified in 1977 when Carter's promise to sign the legislation meant that business's only hope of preventing its passage was to defeat it in the Congress. The NAM and the Business Roundtable had always opposed the agency, and in 1977 they were joined by small firms and agricultural interests. The National Federation of Independent Business, which represented more than half a million small companies, decided to oppose the bill actively on the basis of its members' "painful memory of OSHA."[26] A poll of its membership revealed that 86 percent opposed the creation of the agency. The bill was also opposed by all major farm groups, which feared that the consumers' agency would challenge agricultural price supports. "For the first time in history, you had 'the coalition': National Association of Manufacturers, Grocery Manufacturers of America, the U.S. Chamber of Commerce, National Federation of Independent Business, all together, and thousands of people underneath them, in a highly structured, organized way, taking positions, moving, dividing up the Hill, and lobbying. Tremendous power was brought to bear."[27]

Business political strategists focused their efforts on two categories of representatives: moderate Democrats who had previously supported the bill and new members. Each such representative was visited by industry groups representing various industries from his or her district. These efforts were extremely effective: nineteen representatives who supported the consumers' agency in 1975 reversed their position in 1978, and the freshman class of 1977 opposed the bill by a 3-to-2 margin. The Business Roundtable hired Leon Jaworski, former Watergate special prosecutor, to lobby against the bill and contracted with the North American Press Syndicate to distribute cartoons and canned editorials opposing the bill to newspapers and magazines: approximately two thousand of these were published.

The supporters of the bill were also well organized. The coalition formed to lobby for the bill included representatives from organized labor, the civil rights movement and, most important, senior citizens' organizations. Their lobbying efforts were strongly supported by a number of administration officials, including the president's consumer adviser, Esther Peterson. To mobilize its grass-roots supporters, Congress Watch organized a "nickel campaign": consumers in selected districts were asked to send a nickel to their representatives, based on a calculation that the agency would cost each American an average of five cents a year. Only forty thousand were collected and most targeted congressional offices reported that they had received only a few dollars' worth of nickels.

Citing data from Harris polls in 1975 and 1976 that reported a narrow majority in favor of the establishment of a new federal consumer agency,[28] the bill's supporters blamed its defeat, in Ralph Nader's words, on "the corrupting influence of big business campaign contributions, promised or withdrawn."[29] However, the vote evidently reflected a change in the attitudes of many politicians toward increasing the size and power of government. While the agency would have no direct regulatory authority—its primary role would be to serve as an advocate of consumer interests before other government agencies and in the federal courts—it was viewed by a number of representatives as another example of "the continued intrusion" of government into people's daily lives. One Democratic representative who switched her vote between 1975 and 1978 stated, "Before I support the creation of yet another office, I had better be convinced that first, it is needed, second, it is requested by a substantial number of people, and third, it is going to do some good—or at least enough good to offset the added intrusion."[30] Another Democratic representative noted, "Part of the reason I voted against it was the feeling that 'enough is enough.' "[31]

In fact, support for the creation of a new regulatory agency appears to have been stronger in Washington than in the grass roots. One congressional leader in the fight against it noted that "back home, members heard about antibureaucracy and antigovernment when this came up." Members of Congress received much more mail opposing the agency than supporting it. The *Wall Street Journal* reported, "Many of the bill's opponents reported strong pressure from back home against the consumer agency,"[32] and the *New York Times* noted "representatives were listening to their constituents, and what they were hearing signaled some real changes in their mood. National sympathy has apparently swung against further government growth, and specifically against further regulation."[33] Moreover, in the "post-Watergate era, lack of confidence in government was widespread, and antipathy toward big government and its massive bureaucracy was growing. In these circumstances, consumerists who wanted to use the power of government to reduce the ills of the marketplace suffered a significant erosion of political support."[34]

In addition to being a major political victory for a broad business coalition, the House vote was also an important defeat for Ralph Nader. Nader had been actively campaigning for the agency since 1969 and had personally sought to influence a number of congressional votes in 1977 and 1978.

One of the bill's congressional supporters suggested that "the Nader coalition had badly overplayed its hand and tried to bully legislators into voting for poorly written bills."[35] One corporate lobbyist concluded that the consumer agency's defeat meant that "you didn't have to feel ashamed as a member of Congress to vote against something Ralph Nader wanted."[36] And Nader's credibility was further diminished by his public posture toward a number of liberal Democrats who had decided to oppose the new agency: he accused them of having been motivated solely by a desire to solicit corporate campaign contributions. As one observer put it, the agency's defeat meant that "the age of justified outrage is over."[37]

THE FEDERAL TRADE COMMISSION

Having successfully defeated the consumer movement's effort to establish a new regulatory agency, the business community now went on the offensive: it began a campaign to roll back the authority of an existing regulatory agency, the Federal Trade Commission. One of the oldest federal regulatory agencies, the Federal Trade Commission had accomplished relatively little during its first half-century. In the late 1960s, a joke had circulated around Washington that three museums sat side by side on Pennsylvania Avenue—the National Archives, the National Gallery, and the Federal Trade Commission. Following a devastating report on its efforts to protect the consumer by one of Ralph Nader's task forces, in 1969 President Nixon asked the American Bar Association to examine the agency. Its report essentially echoed Nader's criticisms. Nixon appointed Casper Weinberger to chair the FTC and instructed him to reorganize it. Responding to the leadership of Weinberger and his successors as well as pressures from the FTC's oversight committees in Congress, the commission became a much more aggressive and forceful agency between 1970 and 1977. Reversing its previous policy of responding to individual consumers' complaints, the commission launched a series of major initiatives to curb deceptive national advertising. During the first half of the 1970s it challenged the advertising claims of Wonder, Bufferin, Excedrin, and Listerine as well as various other household brands.

The passage of the Magnuson-Moss Act in 1974 significantly expanded the commission's authority. Now the commission did not have to go after one company at a time; it could instead issue rules that applied to an entire industry. In the next eighteen months, the commission's chairman, Lewis Engman, initiated fourteen rule-making proceedings to protect the consumer. By 1977, the commission had pending before it seventeen separate ruling proceedings affecting major segments of the American economy, including hearing aids, funeral practices, used cars, vocational schools, appliance labeling, eyeglasses, and gasoline station lotteries. A number of the commission's proposed rules directly challenged current industry practices, either by reducing barriers to competition or dictating standards of conduct.

In 1977, President Carter appointed Michael Pertschuk to chair the commission. As chief counsel to the Senate Commerce Committee, Pertschuk had played a critical role in shaping much of the consumer protection legislation enacted during the 1960s. Although the commission was already in the midst of a large number of potentially controversial proposals with a potentially far-reaching effect on a number of different industries, six months after his appointment Pertschuk announced a major new regulatory initiative. He informed the audience at an Action for Children's Television Conference that the "commercial exploitation of children is repugnant to a civilized society" and suggested that "it may be that only a ban on the advertising of these products on programs directed toward the young child can help remedy their inherent defect."[38]

Following his remarks, Pertschuk directed his staff to begin working on a rule designed to regulate television advertising catering to children. Pertschuk selected this issue to demonstrate the seriousness of his commitment to the cause of consumer protection and reassure the consumer movement that he had not become "just another coopted bureaucrat." One of the senior members of his staff, Robert Reich, stated that Pertschuk believed that in "kidvid" he had found "a potent symbol that would probe the frontiers of deception and unfairness and broach the question of protecting the vulnerable." Reich added, "I think he thought that this was a terrific bootstrap issue"—one that would enable him to place his mark both on the commission and the consciousness of the American public and demonstrate his commitment to turning the FTC into "the largest public interest law firm in the U.S." Moreover, at his confirmation hearing, Warren Magnuson, the chair of the Senate Commerce Committee, had told Pertschuk that he hoped he "would take a good long look . . . at the abuses . . . in children's advertising."[39]

In the spring of 1977, Congress began debating the FTC improvements bill. This legislation, which Pertschuk had helped draft while he was working in the Senate, expanded the powers of the FTC beyond those granted by the Magnuson-Moss Act. It authorized groups and individuals to seek redress for violations of FTC rulings in the courts and permitted the FTC to petition the courts to place in receivership companies that faced commission penalties but which were likely to dissipate their assets before paying what they owed. The legislation initially created little controversy and was approved by the Senate with relatively little debate. However, when the improvements bill reached the floor of the House of Representatives in October 1977, it encountered considerable opposition. Both provisions were stricken from the bill by a 2-to-1 margin, and the House also approved an amendment to the commission's authorization bill that gave itself the right to veto any future FTC rule.

In February 1978, the House and Senate met in conference committee to resolve their differing versions of the bill. The Senate members vigorously opposed the legislative veto on constitutional grounds, and it was removed. However, a provision supported by the Senate allowing class-action suits was also eliminated. The Senate approved the conference report by a voice vote the following day, and the conference committee members had every reason to expect that it would be approved by the House by a wide margin as well. But the House of Representatives had just defeated the consumer protection agency bill; and now it was the FTC's turn to become a symbol of intrusive government bureaucracy. The same business lobbyists who had just successfully defeated the new agency mobilized to defeat the conference report.

The debate on the floor of the House over the conference committee report provided an opportunity for scores of members to voice their complaints and those of their constituents with the FTC's enforcement of the Magnuson-Moss Act. One FTC lobbyist observed: "It was just unbelievable. What you don't see in the Congressional Record is that the Republicans were stamping their feet and yelling and cheering. It was really a circus . . . the intensity of the emotion of the people who opposed the agency and the personalized kind of attack that it was—there was really an irrational strain about the debate." The House rejected the conference report by a vote of 146 to 255—a margin significantly larger than the one by which it had defeated the consumer protection agency only a short time earlier. One observer noted: "109 votes is an extraordinary margin for a bill that you planned to win and the other side thinks he's going to lose." The vote constituted a major rebuke to the commission. According to David Dunn, a prominent Washington lobbyist, the FTC's staff had evidently:

. . . underestimated the problems that they were causing the Congressmen back home. They just underestimated the number of complaints that Congressmen were getting back home from their funeral directors, from the used car dealers, and their optometrists and their doctors and dentists and everybody else. The FTC was getting into everybody's business and the FTC became the symbol of big government in the living rooms, in the backyards of all the towns of America.[40]

Meanwhile, the FTC continued to move forward with its rule-making proceedings on children's advertising. Pertschuk was unable to muster a majority of the commission to support an absolute ban on all advertising directed toward children below the age of eight. As a result, the initial notice of proposed rule-making adopted by the commission was actually a set of alternatives to be considered—only one of which banned children's advertising. Other proposals were specifically addressed to the advertising of sugar-coated products consumed by children, including breakfast cereals. The vagueness of these proposals, coupled with the potential threat they posed to millions of dollars' worth of advertising revenues, quickly galvanized business opposition. One Washington lawyer observed: "We could have gotten some of the more enlightened companies to say, let's go in and bargain a little bit, and get half a loaf. But they got everyone 100% against them, willing to commit war chests and time, the personal time of Chief Executive Officers, saying, we cannot allow this to happen. They basically accused well-known businessmen of deliberately trying to foreshorten the lives of kids." Another noted that with the stakes so high, confrontation was inevitable: "When you presented so fundamental a challenge to the broadcasters, they had no choice but to defend themselves in Congress. [The commission] awoke a sleeping giant."[41]

A war chest of $16 million was quickly raised to fight the FTC's proposed restrictions on children's advertising in the Congress. Because of the potentially sweeping implications of the FTC's action, the advertisers of products directed to children were able to secure the support of other major companies, such as General Motors and Bristol-Myers. In all, thirty-two major corporations and trade associations joined the fight against the kidvid rule. Pertschuk told the *Washington Star:* "One of the business lobbyists told me that, because of the ban proposal's first amendment implications, it was easy for the children's lobbyists to raise money from other groups like General Motors and Bristol-Myers, because they saw this as an attack on all advertising."[42]

On March 1, the morning after the House vote on the FTC Improvements Act and the commission announcement, the *Washington Post* ran an editorial entitled, "The National Nanny." It stated that the real purpose of the FTC's proposal was "to protect children from the weaknesses of their parents—and the parents from the wailing insistence of their children." The *Post* concluded that this was "traditionally one of the roles of a governess—if you can afford one. It is not a proper role of government."[43] This editorial, in a newspaper that had long been a strong supporter of the consumer movement, transformed the tone of the public debate. Pertschuk conceded: "The editorial . . . ceded to the opponents of such rule making the single most powerful political symbol upon which we had depended for our political shield against Congressional interference—the defense of the family." He added that the editorial revealed the extent to which "consumer advocates . . . were losing . . . hold on the symbols of the debate. . . . Now it was the Commission—not amoral business—that allegedly threatened to undermine the moral fiber and authority of the family."[44] The phrase "national nanny" was soon picked up by other industry groups who began to portray the FTC as the nanny not only of the nation's children but of business as well.

The kidvid lobby's effort to challenge the commission's rule-making proceedings in Congress became a lightning rod that attracted other businesses whose economic interests were also threatened by the FTC. During the seven days of oversight hearings held in the fall of 1979, scores of industry representatives urged Congress to curb what one representative described as "a rogue agency gone insane."[45] Another suggested that "if it is true that the FTC has become the focal point for critics of government overregulation, then I can think of no federal agency that deserves it more."[46] A supporter of the commission observed "there's almost a lynch mob mentality up here about the FTC." One official of the Chamber of Commerce described the commission as "a notorious agency that has made it the second most powerful legislative body in the country."[47] The chamber took the lead in organizing a group of thirty to forty associations and companies to lobby for a provision for a legislative veto. Mobilizing the business community proved surprisingly easy. As a chamber lobbyist observed: "There wasn't a member of Congress that hadn't been bitched to about the FTC. It was the small industries that were hurt the most. . . . We organized all the groups . . . funeral, insurance, food, toy, used cars. They made their own Congressional contacts. We guided the train."[48] On November 14, 1979, the House voted 223 to 147 to veto the FTC's proposed funeral-cost disclosure rule. One representative explained his vote as follows:

> You know a funeral director can kill you. I go to forty or fifty funerals a year. He decides whether you sit next to the widow or at the back of the room and when you're at a funeral parlor for one funeral and there's another one going on, a friendly funeral director introduces you to the family. . . . They are big joiners. They join the Kiwanis, the Rotaries, and they are very active in the community.[49]

The FTC improvements bill then went to the Senate. Since the mid-1960s the Senate Commerce Subcommittee for Consumers had been one of the strongest supporters of consumer protection. Indeed, as recently as 1974, "the main concern expressed in the . . . Committee hearings on FTC oversight was that the commission *was proceeding too slowly* in its investigations of high food and energy prices, children's advertising and monopolistic practices."[50] But after 1976, congressional support for aggressive consumer regulation declined dramatically. In 1977, twelve of the subcommittee's members left and only three new members took their place, suggesting a significant erosion of interest in consumer protection. Moreover, several of the Senate's most prominent liberal members, including Magnuson himself, were no longer on the committee. Not surprisingly, the bill reported out by the Senate Commerce Committee in 1980 placed extensive restrictions on the FTC's authority. It required the commission to stop or reassess its proposed rules governing children's advertising, used-car sales, and trade groups that set industry standards. However, the Senate bill, unlike the House version, did not contain a provision for a future legislative veto and the two houses were unable to reach agreement.

In April 1980, President Carter invited both Senate and House conferees to the White House. Thanks in large measure to his support of the commission, the resulting bill left the commission's basic authority intact. The commission was explicitly barred only from regulating trade groups that set product and industry standards. It was also forbidden to petition the Patents Commission to cancel a trademark on the grounds that it had become the common name of an item.* While the FTC was allowed to continue its rule-making proceedings with respect to children's advertising, Congress required that any rule be based on whether the advertising was "deceptive" rather than "unfair"—which had the effect of undermining the commission's entire effort. The commission was, however, also given permission to issue its rule on funeral homes—thanks to the refusal of the Senate to go along with the House restriction. Finally, the compromise provided for a veto by both chambers of the legislature. While Pertschuk publicly observed that "the most serious threats to the agency's ability to protect consumers have not materialized,"[51] in fact, the commission had suffered a major political setback. The evident lack of congressional support for its regulatory initiatives not only dramatically slowed down the commission's future rule making but also served to make other regulatory agencies more cautious. As one consumer lobbyist put it, "Other agencies that have not yet provoked Congress may not want to stir up that hornet's nest. Regulators will have to keep more than one eye on what special interests they're antagonizing."[52]

---

*This was the so-called Formica rule.

ECONOMIC DEREGULATION

For all the controversy engendered by the consumer movement's unsuccessful efforts to secure the establishment of an agency for consumer protection and defend the initiatives of the Federal Trade Commission, the most significant changes in regulatory policy during the latter part of the 1970s lay in an entirely different direction. Beginning in the mid-1970s and continuing through the Carter administration, government controls over the terms of competition were significantly reduced in several important sectors of the economy, including airlines, trucking, banking, railroads, and telecommunications. However, it is important to distinguish between the deregulation of banking, telecommunications, railroads, and trucking on one hand, and the deregulation of airlines on the other. In the first group, businesses were on both sides of the issue. Financial institutions, telecommunication firms, and railroads were divided over the merits of deregulation, depending on their particular competitive position. The only industry that took a unified stance in opposition to deregulation was the trucking industry. But it was opposed by a wide array of other industrial groups, including the National Association of Manufacturers, the American Farm Bureau Federation, and the National Federation of Independent Businesses, as well as a number of trade associations and individual firms. The coalition that lobbied for the Trucking Deregulation Act of 1980 was organized in the Washington office of Sears Roebuck.

Still, this situation did not distinguish economic deregulation from many of the other political conflicts whose outcome I have used to trace changes in the political influence of business over time. The interests of businesses are frequently in conflict. What distinguished the politics of economic deregulation is that consumer organizations were *not* active political participants; they neither played an important role in placing the issue on the agenda nor did they significantly affect the outcome. This is not to say that they were indifferent: various consumer groups supported both trucking and banking deregulation and expressed some reservations about the deregulation of telecommunications, but their role was marginal. Individual consumers were not even important users of trucking and railroads. And there was absolutely no evidence of any consumer dissatisfaction with the services provided by AT&T and its affiliate companies prior to deregulation. In short, economic regulation, for the most part, meant neither a defeat for business nor a victory for consumer lobbyists: business was divided and consumer groups were largely indifferent.

Airline deregulation, however, was distinctive. As in the case of trucking, the industry was unified. Each of the scheduled carriers opposed any reduction of government control over the industry. However, although both large and small businesses were among the major consumers of airline services, business was not a part of the coalition that lobbied to curtail the powers of the Civil Aeronautics Board (CAB). The original impetus to deregulate the airline industry came not from business, but from a liberal Democratic senator, namely, Edward Kennedy. And his efforts received the strong and effective backing of a broad range of nonbusiness constituencies.

The deregulation of airlines first appeared on the political agenda in 1975 when the consumer movement was still relatively influential, and the argument for airline deregulation originally reflected the influence and ideology of consumerism. By the mid-1970s, owing in part to the influence of Ralph Nader and streams of book-length exposés of the regulatory process published under his auspices, "the idea that government regulation served business interests penetrated mass attitudes." A 1977 poll for *U.S. News and World Report* reported that 81 percent agreed with the statement that "large companies have a major influence on the government agencies regulating them."[53] Senator Kennedy was attracted to the idea of deregulating the airline industry precisely because he saw the issue as "a response to consumerism, the political movement that addressed the interests of the consumer against big business or, in regulatory regimes, the combination of big business and big government." Among the first individuals to testify at the hearings on airline deregulation held by a subcommittee of the Senate Judiciary Committee in 1975 was Ralph Nader, who stated: "Throughout the land people are repulsed by arrogant and unresponsive bureaucracies serving no useful public purpose, and they are looking to this Congress to get on with the national housecleaning job that is needed. Can you think of a better place to start than the Civil Aeronautics Board?"[54]

The 1975 hearings, held by the Subcommittee on Administrative Practices and Procedures, subjected both the airline industry and the CAB to searching scrutiny. Thanks to the impressive staff work of Stephen Breyer, the subcommittee's special counsel, they publicly exposed the weakness of the case for airline regulation. "It was Kennedy's finest hour as a legislator and his participation guaranteed the hearings wide publicity." Kennedy, like Magnuson and Ribicoff a decade earlier, had almost single-handedly succeeded in placing an issue on the political agenda. By the time President Carter had appointed Cornell University economist Alfred Kahn, a strong proponent of deregulation, to the chairmanship of the CAB, a broad coalition had emerged in favor of deregulation. Consisting of an unusual alliance of liberal and conservative interest groups, it included

Common Cause, the American Association of Retired Persons, the Aviation Consumer Action Project (affiliated with Ralph Nader), the National Taxpayers Union, the Cooperative League of the U.S.A., the American Conservative Union, and the Public Interest Economics Group. One of its members noted, "There is some amount of culture shock, but we all do agree on this issue."[55] Moreover, "the coalition made its lobbying visits to Congressional offices in teams that included representatives of both liberal and conservative groups as well as of business. Instead of an ordinary application of interest group power, this was a form of political theater."[56] Even before Congress began to act on this issue, Alfred Kahn had begun deregulating the industry through the administrative process. In October 1978, Congress passed the Airline Deregulation Act, which effectively ended the federal government's control over airline routes and pricing.

This outcome was an important defeat for the airline industry. Airline regulation appeared to be an exception to the generalization that the power of business vis-à-vis consumer interests increased after 1977. But its dynamics were quite different from the politics of consumer protection during the previous decade. During the 1960s, the unions had been the strongest supporters of consumer protection legislation. But on this issue, the unions representing airline employees were on the side of industry. As a result, airline deregulation was as much a defeat for labor as it was for business; it revealed an important rift in the ranks of consumer advocates. Equally important, Kennedy's challenge to the power of the airline industry was successful because it was consistent with the conservative political climate of the second half of the 1970s. Airline deregulation succeeded because it sought to help consumers by reducing, rather than expanding, government control of industry. In this sense, the willingness of Congress to reduce the power of the CAB in 1978 presaged its challenge to the power of the FTC the following year. While airline deregulation united the liberal opponents of big business and the conservative opponents of big government, it was the conservatives' support that proved critical. Airline deregulation, far from reflecting the continued political influence of the consumer movement, can instead be regarded as its last hurrah.

Finally, in sharp contrast to the consumer legislation of the 1960s and early 1970s, airline deregulation reduced, rather than increased, the prices of products and services: the earlier legislation had been made possible by the prosperity of the 1960s, while the latter reflected the increase in inflation—and stagnating real incomes—that characterized the American economy after 1973. Thus, just as expanding government regulation of corporate social conduct had enabled policymakers to carry on the promises of the Great Society without *increasing* government expenditures, so economic

deregulation provided a way for policymakers to reduce inflation without
reducing government expenditures.

While economic deregulation divided the business community, the politics of social regulation increasingly united it. Around 1978, a flood of
articles began to appear in the business and popular press describing the
impact of social regulation on business. It was blamed for reducing productivity, creating unnecessary paperwork, stifling innovation, delaying plant
construction and expansion, and adding to the cost of consumer products.
Willard Butcher, the president of Chase Manhattan, reported that, according to his company's research, "in 1977 government regulation cost us
more than $100 billion. . . . The trend of ever-growing regulation at all
levels threatens to strangle our market economy and render impotent not
only everything our system stands for but also the capabilities of the
system itself."[57] Goodyear calculated that complying with the regulations
of six of the more demanding federal agencies cost the company $35.5
million each year and that filling out the reports they demanded took
thirty-four employee-years. Hostility to social regulation was particularly
strong among smaller firms. A small manufacturer told the *New York Times:*
"It's become a nightmare. We're spending hundreds of dollars to keep the
Washington bureaucrats happy."[58]

Amid growing business and press criticism of the cost and effectiveness
of government regulation, the issue of "regulatory reform" entered into the
political agenda. Early in 1978, President Carter appointed a Regulatory
Analysis Review Group (RARG) to recommend ways of reducing the cost
of future regulations. In March 1978, he issued an executive order requiring all regulatory agencies of the executive branch to prepare detailed
analyses of future major regulatory rules. ("Major" was defined as costing
more than $100 million a year.) The RARG was charged with its enforce-
ment. In October 1978, he established the U.S. Regulatory Council, composed of thirty-six regulatory agencies, to coordinate federal regulatory
policy. But while the efforts of both the council and the review group to
impose a cost-benefit test on new regulations created considerable controversy, their effect on agency decisions was rather modest. As a result, in
1979, the focus of regulatory reform shifted to Congress.

The *National Journal* wrote that "1979 promises to be the year of . . .
regulatory reform . . . the result of Congressional and Administrative
perceptions of the public mood."[59] The *New York Times* reported that, in

contrast to "those heady days of the late 1960s and early '70s [when] . . . anything and everything could be regulated in the public interest," suddenly in 1979, "all the world seems to be against government overregulation."[60] More than one hundred fifty regulatory-reform bills were introduced, leading *Fortune* to observe that "all of a sudden, just about every Senator and Congressman wanted to get into the act of curbing the regulatory agencies."[61] While the organized political resistance to regulation stemmed primarily from the business community, the popularity of regulatory reform also reflected a shift in public attitudes.

The percentage of those agreeing with the statement that "there is too much regulation of business" increased from 31 percent in 1978 to 33 percent in 1979 to 42 percent in 1980. Indeed, in 1980, support for the view that there is "too much" regulation equaled that for the two alternatives ("not enough" and the "right amount") combined for the first time. The percentage of those reporting that they had personally been made "better off as a result of government control and regulation of the business practices of large corporations" had increased from 37 percent in 1966 to 43 percent in 1970. However, in 1977, it declined to 28 percent.[62] A 1978 poll by CBS News and the *New York Times* reported that 58 percent of the public agreed that government has gone too far in regulating business and interfering with the free enterprise system; only 31 percent disagreed. A Harris poll found that between 1976 and 1978, the proportion of those thinking that "businessmen's complaints about excessive government regulation are . . . justified" had increased from 39 to 44 percent, and disagreement with this position fell from 35 to 32 percent.[63]

In 1979, the administration submitted a regulatory reform bill to Congress that essentially gave the force of law to the president's March executive order on "Improving Government Regulation." The administration acted primarily to head off the efforts of the Business Roundtable and the National Association of Manufacturers, who favored much more sweeping changes, including expanded judicial review of regulations and a legislative veto. In the end, however, the politics underlying the legislation became so complex that Congress was unable to act: senior administration regulatory officials and business lobbyists were unable to agree on a compromise and neither enjoyed enough power in Congress to overcome the other's opposition. The lack of congressional action delighted Ralph Nader's Congress Watch, which had organized a coalition of public-interest organizations to oppose the bill. After Congress adjourned in 1980, they threw a party to celebrate the demise of the regulatory reform legislation. Their victory, however, proved short-lived. The following month a president was elected who was less interested in reforming regulation than in reducing it. In 1981, regulatory "reform" all but disappeared from the political agenda, to be replaced by Reagan's promise of regulatory "relief."

Tax Policy

No area of public policy toward business changed as much during the Carter administration as tax policy. The 1978 Revenue Act was a major milestone in federal tax policy. It dramatically reversed the reform orientation of the 1969 and 1976 revenue acts and thereby laid the groundwork for the even more sweeping changes in federal tax policy that took place in 1981. In a number of significant respects, it also marked the policy debut of supply-side economics.

In his 1976 presidential campaign, Jimmy Carter had described the nation's tax system as "a disgrace to the human race."[64] In January 1978, the administration proposed a comprehensive tax-reform package that was somewhat similar to that offered by President Kennedy nearly two decades earlier. It contained a number of changes designed to make the taxation of individual incomes more progressive. Of particular interest to the business community was an increase in the capital-gains tax for those with higher incomes and a restriction of deductions for business expenses, particularly entertainment expenses. The last was considered particularly important by the president: the infamous "three martini lunch" and the case of the executive who had reportedly deducted 338 lunches costing more than $10,000 in the course of a single year were cited repeatedly in presidential speeches. A few weeks after the administration announced its program, Senator Muskie, chair of the Senate Budget Committee, released a report contending that high-income taxpayers received more than one-third of the nation's "tax expenditures."

It soon became clear that the administration had fundamentally misjudged the climate of public opinion. Articles appeared in two liberal newspapers, the *New York Times* and the *Washington Post,* criticizing the Senate report. The *Times* published an article headlined, "Britain's High Taxes Seen as a Factor in Stagnation," and the *Post* contended that although "wealthier persons . . . enjoy the biggest tax breaks and deductions, they also shoulder a disproportionate share of the tax burden." In June 1978, Proposition 13, which drastically cut property taxes in California, was passed. Suddenly, the "tax revolt" dominated the media. Poll data revealed that there was widespread resentment of tax rates among the middle class. "The mood of Congress and the country was shifting rapidly toward lower taxes and away from tax reform. . . . Never in the history of the income tax were proposals so out of step with Congressional intentions."[65] But even as liberal members of Congress informed Carter that there was no constituency for tax reform and his own secretary of the treasury expressed his lack of enthusiasm for the administration's efforts, the president persisted. Although he revised some of his proposals, he still asked Congress to approve a relatively long list of "reforms," including stiffer taxation of corporate income earned overseas and restrictions on corporate expense accounts.

Following Carter's announcement, the business community decided to take the offensive. Instead of opposing the administration's proposal to increase the tax on capital gains, they decided to press for its reduction. In the spring of 1978, the American Council for Capital Formation arranged a meeting between Ed Zschau, a California hi-tech entrepreneur representing the American Electronics Association (AEA), and Republican Representative William Steiger of Wisconsin. Zschau reported to Steiger a survey conducted by the AEA which demonstrated that the near doubling of the capital-gains tax between 1969 and 1976 had dramatically reduced the availability of venture capital for his industry. Following this meeting, Steiger introduced legislation that rolled back the tax on capital gains to what it had been prior to 1969. By coincidence, Proposition 13 was passed about the same time. As one member of the council put it, "At that time we needed a psychological boost. Proposition 13 gave us a lift. It helped give tax reduction a broader credibility." Charls Walker, who headed the American Council, added, "Within a relatively short period of time, capital formation has entered the lexicon of 'good words.' "[66]

Steiger's bill then became the focus of a massive lobbying and public relations effort. A thousand kits setting forth the case for reducing the capital-gains tax were distributed to individual members of Congress and to the press, while a stream of business-funded academic studies predicted that reducing the capital-gains tax would increase government revenues, accelerate investment, and raise the price of securities.[67] The Steiger amendment took the political initiative out of the hands of the administration. At the same time, Congress was under growing pressure to stimulate the economy and, as in 1964, reducing taxes on business seemed a way of accomplishing this goal. There was significant support in the House of Representatives for the Steiger amendment, and a bill containing it was reported out by the House Ways and Means Committee. However, there remained some concern about its effect on revenue. A compromise was suggested by Representative Jim Jones (Democrat-Oklahoma): it included an across-the-board reduction in individual and corporate tax rates and a reduction of the capital-gains tax to a maximum of 35 percent. This compromise was approved by the full House.

The Senate, however, favored reducing the capital-gains tax to 21 percent. The final version split the difference: the capital-gains tax was reduced to 28 percent. The legislation also provided significant tax relief for established businesses, both by lowering the corporate tax rate and making the 10 percent tax credit for investment permanent. And like President Kennedy, Carter found that Congress, when confronted with the opposition of restaurant and hotel operators and their employees, was unwilling to curb deductions for expense accounts.

Although the administration described the reduction as "tax relief for millionaires," the Jones-Steiger bill received substantial public support. In July 1978, Lou Harris reported that 66 percent of the American public favored the Steiger-Jones compromise and the Opinion Research Corporation revealed that 53 percent of the public wanted to "encourage investment in business by reducing the tax on long-term capital gains."[68] The increase in inflation, which was pushing Americans into higher tax brackets, coupled with stagnating real incomes, had led millions of Americans to sympathize with business's complaints about excessive taxation. Moreover, many Americans, whose homes represented their personal hedge against inflation, saw the high tax on capital gains hurting them as well. Business lobbying, combined with a change in public opinion, proved decisive: the result was the most "pro-investment tax bill since 1964"— one whose passage would have been unthinkable even six months earlier. As one observer put it, "If there ever was a reform era . . . it ended with a bang in 1978."[69]

Energy Policy

The ability of business to affect energy policy did not change as dramatically. In a number of respects the stalement that had characterized energy policy during the Ford administration continued through the Carter administration. Public hostility to the oil industry—particularly after the shortages of 1979—remained considerable, and the energy industry's criticism of federal tax and regulatory policies was not noticeably less in 1980 than it had been six years earlier. However, there was a gradual movement away from price controls in favor of the market.

On November 9, 1978, President Carter signed into law the Natural Gas Policy Act of 1978, thus bringing to an end one of the most complex and complicated legislative battles since the Second World War. While campaigning for the presidency, Jimmy Carter had written a letter to the governors of several Western states promising to deregulate the price of newly discovered natural gas. However, after his election, the president, fearful of the political consequences of the removal of price controls over the nation's most widely used home heating fuel, proposed a compromise. The administration plan liberalized—though it did not abolish—controls over "new" as well as "old" natural gas. The latter came as a pleasant surprise to natural-gas producers, since it actually went beyond Carter's campaign pledge. But much to the dismay of both gas producers and pipeline companies, the administration also proposed to extend federal regulation to the intrastate market, which had previously been exempt from national price controls.[70]

The president's gas bill pleased no one. Citizen and consumer groups representing the consumers of natural gas described it as "de facto deregulation, a cave-in to the monopoly power of OPEC and the major oil companies, and a gross windfall for producers." One consumer organization representative stated, "We believe price to be one of the most regressive techniques for rations and allocation that there is." The gas industry was equally upset with the administration. An official of the Independent Petroleum Association noted that "contrary to what candidate Carter promised, President Carter's proposal would perpetuate controls indefinitely with no hope of achieving competitive market prices."[71]

As the bill worked its way through the Congress, the most powerful opposition came from those forces who favored rather than opposed deregulation—an indication that the industry's political support in Congress had increased since 1975. Indeed, the administration's liberal Democratic supporters in Congress had to fight extremely hard to prevent complete deregulation of gas. While the forces favoring deregulation failed in a close vote on the floor of the House, the Senate, where the heavily populated Northeast consumer states had less representation, adopted an amendment that provided for the deregulation of wellhead prices of new natural gas after two years of gradual increases. In a desperate attempt to save his entire energy package—of which the pricing of natural gas was a critical component—the president made a further compromise: "new gas" would be completely deregulated by 1985.

The White House "pulled out all the stops" to pressure industry to accept this compromise. Reluctantly, the gas-pipeline owners and the distributors, as well as the major oil companies, agreed to withdraw their opposition, though not before a number of them had extracted specific concessions of particular importance to their segment of the industry. Peter Nivola writes: "The tide was turned, in large part by a series of White House conferences with important business leaders. . . . The Department of Energy was able to supply all senators with the names of scores of major corporations, financial institutions and trade associations that were backing the bill."[72] Senator James Abourezk of South Dakota, a bitter opponent of the industry, attempted to filibuster the final bill, but the Senate voted for cloture and, shortly afterward, Congress approved the legislation.

The Natural Gas Policy Act was still a long way from satisfying the demands of the oil and gas industry; in fact, the Department of Energy estimated that, as of 1987, the majority of total sales of gas would still be controlled. In addition, the legislation was extremely complicated: the statute was 66 pages and was accompanied by another 364 pages of regulations describing how it was to be administered. Nonetheless, the bill immediately raised the ceiling price of newly derived natural gas and allowed the prices of various other categories of gas to increase gradually between 1980 and 1985—at which point they would become deregulated. It thus allowed natural-gas prices to move closer to their market levels than they would have without any legislation and in this sense can be regarded as a victory—though clearly an incomplete one—for the energy industry. Not surprising, public-interest groups such as Consumers Union and Energy Action, which had strongly opposed any increase in natural-gas prices, were extremely disappointed by this outcome.

In the last months of 1978, a revolution in Iran reduced that nation's oil production from six million barrels a day to virtually zero. As a result, oil prices, which had been relatively stable since 1974, increased dramatically. The price of oil on the Rotterdam spot market doubled in three months, and once again motorists began lining up at service stations. The public response to the nation's second major energy crisis was even more hostile to the oil companies than it had been five years earlier. A Gallup poll taken in August 1979 reported that 70 percent believed that "the gasoline shortage had been deliberately brought about by the oil companies."[73] Democratic Senator Howard Metzenbaum of Ohio observed that "I don't think an industry could ever have a lower image in the American people's eyes than does the oil industry at this moment." An energy lobbyist for Congress Watch stated, "Whether they like it or not, the oil companies are on trial with the American people, and the people who are going to render that verdict are the people who are waiting in line for gas." The research director of the Consumer Energy Council charged, "During the 1973–74 oil embargo, you would at least say it's mostly the Arabs doing this to us, but now there's no other explanation but the oil companies."[74]

As in 1974, the oil industry mounted a major national effort to attempt to persuade the American public that it had not engineered the gasoline shortage: Mobil spent approximately five million dollars on print ads explaining the industry's position, and 387 of Texaco's employees delivered a total of 2,181 speeches before more than 80,000 members of civic, business, and bar associations. But these efforts had little effect. A representative of Hill and Knowlton, the nation's largest public-relations firm, whose clients included Texaco and Atlantic Richfield, conceded, "I don't think what is being done has accomplished anything. All you can do is keep trying to get across the facts, but the facts alone don't seem to be adequate."[75] The industry's credibility was further damaged in June 1979, when the Department of Energy accused several major oil companies of having overcharged refineries by $1.7 billion since 1973. Compounding the industry's difficulties, senators Kennedy and Metzenbaum introduced legislation prohibiting the sixteen largest oil companies from acquiring any company with assets greater than $100 million.

Yet the government's response to the 1978–79 oil shortages turned out to be rather different from its response to the 1973–74 energy crisis. In a nationally televised speech on April 5, 1979, the president announced that he would gradually phase out price controls on domestic oil over the next thirty months beginning July 1, 1979, thus ending nearly a decade of control of oil prices. He acknowledged that decontrol of prices was a "painful step"—one that would require each American "to use less oil and pay more for it," but stated that it was necessary in order to encourage energy conservation and increase domestic production. The president's decision outraged labor and consumer groups and was bitterly denounced by Democratic representatives in Congress. Representative Dingell and Senator Metzenbaum called for the resignation of Energy Secretary James Schlessinger. But in sharp contrast to the situation in 1975, when a similar proposal from President Ford was immediately overturned by Congress, President Carter suffered no such reversal. The only vote in either chamber to challenge his decision took place in the House of Representatives, which in October 1979 rejected a proposal to retain controls by a vote of 135 to 257. *Congressional Quarterly* concluded, "In the four years between 1975 and 1979, advocates of price controls steadily lost strength as energy prices rose despite controls, inflation continued unabated, and energy supplies diminished."[76]

The president's decision, however, was a mixed blessing for the oil industry, for he also asked Congress to approve a significant tax on the oil companies' profits to prevent the industry from benefiting from the "huge and undeserved windfall profits" that would result from his action. Approximately half of the expected increase in its revenues was to be placed in an Energy Trust Fund which would be used to provide energy credits for the poor, subsidies for mass transit, and funds for development of sources of alternative energy. In urging Congress to enact his tax proposal, the president described the forthcoming legislative battle as a "classic confrontation pitting the common and public good against the enormous power of a well-organized special interest."[77] Not surprising, the oil industry strongly opposed the administration's tax proposal, contending that it needed the additional revenues for energy development.

As Congress began debating the president's proposed tax on windfall profits, the oil companies announced that their first-quarter profits had increased 68 percent from the previous year; their second-quarter profits, announced in July 1979, revealed an even larger increase. These disclosures significantly strengthened Congressional support for an additional tax on the oil companies' profits; indeed, the administration began to fear that Congress would increase their taxes by such a large margin that the industry would have no incentive for domestic exploration. This congressional reaction, in turn, persuaded the major integrated oil companies that "oil price decontrol was politically infeasible without a windfall profits tax."[78] A number of oil executives admitted this in private, and the president of Atlantic Richfield, Thornton Bradshaw, publicly announced that his firm would not oppose a windfall profits tax—if that was the price of decontrol. Tempering the opposition of the industry was the expectation that future increases in world energy prices would result in a substantial increase in company revenues—even if half of them would accrue to the U.S. Treasury. However, the independent oil producers bitterly opposed the tax, claiming that it would severely hamper their exploration efforts.

In June 1979, a National Coalition for a Windfall Profits Tax was formed to mobilize support for the administration's tax proposal. Senator Russell Long, a strong supporter of the oil industry, announced that "if we don't pass a windfall tax, the President is simply going to withdraw the [decontrol] plan and leave us in the mess we are in already." As the Senate Finance Committee began to take up the tax measures, OPEC's prices again increased; they nearly doubled over the next six months, thus increasing the prospective windfall to nearly three hundred billion dollars. At this point, cooperation within the industry completely broke down, as every subgroup and individual firm began "shooting for their own deals and particular needs." The most visible conflict was between the independents and the major producers. The majors, in an effort to switch the burden of taxation to the independents, announced that they would support an increase in the tax to 75 percent, providing the first thousand barrels of each independent producer's daily production was exempted. These and other divisions within the industry severely weakened its efforts to reduce the aggregate effect of the tax, and in March 1980, Senate and House conferees agreed on a formula that would raise an estimated $227 million in revenues by 1988, with the independents taxed at a lower rate than the majors. On the day Congress approved the legislation, The *Wall Street Journal* published its lead editorial with a black border, suggesting that it was "beyond belief that Congress would set about to destroy *this* industry in *this* decade."[79]

Environmental Policy

INTRODUCTION

Compared to both organized labor and the consumer movement, the environmental movement fared relatively well between 1977 and 1980. In 1977, it secured enactment of a bill providing for federal regulation of strip-mining and three years later helped successfully oppose the establishment of an energy mobilization board. And, in the closing days of the Carter administration, Congress approved two major new environmental laws, though in a form considerably weaker than environmentalists preferred. On the other hand, Congress also approved legislation delaying the enforcement of air- and water-pollution standards, including those affecting automobiles, that had been set earlier in the decade.

THE CLEAN AIR ACT AMENDMENTS

In 1977, Congress passed legislation amending two of the most important environmental statutes passed during the preceding decade: the Clean Air Act Amendments of 1970 and the Water Pollution Control Act of 1972. For the most part, these statutes either modified, eliminated, or revised the deadlines enacted at the beginning of what was to be the "environmental decade." The statutes enacted in 1977 climaxed five years of increasingly vigorous opposition by business to the pollution controls imposed at the beginning of the 1970s. The 1977 Clean Air Act Amendments postponed the deadline for achievement of goals for "healthy" air from 1975 to 1982, and in some instances to 1987, and extended the deadline for a 90 percent reduction in automobile emissions by three to six years (depending on the particular pollutant). In the area of water pollution, Congress gave industries that acted in "good faith" an additional two years to meet the 1977 technology deadlines. In addition, those responsible for industrial discharges were given until 1984 to employ the "best conventional pollution control technology," whereas the 1972 statute had required that industry use the "best available technology" by 1983. While officially retaining the goal of "zero discharge" by 1985, the changes in the technological requirements meant that, for all practical purposes, this goal had been abandoned for the 1980s.

As in 1970, the most intense and extensive political conflict over the Clean Air Act Amendments of 1977 revolved around the issue of automobile-emissions standards. A series of postponements—two granted by the Environmental Protection Agency and one extended by Congress as a response to the Arab oil embargo of 1973—had given the automobile manufacturers until the 1978 model year to meet the emissions standards specified by the Clean Air Act of 1970. While the cars produced by the mid-1970s emitted significantly fewer pollutants than those manufactured at the beginning of the decade, as early as 1975 the automobile manufacturers became convinced that they lacked the technology to meet the 1978 deadline—particularly its nitrogen oxide standard. Dr. Fred Bowditch, GM's senior executive responsible for emissions control, stated, "Anything is possible in the technical community given enough time and money. What we are saying is that we don't know how to do it right now."[80] Unless Congress approved legislation that either delayed or reduced the emissions standards it had established in 1970, the industry would find itself unable to begin production in 1977 of its cars for the 1978 model year.

Following a lengthy series of markup sessions, on February 5, 1976, the Senate Public Works Committee granted the automobile industry an initial if modest concession. Responding to the public's heightened interest in fuel economy following OPEC's price increase in 1973, the committee voted to postpone the final auto-emissions standards for carbon monoxide and hydrocarbons until 1979 and relaxed the final standard for nitrogen oxides altogether. Although Senator Muskie had opposed this provision when it had previously come before his subcommittee, he nonetheless indicated his general support for the legislation, regarding it as a reasonable compromise. However, in order to encourage the industry to improve its technology, the bill required the major manufacturers—excluding American Motors and some small importers—to meet all three standards in at least 10 percent of their total output. After rejecting several amendments designed either to strengthen or weaken the auto-emissions standards, the bill was approved by the Senate by a vote of 78 to 13.

Dissatisfied with this compromise, the automobile industry decided to focus its lobbying efforts on the House of Representatives. Even after the House Interstate and Foreign Commerce Committee had voted to extend imposing the final emissions standards beyond the date agreed to by the Senate, the industry launched a major effort to further amend the bill when it reached the floor of the House. Representative John Dingell (Democrat-Michigan), whose district was not only a major producer of automobiles but also included the corporate headquarters of the Ford Motor Company, and James Broyhill (Republican-North Carolina), offered an amendment to postpone the imposition of the final emissions standards until 1982 and to eliminate entirely the standard for nitrogen oxide from the act. Dingell argued that his amendment would "save fuel, reduce consumer costs, promote economy recovery, and reduce unemployment in the automobile and related supplier/service industries."[81] The Dingell-Broyhill amendment which, according to one reporter, "gave the industry virtually everything it wanted," passed the House by a vote of 224 to 169.[82] The automobile industry had scored its first important legislative victory on the issue of air pollution in nearly a decade.

The industry's victory on the House floor, however, proved short-lived. The Senate's conferees refused to compromise on the deadlines for automobile emissions. Faced with the prospect of a relatively stringent bill, the industry reversed its call for the urgent reform of the Clean Air Act and announced that it preferred no bill at all to the one approved by the conference committee. Thanks to a filibuster on an unrelated issue, Congress adjourned without approving new clean-air legislation. The industry's lobbyists were pleased with the outcome: unless Congress acted shortly after its return to revise or delay the requirements of the 1970 act, Detroit would be forced to stop producing automobiles in the fall of 1977, an eventuality that Congress presumably would be unwilling to countenance. Muskie was understandably bitter. Pointing to a Senate gallery filled with lobbyists, he warned: "If they think they can come back in the early months of next year and get a quick fix from the Senate to make them legal, they better take a lot of long careful thoughts about it." Equally defiant, the president of General Motors declared to a wire-service reporter: "They can close down the plants. They can get someone in jail—maybe me. But we're going to make [1978] cars to 1977 standards."[83]

When Congress returned in 1977, Dingell and Broyhill once again offered their amendment to the bill on the floor of the House of Representatives and, following the defeat of a compromise proposed by the Carter administration, it was adopted, 255 to 139. But once again, the automobile industry was rebuffed in the Senate. While a compromise measure, approved by the Senate on June 9, gave the industry until 1980 to meet federal emissions standards and somewhat relaxed the original nitrogen-oxide requirement, it was a setback for the automobile manufacturers in two important respects. First, it required the industry to reduce emissions of nitrogen oxide two years earlier than it would have preferred. Second, it maintained the original emissions standard for carbon monoxide. After a prolonged and exhausting series of meetings between the House and Senate conferees—the final session lasted until after two in the morning—a compromise was reached. The final bill was closer to the Senate than the House version, but the Senate conferees were considerably more conciliatory than they had been in 1976. Their most important concession was to accept a smaller reduction of two of the three major automobile pollutants released by cars produced in the 1980 model year than was specified in the Senate version of the bill. The conference report was adopted by voice votes of both houses two months later.

The most important reason for the increased political effectiveness of the automobile industry was that in 1977, unlike in 1970, the manufacturers were supported by the United Automobile Workers (UAW). As Leon Billings, a Senate Committee staff member, put it, "The auto companies never got to first base in persuading Congress to relax auto emission standards until they got the support of the UAW on the issue of jobs. The UAW has got a credibility up here that the auto companies don't."[84] Another supporter of strict control of pollution asked rhetorically, "What are you going to do when you have Henry Ford and Leonard Woodcock on the same side?"[85] According to the *Congressional Quarterly*, "Virtually all observers of the battle agreed that a union—the United Auto Workers—was the key group in the clean air lobbying fight."[86] A lobbyist from another industry recalled: "The auto companies' success in 1977 was due to one key factor: they employ so many God-damned people."[87]

In 1970, the UAW and six major conservation groups had publicly called for the "creation of air pollution guidelines so harsh that they would banish the internal combustion engine from the automobile within five years,"[88] while the AFL-CIO had publicly opposed industry efforts to weaken Senator Muskie's bill. However, in 1974 the UAW began to shift its position. After commissioning an independent technical study to sort out the conflicting contentions of Muskie and their employers, the union announced its support of a five-year pause in emissions standards—provided that the industry continued to work to develop the technology that would eventually allow clean-air goals to be met.

In 1970, the UAW's support for the Clean Air Act had been relatively perfunctory. But its opposition to strict standards for automobile emissions in 1977 was extremely aggressive. It was Woodcock and the UAW's staff experts who originally sat down with Representative Dingell to develop the specific provisions of the Dingell-Broyhill amendment; the automobile manufacturers, each of whom had earlier publicly advocated even weaker standards, eventually supported Dingell-Broyhill because, in the words of UAW lobbyist Howard Paster, "The companies had nowhere else to go." Imitating the political tactics that public-interest groups had earlier employed so successfully, the UAW, working through its headquarters in Detroit, communicated its position on emissions standards to forty Community Action Program councils. These councils in turn contacted every one of the union's million-and-a-half members, urging them either to write to or meet their senators and representatives. Booklets were distributed to union members with the message: "Congress must be told *quickly* that your job is at stake. . . . Tell Congress you are supporting [the Dingell-Broyhill amendments] because your future depends on protecting air quality without disrupting jobs."[89]

Unlike in 1970, the automobile industry was also able to mobilize other business allies as well. Republican Senator Peter Domenici of New Mexico, a member of the Senate Environment and Public Works Committee, after describing the entire conflict as "a bloody two-year brawl," observed:

By 1975, the automakers had figured something out: Every state in the country has automobile dealers and these dealers have employees. Every state in the country has gasoline stations and they have employees. Every state in the country has automobile parts stores and they have employees. In fact, large segments of each state's economy is based on the health, care, and feeding of the automobile. Most importantly the more rural a state (and thus previously the more immune their representatives to Detroit's pleas), the more they relied on the automobile in their local economy. Accordingly, the auto industry mounted a massive grass-roots campaign. . . . It realized that most representatives will meet with groups of concerned constituents. And that it is very, very tough, in fact painful, for an elected representative to have to tell so many people no.[90]

During the mid-1970s, the National Automobile Dealers Association (NADA) had two thousand members and eight full-time Washington lobbyists. Although the interests of its members and those of the auto manufacturers were frequently in conflict, on this issue they were identical: both were opposed to any public policy that threatened to reduce automobile sales. Not at all active in the deliberations over the 1970 amendments—in part because of the lack of advance warning of congressional intentions—they were well prepared when the Clean Air Act came up for renewal in 1976. In both 1976 and 1977, the NADA sent separate letters to each of its 21,000 members, urging them to make personal contact with their representatives in Washington. As one of its lawyers put it: "Dealers are very effective lobbyists. They are important members of the local community. They serve on hospital boards, lead charity drives. Many are active in local politics and know their congressman by their first name. They tend to be outgoing, friendly. They're salesmen. So it's not surprising that they do a good job."[91] One journalist observed: "The corridors of the House office buildings were as alive with local franchise dealers as if new models were being shown there." Asked to account for the unexpected passage of the Dingell-Broyhill amendment during 1976, a lobbyist for the Friends of the Earth summarized his side's defeat in one word: "Dealers."[92]

OTHER ENVIRONMENTAL LEGISLATION

One important consequence of the environmental laws enacted during the beginning of the 1970s was to delay, and in some cases prevent, a number of construction projects, many of them energy-related. Probably the most celebrated case involved Telleco Dam in Tennessee, whose approval was held up by a federal court on the grounds that it threatened the habitat of the snail darter and thus violated the Endangered Species Act. Congress subsequently enacted legislation authorizing the dam's construction. In March 1979, Standard Oil of Ohio announced that it was abandoning its five-year effort to obtain the more than seven hundred permits it needed to construct a California-to-Texas pipeline. That same year, Dow Chemical stated that it was giving up its effort to construct a new chemical facility in northern California because of the complexity of federal, state, and local pollution-control requirements.

In July 1979 in the midst of the second energy crisis, President Carter stated: "We will protect the environment. But if the nation needs to build a pipeline or refinery we will build them."[93] Reversing his earlier strong support of environmental controls, the president, in a nationally televised speech in the summer of 1979, denounced the "red tape, the delay and the endless roadblocks to completing key energy projects." In addition to calling for federal support of both oil shale and synthetic fuel production, he proposed the creation of an energy mobilization board that would have the authority to expedite the approval of new energy projects. While

Carter promised to be "sensitive to both energy needs and to environmental considerations," the environmental movement felt betrayed by the administration. One of its lobbyists stated that "it takes more than a few vague words to mollify us about the enormous amounts of damage that could be done by [the administration's] energy program."[94] Industry lobbyists were enthusiastic: they began compiling lists of their favorite horror stories about delayed projects.

Initially, there appeared to be little doubt that Congress would approve the president's proposal and, in fact, different variations were approved by both houses within a few months of the president's speech. Nonetheless, in a move termed a "stunning blow" to the president,[95] on June 27, 1980, House Republicans joined liberal Democrats to defeat the president's proposal. Although a coalition consisting of virtually every major environmental organization had lobbied vigorously against the legislation, the bill's defeat had little to do with their efforts. Rather, it was the opposition of House Republicans to the measure that proved crucial. A number of them had concluded that the bill would actually create more red tape than it would cut; several representatives sported buttons with the words "Even More Bureaucracy"—a play on the proposed board's acronym. In addition, the bill was strongly opposed by both the National Governors' Association and the National League of Cities; their arguments that the bill threatened states rights—and indeed the principles of the nation's constitutional system—were persuasive to a number of conservatives. But what finally killed the bill was that many Republicans decided to oppose it in order to embarrass the president. Environmentalists were nonetheless delighted with the outcome.

The same year that the House rejected an energy mobilization board, Congress approved two new important environmental statutes: the Alaska lands bill and the creation of a superfund to clean up toxic wastes. Both were passed by the lame-duck Congress in December 1980.

In 1977, it was discovered that a housing development had been constructed on the top of a former chemical dump in Niagara Falls, New York. A preliminary study indicated that chemical leaks from drums left on the site were poisoning the residents of the Love Canal subdivision and seven hundred families were subsequently evacuated at government expense. Over the next few years, literally thousands of chemical dump sites were discovered throughout the United States, a significant number of which were judged by the EPA to be potentially hazardous. Public pressure began mounting for legislation to provide funding to clean up these sites—about 8 percent of which had been abandoned.

Congress was confronted with several issues, the most important of which was whether the chemical industry or the federal government should pay the cost of cleaning up hazardous wastes sites. In May 1979, President Carter announced his support of legislation requiring that industry pay 80 percent of the cleanup costs and the government 20 percent. This position was strongly opposed by the chemical industry. Although Congress found itself under "increasing pressure from constituents to do something about toxic contaminants in their districts," the Chemical Manufacturers Association was able to prevent any congressional action. One representative who sympathized with the industry complained, "Those who have stonewalled the legislative process have . . . made it very difficult for those of us who wanted to develop a reasonable bill."[96]

However, in April 1980, a massive fire broke out at a dump that had been used by Chemical Corporation in New Jersey; the cost of the cleanup was estimated at more than ten million dollars. At this point, the chemical industry's united front against the superfund began to erode. Some of the major chemical firms now recognized that some regulation was inevitable and that by supporting a compromise they would be in a stronger position to affect its provisions. In August 1980, Irving Shapiro, chairman of Dupont, delivered a speech strongly supporting a superfund bill. The next month, the House approved legislation appropriating a total of $1.2 billion—75 percent to come from industry and 25 percent from the government. But efforts to work out a compromise in the Senate failed because a number of chemical firms, now sensing that Ronald Reagan would soon be elected president, decided to hold firm in the hope that no legislation at all would be enacted.

When the Republicans did capture control of the Senate in November 1980, the bill appeared to be dead. However, in mid-November, several newspapers published articles documenting the chemical industry's contributions to the election campaign of the members of the Senate Finance Committee who had opposed the bill. These disclosures proved highly embarrassing, and the Senate Finance Committee immediately authorized the sum of $4.2 billion. About the same time, Shapiro announced that he preferred that superfund legislation be approved in this session.[97] The next day, three other major chemical firms announced they were also willing to support a compromise.

Finally, in December 1980, Congress approved a drastically scaled-down version of the administration's 1979 proposal. The comprehensive Environmental Response, Compensation and Liability Act established a $1.6 billion emergency superfund to clean up toxic contaminants spilled or dumped into the environment. This fund was to be created over five years and financed primarily by a special tax on the chemical companies and oil companies that produced chemicals. Much to the disappointment of both the administration and environmentalists, the bill excluded oil spills from its purview and prohibited the superfund from compensating those injured by chemical spills or dumping. An earlier version of the legislation had included a provision holding anyone generating or handling hazardous wastes "strictly, jointly and severally" liable for cleanup and damages caused by the wastes.[98] This, however, was vigorously and successfully opposed by the chemical industry; the bill approved by Congress specified that a company would not be held liable if it had exercised "due care" in disposing of its hazardous wastes.

The legislation was reluctantly supported by President Carter and liberal Democrats in both houses on the grounds that some legislation—no matter how limited—was better than none at all. The compromise was also supported by president-elect Ronald Reagan who indicated that he would prefer to have Congress act before he assumed office. The final bill was termed a "significant improvement" over previous versions of the legislation by the president of the Chemical Manufacturers Association, while environmentalists vowed that they would return to Congress the following year to push for stronger legislation.

The lame-duck Congress also approved another important environmental statute: the Alaska lands bill. This legislation, originally proposed in the early 1970s, had been the subject of bitter congressional debate for more than three years. The struggle for strict land-use controls had been led by the Alaska Coalition, a group of fifty-one environmental and wildlife protection groups committed to saving the nation's last untouched frontier—America's "crown jewels." On the other side were most Alaskans, the mining, timber, and oil companies, the United States Chamber of Commerce, the National Rifle Association, and most labor unions. The environmentalists preferred that Congress enact no bill at all rather than a weaker version approved by the Senate, but after the 1980 election, they recognized that this was probably their last opportunity to get any legislation approved, so they reluctantly compromised. The bill restricted economic development of more than one hundred million acres of federal lands in Alaska—larger than California and Maine combined. President Carter, who had declared that passage of this law was his major environmental priority, described the bill as a "truly historic event."[99] While Representative Morris Udall termed it "one of the most far reaching conservation decisions in history," the environmental movement was dissatisfied with the bill: it protected fewer acres and established less severe restrictions on economic development and mineral exploration than the administration had proposed and that they preferred. But in the end, they were forced to bow to "the growing Congressional concern for economic and energy development."[100]

Why was environmental protection the only policy area in which Congress continued to approve new regulatory legislation—albeit in a form significantly weaker than environmentalists wanted—twice even after the 1980 election? One reason has to do with the environmental movement itself: a decade after Earth Day, the environmental movement had spawned a large number of organizations, many of them relatively large, well funded, and politically sophisticated. A *National Journal* survey published in 1980 listed sixteen leading environmental organizations: they had a combined membership of more than half a million individuals and a total budget of approximately $75 million.[101] Many had been actively lobbying Congress, appearing in administration proceedings, and filing lawsuits for more than a decade. *Congressional Quarterly* observed that "the environmental lobby . . . on the whole . . . is an increasingly slick and professional operation."[102] In fact, the most affluent environmental organization, the National Wildlife Federation, employed eight hundred people in its Washington-area offices, about the same number as the American Petroleum Institute.

Equally important, the degree of public support for environmentalism, while less intense than it had been between 1969 and 1972, remained substantial. Between 1973 and 1980, those polled who felt that the country was spending "too little" on the environment declined from 60 to 48 percent and, between 1977 and 1980, the number of individuals favoring the most stringent environmental controls, regardless of cost, diminished from 55 percent to 42 percent. But in 1980, a survey conducted by the Resources for the Future concluded that "environmental protection enjoys continued strong backing."[103] Indeed, between 1978 and 1980 the percentage of Americans believing that the United States could achieve economic growth without sacrificing environmental quality more than doubled— from 18 to 39 percent.[104] Moreover, although air- and water-pollution issues had become less salient than they were a decade earlier, new environmental problems, such as toxic wastes and groundwater contamination, helped sustain the public's commitment to environmental protection. The public may have become more skeptical about the virtues of regulation per se, but it continued to believe in the importance of government intervention designed to protect its health and conserve natural resources. As a result, the relative power of business vis-à-vis the environmental movement changed less than it did vis-à-vis either organized labor or the consumer movement—a pattern that would be repeated under the Reagan administration.

Conclusion

By the time it left office at the end of 1980, the Carter administration had disappointed the interest groups that originally had backed it almost as much as the Nixon administration had disappointed the business community a decade earlier. The administration's inability to secure the passage of labor-law reform, its support for the deregulation of oil prices, its support of regulatory reform, its proposal to streamline the approval of new energy-related projects—all were extremely upsetting to both the public-interest movement and organized labor. The relationship between President Carter and the business community was equally strained. A number of corporate leaders did enjoy access to the Carter White House. Shortly after his election, the president met at the Blair House with fourteen business executives, including J. Paul Austin, the chairman of Coca-Cola; Frank Cary, the chairman of IBM; Henry Ford II; Reginald Jones, the chairman of General Electric; and Irving Shapiro, the chairman of E. I. du Pont. While Jones noted that "initially there was a certain aloofness, a certain stiffness, a certain difficulty in establishing an easy relationship with free-flowing dialogue," during the next two years, the personal relationship between the president and a number of corporate leaders steadily improved. John DeButts, chairman of AT&T, who along with Shapiro and Jones came to constitute "Carter's corporate brain trust," stated, "He's a very easy man to talk to. He always listens."[105] The topics discussed by the president and these business leaders included civil-service reform, the Arab boycott, the Panama Canal Treaty, and corporate taxes.

Nonetheless, in spite of these meetings and the administration's gradual shift to more conservative economic and regulatory policies, in its last two years the business community, like much of the American public, became extremely dissatisfied with the Carter presidency. A number of top executives continued to feel that the president harbored "an innate distrust of the men who run the nation's largest corporations" stemming in part from the "President's background as a small-town businessman." More important, while acknowledging the openness of the administration to their views, they remained troubled by the ad hoc nature of presidential decision making. As Walter Wriston, chairman of Citicorp, complained, "We—and the markets—want a logical consistent strategy. Not conversations about pieces of a plan. . . . They believe they've told us what we want to hear. But the markets say not."[106] A Gallup survey for the *Wall Street Journal* in June 1980 found that "only one in 10 chief executive officers approves of the way the President is handling the economy."[107]

Thus, although business had dramatically increased its influence in Congress between 1977 and 1980, it was not until the election of Ronald Reagan in 1980 that the business community felt it had an ally in the White House, someone who not only understood and shared its political and economic philosophy but also possessed the commitment and the political skills to translate its preferences into a coherent set of policies. However, before examining the Reagan years in detail, I need once again to step back from our chronology and analyze the factors that enabled business to increase its political influence after 1976.

VIII

The Political Resurgence of Business

Introduction

The 1976 election appeared to present both the "old" and "new" politics wings of the Democratic party with an unparalleled opportunity to add to the political gains they had made in the previous decade; for the first time since 1968, the Democrats controlled both houses of Congress and the presidency. Yet by 1978, business had clearly regained the political initiative. Not only had it defeated much of the legislative program of both the public-interest movement and organized labor, including common situs picketing, the consumer protection agency, and labor-law reform, but it had succeeded in reversing some of the legislative defeats it had experienced earlier in the decade. Automobile-emissions standards were reduced, the power of the Federal Trade Commission (FTC) and the Occupational Safety and Health Administration (OSHA) was curtailed, energy prices were deregulated, and corporate taxes were lowered. How had this come about? Why did the political fortunes of business improve so significantly toward the end of the 1970s? My explanation consists of two parts. The first focuses on the efforts of business to increase its political effectiveness and reshape the prevailing political and intellectual climate of opinion. The second has to do with a shift in the attitudes of the public toward both business and government. The two were mutually reinforcing.

The Politicization of Business

INTRODUCTION

During the first half of the 1970s, the business community found itself increasingly frustrated by the decline in its ability to affect the direction of public policy. At a series of private meetings held by the Conference Board in 1974 and 1975, several chief executive officers (CEOs) expressed admiration for the lobbying skills of organized labor and urged their colleagues to intensify their own political activity. As one executive put it, "If you don't know your senators on a first-name basis, you are not doing an adequate job for your stockholders."[1] Thomas A. Murphy, chief executive officer of General Motors, informed a gathering of CEOs, "The truth is that we have been clobbered. As a result, we have not been able to do our best in the more traditional areas of competition as well."[2] John Harper, chairman of Alcoa, recalled: "We were not involved. What we were doing wasn't working. All the polls showed business was in disfavor. . . . We were getting short shrift from Congress. I thought we were powerless in spite of all the stories of how we could manipulate everything."[3] James Fergson, chairman of the board of General Foods, added: "Business was getting kicked around compared to labor, consumer and other groups and the constant cry within the business community was, 'How come we can't get together and make our voices heard?' "[4] Jeffrey Joseph, chief lobbyist for the U.S. Chamber of Commerce, noted that during the late 1960s and early 1970s, "business didn't even want to try to fight against something with a consumer handle on it. . . . I think a lot of people were concerned about their image."[5]

The results of the 1974 and 1976 elections further heightened the business community's sense of vulnerability. In 1974, the Democratic party, only two years after its resounding defeat in the 1972 presidential election, gained forty-nine House and five Senate seats, thus creating the possibility of a veto-proof Congress. Bryce Harlow, a senior Washington lobbyist representing Procter & Gamble recalled, "We had to prevent business from being rolled up and put in the trash can by that Congress."[6] The *New York Times* reported in 1976, "As businessmen see things, the attitude among Congressmen towards business today is less favorable than at any time since the Depression. Congress is awash with proposals, they complain, ranging from national economic planning to energy controls, that would severely restrict the free enterprise basis of the American economy."[7] After

President Ford's defeat for reelection in 1976, business became even more pessimistic. One business lobbyist recalled that, in November 1976, "We suddenly realized that we would be fighting for our lives." Mark Green, a close associate of Ralph Nader, stated:

> When they lost the Republican veto, they realized that they had to do it themselves. If the business groups tried to arouse all their constituencies when the Republicans were in power, it would have been greeted with a yawn. But when the Business Roundtable and the Chamber of Commerce sabre-rattled and yelled about a Democratic President and a two-to-one Democratic Congress, then their constituents get aroused and roll up their sleeves.[8]

CORPORATE POLITICAL ACTIVITY

Although by 1970 a majority of large corporations had begun to monitor the legislative process closely, relatively few Fortune 500 firms had formal public-affairs offices. Ten years later, more than 80 percent of the Fortune 500 companies had established a unit responsible for managing the "external environment." A survey of four hundred large and medium-sized U.S. business firms conducted in 1981 found that 361 had public-affairs units, that more than half of these had been created since 1970, and that nearly one-third were established between 1975 and 1979. Nearly a third were staffed by more than ten individuals and the majority had annual budgets of at least a half-million dollars.[9]

Not only did government-relations units increase in number and size, but the individuals who managed them gained greater status within the corporate hierarchy. Allan Cors, vice president of government affairs at Corning Glass Works, noted, "In the 50's and 60's, the business community was primarily interested in keeping government at arm's length. [Now] . . . corporate leaders demand and expect a more effective relationship between business and government, and that's why more companies are putting a corporate officer in charge."[10] The *Wall Street Journal* noted that "the post of government-affairs executive has taken on an added luster. A tour through the government-affairs department can be a quick route to the top."[11] A 1979 study by Galightly & Co. International reported that three-fourths of the Fortune 500 companies surveyed had promoted their senior officers responsible for government relations to vice president during the previous five years. Most of them attributed this in part to "the need to give more visibility to the function throughout the company," and 86 percent stated that these positions had been upgraded because of their increased importance to top management.[12]

A manager of an executive recruiting firm observed in 1977: "We get calls to fill jobs paying as much as $200,000 for people who can coordinate corporate affairs, public relations, financial affairs, and Washington relations. Companies want executives who can manage Washington almost like a profit center."[13] In addition, many firms established formal mechanisms for monitoring and managing changes in the political environment. Through the development of techniques of "issues management," companies attempted to anticipate changes in the political agenda and to develop contingency plans for responding to them.[14]

Another sign of the increasing importance of politics to business was an increase in political activity on the part of chief executive officers. A Conference Board study noted that "one of the most striking developments in recent years has been the increasing participation of the chief executive officers in the government relations effort."[15] A 1976 study reported that 92 percent of the CEOs polled indicated that they were spending more time on external relations than they were in 1972 or 1970, and a 1978 survey revealed that the CEOs of the Fortune 1000 were devoting approximately 40 percent of their time to "public issues"—twice that spent only two years earlier.[16] Another estimate placed this number as high as 50 percent for "the top people in most large companies."[17] John deButts, former chairman of AT&T, remarked in 1978: "So vital . . . is the relationship of government and business that to my mind the chief executive officer who is content to delegate responsibility for that relationship to his public affairs experts may be neglecting one of the most crucial aspects of his own responsibility." Irving Shapiro, the CEO of E. I. du Pont de Nemours & Co., observed: "In recent years, there's been a fundamental change in the approach taken by many chief executive officers. They've become personally involved in the governmental process. Because of the increasing impact of government actions on business operations, this is just as important as being skilled in knowing how to manufacture a product or administer a payroll."[18]

This change in the willingness of the chief executive officer to become personally involved in the government process was accompanied by a shift in the background and training of CEOs. The individual who epitomized the "modern business leader," "with one foot in the boardroom and the other in Washington," was Irving Shapiro, who became chairman and chief executive officer of Du Pont in 1974.[19] What distinguished Shapiro was that he was chosen largely because of his skills in government relations. The first individual with no background in science, engineering, or finance to become head of Du Pont in the firm's nearly two-hundred-year history, he rose through the company's legal department. Not surprisingly,

Shapiro emerged as one of the most visible and influential public spokespersons for the business community, enjoying particularly close ties with President Carter.[20] In June 1978, Thomas Murphy of General Motors told a gathering of fellow CEOs: "Look at what Irv Shapiro and Reg Jones [CEO of GE] have been doing—making the rounds of Washington, from the President on down. They should serve as models for top management throughout the business community."[21]

Corporations also established a larger physical presence in Washington. Between 1968 and 1978, the number of corporations with public-affairs offices in Washington increased from one hundred to more than five hundred. The size of their offices also became larger: at the beginning of the decade the typical Washington corporate office had only one or two individuals; by the late 1970s, it consisted of six or seven. For example, the Washington office of General Motors increased from three to twenty-eight people between 1968 and 1977. In addition, both the nature and the focus of the corporate Washington office changed. In 1979 the president of an executive recruiting firm remarked, "Companies used to staff their offices with unelected congressmen or other members of the 'old boy' network, but now they need people who can put forward an intelligent case on complex issues." One longtime Washington lobbyist observed, "My job used to be booze, broads and golf. . . . Now it is organizing coalitions and keeping information flowing."[22] In 1969, the Chamber of Commerce's biweekly breakfasts for the Washington representatives of major firms attracted fewer than seventy-five people; a decade later they were drawing two hundred.

In 1971, only 175 business firms had registered lobbyists; by 1979, 650 had them. According to *Washington Representatives,* which counts registered as well as unregistered lobbyists, by 1982 a total of 2,445 firms had some form of political representation in Washington.[23] In 1973, the National Association of Manufacturers moved its headquarters to Washington in order to increase the political influence of its 12,100 corporate members, and a number of trade associations subsequently made a similar move. In 1977, the number of trade associations with Washington offices increased by 21 percent; by 1978, nearly 2,000 trade associations had their headquarters in the nation's capital. The budgets of trade associations also increased substantially and a number, including the Chemical Manufacturers Association, were reorganized in order to increase their political effectiveness. By the end of the decade, "Washington knowledge" had replaced industry familiarity as the most important qualification for trade-association directors.

All told, as of 1980 there were in Washington 12,000 lawyers representing business before federal regulatory agencies and the federal courts, 9,000 business lobbyists, 50,000 trade-association personnel, 8,000 public-relations specialists, 1,300 public-affairs consultants, and 12,000 specialized journalists reporting to particular industries on government developments affecting them.[24] The number of individuals employed by the "private service industry" exceeded the number of federal employers in the Washington metropolitan area for the first time since before the New Deal.

Each reform period has witnessed the formation of new organizations representing large cross-sections of business. The Chamber of Commerce and the Conference Board were formed during the Progressive Era; the New Deal inspired the establishment of the Liberty League, the Business Council, and the Committee for Economic Development. The most important new peak organization of business established during the 1970s was the Business Roundtable. The Roundtable was formed in 1972 out of a merger of three small ad hoc groups: the Construction Users Anti-Inflation Roundtable, the March Group—an informal group of CEOs established to increase the political effectiveness of business, and the Labor Law Study Committee, which was created to counterbalance the political influence of organized labor. What made the Roundtable unique was that it was the first business lobbying organization whose membership was restricted to the CEOs of major corporations. In 1977, it consisted of 180 chief executive officers, representing 180 of the nation's largest firms.

Much of the Roundtable's lobbying was conducted by the Washington representatives of the companies whose CEOs belong to the organization; they also advised the organization of the kinds of positions likely to be politically acceptable, in effect serving as the organization's "eyes and ears." In addition, they staffed the Roundtable's task forces and prepared the organization's policy papers. But the organization's effectiveness was due to its "unique mobilization of the talent and prestige of the nation's top corporate heads." In 1977, ten chief executives met with the Democratic leadership of Congress in order to communicate the Roundtable's legislative priorities, and its members frequently personally lobbied individual representatives. As one senior legislative aide put it, "The conventional wisdom is that they're extremely effective, for the very reason that they put themselves together. When they come in here, it's not some vice president for public relations, but *the* president of GM, Du Pont or another corporation coming in themselves. That has a hell of a lot more impact than some lobbyist." Another noted, "You can be sure that there would be very few members of Congress who would not meet with the president of a

Business Roundtable corporation, even if there were no district connection."[25]

The increased mobilization of business's political resources was not confined to large companies.[26] During the 1960s, small business had virtually no political presence in Washington. Albert Liebenson, the president of the National Small Businesses Association, observed, "In the past, especially on broad economic issues—labor, social security—there was literally no input from small business because none of the associations had the money or the staff." But following the passage of the Occupational Safety and Health Act and the Employee Retirement Income Security Act (ERISA), many small business owners found themselves subject to federal regulation for the first time. Lieberson noted, "The more they got hit over the head, the madder they got."[27] Between 1970 and 1979, the membership of the National Federation of Independent Business grew from 300 to 600,000. Based in California, the Federation had 600 full-time employees, including 400 field agents located throughout the United States responsible for recruiting new members and serving as a communications link between the membership and government officials. In 1978, its Washington office consisted of twenty individuals, including eleven full-time registered lobbyists, and had a budget of $500,000. In 1977, the Small Business Legislative Council (SBLC) was established to direct and coordinate the lobbying efforts of small firms. Originally composed of twenty trade associations, by 1980 the SBLC included seventy-five national trade associations and a number of state trade groups—which together represented more than four million companies, nearly one-quarter of all businesses in the United States. The *Wall Street Journal* noted in 1979: "Tough-minded, politically wily and backed up by the increasingly vocal little guys of the business world, [small-business] operatives have emerged as a force to be reckoned with on Capitol Hill."[28]

The United States Chamber of Commerce was also revitalized. During the 1950s and 1960s, the Chamber of Commerce was poorly regarded in Washington, but its stature and membership increased dramatically during the 1970s. In 1967, the Chamber had 36,000 members; in 1974, 80,000 companies belonged. Between 1974 and 1980, the Chamber's annual budget tripled and its membership more than doubled. In 1980, it had a budget of $55 million and employed 45 full-time lobbyists. In addition, more than 76,000 individuals were participating in Chamber activities through a subsidiary organization, Citizens' Choice, organized in 1977. The National Association of Manufacturers also upgraded its government-relations efforts after its relocation to Washington, D.C.

Business did not simply increase the resources it devoted to the government process during the 1970s; it also changed the way these resources were deployed. One aspect of this change was an increase in political alliances among different segments of the business community. One executive observed in 1975, "We don't have a business community. Just a fragmented bunch of self-interested people. When a particular industry is in trouble . . . it fights alone and everyone else turns their back."[29] A building contractor complained, in 1976: "It took us three or four months just to get business to understand that common-situs picketing was their fight. We worked harder on the business community during that time than on Congress."[30] Yet a year later, an official of the Association's General Contractors of America noted, "We've learned how to cooperate, how to share the credit when we're successful and try not to hog the limelight. We've decided it's better to win together than lose individually."[31] He explained, "Frankly, we are just doing what labor did so well for so long."[32] Another corporate lobbyist observed that individual companies finally

> learned not to try to fight by themselves. They learned to find people who were similarly situated and form ad hoc committees with these people and have a concerted, organized effort across the board of a number of industries who were similarly situated to fight the thing together. If you put ten different companies or ten different trade associations in one room you're bound to have a plant in a lot more Congressional districts and a lot more states than if you're just one person.[33]

As with the increase in corporate political activity itself, corporate coalition building reflected, in part, the shift in the nature of government regulation. Prior to the 1970s, virtually all regulatory agencies and statutes affected only one or at most a handful of industries. Accordingly, the trade association was the logical unit for most corporate political activity. However, with the emergence of the new social regulation beginning in 1970, a much larger proportion of regulatory policies began to affect firms in a wide variety of different industries, which in turn required a different way of organizing business political activity. Significantly, the first serious and sustained effort at corporate coalition building involved the legislative battle over the proposal to establish a consumer protection agency—a regulatory agency that would have affected firms in hundreds of different industries. In a sense, the public-interest movement was a victim of its own successes. As long as the regulatory statutes it proposed affected only one industry, the extent of political cooperation among business remained limited: individual industries could be defeated one at a time. But once the movement began to propose legislation that affected substantial numbers of companies, firms in different industries found it in their interest to cooperate with one another.

Moreover, political conflict between labor and business, which had been relatively dormant since the 1940s, intensified in the mid-1970s. Between 1966 and 1973, labor's share of income increased significantly while the growth of productivity began to decline. As a result, "corporate profitability was squeezed by rising labor costs from 1966 to 1973."[34] This development, along with increased foreign competition, led many firms to seek to limit the power of unions. While unions did not affect all firms equally, wages and work rules affected the economy as a whole—thus making them important to virtually all companies. Not coincidentally, it was the effort to reduce construction wages that, in part, led to the formation of the Business Roundtable. And two of the most extensive efforts at building business coalitions during the second half of the 1970s involved the battles over labor-law reform and the legalization of common situs picketing.

The formation of the Roundtable can be seen as an effort on the part of business firms to institutionalize the process of coalition building. The Roundtable was very selective about the issues on which it took positions. Instead of functioning simply as one big trade association, it made a conscious effort to define political positions that were in the interest of business as a whole—even if they were not necessarily in the interest of each individual firm. For example, the Roundtable opposed subsidies for the merchant marine industry as well as the bailout of Chrysler (a decision that prompted Lee Iacocca's resignation). And, significantly, even firms that supported labor-law reform committed their resources to lobbying against it when the Roundtable decided to oppose the bill.

The efforts of different business organizations to cooperate were not free from tension, of which the Roundtable was one of the most persistent sources. In contrast to most individual corporations and trade associations, the Roundtable attempted to come up with "positive alternatives" to policies with which it disagreed, rather than simply opposing them—a strategy described as "Yes, but . . ." In the words of George Schultz, who served as labor and treasury secretary during the Nixon administration, "It . . . means looking beyond the very narrow interests of the individual firm or industry and offering some connection between what you want and the broader public interest."[35] As a result of its willingness to compromise and the sophistication of its staff work, the Roundtable was able to develop a relatively good working relationship with the Carter administration. For example, it played a critical role in the negotiations that helped fashion the legislation restricting corporate compliance with the Arab boycott of Israel.

But the Roundtable's relationship with Carter's White House created considerable resentment in other segments of the business community: it was accused of being too willing to sacrifice the long-term economic interests of business in order to achieve immediate political gains. One corporate lobbyist criticized the Roundtable for "naively cutting deals with the Administration" that can't be kept in Congress, adding that "the Roundtable sometimes paints itself into a corner and causes a lot of resentment in the business community."[36] Both *Fortune* and the *Wall Street Journal* strongly criticized the Roundtable's endorsement of President Carter's wage-and-price guidelines. *Fortune* observed: "Many large companies are pursuing a strategy that can be described only as one of accommodation and concession. They acquiesce to unwarranted demands by regulators and the White House, and they frequently take positions that are inimical to their long-term interests."[37]

Not only did the Roundtable's "pragmatism" help strain relations between it and other business organizations such as the National Association of Manufacturers (NAM) and the U.S. Chamber of Commerce but it also exacerbated the tensions between large and small companies. In fact, much of the mobilization of small-business owners was due to their resentment of larger firms, which they frequently accused of being too willing to compromise. As one small-business lobbyist put it, "[Large firms] think anything coming from Capitol Hill actually comes from heaven: You can't block it, you can only compromise. So when the sword comes down, all you can do is to ask that it be thrust through you a little slicker, a little cleaner." John Lewis, the president of the Small Business Association, noted, "Big business is a team-mate of big government. . . . But small business is the one element in society that's truly endangered."[38] In general, the newer small business lobbies such as the National Federation of Independent Business (NFIB) tended to be more critical of larger firms than the more established lobbies, such as the Chamber of Commerce and the NAM; indeed, representatives of the former frequently accused the latter of being "tools of big business."

Corporate coalition building—among both firms and business associations—was instrumental in the defeat of common situs picketing, the consumer protection agency, and labor-law reform and in the rollback in the powers of the FTC. The effort of the automobile manufacturers to reduce automobile-emissions standards was, in part, made possible by the support they received from the dealers. On each of these issues, large and smaller firms closely cooperated with one another. On other issues, however, the business community was divided, thus weakening its overall political clout. The conflict between the interests of large and small companies, for example, made it impossible for the oil industry to develop a common position on both energy price decontrols and the windfall profits tax, and the business community was divided over natural-gas deregulation. Likewise, the chemical industry broke ranks over superfund and the business community was unable to agree on a common legislative approach to regulatory reform.

GRASS-ROOTS ORGANIZING

Many of the political defeats experienced by business in the 1960s and 1970s were made possible by the fact that power in Congress had become more evenly distributed. The chairs of committees and the House and Senate leadership no longer were able—even if they were so inclined—to control the flow of legislation. This first became apparent during the second half of the 1960s in the Senate where, not coincidentally, business first experienced many of its most important defeats. The decentralization of power in the Senate made it possible for a relatively large number of individual senators to play an important role in initiating and strengthening legislation. Subsequently, power in Congress became even more fragmented. The number of the Senate's committees and subcommittees increased from 155 in 1967–68 to 205 in 1975–76; in 1979, every Democratic senator save one chaired at least one subcommittee or committee. Following the congressional reforms of 1974, the distribution of power in the House of Representatives began to resemble that of the Senate. The number of committees and subcommittees in that body grew from 175 in 1971–72 to 204 in 1975–76; during the mid-1970s, one of every two Democrats in the House chaired a subcommittee. At the same time, in both Houses, party loyalty declined, thus further weakening the power of the congressional leadership. The result was a Congress increasingly dominated by independents and mavericks. As one political scientist put it, "There are more power bases on the Hill than ever before."[39]

Yet, while these developments made individual representatives more independent of both congressional leadership and their local party organizations, it also made them more susceptible to the pressures of interest groups. Local party organizations and the seniority system had both been a source of stability; they provided individual representatives with a political orientation and frequently served to protect them from external pressures. By contrast, the typical representatives of the mid-1970s—particu-

larly those who had served in the Congress only a short period of time—
were, in effect, free agents. They lacked the support of a political party as
well as its political guidance. Gary Jacobson writes that "members of
Congress accepted, willy-nilly, a kind of Faustian bargain: greater power
over their own electoral fortunes, but at the price of being condemned to
unrelenting entrepreneurial effort."[40]

Following the Second World War, the relative centralization of power
in Congress had favored business, since companies were able to rely on the
support of a handful of strategically placed representatives and senators to
defend their interests, which more often than not involved preserving the
status quo. The shift to more decentralized decision making in Congress
initially favored the public-interest movement. Its leadership was among
the first to recognize that this shift in the distribution of power in Congress
called for a new kind of lobbying strategy—one that emphasized the
mobilization of grass-roots pressures on individual legislators. This new
style of lobbying was used effectively by both the environmental and
consumer movements during the early 1970s. By comparison, business was
somewhat slower to adjust, in part because its insider strategies had
worked so well for so long. But by the second half of the 1970s, business
had become more sophisticated at grass-roots organizing. As *Fortune* noted
in 1978, "Business's greatest new discovery . . . is its power to mobilize
opinion out there in the districts where the 'permanent interests' are
formed."[41] A congressional subcommittee estimated that by 1978, corporations and trade associations were spending between $850 million and
$900 million a year on mobilizing their supporters throughout the United
States.

Business associations that represented large numbers of small firms
made the most extensive and effective use of grass-roots lobbying. As one
liberal Democrat from Nebraska told the *Wall Street Journal* in 1978, "When
a small businessman shows me his books to illustrate what he's up against,
that's a lot more effective with me than some Washington professional in
a three-piece suit."[42] Both the NFIB and the Chamber of Commerce developed extremely sophisticated grass-roots networks. Most of the NFIB's
members were located in suburban and rural districts of the Midwest.
According to *Consumer Reports,* "As merchants in districts with few large
corporations, they are big fish in little ponds." When the NFIB was seeking
to persuade Wisconsin Democrat Alvin Baldus to vote against the establishment of a consumer protection agency, the Chamber located three
prominent small-business owners in his district and arranged for them to
meet with him. The legislator was also presented with a computer printout
listing the names of merchants in his district who had voted in the NFIB

poll against such an agency. He noted, "You give a Congressman a list of people in his district, he invariably looks down it to see whom he knows. He knows the prominent business people in his district. He can't ignore them. Anytime you give him an expression of how they feel, he's going to think twice."[43]

The most effective and sophisticated practitioner of grass-roots lobbying was the Chamber of Commerce: "The network of 2,800 state and local Chambers of Commerce in cities and towns across the country, the 210,000 corporations that are members, and the 1,400 professional and trade associations provide an ideal base for grass-roots lobbying, particularly when the issue before Congress is perceived as a threat by the business community."[44] By 1980, the Chamber of Commerce had established 2,700 "Congressional Action Committees," each made up of about thirty executives who were personally acquainted with their representatives or senators. They were kept informed of developments in Washington by a stream of ACTION bulletins from the Chamber's Washington office and were in turn responsible for maintaining close and continuous contact with their representatives. The Chamber's efforts became so effective that "within a week it can carry out research on the impact of a bill on each legislator's district and through its local branches mobilize a 'grass roots campaign' on the issue in time to affect the outcome of the vote."[45] Citizens' Choice, the Chamber's public-interest lobby, was capable of generating twelve thousand phone calls to legislators in twenty-four hours.

While most grass-roots organizing involved the mobilization of small businesses, a number of large firms also attempted to mobilize both their stockholders and employees. A quarter of the firms polled by the Conference Board in the late 1970s had recently developed a stockholders' program, and the majority of large firms had also developed programs aimed at mobilizing their employees.[46] By 1980, more than 260 major corporations had established grass-roots political organizations. According to one student of grass-roots organizing:

> a prudently managed grassroots program can be a team-building exercise.
> Providing information about legislation that will affect current and future
> company activities will be of interest to many employees at all ranks. . . .
> Building a grassroots program with employees makes them part of the team.
> In Tom Peters' words, we are "making everybody part of the strategic infor-
> mation stream of the business; making everybody an owner."[47]

The company in the vanguard of this effort was Atlantic Richfield (Arco) which in 1975 organized 53,000 of its individual shareholders, 6,000 employees, and 2,000 retired employees into forty-five regional committees. These committees were encouraged to take stands on public policy issues paralleling those of Arco's management and to become politically active in their communities; during the late 1970s, the company spent $750,000 a year on this program.[48] In 1978, the Fluror Corporation of Irvine, California, urged its 20,000 employees to write to their representatives in support of arms sales to Saudi Arabia, and Rockwell provided its headquarters employees with printed postcards so they could urge Congress to support continued production of the B-1 bomber. In 1979, several major oil companies employed a variety of strategies—ranging from pep talks over plant intercoms to company newsletters—to persuade their employees to write their representatives to urge them to oppose the windfall profits tax.

Grass-roots organizing did not make Washington lobbyists obsolete. On the contrary, individual lobbyists such as Thomas Boggs and Charls Walker played an important part in the resurgence of the political power of business in Congress. But their role changed. During the 1950s and 1960s, they or their counterparts had relied upon their access to "key" senators or representatives to advance the interests of their clients. Now their value was based on their ability to orchestrate a grass-roots campaign and to advise companies as to the kinds of strategies likely to appeal to particular representatives and senators. Boggs observed:

Instead of 10 committee chairmen, you now have 70 people running the House and a hundred people running the Senate. In the past, a lobbyist needed to know only about 10 people on the House side. He could call the Speaker of the House or Sherman Adams [an aide to President Eisenhower] at the White House and say, "Help me." All that has changed as power has dispersed. Now you need a law firm to . . . [know] how to use the whole system.[49]

POLITICAL ACTION COMMITTEES

Many of the political strategies developed by business during the 1970s were similar to those that had earlier been successfully employed—and in some cases even pioneered—by the public-interest movement. It was public-interest organizations that first established a substantial physical presence in Washington, that pioneered the art of coalition building, and that made the first effective use of grass-roots lobbying. However, one important political strategy employed by business during the 1970s came not from the public-interest movement but from organized labor. This was the formation of Political Action Committees (PACs) to raise and disperse campaign funds.

Although both the 1971 and 1974 Campaign Finance Amendments had provided the legal authority for corporations to establish PACs, few did so: only 89 companies had established PACs by December 1974 and a year later the number of corporate PACs stood at 139.[50] However, following the Federal Election Committee's (FEC) ruling in SUN-PAC (see chapter 6), which liberalized the use of PACs by corporations, the number of corporate PACs exploded: in the six months following this decision more than 150 corporations established PACs, bringing their total to 294 by May 1976. By December 1976, 433 firms had PACs; two years later there were 784 corporate PACs, and, as of July 1, 1980, 1,204 corporations had them. In 1976, less than a quarter of Fortune 500 companies had PACs; by 1978, 39.6 percent had them; and by 1980, more than half had them.

Both corporate and trade-association PACs played a modest role in financing the 1972 and 1974 elections: together they contributed only $2.7 million to congressional candidates in 1972 and $4.4 million in 1974. Their role became much more important in the 1976 election, when they contributed $10 million—making business for the first time a more important contributor to congressional elections than organized labor. The contrast in the level of corporate campaign contributions between 1976 and 1978 is particularly striking. In 1976, only nine company PACs had receipts and expenditures totaling more than $100,000; two years later twenty-eight companies fell into that category, six of which collected and dispersed more than $200,000. In 1978, business-related PACs contributed $9.8 million to congressional candidates; in 1980, their contributions totaled $19.2 million.[51]

However, the effort of corporations and trade associations to use campaign contributions to influence elections and congressional decisions faced two major obstacles. First, each PAC was limited by law to contributing $5,000 to each candidate, and most actually contributed far less. Throughout the 1970s, the vast majority of corporate PACs raised less than $100,000 per election cycle and in the 1979–80 election cycle, the average corporate PAC contributed only $19,580 to all candidates for federal office. This sum was too modest to have much effect, especially since between 1974 and 1978 *all* PACs contributed less than one-quarter of the funds received by House candidates. Second, most of the executives responsible for administering PAC funds lacked sufficient information about the details of individual races to be able to decide where their funds could be employed most effectively.

To address this problem, the business community established a number of mechanisms to coordinate its campaign spending and thus increase its effectiveness. The most important of these was the Business-Industry Political Action Committee (BIPAC), which had been founded in 1963 by the NAM as a response to the AFL-CIO's Committee on Political Education (COPE). While BIPAC itself contributed directly to candidates, its more important role was to endorse candidates and identify "close races." During each election year, the organization held monthly briefings for 100 to 125 managers of PACs and operated a recorded telephone service that provided daily updates on key congressional races. "A BIPAC endorsement is highly prized by candidates since it sends a signal to other PACs that the selected contender is 'right' on the issues and has a reasonable chance to win."[52] Sixty-one percent of all corporate PACs became affiliated with BIPAC. In addition, the U.S. Chamber of Commerce's PAC—known as the National Chamber Alliance for Politics—issued an "opportunity race" list of its preferred candidates in close races; 59 percent of corporate PACs belonged to the chamber. Four trade-association PACs were also established to coordinate and serve a clearing house for other corporate trade PACs. One, the National Association of Business Political Action Committees, was founded in 1977 as a service organization to provide research and information to the staffs of business PACs; 225 PACs each paid $400 a year for its services, which included evaluating the fifty most important campaigns during each election. Thus, ironically, the restrictions placed on the amount that any one PAC could contribute helped encourage the business community to coordinate its campaign spending—something that individual businessmen had only infrequently attempted to do prior to the legalization of PACs.

Business-affiliated PACs faced another dilemma: Should they use their funds to secure access or to influence electoral outcomes? Should they adopt a low-risk strategy and direct their contributions to candidates whose victory was virtually reassured? Or should they employ a more aggressive approach and seek to transform the partisan and ideological makeup of Congress? In short: To whom did they owe their primary loyalty, their stockholders or the business system? To choose the former would result in most business funds going to incumbents, who during the 1970s were disproportionately liberal Democrats. The latter choice would mean giving relatively large sums to challengers, who were likely to be conservative Republicans.

The business community was deeply divided on this issue. Executives from PACs who chose a "pragmatic" strategy argued that "moderate Democrats are to be preferred to Republicans who are to the right of Franco," and worried that a "hit list" approach to politics "could bring public and Congressional outrage down on all their heads." In turn, the managers of "ideological" corporate PACs countered that pragmatic corporate PACs were "contributing to the enemies of business."[53] In general, companies from traditionally regulated industries such as finance, transportation, utilities, and communication tended to adopt a pragmatic strategy while firms from sectors that were disproportionately affected by the new social regulations—construction, chemicals, rubber, machinery, oil, and lumber and paper—were more ideological in their orientation. The latter viewed the formation of PACs as a way of responding to the recent intrusion of government into their day-to-day operations—an intrusion that many regarded as both burdensome and illegitimate.

In 1976, three-quarters of all contributions by business PACs went to incumbents. A major share of these funds went to chairs of House and Senate committees—all of whom were assured of reelection and most of whom were liberal Democrats. *Congressional Quarterly* noted, "The link between large corporations and conservative Republicans is just about gone. Disaffection between the corporations and the right, smoldering for years, turned into open hostility after campaign finance reports for the 1976 elections showed conservatives just where business was putting its money." This strategy created considerable resentment among Republicans. One conservative Republican complained that "corporate managers are whores. They don't care who's in office, what party or what they stand for. They're just out to buy you."[54] Ronald Reagan told a meeting of business people, "I don't think the Republican Party has received the kind of financial support from corporate PACs that its record deserves. Why does half of the business PAC money go to candidates who may not be friends of business? The best thing that you can hope for by following an anti-business, incumbent contribution policy is that the alligator will eat you last."[55] Another Republican representative observed: "The irony here is that although the public perceives us as carrying business's water, much of big business is really supporting our enemy. Many of these groups care more about buying access to incumbents than any philosophical principles."[56]

In 1978, the strategy of business PACs began to shift—in part as a reflection of the business community's increased political self-confidence and in part as a response to criticism from Republican politicians. Most of this shift occurred in the last months of the 1978 campaign. Through September 30, 1978, Democrats had received nearly half of all corporate PAC contributions. But between October 1 and 23, they received only 29 percent. While 61 percent of all corporate PAC contributions wound up going to incumbents, many were Republicans who faced challenges from liberal Democrats. Sixty-one percent of all corporate contributions to the 1978 campaign—$6.1 million—went to Republicans and only $3.6 million went to Democrats.

What role did campaign spending play in the resurgence of business influence in Congress between 1977 and 1980? It is difficult to disentangle the impact of business campaign contributions from the other components of corporate political activity. It is also hard to distinguish the relative importance of business-related PAC money compared to other sources of campaign financing. Business and trade-association PACs have always given less than a fifth of all funds raised by congressional candidates. The largest single source of campaign financing continues to be individuals who may or may not be interested in the welfare of business. At the same time, many other important sources of campaign funding, such as the monies contributed by professional associations or the funds distributed by right-wing, ideologically oriented PACs such as the National Conservative Political Action Committee, have gone to support candidates who are also likely to be sympathetic to business.

Campaign contributions do not appear to have significantly affected the balance of power between business and the environmental movement; the latter's support in the Congress remained substantial. Nor does the pattern of business campaign spending appear to have had a major influence on energy policy; regional interests remained far more decisive. Corporate campaign contributions did play a role in reducing congressional support of consumer initiatives. However, their most important political effect was to reduce the political influence of organized labor—which ironically had initiated the legislation that legalized their use by business in the first place. Trade unions contributed far more than business to congressional races in 1972 and 1974, slightly less in 1976, and approximately as much in 1978. But after 1978, business pulled far ahead: between 1978 and 1982, campaign contributions from trade unions doubled while business funding tripled. Labor accounted for half of all PAC contributions in 1974; in 1980 and 1982, it accounted for less than a quarter.

Business campaign contributions played a role in making several of the Democratic representatives first elected in 1974 less sympathetic to the political objectives of organized labor than they might otherwise have been—though it should also be noted that most came from districts that had traditionally been Republican.[57] One crucial vote during the 1970s that appears to have been affected by business contributions was the defeat of common situs picketing in the House of Representatives in 1977. The eleven Democrats who voted for the legislation in 1975 but against it in 1977 experienced a decline in financial support from organized labor in 1978. This was more than made up by an increase in contributions from businesses and trade associations; the latter gave twice as much to these candidates in 1978 as they had in 1976. Equally important, during the second half of the 1970s, labor unions provided a decreasing share of funds to Democratic candidates: two-thirds of the PAC money received by Democrats came from organized labor in 1976 and 1978, but by 1980 this figure had declined to 43 percent. In 1980, corporate, trade, and professional PACs supplied more money to Democrats than did organized labor—a development that helped make many Democrats more independent of trade unions and thus more responsive to pressures from business than they would otherwise have been. Charls Walker, a corporate lobbyist, observed that the rise of corporate PACs was "very important in affecting the ideological balance in Congress. Members now have alternative places to look for campaign contributions" and this has helped bring about "a dramatic decline in the influence of the AFL-CIO on Capitol Hill."[58]

The resurgence of corporate power in Congress during the latter 1970s was not due to a change in its partisan composition. The relative strength of the two parties in Congress did not change at all in 1976 and, while the 1978 elections did produce fifteen more Republican representatives and three additional Republican senators, that increase was hardly sufficient to account for the dramatic improvement in the political influence of business in 1979 and 1980. But thanks to the rise of business PACs, it became "possible to have policy realignments without having partisan realignments." Political scientist Gary Jacobson adds, "Democrats are perfectly capable of pursuing [conservative] objectives if they find political profit in doing so. . . . [C]orporations and other business-oriented groups need [not] elect Republicans to have friends in Congress. They can influence policy just as well by helping to elect and reelect cooperative Democrats."[59]

Campaign spending also appears to have played a role in advancing the interests of particular segments of the business community. While partisan identification, constituency interests, and political orientation remain the most important factors in shaping congressional voting patterns, there have been occasions when campaign contributions from business appear to have been decisive in affecting particular outcomes. For example, there was a strong relationship between votes for milk price supports and trucking deregulation and campaign contributions by the dairy and trucking industries, and contributions by the National Automobile Dealers Association appear to have made a decisive difference in the House's decision to veto the FTC's "lemon rule" in 1982.[60]

On balance, however, more sophisticated and intensive business lobbying, and the ability of business to mobilize its supporters in the "grass roots" proved more important than campaign contributions in strengthening the influence of business during the second half of the 1970s. Significantly, companies committed far more resources to lobbying than to funding campaigns; far more firms have hired lobbyists than have organized PACs. In 1978, business spent approximately $5 million on its grass-roots effort to defeat one law, labor-law reform in the Senate. By contrast, all corporate PACs contributed only $10 million to candidates in the 1978 congressional elections. The limited importance of PACs as a vehicle for corporate political influence is further suggested by the decline in their rate of growth after 1980. While the number of corporate PACs nearly tripled between 1976 and 1980, between 1980 and 1984 their number increased by only 30 percent; virtually no new corporate PACs have been established since 1984.

The real significance of corporate PACs may lie in the extent to which they reinforced the other critical changes in corporate political activity that occurred during the 1970s. Thus, corporate PACs can be seen as an extension of both grass-roots organizing and the increased interest in politics on the part of corporate managers. Approximately 150,000 individuals—virtually all of whom were corporate employees—contributed to the political action committees established by the firms for which they worked in 1978 and 1979. Many of these individuals had not previously contributed to a candidate for public office, and two-thirds gave less than $100.[61] Whether or not there was an actual increase in business campaign spending between the 1960s and the 1970s, its character certainly changed. Prior to the legalization of PACs, contributions from business primarily came from a relatively small number of wealthy individuals and senior executives. But PACs enabled many more managers to become politically active. According to one executive, PACs are "one of the most effective vehicles to generate individual participation in the political process to come along in a long time." Another observed, "Our first goal is to involve our people in the political process. Only about five percent of our time is devoted to fund raising and the distribution of funds; 95 percent is devoted to political education. Our philosophy is to encourage long-term understanding and continuing involvement in the political process."[62]

PACs also encouraged companies to coordinate their electoral strategies and thus provided another vehicle for cooperation among different companies and trade associations. In addition, the emergence of corporate PACs reflected both the institutionalization and the professionalization of corporate political participation. Establishing a corporate PAC, soliciting contributions from managers and stockholders and, most important, determining to whom and how much the firm should contribute—all required not only a substantial commitment of corporate resources (while corporations remain legally prohibited from contributing to candidates for federal offices, they are allowed to pay the administrative costs associated with the operation of a PAC) but a substantial degree of political expertise as well. The limited knowledge we have of campaign contributions by businesses prior to 1974 suggests that much of it was ad hoc and personal in nature. For example, there appears to be no pattern underlying business contributions to Richard Nixon's presidential campaign in 1972. By contrast, the formation of PACs by companies has been much more systematic: it is highly correlated with three variables: firm size, industry concentration, and the degree of government regulation.[63]

Redefining the Political Agenda

INTRODUCTION

Increased and more sophisticated political activity constituted one aspect of the effort of business to improve its political effectiveness during the 1970s; the second involved an effort to influence the climate of public and elite opinion. During the 1970s, business leaders became increasingly concerned about the depth and persistence of negative public attitudes toward them. As the chairman of Westinghouse Electric Corporation put it:

> This hostility is real. College professors don't love us. The news media don't trust us. The government doesn't help us. Some special interest groups wish we weren't around. And each of these creates an ever expanding ripple of hostility—professors to their students, citizens' groups to the government, government to the news media and media to the general public. Suddenly we look around and wonder why it's so lonesome out here in business land.[64]

Many executives were genuinely bewildered by the increase in public hostility toward business that had taken place between the mid-1960s and the mid-1970s. After all, were they not providing the public with what it most wanted, namely, economic prosperity? Why, then, had public attitudes toward business become so much more negative? They concluded that the reason business had become less popular was because the public was receiving a distorted view of its economic and social performance. Specifically, the institutions responsible for the production of ideas, namely, the media and the universities, had become dominated by its critics. Accordingly, business had to learn how to compete more successfully in the marketplace of ideas. As one columnist quipped, "If American corporations sold their products as ineptly and clumsily as they have been selling their politics, America's gross national product would be less than Iceland's codfish catch."[65]

The effort of business to change the climate of public and intellectual opinion took place on two levels: one focused on the press and public opinion, the other on the intelligentsia.

BUSINESS AND THE PRESS

It is difficult to exaggerate what one business editor described as "the visceral hatred and contempt that most businessmen had for the media" during the 1970s.[66] An executive in the steel industry informed the American Newspaper Publishers Association in 1976, "People in business have a lot of gripes about the press. Any time a bunch of executives get together these days, you can be sure somebody will start talking about what's wrong with the news media."[67] At the Conference Board meetings of corporate CEOs held in 1974 and 1975, one executive described the press as "forever at war with the creative minds of free men," while another criticized the media for being "destructive and misinformed," and a third asked, "What good is it to have a story if the media won't let you tell it?"[68] A survey of top executives in 1974 reported that 95 percent felt that business did a poorer job than its critics in communicating with the general public,[69] and a survey of large-firm executives conducted in 1979–80 reported that "they perceive the media to be the single most influential institution in America."[70]

The most commonly cited explanation of the poor quality of press coverage of business was the political bias of reporters. W. O'Conner, chairman of the American Association of Advertising Agencies, claimed that "when dealing with business, the news media more often than not are antibusiness," and the editor of *Barron's* noted, "there is no doubt in my mind that there is antibusiness bias in a good deal of reporting. Television, notably the network news programs and documentaries, goes out of its way to exaggerate the flaws of business and minimize the achievements."[71] This contention was supported by a number of studies—frequently cited by executives—indicating that individuals who worked for the nation's most influential news media held social and political views that not only differed sharply from their counterparts in the business community but were considerably more liberal than the nation as a whole.[72]

Other explanations of the perceived bias of the press included the inherently superficial nature of television reporting, the ignorance of most reporters about business, and the interest of the media in "sensationalism." Louis Banks observed:

> Some of these newsmen are like kids with loaded pistols, prowling through the forests of corporate complexity to play games of cowboys and Indians or good guys and bad guys. Their only interest in business is to find a negative story that will get them promoted out of business into Woodward and Bernstein. And by and large this is what too many of their editors also want.[73]

One executive added, "The reporters and the editors in the general media are woefully ignorant of the complexities and ambiguities of corporate operations, and being so, are easy targets for politicians or pressure group partisans with special axes to grind at the expense of business." While many executives had complaints about the print media, most of their ire was directed against television reporting. A manager complained, "Sixty seconds on the evening news tonight is all that is required to ruin a reputation, turn a politician out of office, or impair a company's profitability. The power of the press with today's methods of mass communication has become, in short, the power to destroy." Donald MacNaughton, chairman of Prudential Insurance Company of America, stated, "Most of us are fed up with glib, shallow, inaccurate reporting and editing—tired of journalistic tastes which prefer sensationalism above the fundamentals— which allow a thespian to pose as a newsman."[74] David Mahoney, the CEO of Norton Simon, wrote in the *New York Times* in 1977, "We're not going to suffer silently while being blamed for the sins of the world by self-styled adversaries who substitute a trendy distrust for objective standards of accountability."[75]

One way for executives to improve the public image of business was to become more personally visible. During the postwar period, most CEOs had adopted a low public profile and, as a result, few Americans knew the names of the individuals who managed American corporations. On the other hand, many of business's critics, most notably Ralph Nader, had become household names. Thomas Murphy of General Motors told a meeting of fellow CEOs:

> Many of us are not comfortable in the spotlight—or on television. But, since we are intent upon developing a healthier relationship of mutual respect and

confidence with the government and the public, it is the individual—the flesh-and-blood man who exhibits such qualities himself—who must humanize the corporate image. Through us, the public must see corporations in the same human terms that they see the President, George Meany, or Ralph Nader.[76]

Beginning around 1973, senior executives and plant managers began to solicit the assistance of consultants that specialized in advising executives how to deal with the press. The president of Shell Oil, who had taken J. Walter Thompson's Dialog Telecommunications Development Course, told *Business Week,* "I enrolled because I am not a natural to appear on the television set or to be publicly interviewed. This business of communicating has become as important as finding oil." A public-relations executive added, "Our greatest market seems to be among the companies where Ralph Nader has just been."[77] More than half of the chief executive officers of four hundred large corporations surveyed in 1979 felt that they should take their "views on public policy issues" to "the people" through personal media appearances.[78]

Another strategy was to appeal to the public through advertising. Between 1970 and 1978, annual expenditures for advertising to improve the corporate image or promote goodwill increased from $149 million to $330 million. The primary purpose of these expenditures was to enhance the company's reputation among specific constituencies. Most of these ads tended to be relatively uncontroversial, generally emphasizing the firm's technological leadership, its commitment to public and community service, and the contribution of its products and services to the quality of American life. Corporate sponsorship for noncommercial public television can also be seen as a form of image advertising. While its audience is relatively small, it is composed of people whose opinions matter to business—highly educated and relatively affluent individuals with an interest in current events. Corporate grants to the Public Broadcasting System (PBS) increased from $3.3 million in 1973 to $22.6 million in 1979. Approximately half of all corporate funds contributed to public television during the 1970s came from the oil industry—leading to the suggestion that PBS actually stood for "Petroleum Broadcasting Network."

Companies and trade associations also began to make greater use of "advocacy advertising," a specialized form of institutional or corporate advertising whose purpose is to persuade the public of the merits of the corporation's view on a particular issue. While individual companies have been running advocacy ads for several decades, its use by business began to increase markedly in the early 1970s. The oil industry responded to public criticism during the first energy crisis by undertaking an extensive advertising campaign that explained its position on divestiture, government regulation, and company profitability. Subsequently, scores of companies and industries began to run such campaigns. A survey by the Association of National Advertisers, in 1974, of 114 large companies found that 30 to 35 percent of corporate advertising addressed environmentalism, energy-related issues, or the capitalist system.[79] Corporations spent approximately $100 million on advocacy advertising in 1975 and $140 million in 1976. Several steel firms bought advertising space to explain their position on import restrictions and pollution controls. Union Carbide ran a highly visible campaign on energy conservation policy, and Chase Manhattan purchased a series of advertisements to show the need for greater capital formation by business.

In the mid-1970s, the American Electric Power Company ran a multimillion-dollar campaign opposing the use of scrubbers and a number of other utilities placed ads stressing the importance of coal and nuclear power as sources of energy. In 1976, the Advertising Council launched a multimillion-dollar, multiyear campaign designed to inform the American public of its stake in the preservation and prosperity of the American economic system. In 1977, one trade association, the Caloric Control Council, employed advocacy advertising to build grass-roots support for legislation aimed at overruling the Food and Drug Administration's (FDA) ban of the use of the artificial sweetener saccharin. That same year, the chemical industry spent more than $10 million to counter its poor public image in an unsuccessful attempt to head off a congressional effort to create a $6 billion "superfund" to clean up spills and waste sites.

Mobil's use of advocacy advertising was particularly visible. In 1969, Mobil concluded that an energy crisis was likely to emerge within a few years and that the oil industry would find itself politically vulnerable. Its newly appointed vice president for public relations, Herbert Schmertz, decided that the industry needed to improve its credibility with the public. In 1970, the *New York Times* announced that it would sell advertising space on its op-ed page, and Mobil, recognizing that this page was regularly read by the nation's opinion leaders, decided to purchase space in the lower right-hand corner. Its first ad was intentionally provocative: it urged the nation to devote more resources to constructing mass transit. It also attracted considerable attention: Mobil, in Schmertz's words, had "crossed the line from low profile to going public."[80] The ads ran at irregular intervals until the end of 1971. In the middle of 1971, the firm, faced by growing pressures from the environmental movement, decided to run the ads weekly, making Mobil, in effect, a regular *Times* columnist. Subsequently, weekly space was also purchased in the *Washington Post*, the *Boston Globe*, the *Chicago Tribune*, the *Los Angeles Times*, and the eastern edition of the *Wall Street Journal*. During the first energy crisis, Mobil's op-ed ads appeared in 103 newspapers around the United States.

While a large portion of Mobil's ads dealt with issues of particular concern to the oil industry, they also addressed a variety of other issues, including government spending, tax and trade policy, government regulation of industry, and the liberal bias of the media. About two-thirds expressed Mobil's viewpoint on specific public-policy issues. Their underlying theme was the contribution that business makes to the welfare of society and the need for public policies that recognized that contribution. The ads themselves were argumentative—and occasionally strident—but written in a style designed to make them as readable as the columns that surrounded them. In an ad published in 1984, the company wrote that Mobil continues its campaign because it does not "want to be like the mother-in-law who comes to visit only when she has problems and matters to complain about. We think that a continuous presence in this space makes sense for us. And we hope, on your part, you find us informative occasionally, or entertaining, or at least infuriating. But never boring. After all, you did read this far, didn't you?"[81]

Mobil's public-relations efforts have been highly controversial. While some executives have applauded the company for "recognizing opposing views and presenting corporate positions in a positive way," others have accused the firm of being "too strident" and of "preaching to the converted." Clearly, the ads have given Mobil a distinctive corporate identity, but it is unclear whether they have helped it politically. One survey of congressional and other government leaders found that while virtually all read them, the majority felt that the ads contained little information of value and that they lacked credibility. On the other hand, according to Schmertz, "If you went back over ten years you would find that many of the things that we have espoused and which were unpopular or criticized at the time have now become pretty well accepted."[82] He added, "We have established a franchise for a particular kind of view and have developed a free-market constituency that is growing. We're practicing the ancient and honorable art of pamphleteering. It goes back hundreds and hundreds of years. I look at newspapers merely as a delivery vehicle for our pamphlets."[83]

Schmertz also became involved in a number of well-publicized quarrels with the television networks. The company's public-relations department closely monitored everything written or broadcast about the oil industry and Schmertz repeatedly challenged the accuracy of television coverage.

Schmertz also repeatedly attempted to purchase time on television to counter the descriptions of the industry on the television news, but the networks refused to sell it to him. (As a general rule, the networks have not allowed corporations to purchase time to present their positions on controversial issues—a position that was upheld by the Supreme Court in 1973.[84] Only product and noncontroversial "image" advertising by business have been permitted.) Schmertz labeled this policy "repressive censorship," and even offered to purchase time for rebuttal by the industry's critics. In 1980, Mobil attempted to buy time for a one-minute commercial to show that Mobil's return on equity was less than that of ABC, CBS, and NBC, but all three networks refused to run it. That same year, Schmertz also protested Ralph Nader's appearance on "Saturday Night Live," claiming that the show was providing Nader with a forum for his political views. Schmertz wanted to purchase commercial time in the following week's program to reply to Nader's criticism of the energy industry, but NBC refused to sell it to him. The network did offer Schmertz a guest spot on the comedy program, but he turned down the offer, claiming that this forum was inappropriate.

Mobil was not the only firm to quarrel with the television networks. Both Exxon and Shell filed formal complaints about NBC's unflattering coverage with the National News Council, an independent group established to monitor media performance. Bristol-Myers sued CBS for $25 million over a report on the network's New York station that questioned advertising claims for two of its products. The American Family Life Assurance Company filed a $275 million libel suit against ABC-TV, claiming it had used hidden cameras to present a deliberately distorted coverage of cancer insurance, and Kaiser Aluminum and Chemical Corporation sued ABC for $40 million on the grounds that its "20/20" program had presented misleading information to the public about the safety of aluminum electrical wire sold by the firm. All of these cases were settled out of court.

After Kaiser ran full-page ads in ten newspapers alleging that the "20/20" report constituted "Trial by Television," ABC, in an unprecedented move, allowed the company to air an unedited four-minute rebuttal on a subsequent episode of "20/20." The Illinois Power Company, after being criticized by "60 Minutes" for its management of the construction of a nuclear power plant, got "60 Minutes" to retract two of its allegations on the air. Illinois Power also produced a forty-two-minute rebuttal of the "60 Minute" episode, entitled "60 Minutes: Our Reply," and distributed more than two thousand copies to corporations, trade associations, journalism schools, and community organizations. While the utility's video was never shown on television, another video rebuttal, a one-hour film that challenged ABC's documentary on the health hazards created by the production of uranium, was shown on a few local stations in the Midwest.

In 1976, a number of corporations and foundations joined together to establish the Media Institute to monitor the media's coverage of business. The institute published a biweekly summary of economics and business reporting on network evening news and, in 1973, issued a handbook on communications law reviewing "administrative and judicial remedies available to individuals and corporations who are the subject of biased, distorted, or inaccurate media coverage."[85] It also published a highly critical study of television's coverage of the 1973–74 and 1978–79 oil crises.

It is difficult to assess the political impact of all these efforts. Notwithstanding the vast sums spent on improving the image of business, public attitudes toward business were only slightly more positive in 1980 than they were in 1974. The complaints of business executives about the "bias and ignorance" of press and media coverage may have had a more discernible impact: during the late 1970s, the quality of business reporting did improve and much of the media became somewhat less critical of business. However, this latter change may have been primarily a response to a more conservative political climate: on balance, the media appear less to have shaped changing public attitudes toward business over the last two decades than to have reflected them.

THE INTELLECTUAL DEBATE

The decline in the political fortunes of business from the mid-1960s through the mid-1970s was accompanied not only by an increase in popular antagonism to business, but also by a shift in the political tone of intellectual and academic discourse. Like journalists, the social-science faculty at the nation's elite universities held political views that were significantly more liberal than those shared by business executives, as well as the American public as a whole.[86] Consequently, many executives blamed the nation's universities, along with the press, for their loss of political influence. One senior manager noted that "a large portion of our educational faculties throughout America have an anti-establishment bias." Another complained, "I asked a college professor I know to suggest a book to me that defends the free enterprise system. You know all he could suggest to me? Adam Smith!"[87] A survey of corporate executives, conducted in 1979, reported that 80 percent believed that "academics were too critical of business, and 75 percent contended that social-science programs in universities are 'so slanted on the liberal side as to seriously impair the future objectivity and judgment of college graduates.' "[88] Walter Wriston, the CEO of Citibank, observed, "It takes about twenty years for a research paper at Harvard to become a law. There weren't any people feeding the intellectual argument on the other side."[89] In 1977, Henry Ford II resigned from the Ford Foundation's board of trustees, contending that while the "Foundation is a creature of capitalism . . . it is hard to discern recognition of this fact in anything the Foundation does [or in] the universities that are the beneficiaries of the Foundation's great programs."[90]

In sharp contrast to its critics, the business community was slow to appreciate the political significance—and power—of ideas and intellectuals. William Broody, Jr., whose father founded the American Enterprise Institute in the early 1960s, recalled, "The great frustration my father faced was convincing the business community of the relevance of ideas to the practical world of American society. That wasn't what they were about. They were about business." John Post, the executive director of the Business Roundtable, stated: "I can remember the early days [of the American Enterprise Institute], when chief executive officers didn't want to have anything to do with these goddamned professors. Now we understand more about the impact of ideas."[91] Irving Kristol observed in 1977:

> Businessmen who cannot even persuade their own children that business is a morally legitimate activity are not going to succeed, on their own, in persuading the world of it. You can only beat an idea with another idea, and the war of ideas and ideologies will be won or lost within the "new class," not against it. Business certainly has a stake in this war, but for the most part seems blithely unaware of it.[92]

Both Irving Kristol and William Simon played an important role in persuading the business community that ideas had political consequences and that the business community should use its philanthropy to advance its political goals. Kristol wrote in the *Wall Street Journal* in 1977 that it was "absurd" for business persons or corporations to "give money to institutions whose views or attitudes they disapprove of." He urged "corporations to give support to those elements of the 'new class'—and they exist, if not in large numbers—which do believe in the preservation of a strong private sector."[93] In *A Time for Truth,* published the following year, William Simon argued that "American business was financing the destruction of free enterprise." He stated: "Funds generated by business (by which I mean profits, funds in business foundations and contributions from individual businessmen) must rush by multimillions . . . to funnel desperately needed funds to scholars, social scientists, writers and journalists who understand the relationship between political and economic liberty."[94]

It was Kristol who, according to one of his colleagues, "put spine into the business community."[95] Once described as "the godfather" of the neoconservative intelligentsia, he co-founded and edited one of its most influential journals, *The Public Interest*, was a senior fellow of the American Enterprise Institute, and contributed regularly to the editorial page of the *Wall Street Journal*.[96] Equally important, he played a key role in matching foundation dollars to promising projects and writers. Kristol persuaded the Smith Richardson Foundation to fund the writing of Jude Wanniski's *The Way the World Works*, which popularized the ideas behind supply-side economics.[97] He also served on the board of directors of five corporations. In his own words, "I am a liaison to some degree between intellectuals and the business community."[98] William Simon's importance came from his position as president of the John Olin Foundation, a post he assumed in 1977. Under his leadership, the foundation began to play a large role in supporting conservative research and scholarship. It endowed chairs and fellowships at the Heritage Foundation, the Hoover Institution, and the American Enterprise Institute. It also provided funds for the Media Institute, the Law and Economics Center at Emory University, and the Center for the Study of American Business at Washington University. The foundation disperses about $3 million a year.

In 1978, Simon and Kristol helped establish the Institute for Educational Affairs. Its purpose was to serve as a clearinghouse for corporate philanthropy, helping to connect corporations and foundations with conservative thinkers in need of funds. It financed more than fifty new conservative student newspapers and journals and provided grants to established journalists and to editorial interns at various conservative publications. In 1981, the institute dispersed about $4.7 million directly and served as a broker to smaller companies that contributed an additional $2 million.

A number of other foundations, besides the John Olin Foundation, have provided funds to support various business-oriented programs.[99] After R. Randolph Richardson assumed the presidency of the Smith Richardson Foundation in 1973, that foundation's funds were redirected to conservative causes. Smith Richardson provided funds to enable George Gilder to write *Wealth and Poverty*, an intellectual defense of capitalism published in 1981. In 1973, Richard Scaife, an heir to the Mellon family fortune, became chairman of the Sarah Scaife Foundation, which in the next seven years gave $3 million to the Law and Economics Center, $4 million to the Heritage Foundation, and $2 million to various media projects, including Accuracy in Media. Scaife also provided $500,000 to a TV station in Erie, Pennsylvania, WQLN, to underwrite Milton Friedman's TV series, "Time to Choose," and nearly $4 million to conservative public-interest law firms. It has also been a major financial supporter of *The Public Interest.* Other prominent conservative foundations include the Adolph Coors Foundation, the J. Howard Pew Foundation, and the Bechtel Foundation. In addition, the Smithkline Beckman Corporation, a pharmaceutical company, donated $500,000 a year to public policy research.

In spite of Kristol's and Simon's admonitions, most corporate giving to universities was not politicized.[100] Corporations continued to support schools, centers, and research programs that addressed subjects of particular importance to firms, primarily in the sciences and engineering. However, a number of firms did make a conscious effort to create a more probusiness climate on the nation's campuses. Between 1974 and 1978, companies endowed more than forty chairs of "free enterprise." While a few were in business schools, most were in liberal undergraduate colleges; their purpose was to improve the reputation of business among students. As an Alabama bank president who endowed a chair put it, "I'd like my children to be able to do in business what I've done. And the way things are going in this country, misinformed attitudes on the part of the public, combined with increasing government regulation of the economy, will soon make this impossible."[101] A number of business schools also received funds to conduct "executive in residence" programs. According to the Council for Financial Aid to Education, in 1978 there were approximately 100 programs linking corporations and campuses, and firms were spending approximately $10 million to influence the teaching of business and economics in the nation's high schools. The Phillips Petroleum Company donated $800,000 to produce five films on "American Enterprise" that were seen by more than eight million students.

In the Fall 1986 issue of *Dissent,* the magazine's editor, Irving Howe, recalled that "some nine or ten years ago" he had noticed in a corporate institutional advertisement on the op-ed page of the *New York Times* a quotation from the literary critic Lionel Trilling. Howe observed, "This struck me as a turning point in intellectual life . . . corporate America [had] discovered the pragmatic uses of ideology, the importance of entering intellectual debate."[102] Howe's observation was an insightful one. As one corporate president put it, "business is slowly coming to realize that the long-term success of their companies depends just as much on social policy as on management. Think tanks are useful tools."[103] Owing to the willingness of a handful of foundations and a large number of corporations to fund conservative research, by the end of the 1970s there were a number of think tanks sponsoring studies and publishing research that frequently lent support to public policies favored by business.[104]

The most important conservative think tank was the American Enterprise Institute (AEI) which became a kind of right-of-center counterpart to the more liberal and older Brookings Institution. In 1970, the AEI had a budget of less than $1 million and a staff of only 19. A decade later, it had a budget of $10.4 million and a staff of 135. In 1977, the AEI released 54 studies, organized 22 conferences, prepared 15 analyses of important legislative proposals, published 7 journals and newsletters, sent a series of editorials to 105 newspapers, and produced a public-affairs program that was aired on more than 300 television stations. A major share of the AEI's efforts focused on government regulation. It published scores of research monographs on this topic, and in 1977 began to publish a bimonthly magazine called *Regulation*. The Center for the Study of American Business at Washington University was founded in 1973 by Murray Weidenbaum and has an annual budget of approximately $750,000. Its primary output consists of research monographs on economics and regulatory policy. During the second half of the 1970s, Weidenbaum emerged as the leading academic critic of government regulations. In 1978, he and his associates at the center estimated the total cost of all government regulation—economic as well as social—at $100 billion. Their analysis attracted considerable public attention: a version of it was published in *Reader's Digest*. Although its methodology was sharply criticized by public-interest groups, Weidenbaum's figure became virtually a symbol of the "excessive" cost of government regulation of business.[105]

The Heritage Foundation was founded in 1973 with a grant from Joseph Coors. It grew rapidly: by 1980–81, its annual budget was $5.2 million. (Heritage is unique among conservative research institutions in that it also relies heavily on direct mail: 140,000 individuals each contribute a minimum of $25.) Heritage is also primarily policy-oriented. At the heart of the organization are several dozen policy analysts, each of whom specializes in a particular policy area. They work closely with the staffs of sympathetic members of Congress, tracking the progress of particular legislation and preparing position papers to influence the policy debate on relatively short notice. This foundation also developed an Academic Bank, composed of approximately 1,600 scholars. It "was instrumental in transforming isolated conservative intellectuals into a network," by providing a way for them to have a direct influence on the shaping of policy in Congress.[106]

The interests of institutions such as AEI and the Heritage Foundation extend far beyond business-government relations. They have addressed issues ranging from American foreign policy to the relationship between religion and capitalism. In the area of business-government relations, a disproportionate amount of their efforts have been focused on government regulation. These studies can be viewed as a direct counterpart of the various reports, studies, and publications of public-interest groups in the late 1960s and early 1970s that played an important role in promoting and legitimating expanded government controls over business. They argued that the proponents of regulation had in many cases exaggerated the significance of the problems they were trying to ameliorate and that many of the government rules and regulations were both inefficient and ineffective—in some cases even exacerbating the problems they were designed to reduce. These studies proposed a large number of regulatory reforms, the most important of which was for government to carefully weigh the costs and benefits of regulations before issuing them.

A decade earlier, virtually the entire corpus of writing on such topics as occupational health and safety and consumer and environmental protection was aimed at making a case for additional government control of business. By contrast, the arguments against regulation advanced by trade associations tended to be both poorly researched and unpersuasive. But by the end of the 1970s, corporations and trade associations could draw upon an extensive body of literature—much of it professional and competent—that, in many important respects, buttressed their political positions. Thus, for every horror story about corporate irresponsibility that had circulated at the beginning of the decade, by its end there was a matching horror story about the shortcomings of government regulation. The movement for regulatory reform, the case for lower taxes on business, and the impetus for economic deregulation—all of which moved to the forefront of the domestic political agenda toward the end of the 1970s—owed much to the scholarship funded by these conservative think tanks. They also provided many of the people who played an important role in shaping and implementing the Reagan administration's regulatory policies, and they played a decisive role in both formulating and publicizing what became the Reagan administration's most important contribution to economic policy, namely, supply-side economics. More generally, they contributed to the growth of public skepticism about the appropriateness—and effectiveness—of government intervention in the economy.

Not all of their studies endorsed the positions of the companies that helped fund them. Both *Regulation* and *The Public Interest* repeatedly published articles that opposed subsidies for particular industries, and virtually every conservative think tank remained firmly committed to both free trade and economic deregulation. In this sense, they were not so much probusiness as they were antigovernment and promarket. At the same time, they also helped change the tone of political discourse within the business community. During the 1950s, the political positions of business tended to be expressed in highly ideological terms: they consisted largely

of denunciations of "creeping socialism" and praises of "free enterprise."[107] During the 1970s, the business community did not become less
antagonistic toward government; if anything, thanks to increased government regulation, business distrust of government increased. But the hostility of business to government was now articulated differently: instead of
rhetorical denunciations of big government, it now was expressed in terms
of relatively sophisticated and well-documented analyses of the economic
effect of specific government policies on business and of criticisms of the
scientific basis of health and safety regulations. Both these perspectives
were consistently articulated by the *Wall Street Journal,* whose editorial page,
under the direction of Robert Bartley, became a leading forum for business
views on economic and regulatory policy.

At the same time, a mutually supportive relationship developed between conservative intellectuals and business. During the 1960s, corporate capitalism had relatively few defenders among the intelligentsia.
Conservatives such as William Buckley, Jr., and Clinton Rossiter had not
been particularly interested in business-government relations. While *Capitalism and Freedom* by Milton Friedman, which was published in 1962, did
attract considerable attention, its ideological rigidity limited its intellectual appeal.[108] Friedman, like Friedrich von Hayek, who had published
the *Road to Serfdom* almost two decades earlier, was still fighting the battles
of the 1930s: their free-market philosophy was well outside the then-
prevailing political and intellectual consensus.[109] The result was a business ideology—described in such studies as *The American Business Creed*—
that was remarkably out of touch with the political and economic
realities of post–New Deal America. It subsequently proved woefully
inadequate to respond to the arguments for greater government intervention made by social critics such as John Kenneth Galbraith and Robert
Heilbroner.

However, beginning in the early 1970s, a number of liberal intellectuals
became more conservative. At first, neoconservatism had little to do with
business or economics; it largely represented a response to the failures of
the Great Society, the youth culture of the 1960s, and the New Left's
criticism of American foreign policy. But about the middle of the 1970s,
the neoconservatives began to discover the business corporation. Initially,
they were not so much supportive of business as they were opposed to its
critics. They recognized that both they and business had the same "enemies": namely, the "new class." The writings of these intellectuals on
business emphasized less the economic impact of regulation than its political significance: they viewed government regulation of corporate social
conduct as an effort by this "class" to remove the control of the nation's

economy from the hands of "ordinary" consumers and workers in order to increase their own power and status. This thesis of a new class defended business, but in a roundabout way. Its primary objective was to attack the motives of the corporation's critics by suggesting that they were in fact no more public-spirited than the business people whose motives they routinely castigated. It was essentially a defensive position that reflected the intellectual climate of the 1970s.

In 1981 and 1982, two important books were published that advanced a serious intellectual justification for capitalism: *Wealth and Poverty* by George Gilder and *The Spirit of Democratic Capitalism* by Michael Novak.[110] Gilder, who had previously written on welfare policy, emphasized the importance of entrepreneurship and described the creation of wealth as not simply an economic process but a spiritual one. His book sold 500,000 copies throughout the world. Novak, who was a resident scholar at AEI and had written widely on religious issues, stressed the links between democratic capitalism and social pluralism. Unlike Kristol, who had only "two cheers" for capitalism, these authors had three. Both works were widely discussed and debated: President Reagan handed a copy of *Wealth and Poverty* to each member of his newly appointed cabinet. By the early 1980s, "capitalism" had once again become a reputable term in American political and intellectual discourse—a development that Kristol subsequently attributed to "a conspiracy among a handful of conservative intellectuals to come up with a 'word to describe the kind of economic and social order we favored.' "[111]

Business was not responsible for the revival of conservative ideology. Nor did it play a role in making many economists more critical of government intervention in the economy. The rise of neoconservatism and the revival of market-oriented economics would have occurred in any event. Rather, the role played by business and by conservative foundations was that of a catalyst: they accelerated the rate at which neoconservative and market-oriented studies were produced and gave them far more visibility and influence than they might otherwise have received. On balance, business did not so much reshape the climate of intellectual debate as it benefited from and, in turn, helped promote a shift that was already occurring.

The Limits of Reform

The effort of business to counter the political influence of the public-interest movement and organized labor in Washington and to reshape public attitudes and intellectual discourse played an important role in the political resurgence of business in the late 1970s and early 1980s. But the increase in the political effectiveness of business was not entirely due to its own efforts. Like the public-interest movement a decade earlier, business was the beneficiary of developments beyond its control.

ECONOMIC DECLINE

The most important of these developments was a change in the public's perception of the performance of the American economy. During the first three years of the Carter administration, the economy actually performed rather well; real GNP growth averaged more than 4 percent. But this growth was accompanied by two highly visible developments which undermined public confidence in the essential strengths of the American economy. The first was inflation, which increased each year between 1976 and 1980, and remained at double-digit levels for three years. The second was a deterioration in the nation's trade balance. After accumulating a surplus in all but three years between 1960 and 1974, the trade balance significantly deteriorated after 1975. The U.S. merchandise balance of trade ran a $9.5 billion deficit in 1976, a $31.1 billion deficit in 1977, a $34 billion deficit in 1978, a $27.6 billion deficit in 1979, and a $25.5 billion deficit in 1980.

Both of these developments had important political consequences. The steady increase in the rate of inflation between 1976 and 1980 created considerable anxiety among the middle class, which had constituted the political base of support for additional government controls over business. While its after-tax income did not decline, since wages also increased, the middle class's confidence in its economic future did. According to a University of Michigan survey of families with incomes of more than $20,000, conducted shortly after Reagan's election, "Their assessment of their current situation is less favorable than in the past three to four years, and it is reaching its lowest level in thirty years. That is the result of decreased expectation plus the cumulative strain of a decade of inflation and sluggish growth in real incomes." *Business Week* observed that this squeeze on the "middle class's standard of living . . . has all but destroyed its confidence in the traditional American dream that if you work hard, you will get ahead."[112]

The immediate political consequence of the middle class's growing anxiety was the so-called tax revolt. It began as a grass-roots movement in cities and states throughout the United States and reached political prominence with the passage of Proposition 13 in California in 1978. Taxes were not a significant cause of the stagnation of real income during the latter part of the 1970s. But because of "bracket creep," Americans were paying more taxes to state and local governments at the same time that their real incomes had stopped increasing. Taxes were thus a convenient scapegoat. Bracket creep created a commonality of interest between the middle class and business: both came to view excessive taxation as the cause of their own economic difficulties. Without this indigenous tax revolt, it is unlikely that the efforts of business to reduce corporate taxes in 1979 would have been as successful. One observer noted that "the tax revolt leaves one with the conviction that the era of steady government expansion in the United States is quite finished."[113]

During the second half of the 1960s, a modest increase in inflation had helped turn the middle class against business. But the persistently high rates of inflation of the second half of the 1970s had precisely the opposite political effect: they helped turn the public against government. Whether or not government spending was a cause of the high rates of inflation in the late 1970s, the public certainly viewed it as such. As a result, people began to sympathize with the argument of business executives that the expansion of government had gone far enough. The result was substantial political support in favor of curbing the size and power of government—a political shift that clearly benefited business. Robert Kuttner noted, "The signal success of political conservatives was to convince a growing public that stagnation resulted from excess government size as well as from misguided government policy."[114]

There was a second important change in the economy during the 1970s. This had to do with the relative salience of international competition. While the 1974–75 recession was certainly provoked by international economic developments, the oil crisis was not generally attributed to any weakness in the relative economic position of the United States; indeed, the first oil shock hurt West Germany and Japan far more than it did the United States. But, throughout the 1970s, imports of manufactured goods steadily increased in a large number of sectors. In spite of the depreciation of the dollar at the end of the 1970s, America's share of the world market for manufactured goods declined by 23 percent in the course of that decade. Between 1975 and 1977, imports of steel increased from 13.5 percent of domestic consumption to 17.8 percent. Likewise, the number of imported cars grew significantly during the second half of the 1970s; by 1979, foreign automobile producers had captured nearly 22 percent of the American domestic market—as compared with 8 percent in 1970. Each American manufacturer announced major layoffs and the nation's third largest automobile firm, Chrysler, tottered on the verge of bankruptcy. Numerous articles documented both the superior quality of Japanese-made products and the growing trade deficit of the United States vis-à-vis Japan. Robert Reich wrote that, as of 1980, the United States had "the highest percentage of obsolete plants, the lowest percentage of capital investment, and the lowest growth in productivity of any major industrial society other than Great Britain."[115]

The nation's economic difficulties during the late 1970s and early 1980s became associated with what *Business Week* characterized in its special issue on "The Reindustrialization of America," published on June 30, 1980, as a "drastic new loss of competitive strength." The magazine's editors argued that "the decline in the U.S. economy had advanced so far that the public as a whole has begun to sense a need for change" and went on to suggest that "the jolt provided by the current recession has created an environment in which the public is ready to reindustrialize America." The pollster Daniel Yankelovitch observed, "The state of mind of the public is worried sick and in a panic . . . people know there is something wrong. That pushes them into working out accommodations that make economic sense."[116]

Notwithstanding Yankelovitch's prediction, no consensus emerged about how the United States should go about reindustrializing itself. But the sudden increase in the public's awareness of the vulnerability of American industry to competition from firms in other industrial nations had an important influence on the public's perception of business: it meant that for the first time since the 1930s the future of the large American corporation could no longer be taken for granted. Far from being a "private government" with the ability to dominate its external environment, the large business corporation now appeared quite vulnerable to market forces. Henceforth, instead of being almost exclusively preoccupied with how to control the large industrial corporation, the American public would now also begin to discuss what measures were needed to assure its survival. As one observer put it: "Big business in America is no longer viewed as all-powerful; it is more often seen as bloodied by foreign competition and in need of all the help it can get."[117]

The deterioration in the performance of the American economy also made the public more sympathetic to business criticisms of government regulation. Prior to the mid-1970s, few Americans had any reason to be concerned about the effect of regulation on the profitability of particular sectors of the economy. It was only when business began to talk about the "macro" effects of government regulation that its criticism of regulation began to make political headway: "The significance of this ideological redefinition cannot be overemphasized."[118] The public-interest movement had earlier contended that increased government regulation was necessary because of market failures. Now business stood this argument on its head: its supporters contended that it was government regulation that threatened the success of the market system as a whole. Whether or not this analysis was correct, it was certainly made credible by the evident economic difficulties that highly visible sectors of the American economy, such as autos and steel, were experiencing at the end of the 1970s. Lipset and Schneider wrote in 1979: "During the second half of the 1970s a majority of the public believed that government regulation increased inflation . . . and most . . . believed that money spent by companies in meeting government regulatory requirements 'has significantly reduced the amount business can invest in the expansion and modernization of plant and equipment.'"[119]

As long as the political agenda was dominated by a concern about "micro" market failures, the public-interest movement was in a position to offer a politically coherent and economically plausible policy alternative, namely, increased regulation. But once the public became concerned about long-term economic growth, public-interest activists found that they had become largely irrelevant: having based their political program on policies designed to ameliorate the effect of economic growth, they had no practical solutions to offer when that growth appeared to have become problematic. They did, of course, vigorously challenge the contention of business that social regulation was a cause of the nation's economic difficulties. But the burden of proof had shifted: now it was government, not business, that was forced to justify itself.

The growing saliency of economic issues during the latter part of the 1970s also affected the political outlook of the "baby boomers," who during the previous decade had been far more hostile to business than the public as a whole. The kinds of government solutions to the nation's economic difficulties advanced by some social critics and trade unions threatened not only the autonomy of business people, but also the baby boomers' own aspirations for individual economic success as well. In particular, they emphatically did *not* favor "New Deal type" solutions to the nation's economic difficulties—a perspective that was reinforced as they became older and moved into the labor market. Pat Caddell reports:

It is a cliche to say that baby boomers are essentially more liberal on social and cultural matters and more conservative on economic issues, but the truth of the matter is, that is what they are. . . . The baby boomers were . . . anti-New Deal in terms of their suspicion of the size of government and of government solutions to economic problems. . . . It partly had to do with a philosophy . . . of "anti-bigness." It had to do with a discomfiting feeling about the government, and a yearning for individual success.[120]

Moreover, by the late 1970s, the baby-boom generation had grown up. Robert Samuelson observed in 1978:

People grow older, and as the "baby boom" generation—which exerts a profound influence on public opinion—enters its late twenties and early thirties, it may relax its reflexive anti-business attitudes, if only out of self-defense. Even those who have not gone to work for corporate America know many who have. It is difficult to consider all your friends monsters.[121]

The economic conservatism of much of the upper middle class drove a wedge between it and organized labor. While the former was a strong proponent of economic deregulation, trade unions preferred the status quo: unions worked closely with their respective industries to oppose reductions in the government's authority over prices and service. Likewise, while unions favored assistance to industries in economic difficulty, the baby boomers generally opposed restrictions on imports and bailouts. And whereas a decade earlier, a significant segment of the middle class had blamed business for many of the nation's economic problems, now they began to attribute to labor at least a portion of the blame for the inability of American firms to compete successfully in world markets.

Unions had been able to use their strength within the Democratic party during the first part of the decade to press for policies such as maintaining price controls on energy and increasing government's expenditures to reduce unemployment. But by the end of the decade, the ability of unions to shape the domestic political agenda of the Democratic party in Congress had eroded. Democratic representatives were now more responsive to the demands of their middle-class constituents for economic deregulation, lower taxes, less government spending, and free trade—policies sharply at odds with those of the trade-union movement. The trade-union movement had enjoyed considerable political influence when its demands and those of the new class coincided. But when the unions sought to advance their own legislative agenda after 1976, they were remarkably unsuccessful.

On the other hand, trade unions, which prior to 1973 had been relatively strong supporters of environmental regulation, faced with stagnant real wages and increased unemployment, now increasingly began to side with business. Significantly, it was the United Auto Workers' support of the relaxation of automobile-emissions standards which handed the environmental movement its most important legislative defeat during the second half of the 1970s. As a result, by the end of the 1970s, the alliance between the trade-union and public-interest movements that had been so successful in challenging business between the mid-1960s and the mid-1970s had become severely strained: now it was the turn of business to divide and conquer.

THE BACKLASH AGAINST REGULATION

The increased public support for business criticisms of regulation during the second half of the 1970s was due not only to the performance of the economy. It was also a response to increased public awareness of its shortcomings. There is a striking parallel between the public's reaction to the Great Society in the early 1970s and its perception of government regulation of corporate social conduct later in the decade: in each case, the expansion of government led to consequences that were unanticipated— and in some cases even perverse. By the late 1970s, government regulation was no longer seen simply as a solution to the problems created by business: it had become a problem in its own right as well.

In some cases, regulatory officials had sought to impose restrictions on business that significant segments of the public regarded as constituting an unnecessary interference with their freedom of choice. The first popular backlash against regulation was in response to a 1974 National Highway Traffic Safety Administration (NHTSA) requirement that all automobiles be equipped with an interlock system to prevent them from starting if the driver had not put on a seat belt. Popular resentment against the interlock was so overwhelming that Congress immediately passed legislation that voided it. Three years later, in 1977, an identical public reaction occurred in response to the FDA's decision to ban the use of the artificial sweetener saccharin. Once again, Congress quickly enacted a statute limiting the authority of a regulatory agency over business.

In other cases, the public-interest movement and its political allies appeared to be supporting regulation for its own sake. While the regulatory statutes initiated by Michael Pertschuk when he worked for the Senate Commerce Committee represented a response to real, widely recognized problems, his proposal, as chair of the FTC, to restrict advertising on children's television programs struck many as gratuitous and unnecessary. The consumer movement's most important political priority in 1977, namely, the establishment of a consumer protection agency, was viewed in similar terms. In contrast to the EPA or OSHA, it was seen as simply adding another layer of government bureaucracy. Likewise, while there was a broad consensus about the need to protect endangered species at the time that statute was enacted in the early 1970s, the June 1978 decision of the Supreme Court, which halted construction of the Tennessee Valley Authority's $100 million Tellico Dam in order to save the habitat of a tiny species of minnow of which few had ever heard, struck many as a kind of parody. In response, Congress soon declared the Tellico Dam to be in compliance with the Endangered Species Act. The cumulative effect of all these events was to weaken the credibility of advocates of regulation.

At about the same time, evidence began to accumulate that government regulation had sometimes produced results that were both unanticipated and undesirable. For example, the enactment of the "sunshine laws," which had opened up committee legislative drafting sessions to the public in order to dilute the power of business lobbyists, had precisely the opposite effect. They enabled business lobbyists to monitor the votes of each elected official more closely. Similarly, Common Cause's success in imposing a ceiling on the outside income of members of Congress helped make that legislative body a preserve for individuals of inherited wealth. Likewise, in the two years following the passage of the ERISA, more than ten thousand companies dropped their pension plans and 320,000 workers lost their pensions, owing to the fact that the cost of compliance with the statute's extremely complex requirements was considered too great by many smaller firms.

In 1972, the Consumer Product Safety Commission (CPSC) required that all children's sleepwear be treated with a flame retardant chemical, a rule which was mandated by the Flammable Fabrics Act. The immediate effect was to increase the cost of children's pajamas and nightgowns. Its long-term impact was revealed in the spring of 1977 when the CPSC banned the chemical Tris, which had been used to treat over 40 percent of the garments, on the grounds that it caused cancer. Parents had been paying a higher price in order to expose their children to a carcinogen. The Poison Prevention Act made it extremely difficult for elderly people with arthritic fingers to open bottles containing over-the-counter medicines. And the Truth in Lending Act, which was enacted in order to enable borrowers to understand better the full costs of credit, resulted in a set of requirements so complex as to make the resulting disclosures unintelligible. The liberal *Washington Monthly* commented, in the fall of 1977, that "these unintended effects, which range from the laughable to the horrendous . . . eat away at the confidence of citizens in their government . . . add[ing] up to a disillusionment that's quite widespread."[122] As a result, by the end of the 1970s the public-interest movement had lost much of the moral halo that had been the source of its earlier success: the political objectives of the movement, and the public in whose name it spoke, no longer appeared to be identical.

Government regulation had another equally unanticipated effect: it had increased federal controls over many of the nation's nonbusiness institutions, most notably local governments and universities. By the late 1970s, many of the complaints of mayors and college administrations regarding the regulations imposed by the federal government echoed those of corporate executives. In 1979, the Institute for Contemporary Studies, a conservative think tank based in San Francisco, published a collection of essays on government regulation of universities.[123] In the book's introductory essay, Robert Hatfield, the chief executive officer of the Continental Group, after noting that "between 1965 and 1977, the number of pages in the Federal Register devoted to regulations of higher education grew from 92 to more than 1,000," concluded that, "many members of the university community have come to share business and industry's view of the excesses of government."[124] While the alliance between academics and business people hoped for by both Hatfield and the institute's president, H. Monroe Browne, never took place, the volume's publication revealed that complaints about government regulation no longer came exclusively from the business community. At the same time, federal regulatory requirements imposed on cities, most notably the rule requiring access to transportation facilities for the handicapped, made many big-city mayors —virtually all of whom were liberal Democrats—much more critical of federal regulation as well. The growing backlash against school busing also contributed to public skepticism about the cost and benefit of federally imposed rules and regulations.

At the same time, the public-interest movement began to experience some organizational difficulties: it was finding it more difficult to generate financial resources. Ralph Nader's Public Citizen raised the greatest amount in its history in 1977: $1.3 million. But in 1979, it received less than $1 million. It cost the organization approximately $300,000 to generate this sum, leaving Nader and his associates with only $700,000 to spend on political activity. The membership of Common Cause peaked in 1974. By 1980, the organization had lost nearly one-third of its members. While the overall membership of the nation's environmental movement remained relatively stable, individual organizations did suffer a loss of membership. Membership in the Wilderness Society declined from a peak of 64,000 members to 48,000 in 1979, and the National Parks and Conservation

Association lost more than one-third of its members between 1971 and 1979.

Although the number of Americans willing to contribute to public-interest groups did not decline, the significant increase in the number of such groups meant each individual organization was finding it more difficult to secure public support. One observer noted, "Competition is getting very tight because of the vast increase in use of the mails." Nader observed, "You've got over 100 groups out there competing and the [mailing] lists don't get any bigger."[125] As a result, the rate of response to the movement's direct mail appeals declined to less than 1 percent. This in turn required a number of organizations to increase their annual dues—thus further reducing their response rate. Compounding the financial difficulties of the movement was the decision of the Ford Foundation in 1979 to phase out its financial support of public-interest law firms. While the foundation did provide each of the groups that it had previously sponsored with a significant endowment grant, in most cases the income from the grant was not sufficient to enable them to maintain their current level of activity.

The movement's public image was also damaged by a highly publicized squabble that broke out in 1977 between Ralph Nader and Joan Claybrook, a former Nader aide whom Carter had recently appointed to head the NHTSC. When Claybrook decided to go along with the Carter administration's decision not to require airbags until 1981, Nader publicly accused her of giving in to industry pressure and demanded her resignation. One political scientist observed, in the *New York Times:* "Contemporary American reformism is in the act of consuming its young."[126] Ralph Nader's subsequent reaction to the defeat of a consumer protection agency, which he attributed solely to the desire of House members to solicit campaign contributions from business, did little to improve his image.

The public-interest movement made one spirited effort to recapture the political initiative. On April 17, 1980, a number of organizations sponsored Big Business Day in order to call public attention to the dangers posed by large corporations to the American public and to create public pressure for the passage of a Corporate Democracy Act which would require each of the various constituencies affected by a firm to be represented on its board. This effort received considerable press coverage. To counter it, a group of corporations and foundations designated April 17, 1980, as Growth Day. The results of Big Business Day, however, sharply contrasted with Earth Day, which had been celebrated exactly ten years earlier: within a few weeks hardly anyone recalled that it had taken place.

Finally the public-interest movement was also the victim of its own antigovernment rhetoric. For all its support of additional government controls over business, the public-interest movement had always remained extremely suspicious of government, particularly of regulatory bureaucracies. This, in fact, is what distinguished the public-interest movement from the traditions of New Deal liberalism. It was precisely its mistrust of both government and business that had led the public-interest movement to favor a series of legal innovations aimed at reducing the autonomy of regulatory officials. But as Pertschuk observed, "Nader's attacks on the unresponsive regulatory bureaucracy had the unintended side effect of feeding public disaffection and distrust of government." The public-interest movement's strong support of economic deregulation had a similar effect. It helped undermine public support of regulations which the movement strongly favored: "The deregulatory yeast, once risen, was hard to contain."[127] Watergate had a similar, equally unintended consequence. Its immediate effect was to weaken still further public confidence in business; its more long-term consequence was to increase public suspicion of government—a change in attitude that ultimately benefited business.

Conclusion

Both the decline and rise of business power in the last three decades have been characterized as a kind of power grab by elites. During the 1970s, Irving Kristol and Paul Weaver argued that the expansion of government regulation was due to the efforts of a new class to increase its own power and privileges at the expense of "ordinary workers and consumers."[128] During the 1980s, critics of business made a similar argument. Thomas Edsell, Thomas Ferguson, and Joel Rogers contended that the "right turn" of American politics was due not to a shift in public attitudes toward business or government, but rather to a decision by the nation's corporate elite to reverse the direction of economic and social policy.[129]

Both of these explanations are incomplete. New-class activists and corporate executives did work hard to reshape public attitudes and policies toward business. But the success of each was, in turn, made possible by the fact that their objectives and those of a substantial segment of the American electorate coincided: the prosperity of the late 1960s made much of the American middle class relatively indifferent, if not hostile, to corporations, while the economic stagnation of the mid-1970s made them more supportive. Charls Walker could have no more secured the passage of the 1978 Revenue Act in 1970 than the Sierra Club could have persuaded

Congress to adopt the 1970 Clean Air Act Amendments in 1977. The nation's workplaces had not become any less safe during the late 1960s, yet Congress reacted to reports of a crisis in the workplace by establishing the Occupational Safety and Health Act in 1970. Likewise, there is no evidence that government regulation of business contributed significantly to the nation's economic difficulties during the 1970s. Yet during the latter part of that decade, both Congress and the Carter administration embraced the cause of regulatory reform. Both these outcomes were due to orchestrated campaigns: the first by Ralph Nader and the public-interest movement, the second by business and conservative think tanks. But both efforts were successful because changing economic conditions made the public predisposed to accept their arguments. Had *Bitter Wages* been published in 1960 or 1980, it would hardly have led to a major expansion of federal controls of the nation's workplaces any more than Murray Weidenbaum's study of the costs of government regulation would have helped spawn a backlash against government control of business had it been released in 1970.

Nonetheless, it is clear that political mobilization did play a more important role in the resurgence of business power than in its decline. The growth of social regulation in the late 1960s and early 1970s was in large measure due to changes in public attitudes: politicians responded less to lobbying or grass-roots organizing by either organized labor or the public-interest movement than to their perception of the kind of public policies toward businesses that their constituents favored. In fact, the political mobilization of the educated middle class by the public-interest movement followed, rather than preceded, many of business's most important political defeats. And although public-interest lobbyists did play a more important role in the political process after 1970, they did little to shape the response of Congress to either the energy crisis or Watergate. In both cases, politicians responded primarily to their perceptions of the preferences of their constituents.

On the other hand, the political triumphs of business between 1977 and 1980 were significantly affected by its superior political resources. The poor public image of trade unions certainly contributed to the defeat of both common situs picketing in 1977 and labor-law reform the following year, but Congress could just as easily have approved these statutes. It was business lobbying that made the decisive difference. Similarly, while there was a notable lack of public enthusiasm for the creation of a consumer protection agency, a majority of the public did in fact support it; it was defeated in 1978 because of a skillful lobbying effort on the part of business. Proposition 13 may have facilitated the passage of legislation reducing the tax on capital gains in 1978, but its approval also owed much to the efforts of Charls Walker and the American Council for Capital Formation. While there was little public enthusiasm for Pertschuk's "kidvid" initiative, the passage of the FTC Improvements Act was made possible only by a determined lobbying effort on the part of the various trade associations threatened by the commission's enforcement of Magnuson-Moss: there was certainly no groundswell of public support for exempting funeral directors or used-car salesmen from the jurisdiction of the Federal Trade Commission.

But, while the political mobilization of both large and small businesses may have been a necessary condition for the revival of the political influence of business after 1976, it was not a sufficient one. Like the public-interest movement earlier in the decade, the business community was the beneficiary of developments beyond its control. Double-digit inflation, accompanied by bracket creep, made significant segments of the middle class more sensitive to the cost of social regulation and more supportive of the effort of business to reduce taxes. The growth of imports also made many Americans more aware of the vulnerability of large corporations to economic pressures than they had been a decade earlier. At the same time, the baby boomers of the 1960s had grown up: they were less antagonistic to business in their thirties than they had been in their twenties. Their views about economic policy tended to be similar to business's: they did not favor solutions to the nation's economic difficulties that involved increasing the size and power of government. This, in turn, drove a wedge between them and organized labor.

It is also important to note that while business people may constitute a minority of the American electorate, the number of individuals who fall into this category is far from trivial. "Business" should not be confused with Fortune 500 firms. There are approximately fifteen million businesses in the United States. A number of these exist primarily on paper, and not all their owners identify politically with "business." At the same time, many of these firms employ a large number of managers who regard themselves as business people, as do their major stockholders. Thus, to regard the political gains of business as necessarily elitist is simplistic; a significant share of the American electorate does in fact consist of owners, managers, and their families. Had substantial numbers of these individuals not become politically mobilized during the 1970s, it is unlikely that business lobbyists in Washington would have been so effective. American politics may have many faults, but indifference to the preferences of substantial segments of the American electorate is not among them.

IX

Business and the Reagan Administration, 1981 to 1988

The 1980 Election

Ronald Reagan was not the Republican presidential candidate initially preferred by the American corporate community. While he did receive substantial backing from many small businessowners and middle managers, most corporate executives supported either George Bush or John Connally. Many executives worried about Reagan's lack of experience. They also feared that the candidate's advocacy of the Kemp-Roth plan to cut federal individual income taxes by 30 percent would increase the budget deficit and prevent a reduction in business taxes. However, once it became clear that Reagan would be the Republican nominee, the business community strongly supported his candidacy, particularly after the candidate expressed his support for cutting corporate taxes. Each of 865 "Republican Eagles" contributed $10,000 to the Republican National Committee, and independent expenditures, many of which came from business people, were 382 times greater for Reagan than for Carter. On October 30, a Gallup poll for the *Wall Street Journal* reported that an overwhelming majority of chief executive officers (CEOs) believed that Reagan would do a better job than Carter in handling the economy.[1]

Business played an extremely active role in the 1980 campaign. Corporate PACs contributed a total of $19.2 million to congressional candidates, twice as much as they had contributed in 1978. The 1980 campaign was also unique in the amount of resources that business mobilized to defeat incumbents, most of whom were, of course, Democrats.[2] The Republican party fielded a relatively large number of politically experienced challengers, and the National Republican Committee invested its considerable resources in recruiting effective candidates for House seats and teaching them how to campaign effectively. In turn, a significant number of companies and trade associations made a determined effort to change the ideological composition of the Congress. Republican National Chairman William Brock noted, "We really worked on that in 1980. We said 'the business of business is to take risks.' " As a result, "the partisanship and risk taking of corporate PAC's in the 1980 election have not been matched before or since."[3] Eisneier and Pollack write, "An unpopular president, a worsening economy, a strong crop of Republican challengers, and a set of vulnerable Democrats in the Senate all tempted corporate PACs to throw caution to the wind and invest heavily in Republican challengers."[4] Approximately one-third of all corporate PAC money went to support conservative Republicans who were challenging incumbent liberal Democrats.

There is a marked contrast between the pattern of corporate campaign contributions in 1976 and the pattern in 1980. Corporate PACs gave 31 percent of their donations to challengers in 1980, compared with 18 percent in 1976. Business support for Republican incumbents was not reduced; indeed, they continued to receive about twenty times as much money as their Democratic challengers. However, business contributions to Democratic incumbents declined dramatically. In 1976 the typical Democratic incumbent received about twice as much corporate money as his or her Republican challenger; in 1980 Republican challengers received, in the aggregate, more corporate support than did the Democratic incumbents they were trying to unseat.[5] On balance, the business community displayed a remarkable degree of unity in 1980.[6] In nearly three-quarters of all congressional races, business gave at least nine times as much to one candidate as another, and in every close race, corporate giving went exclusively to Republicans.

A revitalized Republican party, a network of conservative corporate PACs, and the independent expenditures of ideological PACs—all reinforced one another; the candidates nominated by the Republican party to oppose Democratic incumbents also received a disproportionate share of the contributions of both corporate and conservative PACs. The latter PACs raised and dispersed substantial sums in an effort to defeat six liberal Democratic Senators, and one PAC—the National Conservative Political Action Committee—spent a total of $1.2 million. These efforts were extremely successful. Not since 1974 had the partisan composition of Congress changed so substantially. The Republicans captured control of the

Senate for the first time since 1955 and gained thirty-four seats in the House, producing the most conservative Congress in a generation.

Reagan's victory in 1980 had at least as much to do with public dissatisfaction with President Carter and the performance of the economy as with public support for the probusiness planks of the 1980 Republican platform. Nonetheless, the business community viewed his election as a major political victory. The *New York Times* reported after the November election that "Wall Street and the business community yesterday welcomed the election of Ronald Reagan, amid predictions that the President-elect would oversee the most probusiness administration since that of Dwight D. Eisenhower." Reginald Jones, chairman of the Business Roundtable, predicted that "this conservative landslide should provide considerable encouragement for the private sector, resulting in increased economic activity."[7] Although *Business Week* cautioned that "relations between business and government cannot go back to what they were in Eisenhower's Administration," it expressed the hope that the "Reagan Presidency can end the long adversary relationship between business and government in the U.S."[8] This new rapprochement between business and government was symbolized by the president's inaugural ball; hundreds of corporate executives flew to Washington to celebrate the Reagan victory at a series of lavish parties bankrolled by the private sector. A month later, Wayne Valis, a presidential assistant responsible for relations with business, informed hundreds of corporate lobbyists who had gathered in the old Executive Office Building: "Like the Confederacy, you have only won defensive victories. That leads to defeat. If you will march with us this time, you will win offensive victories."[9] The applause was thunderous.

The 1981 Tax Cut

Five years earlier, in 1975, a group of tax specialists for a number of major business organizations had begun to meet informally over breakfast at the Carlton Hotel. The Carlton Group included Charls Walker, who had played a critical role in lobbying for the 1978 tax cut, as well as representatives of the U.S. Chamber of Commerce, the Business Roundtable, the National Federation of Independent Business, the Council for Capital Formation, and the Committee for Effective Capital Recovery. In 1980, a new business organization, the American Business Conference, composed of the chief executives of 100 "growth" companies, also began to send representatives. The 1978 legislation had lowered the capital-gains tax, primarily benefiting investors, entrepreneurs, and wealthy individuals. However, it had not significantly lowered corporate tax rates. The Carlton Group focused its efforts on reducing the corporate tax rate, primarily through more generous depreciation allowances.

To increase their political effectiveness, the members of the group agreed on a single proposal. As one participant recalled, "It was like the Paris peace talks; we all sat around the table and argued . . . and we hammered something out that we could all live with." Eventually, they agreed on the following formula: buildings would be written off in ten years, light trucks and automobiles in three, and all other capital equipment in five. Subsequently, "every business advocate began chanting the same refrain: 10:5:3."[10] The Carlton Group's unanimity had a political impact. As one representative put it, "When every businessman in my district takes the same position on a tax issue, I'll tell you I'm impressed."[11] In 1980, 10:5:3 began to pick up significant support from the Democrats who controlled the House Ways and Means Committee and the Senate Finance Committee—an indication of how the politics of corporate taxation were changing.

During his presidential campaign, Reagan had made individual tax cuts based on a proposal by Republican Representative Jack Kemp of New York and Republican Senator William Roth of Delaware a centerpiece of his program to revitalize the American economy. Shortly after his election, he appointed Charls Walker to head his transition team on tax policy. Working closely with Walker, the U.S. Treasury submitted a proposal to cut back individual tax rates by 30 percent during the next four years, to liberalize depreciation rates—though not quite as much as 10:5:3—and to phase out the distinction between the tax treatment of earned and unearned income in three years. While Reagan defended the tax proposal on the grounds that an "equal reduction in everyone's tax rates will expand our national prosperity, enlarge national income and increase opportunities for all Americans," his budget director, David Stockman, subsequently admitted that the administration's real objective was to reduce the top marginal rate, but that "in order to make this palatable as a political matter, you had to bring down all the brackets."[12] However, several groups representing large companies, led by the Business Roundtable, expressed concern about the projected loss of revenue stemming from the administration's proposal and urged that the individual tax cuts be scaled back.

The House Ways and Means Committee drafted a bill that generally reflected the Roundtable's recommendations. However, the president then announced a revised plan in order to enlist the support of conservative House Democrats worried about future deficits. It cut back on the individ-

ual cuts associated with Kemp-Roth and reduced some of the more significant changes in depreciation schedules that had been part of the original
Treasury proposal. The reaction of the corporate community to this threat
to its depreciation allowances was immediate. On what became known as
"Lear Jet Weekend," scores of corporate CEOs flew to Washington to meet
with Treasury and White House officials. Their pleas proved extremely
effective. Not only did the administration restore many of business's tax
breaks, but Treasury officials promised to explore ways in which the tax
bill could be modified to provide benefits for companies that would not
gain from tax reductions—either because they were losing money or had
no past losses to offset their future tax liabilities.

The Democrats in the House of Representatives, eager to attract some
of the corporate PAC money that had gone to Republicans in 1980, countered by proposing a set of provisions that were even more generous to
business: instead of a more generous depreciation schedule, the House
Ways and Means Committee reported out a bill that moved toward the full
expensing of capital investments. Richard Rahn, the chief economist for
the U.S. Chamber of Commerce and an original member of the Carlton
Group, characterized this development as "nothing short of astounding,"
adding that, "If you'd told me a few years ago that the Democrats would
propose expensing, I would have said you were out of your mind."[13] The
Democratic proposal also added a number of benefits targeted to specific
sectors. For example, depressed industries could have their unused investment credits refunded to them, provided the monies were reinvested. The
administration responded by further broadening the accelerated depreciation schedules for companies and added a number of additional tax breaks
for specific sectors of the economy. As David Stockman subsequently
recalled, "The hogs were really feeding. The greed level, the level of oppor-
tunism, just got out of control."[14] A particular beneficiary of this bidding
war was the energy industry, whose taxes had increased substantially
between 1969 and 1979. In 1981, Congress reduced taxes for owners of oil
royalties, independents, and those who operated strippers. It also halved
the windfall profits tax on newly discovered oil over the next six years. The
combined revenue gain for the oil industry from these provisions was
estimated at $1.3 billion in 1982 and $1.7 billion the following year.

As a consequence, the Economic Recovery Act of 1981 that emerged
from the conference committee provided tax breaks for both individuals
and businesses far greater than anyone had earlier advocated. Although
some executives and administration officials were worried about its impact
on the budget deficit, every major business organization strongly backed
the final legislation, since, with the economy now moving into a recession,

the bill provided businesses with much needed additional revenues. For its part, the administration hoped that the ensuing deficit would abet its long-range campaign to reduce nondefense spending.

The 1981 tax cut was clearly affected by the momentum generated by Reagan's election and the Republican party's unexpected capture of the Senate. Yet while its magnitude was unprecedented, it was also a continuation of a trend that had begun during the Carter administration when Congress had reduced the capital-gains tax in an effort to encourage capital formation. What was unusual about the 1981 legislation was the strong support for reductions in business taxes from congressional Democrats, many of whom, having, in the words of the Democratic Congressional Campaign Committee Chairman Tony Coelho, "had our access kicked" in 1980, were now eager to identify themselves as "business democrats."[15] Their shift was at least as politically significant as the Republican capture of the presidency and the Senate in 1980. Little more than a decade earlier, the automobile industry had found itself caught in a bidding war between the Nixon administration and the Democrats in the Senate. Each had tried to outdo the other in demonstrating its commitment to strict pollution-control standards: the result was the 1970 Clean Air Act Amendments. In 1981, a Republican president and a Democratic House also found themselves in a bidding war, this time to demonstrate their commitment to cut corporate taxes. The result was a reduction of $151 billion in business taxes over the next five years—the most significant cut in the history of the federal income tax.

The magnitude of the business community's victory on tax policy was also facilitated by its unusual degree of unity. As Representative Barber Conable (Republican-New York) observed, "There have been sweetener offers throughout the tax negotiations, but the business response has been to stand together. It's a good example of how to lobby effectively. I think it has been extraordinary."[16] Not only had virtually the entire business community been able for the first time to agree on a program for tax relief, but a broad coalition of firms and trade associations also worked closely with the administration to persuade Congress to approve substantial cuts in nondefense spending. More than one hundred companies urged their employees and stockholders to write letters in support of the president's economic program, while an ad hoc Budget Control Working Group, composed of four hundred corporations, lobbied extensively for congressional approval of the administration's budget proposals. Several firms took out full-page ads supporting the Reagan program; one, W. R. Grace & Co., spent $200,000 in the space of a few months. In spite of the fact that the president's proposed budget adversely affected a number of different firms and industries, his economic program received the blanket endorsement of the National Association of Manufacturers (NAM), the American Farm Bureau Federation, the National Federation of Independent Business, and the American Business Conference. As one NAM official put it, "It's time for us to put our legislative muscle where our rhetorical mouths have been for the last 20 years."[17]

Jeffery H. Joseph, the manager of the business-government affairs division of the Chamber of Commerce, concluded in 1981 that "business lobbyists were very successful this year because after years of assuming a defensive posture we went on the offensive. . . . We hope to be pushing for other initiatives, because now we know that the coalition technique can work." Alexander Trowbridge, the president of the NAM, observed, "Now we're in a new mode. We're able to go affirmative. The business community strongly formed coalitions in the budget fight and the tax cut fight, and we will retain that ability to put coalitions together on an issue-by-issue basis." Trowbridge added, "Everybody's still in a state of recovery from the exhaustion of the last six months. We know we've come a long way, but we also know we have a long way yet to go."[18]

Deregulation, 1981–82

During his presidential campaign, Ronald Reagan had repeatedly criticized government regulation of business, promising business audiences that if elected he planned to "turn you loose again to do the things that I know you can do so well."[19] Indeed, Ronald Reagan devoted more attention to the subject of government regulation than had any previous presidential candidate. The president stated, in September 1980, "When the real take-home pay of the average worker is declining steadily and eight million Americans are out of work, we must carefully reexamine our regulatory structure to assess to what degree regulations have contributed to the situation."[20] The candidate's well-publicized gaffes on environmental policy—on one occasion Reagan, confusing nitrous oxide with nitric oxide, stated that nature, rather than industry, was the chief cause of air pollution—provided a further indication of his strongly held views on regulatory policy.

In a memo circulated among the president's key advisers shortly before the administration took office, the president's budget director, David Stockman, warned of a "ticking regulatory time bomb." He argued that

"unless strict, comprehensive and far-reaching regulatory policy correc-
tions are undertaken immediately, an unprecedented, quantum scale-up of
the much discussed 'regulatory burden' will occur in the next 18–40
months."[21] Stockman further suggested that a substantial and dramatic
reduction of regulatory burdens was necessary "for the short-term cash
flow relief it will provide to business planners and the long-term signal it
will provide for corporate investment planners," adding that, "a major
'regulatory ventilation' will do as much to boost business confidence as tax
and fiscal measures."[22] The president subsequently made deregulation,
along with tax cuts, spending cuts, and stable monetary policy, one of the
four key components of his program to spur economic recovery. In sharp
contrast to presidents Ford and Carter, both of whom had sought to "reform" federal regulation, Reagan came into office explicitly committed to
reducing it.

The president moved rapidly to deliver on this commitment. The day
after his inauguration, he established a Task Force on Regulatory Relief.
Headed by Vice President George Bush, it was charged with reviewing all
existing regulatory statutes and rules in order to determine which needed
to be revised or abolished. By naming the vice president to chair this
oversight body, Reagan sought to give it more authority and visibility than
similar bodies that had been established during the Ford and Carter administrations. A month later, on the recommendations of the vice president's task force, the White House issued an executive order requiring all
agencies to undertake a cost-benefit analysis before issuing any new rules,
and then to adopt the least costly alternative. Each regulatory agency was
also ordered to reexamine all rules currently in effect, and prepare "regulatory impact analyses" for those deemed of major significance. An Office
of Information and Regulatory Affairs was created within the White
House to enforce this order. By giving the White House the final authority
to approve both new and existing regulations, it turned federal agency
heads from "policy makers to policy pleaders in a tough, unsympathetic
court."[23]

In its first six weeks in office, the administration made a number of
changes in regulatory policies. It lifted price controls on domestic crude oil
eight months ahead of schedule, froze dozens of "midnight" regulations
promulgated by the Carter administration in its last days of office, and
dropped energy efficiency standards for appliances. In addition, it proposed curbs on the antitrust powers of the Federal Trade Commission
(FTC) and the Interstate Commerce Commission (ICC) and targeted thirty-
four safety and environmental standards affecting the automobile industry
for immediate delay or repeal—including a year's postponement of federal

regulations requiring the installation of air bags or other "passive re-straints." The administration predicted that these changes would reduce the production costs of autos by $150, save the financially hard-pressed automobile industry $1.4 billion in capital expenses, and reduce the cost of automobiles to consumers by nearly $1.9 billion a year.

In addition to attempting to centralize control over regulatory policy making in the White House, the Reagan administration, like its predeces-sor, appointed regulatory officials who shared its political philosophy. While the Carter administration had largely staffed the social regulatory agencies with representatives of the public-interest movement and orga-nized labor, Reagan's appointees tended to be either business executives or individuals who had worked closely with the business community. To head the Department of the Interior, the president appointed James Watt, who had previously served as director of the Mountain States Legal Foun-dation, a conservative public-interest law firm that had challenged federal restrictions on land use in the western states. Anne Gorsuch (later Burford) was appointed to head the Environmental Protection Agency (EPA). As a member of the Colorado state legislature, she had been part of a group of conservative Republicans who had opposed many of the environmental regulations imposed on the states by the federal government. The presi-dent appointed Thorne Auchter, a Reagan campaign official who had pre-viously managed a family construction company in Florida, to head the Occupational Safety and Health Administration (OSHA). To chair his Council of Economic Advisors, the president appointed Murray Weiden-baum, the director of the Center for the Study of American Business, who had become one of the foremost critics of government regulation. Another prominent critic of government regulation, James Miller III, was selected to head the Office of Regulatory Affairs in the Office of Management and Budget (OMB). Shortly afterward, he was appointed to replace Michael Pertschuk as chair of the FTC.

The administration also reduced both the size and budget of federal regulatory agencies—thus reversing a trend that had begun under the Nixon administration. The budgets of the federal government's forty-two regulatory agencies had grown, in real terms, nearly fourfold between 1970 and 1980. In fiscal year 1981, they did not increase at all when measured in constant dollars, and in fiscal year 1982, they decreased by 9 percent. While the agencies most severely affected by these budget cuts were the economic regulatory bodies, a number of social regulatory agencies also suffered budgetary reductions. The budget of the Consumer Product Safety Commission (CPSC) was reduced by 38 percent, the FTC's by 28 percent, the EPA's by 10 percent, and the National Highway Traffic Safety

Administration's (NHTSA) by 22 percent. The number of individuals employed at the nation's major regulatory agencies had increased three-and-one-half times between 1970 and 1980, but it declined 4 percent in fiscal 1981 and an additional 8 percent in fiscal 1982. At the EPA, the staff fell from 14,075 in 1981 to 10,396 in 1982, and at the Department of the Interior, the staff of the Office of Surface Mining was reduced from 1,000 to 628.

As a consequence of these budget and staff reductions as well as the political orientation of the administration's appointees, there was a marked reduction in the use of legally oriented enforcement mechanisms and a shift toward a more cooperative approach. James Watt initiated a general overhaul of strip-mining regulations to eliminate the "how to comply" details, ordered his solicitor to settle court suits that had delayed enforcement of the 1977 statute, moved to give the states more leeway in adopting their own strip-mining laws under the federal act, and reorganized the surface mining office by eliminating its five regional offices and reducing its enforcement staff by 57 percent during the next twelve months.[24] Auchter told the *Washington Post*, "Our philosophy is one of safety and health and not one of crime and punishment."[25] The number of OSHA's inspectors was reduced by four hundred between 1980 and 1981. Between 1980 and 1982, inspections of work sites declined 15 percent, citations of employers for serious hazards declined 47 percent, and fines were reduced 69 percent. This represented "the most radical shift in the enforcement of worker health and safety laws since Congress passed the Occupational Safety and Health Act in 1970" and marked a striking contrast to Bingham's performance, whose aggressive enforcement policies had made her "a pariah in business circles."[26] A labor attorney for the United States Chamber of Commerce stated in November 1981, "We're very positive on what Auchter has done so far. We think he's a very quick study."[27] He added, "No other agency has successfully provided the type of regulatory reform and eased the regulatory burden in the minds of employers the way OSHA has."[28]

At the EPA, Gorsuch first abolished the Office of Enforcement, then reestablished it with a reduced staff and then reorganized it again. Between 1981 and 1982, the number of cases referred to the Justice Department for prosecution by the EPA declined by 84 percent from the previous year, and the number of civil penalties imposed by the EPA dropped 48 percent. Between 1980 and 1982, the number of administrative enforcement orders issued by the EPA declined one-third. Likewise, the number of formal investigations into potential car defects by the NHTSA fell from eleven during the Carter administration's last year in office to four in 1981.

There were also a number of substantive changes in regulatory policy. The Food and Drug Administration approved more new drugs in 1981 than in any year since the passage of the 1962 Drug Amendment, and the number of "emergency exceptions" from restrictions on the use of pesticides tripled during the administration's first term. While the Carter administration had listed one hundred and fifty species as "endangered" during its four years in office, the U.S. Fish and Wildlife Service listed only one in 1981. In his first two years as secretary of the interior, Watt leased one-and-one-half times more public land for offshore oil and gas development than was leased during the entire Carter administration. The sale of 2.24 billion tons of coal in the Powder River Basin in Wyoming and Montana was the largest coal sale in history and represented a major shift in the public policy toward leasing coal on federal land. On balance, in his first two years Watt did more to open up the nation's federal supplies of oil, gas, coal, and geothermal energy than any other secretary of the interior in history: "Through budgetary maneuvering, rules changes and a thousand small decisions lost to national view, he has dramatically shifted the balance between use and preservation that had existed for the past four Administrations."[29]

The administration's two "oversight" bodies had a more modest effect. In its first year of operation, OMB declined to approve 91 of the 2,781 regulations forwarded to it. Many were only relatively minor, including the midnight regulations of the Carter administration. Others were more significant. For example, the EPA was forced to withdraw a set of rules governing the disposal of hazardous chemical wastes. The Presidential Task Force on Regulatory Relief focused on regulations that business leaders viewed as particularly burdensome. It prodded regulatory agencies into changing or revising thirty-seven rules, about a third of which affected the automobile industry. The latter included the NHTSA's fuel-economy standards for 1981 automobiles as well as a rule requiring the installation of passive restraints. In addition, the Agriculture Department was persuaded to loosen its standards for labeling and marketing mechanically deboned meat.

Overall, the administration's regulatory policies in its first year in office, like its tax policies, delighted the business community. An executive of General Motors informed the *Wall Street Journal* that the change in attitudes of regulatory officials between the Carter and Reagan administrations was "like the difference between night and day."[30] The chairman of Amway noted, "A lot of overregulation is still in place, but there is a different attitude on the part of the people who are doing the regulating."[31] As the director of the Presidential Task Force on Regulatory Relief put it, "at the level of inspection and enforcement, businessmen today are much less likely to mistake a visit from EPA or OSHA for a visit from the FBI."[32] Although the regulatory statutes enacted during the previous decade remained on the books, the number of rules issued under them measurably declined: the total number of rules published in the *Federal Register* was 25 percent less in 1981 than in 1980, and the number of major rules issued was cut in half.[33] Not only had the relationship between business and government improved dramatically at most regulatory agencies, but the business community now had a sympathetic "appeals court," namely, the Task Force on Regulatory Relief, whose counsel, C. Boyden Gray, actively encouraged corporations to bring the decisions of regulatory agencies to the task force's attention. Gray told a meeting of the Chamber of Commerce:

> If you go to the agency first, don't be too pessimistic if they can't solve the problem there. If they don't, that's what the task force is for. Two weeks ago [a group] showed up and I asked if they had a problem. They said they did, and we made a couple of phone calls and straightened it out, alerted the top people at the agency that there was a little hanky-panky going on at the bottom of the agency, and it was cleared up very rapidly—so the system does work if you use it as a sort of an appeal. We can act as a double check on the agency that you might encounter problems with.[34]

One Washington lawyer concluded, "It has been non-factitiously suggested that the lawyer who does not argue all the way to Vice President Bush may be subjecting himself to a malpractice charge."[35]

A CEO told the *U.S. News and World Report* in the fall of 1981, "I see a dramatic difference in business's relations with Washington. Here you've got an administration that is moving just as fast as it can in the direction we want to move. Top officials are now saying the kinds of things that we have been saying for years. It used to be we were prepared to try to fight off whatever government wanted to do. Now that's changed. I told a friend recently, 'I almost feel like I've died and gone to heaven.' " Another observed, "A basic difference in this administration is that business is not viewed as an adversary from the instant we walk in the door."[36]

The 1982 Tax Increase

Yet within a year, the honeymoon between business and the Reagan administration had ended. For no sooner did the 1981 tax cuts go into effect than pressure began to mount for their modification. This was prompted by the fact that the federal deficit was projected to reach more than $100 billion in 1983. In addition, as the implications of the 1981 tax cut began to become clear, one provision—though uncontroversial at the time of its enactment—attracted particular notoriety. "Safe-harbor leasing" allowed companies to, in effect, sell their investment tax credits and depreciation allowances to other firms. As a result, companies that lost money in 1981, such as Ford and Chrysler, received hundreds of millions of dollars in refunds, while highly profitable firms such as IBM and Metromedia were able to buy their way out of most of their tax bills. In April 1982, General Electric touched off a public furor by disclosing that, through leasing deals, it had not only wiped out most of its 1981 tax liability but also picked up $110 million in refunds for previous years, leading some Washington lobbyists to dub the firm "Greed Electric."[37]

The 1983 congressional budget resolution called for $98.3 billion in new taxes over three years and approximately $16 billion in spending cuts. The administration reluctantly concurred. In his 1982 State of the Union Address, the president called for additional tax revenues, and the White House subsequently outlined a package of $86.6 billion in new taxes for the fiscal years 1983 through 1987. The president, however, refused to make any substantial modifications in individual tax cuts since he considered them central to his long-term plan for economic recovery. Instead he asked Congress to "plug unwarranted tax loopholes"[38] and to strengthen the law requiring corporations to pay a minimum income tax. The president also proposed to withhold 5 percent of taxable interest and dividends in order to reduce tax evasion.

The president's proposal completely shattered the business community's unified position on taxes, as each firm and sector began to battle to hold on to as many of the tax breaks it had received in 1981 as possible. Robert Lighthizer, chief counsel for the Senate Finance Committee, observed, "The biggest difference between last year and this year is that last year we were giving it away and this year we're taking it back."[39] Virtually all companies agreed that the best way for the government to reduce the deficit was to lower spending. But with the important exception of the U.S. Chamber of Commerce, whose president, Richard Lester, opposed any tax increase, most business organizations were willing to support some increase in taxes—providing the burden fell primarily upon other firms or individuals.

In March 1982, the Policy Committee of the Business Roundtable met to formulate its position. After a long and bitter meeting—described by some participants as "one of the group's stormiest ever"—the organization voted to support a range of tax increases, including an increase in personal taxes. However, it urged that business tax cuts be maintained—though it did agree to support the elimination of some of the abuses in leasing. The Roundtable's statement drew strong criticism from the White House. Treasury Secretary Donald T. Regan responded that "it's somewhat ironic to hear $200,000 executives saying, 'Don't give a tax cut to $20,000 workers'" He asked Theodore Brophy of General Telephone and Electronics, who had delivered the Roundtable's position to the White House: "Tell me, which Congressman is going to vote to take away a tax cut from the little guys and let you keep everything?"[40]

The American Business Conference (ABC) organized a coalition in favor of a tax increase labeled the Deficit Reduction Action Group. Its president, John Albertine, stated that while there was no good economic justification for a tax increase, it was politically necessary in order to persuade liberal Democrats to vote for spending reductions. The ABC, which represented 100 medium-size, high-growth companies, called for a repeal of the safe-harbor provision (which didn't provide many benefits for its members) but urged that the individual tax cuts (which did) be preserved. The National Federation of Independent Business (NFIB) took a similar position: it opposed the safe-harbor provision on the grounds that it benefited only larger firms and strongly endorsed retention of the individual tax cuts since most of its members were business people who filed individual rather than corporate tax returns.

The Reagan administration lobbied hard to secure business support for its tax package. Much of the White House's effort was directed at the U.S. Chamber of Commerce, the business organization most opposed to the president's position. The White House issued urgent appeals to the officials and members of approximately twelve thousand state and local chambers, requesting that they ignore the calls to oppose the tax increase coming from Lester and his Washington office. While only twenty individual chambers backed the president, many agreed to remain neutral and thirty-two of the Chamber's sixty-one board members eventually agreed to back a tax increase. The Independent Petroleum Association subsequently agreed to support the president's proposal, in exchange for a provision exempting independent oil companies from new taxes on oil. The president was also eventually supported by all but two of the twenty-four members of the executive committee of the NAM as well as by all but a handful of members of the policy committee of the Roundtable.

The tax bill enacted in 1982 raised taxes by a total of $18.3 billion over the next three years. Approximately half of this sum came directly from the private sector: the 1982 legislation effectively eliminated half of the incentives for capital investment enacted a year earlier. One of business's few victories was the prevention of a minimum corporate tax. John Albertine was philosophical: "When you look at the specifics, there's no question but that this bill was not good for business. But a drop in interest rates far, far swamps any negative effects of the bill."[41] Nonetheless, corporate taxes remained far lower than they had been when President Reagan came into office. Even after the 1982 increase, corporate tax liabilities were $10 billion less in February 1983 and were expected to fall by $17 billion in February 1986, compared to what they would have been prior to 1981. In 1980, the effective federal corporate tax rate was 33.3 percent; it had declined to 4.7 percent in 1981 and was still only 15.8 percent in 1982.[42]

In spite of their disappointment with the 1982 legislation, when asked in the fall of 1982 "if they think business is better able now to get its message across in Washington than it was five years ago, 90 percent of all executives said yes." Louis Harris observed, "They are purring. Business is much more self-confident about its power than it was."[43] However, many corporate executives continued to be troubled by the increasing size of the deficit in the federal budget. The *National Journal* reported in January of 1983:

> The business community today seems united as never before by its concern over how much harm the federal government is causing as a result of the ever-larger deficits that it is running. . . . Business representatives seem much less worried about what the government is doing to them directly, with its regulations, as they are by what the government is doing to them indirectly, by borrowing so much money.[44]

A series of two-page newspaper ads sponsored by "The Bipartisan Budget Appeal" and signed by five former treasury secretaries and several dozen CEOs, appealed to the president and Congress for dramatic and immediate steps to cut federal spending. The ad stated: "Tomorrow's big deficits, and the high long-term real interest rates that will accompany them, are already doing serious damage now and will wreak even more havoc in the coming decade and beyond. Without savings available to fuel productive investments, the economy will face nearly perpetual stagnation."[45] On January 18, 1983, three large business organizations, the NAM, the ABC, and the NFIB, held an unusual joint press conference to urge deficit-reducing actions in the fiscal 1984 budget cycle. A similar theme was echoed at conferences sponsored by the Conference Board and the Center for the Study of American Business. A survey of executives conducted by Louis Harris in January 1983 reported that 74 percent regarded the size of the deficit as "very serious," while 86 percent expressed their belief that the private sector would soon begin to have trouble competing with the U.S. Treasury for capital.[46]

Yet there was in fact little business could do to reduce federal spending. The Congress was unwilling to approve any additional cuts in domestic social spending, and the Reagan administration refused to scale back its plans to substantially increase defense spending—even when repeatedly urged to do so by a number of business leaders, including those representing major defense contractors.[47] This realistically left only one alternative: increased taxes. Yet on this issue, the business community remained divided. The organizations that had initially opposed the 1982 tax bill, such as the Chamber of Commerce and the NFIB, as well as those that had supported it, such as the NAM and the ABC, all expressed their strong opposition to additional tax increases. Only the Roundtable, along with the executives associated with the bipartisan appeal, indicated its willingness to support some increase in taxes. The administration, however, remained opposed to any additional taxes and as a result there was no significant change in federal tax policy during the remainder of its first term.

The Politics of Recession and International Competition

The debate over tax policy was however soon overshadowed by the deterioration in the performance of the economy. During the Reagan administration's first three years, the Federal Reserve continued the tight monetary policy it had begun in 1979. Real interest rates rose substantially and the nation plunged into its worse recession in the postwar period: GNP declined by 2.1 percent in 1982, the largest one-year decline since the 1930s. More than 25,000 firms failed in 1982 and another 31,000 declared bankruptcy in 1983—the highest level of business failures since the Great Depression. High American interest rates also led to a significant increase in the value of the dollar, thus increasing the nation's trade deficit. The merchandise balance of trade deficit stood at $25.5 billion in 1980; by 1983, it had increased to $60.6 billion. A year later, it had doubled to $123 billion. Between 1980 and 1983, the trade deficit resulted in a shift in annual production, from U.S. plants to producers overseas, of roughly $50 billion worth of goods. As a result of economic deregulation, recession, and high interest rates, the profits of financial-service companies fell 75 percent between 1979 and 1982, reaching their lowest level in real terms since 1933. Bank failures stood at their highest levels since 1940. The only Reagan policy that mitigated the short-term effect of the recession was the sharp increase in defense spending.

Unemployment also increased substantially between 1980 and 1983. It rose to 7.5 percent in 1981, and remained at 9.5 percent throughout 1982 and 1983. The effect of the recession and the growing trade deficit on workers employed in the manufacturing sector was severe. The United States lost two million manufacturing jobs between 1981 and 1984. In 1982, unemployment in the textile industry averaged 14.8 percent; in the apparel industry it stood at 15 percent. Public support for business plummeted: in October 1982, only 12 percent of Americans expressed a "highly favorable opinion of business," a drop of 6 percentage points from the previous year. As one political observer noted: "The president's pitch in 1981 was that the rising tide of prosperity will carry all boats. With the sour economic performance of 1981 and 1982, that appeal has been discredited in the public. The group much identified with the unfairness aspects of Reaganomics is business."[48]

In spite of the hardships associated with the 1981–82 recession and the accompanying structural readjustments of the American economy, the business community continued to support the president's economic program. A survey of executives taken in the spring of 1982 reported that two-thirds believed that the president's economic program was working well, and 64 percent endorsed the view that "the fight against inflation must continue even if that means high unemployment and more small business bankruptcies."[49] And a majority of the 800 executives at large and medium-sized companies surveyed in 1984 responded that the recession had been a good thing for the country. They argued that it had been effective in fighting inflation, which after climbing to 10.4 percent in 1981, dropped to 6.1 percent in 1982, and to 3.2 percent in 1983, although increasing slightly to 4.3 percent in 1984.

An important reason for business's support of the president's economic policies was their effect on wages. There were fewer work stoppages in 1982 than in any year in the postwar period. While U.S. labor costs had increased at an annual rate of 8.3 percent between 1973 and 1981, in 1983 they rose only 2.5 percent. Moreover, even as the economy began to recover, wage settlements remained modest. In 1983, wages and salaries increased by their lowest percentage since 1966. In fact, the major collective bargaining agreements concluded in the fall of 1983 resulted in an average net reduction in wages of 1.4 percent for the first contract year— the first such negative figure recorded in fifteen years.[50]

The trade-union movement and its liberal allies had responded to the 1974–75 recession by pressuring for the enactment of the Humphrey-Hawkins full employment bill. Their response to the 1981–82 recession was somewhat different, but no more successful. Responding to changes in the international economic position of the United States that had taken place during the intervening years, a number of unions, particularly in the manufacturing sector, became vigorous supporters of protectionist policies. In particular, the United Automobile Workers (UAW) waged a determined effort to persuade Congress to approve legislation requiring that a specified percentage of the content of all automobiles sold in the United States be made in the United States.

The battle over domestic-content legislation was an extremely bitter one. While it originally appeared that the legislation had little chance of being approved, the UAW's argument that the law was needed to protect American jobs and industry against Japanese imports was persuasive to many members of Congress, particularly in the depths of the 1982 recession. Opposition to the bill was led by Toyota, which in addition to hiring its own lobbyists, mobilized the seven thousand members of the American International Automobile Dealers Association to contact their representatives; the latter gathered more than a quarter-million signatures from their customers. The Chamber of Commerce also lobbied against the bill, as did those labor unions that had a stake in automobile imports. On December 11, 1982, the lame-duck House of Representatives approved domestic contents legislation by a vote of 215 to 188, but the vote was largely symbolic since it had earlier approved an amendment that effectively gutted the bill. Moreover, neither the bill's sponsors nor opponents expected it to be voted on by the Senate. The bill was again approved by the House in 1983, this time without the weakening amendment. The willingness of the House to pass a tougher bill in 1983 appears to have been in part due to the decision of the Ford and Chrysler companies to reverse their position and back the legislation. Their strategy appears to have been motivated by their desire to "send a signal" to Tokyo to renew the voluntary agreement restructuring the import of Japanese cars. The Japanese did in fact renew their agreement and the bill never made it to the floor of the Senate.[51]

The administration did respond to pressures from industries hard hit by foreign competition by enacting a number of restrictions of imports. Trade barriers were imposed on imported automobiles in 1981, on carbon steel in 1982 and 1983, and on speciality steel and motorcycles in 1983. These, however, were comparatively modest and the administration vigorously—and successfully—opposed the passage of legislation that would require the government to restrict the imports of particular products from countries that restricted American exports. In general, Congress and the administration were responsive to demands for protection only when they came from business. On its own, organized labor had virtually no effect on trade policy, or indeed on any aspect of economic policy.

As in 1974 and 1975, the difficulties experienced by the American economy in the early 1980s prompted a lively debate about the appropriate scope and purpose of government intervention in the economy. A decade earlier, proponents of an expanded role for government had advocated a form of national economic planning; during the early 1980s, they began to urge that the government adopt a form of national industrial policy. The former was essentially motivated by the desire to shield the American economy from the impact of international economic forces; the latter by an effort to enable American business to compete better internationally. In a series of articles published in the early 1980s, Robert Reich of the Kennedy School of Business and Lester Thurow of MIT argued that the American government already had a de facto industrial policy, since its tax spending and trade policies clearly favored some industries over others.[52] They contended that if American industry was to become more competitive, particularly vis-à-vis Japanese companies, the American government needed to be given a more explicit role in determining which sectors of the economy merited additional assistance and which did not. Critics of their ideas, such as Charles Schultze of the Brookings Institution, countered: "The surest way to multiply unwarranted subsidies and protectionist measures is to legitimize their existence under the rubric of industrial policy."[53]

As the recession deepened and the 1984 election approached, a number of Democratic members of Congress became attracted to the idea of an industrial policy. They viewed it as a viable liberal Democratic alternative to the Reagan administration's economic policies and hoped that it would become a central issue in the next presidential election. In June 1983, Representative John J. LaFalce, a Democrat from upstate New York, announced that the Subcommittee on Economic Stabilization that he chaired would hold a series of hearings on industrial policy. LaFalce contended that he "was not talking about government planning." Rather, he wanted to reexamine the nation's current tax, trade, and credit-allocation programs in order to determine how they could become better "suited to an increasingly competitive world economy."[54]

The following year, Democrats in Congress came up with two concrete proposals. One was to establish a national industry bank to provide loans or guaranty loans to companies in exchange for various concessions, such as cutting labor costs or increasing their level of investment, that would make them more internationally competitive. A "high production strategy" paper outlining this proposal was endorsed by 150 House Democrats.[55] A second was to establish a council of industrial competitiveness to recommend strategies to enable American firms to compete more effectively both in the United States and overseas. Neither proposal ever made it to the floor of the Democratic-controlled House of Representatives, and with the rapid growth of the economy in 1984, industrial policy disappeared from the political agenda. It was not an issue in the 1984 presidential campaign. As Reich later put it, the notion of an industrial policy had gone "from obscurity to meaninglessness" in just a few months.[56]

Nonetheless, the brief flurry of enthusiasm demonstrated for the idea by a number of Democratic politicians was itself significant: it revealed the extent to which a number of the latter—dubbed "neoliberals"—had become more sympathetic to the needs and interests of business. For while neoliberals and conservatives might strongly disagree about what changes in public policy were needed—in general, the former wanted to expand the ability of the government to assist particular sectors while the latter wanted to minimize it—both shared a similar objective: to help American business become more competitive internationally. As Representative Stan Lundine, a Democrat from New York and cosponsor of legislation to establish an industrial development bank put it, "Government has to be on the side of industry."[57]

While the globalization of the American economy during the previous decade may have had an adverse economic impact on American industry, it had clearly shifted the terms of national political discourse. Whereas during the 1974–75 recession, the advocates of national economic planning wanted to enable the government to control business investment decisions more effectively, the advocates of industrial policy in the early 1980s wanted to use the government to more effectively assist business to compete with foreign firms that received extensive government assistance. The former had taken as their model Europe's social democracies, in which labor unions wielded considerable political influence; the latter looked to Japan, a nation whose government had made helping business an important national priority. Not surprisingly, the ideas of neoliberals were strongly criticized by the trade-union movement, which was interested less in making American industry more competitive in global markets than in preserving the jobs and wages of its members. Thus, the 1981–82 recession drove a further wedge between trade unions and segments of the Democratic party.

However, for all its public hostility to the idea of an industrial policy, the Reagan administration in fact dramatically expanded the scope and extent of government assistance to industry, particularly in the area of high technology. The Department of Energy approved a $4.4 billion plan to build a "superconducting supercollider." The Pentagon increased its support for research designed to develop practical applications for superconducting materials and agreed to help fund Sematech—a joint venture of American semiconductor manufacturers. The National Security Agency established a Supercomputer Research Center, and the National Aeronautics and Space Administration agreed to support the design and construction of a space plane, dubbed the "Orient Express." What is significant about these initiatives is not that they occurred. After all, government assistance to industry, particularly under the rubric of national security, has a long history in the United States. It is rather that they evoked virtually no political opposition. Thanks in part to Japan's MITI, fifteen years after Congress had refused to appropriate funds to construct a supersonic transport, the American electorate appeared to have shed much of its hostility toward government support of high technology. The globalization of the American economy also affected antitrust policy. In 1984, Congress approved, with little controversy, legislation making it easier for U.S. companies to cooperate on research and development projects.

Regulatory Policy, 1982–84

Yet while the politics of economic and industrial policy was moving in a direction that was more favorable to business, the politics of deregulation was moving in the opposite direction. After a promising start in 1981, the administration's deregulatory effort began to falter. By 1983, it was clear that the administration had all but abandoned its attempt to bring about major changes in federal regulatory policies. Simon Lazarus, who had worked on regulatory policies in the Carter White House, noted in the spring of 1983, "It's incredible that with a Republican Senate, business groups up in arms and a committed administration, they achieved so little."[58] What accounted for the administration's inability to sustain its deregulatory initiative after 1982?

Part of the explanation has to do with its own political priorities. In spite of the president's pledge to "examine all legislation that serves as the foundation for major regulatory programs,"[59] the administration actually made no effort to repeal or even amend a single major regulatory statute. Christopher Demuth, who headed OMB's office on regulation, admitted, "we have not advanced a single detailed proposal of our own for reform of any of the major health, safety, or environmental statutes." Instead, the administration focused its legislative efforts on other issues. Jerry Jasinowski, an official at the U.S. Chamber of Commerce, recalled: "When senior leaders of the White House staff were asked when there would be a big push in a specific area of regulatory legislation, their reply was invariably, 'after we finish the tax and budget issues'; [but] the tax and budget agenda never ended."[60] The head of regulatory affairs of the NAM complained, in 1983, "We've been working on [regulatory reform] for four years. We had the thing greased to go in 1981. If they had jumped on it early, it would be law today. Instead, the White House had lower echelon people working on it. Legislatively, they've flunked."[61]

The most obvious candidate for revision was the Clean Air Act, which was costing business more than $25 billion a year by the early 1980s and whose ineffectiveness and inefficiency had been exhaustively documented by numerous studies.[62] Ever since 1977, a group of companies and trade associations had been meeting weekly to prepare for the next round of amendments. President Carter's defeat in 1980, along with the Republican capture of the Senate, had provided them with their most important political opening since the adoption of the 1970 amendments a decade earlier. Yet, the White House failed to come up with its own legislative proposal, and in the absence of presidential leadership, business's effort to revise the legislation floundered.

However, even if the administration had decided to press for a substantial revision of the Clean Air Act or any other of the nation's major environmental laws, it is by no means clear that it would have succeeded. Ironically, the environmental movement's political strength had actually grown as a result of the 1980 elections.[63] In response to the fears aroused by the president's campaign rhetoric on environmental issues and his appointment of James Watt as secretary of the interior, the membership of the nation's environmental groups began to increase once again. After remaining stable for three years, between 1980 and 1983, the Sierra Club's membership grew from 180,000 to 335,000.[64] In 1981, the public's response to mail solicitations by the Sierra Club, the Wilderness Society, and the Natural Resources Defense Council increased 30 percent.

Just as businesses began to cooperate more closely with each other following Jimmy Carter's election to the presidency, after 1980 the leaders of the nation's ten major environmental organizations began to meet regularly to discuss common problems and strategies. One activist noted that in contrast to the 1970s, when "there was a lot of turf fighting, . . . the leaders have made a special effort to work together."[65] At the same time, they also became more aggressive. The Sierra Club collected more than a million signatures on a petition calling for Watt's resignation and the Friends of the Earth ran a series of expensive advertisements in a number of major newspapers that blamed the president for Ann Gorsuch's policies. These ads generated thousands of dollars in contributions. In the 1982 congressional election, environmental groups spent $42 million—double the sum in 1980—on organizing volunteers who participated in more than seventy campaigns.

The movement's political effectiveness was also enhanced by a number of widely publicized public-opinion polls that revealed that the public continued to support strong controls over pollution. A Roper survey conducted in September 1982 reported that only 21 percent thought that "environmental protection laws and regulations have gone too far." By contrast, 69 percent agreed that "they are about right or haven't gone far enough."[66] The pollster Louis Harris testified before Congress that "clean air happens to be one of the sacred cows of the American people."[67] A Harris survey conducted in 1982 reported that 95 percent of those polled considered "disposal of hazardous wastes" to be a serious problem, while an ABC News–*Washington Post* poll in April 1983 found that "even though the large majority of Americans believe compliance with antipollution laws costs business firms at least a fair amount of money, more than three out of four say these laws are worth the cost."[68] The portion of Americans agreeing with the statement that "protecting the environment is so important that requirements and standards cannot be too high" increased from 45 percent in September 1981 to 58 percent in April 1983.[69]

The environmental movement's strength in the Congress during the 1980s was first revealed in 1982 when Congress overwhelmingly voted to extend the Endangered Species Act without making any significant changes in it. This extension took place only a few years after the nation appeared to have been outraged by the use of this statute to delay the construction of a dam in Tennessee. The following year, congressional pressure forced the EPA to withdraw its suspension of a ban on liquid wastes in landfills and to strengthen, instead of weaken, limits on the lead content of gasoline. In May 1982, the head of the Business Roundtable Task Force on the environment sent a telegram to the members of the Roundtable warning them that, if the business community did not press its views more effectively, "it is possible that the environmental community will have earned a highly publicized and stunning victory that could frustrate regulatory reform efforts for the balance of this administration."[70] These fears proved well founded. Not only did Congress leave the Clean Air Act intact, but between 1981 and 1983, it repeatedly approved legislation that restricted the Department of the Interior's plans to lease federal wilderness areas to developers.

The resistance of the Congress to the administration's deregulatory initiatives was not confined to environmental policy. In spite of the OMB's efforts to cut off all funds for the CPSC, Congress continued to renew the commission's appropriations, though the commission was forced to close a number of its offices. Despite heated congressional criticism of the FTC in the late 1970s, Congress refused to go along with James Miller's proposal that its ten regional offices be abolished; it continued to provide funds to keep most of them open, though their size was reduced. And after 1981, Congress repeatedly appropriated more funds for social-regulatory agencies than the administration requested.

Initially, the FTC found itself on the defensive. In 1981, after a decade of deliberation, it finally issued a rule that required used-car dealers to place a sticker on each used car that stated whether a warranty was offered on the vehicle and if the dealer knew of any defects. The following year, the National Association of Car Dealers, taking advantage of the momentum generated by congressional opposition to the FTC two years earlier, persuaded Congress to exercise its legislative veto. On May 18, 1982, by a vote of 69 to 27, the Senate adopted a resolution expressing its disapproval of this rule; the next week, the House endorsed the Senate action by a vote of 286 to 133.

Congress's decision appeared to open the way for an additional round of challenges to the commission's authority. As one congressional staff member put it, "politically speaking, if you can't muster votes against used-car dealers, you can't do anything."[71] Almost immediately, a number of professional trade groups, led by the American Medical Association (AMA) began lobbying for an amendment to the commission's reauthorization act that would exempt doctors, dentists, and other professional groups from the commission's jurisdiction. This effort was strongly opposed by James Miller, the FTC's chair, on the grounds that professional restraints on competition were inappropriate. As in the cases of airline and trucking deregulation, free-market conservatives and liberal consumer activists found themselves on the same side: the former opposed all forms of market regulation, including self-regulation, while the latter were concerned about price fixing and monopolization. The *Wall Street Journal* editorialized: "Generally, more power to the FTC has meant more punitive and unnecessary regulation. But this time the Commission is on the side of the markets. . . . On this one we are on the side of the Feds."[72] All of the 154 newspapers that published editorials on the issue supported Miller's position.

It turned out that Congress's overturning of the FTC's used-car rule was the high point of anti-FTC sentiment in the Congress. On December 17, 1982, following a dramatic all-night session, the Senate, by a vote of 59 to 37, rejected the request of the AMA and its allies. The vote came somewhat as a surprise, since the Senate Commerce Committee had previously approved the exemption by a two-to-one margin. What accounted for it? First, in contrast to the effort to curb the commission's authority in 1979 and 1980, the business community was not unified. The major business lobbies, such as the Chamber of Commerce, were neutral, while the Washington Business Group on Health, which represented two hundred large firms, opposed the exemption on the grounds that it would increase the cost of health care. Second, a powerful lobby, the American Association of Retired Persons, vigorously opposed the exemption, as did a coalition composed of the American Nurses Association and thirty other professional associations. Finally, an important role was played by Ralph Nader's Congress Watch, which had released a series of studies that documented the AMA's extensive campaign contributions while the debate was proceeding. Congress Watch revealed that the AMA had contributed $1.7 million to the 1982 congressional campaign—more than any other PAC—and that of the exemption's 192 congressional cosponsors, 186 had received an average of $6,145 from each of the three trade groups "that stood to benefit from its enactment."[73] These disclosures received extensive press coverage and proved embarrassing to many members of Congress.

Following the critical Senate vote, Jay Angoff, a lawyer with Congress Watch, observed, "Congress has been beating up on the FTC since 1979, and they've finally said, 'Enough.' " The legislative director of the Consumer Federation of America stated, "I think maybe Congress is finally starting to get a sense of what this agency's mission ought to be."[74] Their optimism proved well founded: while consumer organizations remained extremely critical of Miller's performance as commission chair, Congress never again seriously debated placing any additional limitations on the FTC's authority. The following year, a commission rule governing sales practices in the funeral industry went into effect—the first new FTC regulation to survive congressional scrutiny in almost three years.

But Congress was not the only obstacle to major changes in regulatory policies. A number of the Reagan administration's deregulatory initiatives were also overturned by the courts. In 1981 and 1982, four major changes of rules proposed by the EPA were declared illegal by various federal courts on the grounds that the administration lacked either the legal authority or the scientific basis to enact them. In December 1982, a federal district court judge, in a case brought by a Tennessee environmental organization, criticized Watt for "flouting" the enforcement of the 1977 Surface Mining Control and Reclamation Act and ordered the secretary to enforce 1,700 case-operations orders against derelict coal-mine operators and collect some $44 million in back penalties.[75] And in 1983, the administration's most important deregulatory initiative, NHTSA's decision to rescind the passive-restraint standards for automobiles, was held to be "arbitrary and capricious."[76] The Supreme Court also frustrated an attempt by OSHA to apply a cost-benefit test to a rule establishing cotton-dust standards for textile workers.

However, probably the most important reason for the failure of the administration and the business community to reverse significantly the direction of federal social regulation was due to the controversy that surrounded the management of the EPA and the Department of the Interior. From the outset, Gorsuch's "tough and often condescending manner" alienated both the environmental community and the congressional committees that oversaw the agency.[77] Her strained relations with the EPA's professional staff, along with her repeated reorganization of the agency and the administration's substantial budget cuts, threw the EPA into chaos. Even business was appalled. Less than a year after she assumed office, a writer in *Automotive News*, the trade journal of the automobile industry, observed:

In the ten-year history of EPA, there have been periods of turmoil, but none rivals what is happening now under the reign of Anne Gorsuch. What was once a robust, dynamic entity has shriveled to a gray shadow of its former self, wracked by internal dissension, run by people with little expertise in environmental issues, and dogged by a paranoia that has virtually brought it to a standstill.[78]

Gorsuch's erratic administration—between July 1981 and May 1982, the enforcement division went through a major reorganization every eleven weeks—was as bewildering to business as it was to environmentalists. A

Washington attorney who represented the Chemical Manufacturers Association stated, "The chemical industry certainly doesn't want to see EPA dismembered."[79] Another business lobbyist noted, "We're in favor of intelligent implementation of the laws, but an agency in disarray can't do that."[80]

At the same time, many industries feared that a sudden decline in federal enforcement of environmental regulations would result in more vigorous regulatory activity by the states—thus confronting them with fifty sets of rules instead of one. In 1982, Jeffrey H. Joseph, the vice president for domestic policy of the Chamber of Commerce, stated that "many business leaders are concerned that the New Federalism, along with the President's strong conviction that states should play a larger role in regulation and his decision to reduce federal agency staffs and budgets, could lead states to believe there is a regulatory vacuum to be filled."[81] Their concerns were well founded: many of the administration's deregulatory initiatives did create a "regulatory vacuum" which was to some extent filled by more vigorous regulation by a number of states.[82] Moreover, some of the firms that had already complied with various environmental rules and regulations did not want to see them relaxed, lest their competitors not have to undertake the same expenditures. For example, in 1980, the manager of government relations for Texaco criticized the EPA for "rewarding those companies that failed to comply."[83]

In 1982, the agency's management of the "superfund" program came under congressional scrutiny. It was discovered that in the course of two years, the EPA had managed to clean up only two sites. A subsequent House audit revealed that the agency could not account for nearly one-third of the 1982 appropriations for the superfund. By the end of 1982, more than six congressional panels were investigating charges that the EPA had made "sweetheart" deals with various companies, delayed clean-ups for political reasons, and destroyed documents regarding its management of the $1.6 billion fund. On December 16, 1982, the House of Representatives cited Burford (née Gorsuch) for contempt of Congress after she refused to turn over documents sought by a House subcommittee examining the EPA's management of the nation's hazardous waste cleanup program. Two months later President Reagan was pressured into firing Rita Lavelle, the official responsible for the management of the superfund. She was accused, among other things, of preventing the EPA's general counsel from filing suits against twenty-four companies in order to force them to clean up a dump near Seymour, Indiana, and of harassing an EPA official who had criticized the enforcement of the superfund on "60 Minutes." Lavelle was subsequently convicted of lying to Congress under oath and served time in federal prison. A month later, amid mounting public and congressional questioning of Burford's competence and integrity, she, along with twenty of the agency's twenty-one senior officials, was forced to resign.

Thanks to Burford and Lavelle, not since the early 1970s had environmental regulation been as politically salient as it became in late 1982 and early 1983. The scandals surrounding Burford's management at the EPA dealt a severe blow to the Reagan administration's efforts to change the nation's environmental laws. According to one policy analyst, the Reagan administration "destroyed for a decade the ability to think about reform in a nonpartisan way. You can't talk intelligently about changing the Clean Air Act because the first question is how Anne [Burford] will enforce it. And that's the end of the discussion."[84] Murray Weidenbaum wrote that, as a result of Burford's scandal-ridden reign, "Just try to change a comma in the Clean Air Act and you lay yourself open to charges that you want to 'gut' environmental protection."[85] Consequently, environmentalists were once again able to occupy the high ground. They were not powerful enough to get Congress to amend the Clean Air Act to include controls over the emissions that contributed to acid rain, in part because of a regional conflict among the nation's utilities about who should pay the costs of abatement. But in 1984, Congress, for the first time since 1980, did approve a new regulatory statute. The Resources Conservation and Recovery Act brought tens of thousands of small businesses, from dry cleaners to gas stations, under the EPA's jurisdiction. Its passage reflected the potency of toxic waste as a political issue as the 1984 presidential election drew near. Also in 1984, Congress increased the EPA's appropriations, bringing them to their highest level in three years, though still below their level in President Carter's administration. One corporate lobbyist noted, "There's been a shift in the climate," and the director of the Washington office of Consumers Union stated that lawmakers now realize that there are "very substantial, valid federal responsibilities in the areas of health, safety and consumer protection."[86]

Nor was the impact of Burford's resignation confined to environmental policy. Just as congressional hostility to Pertschuk led to the retrenchment of other social regulatory agencies after 1978, Burford's resignation had precisely the opposite effect four years later. Shortly after she was removed from office, the administrator of OSHA, Thorne Auchter, proposed to tighten standards of exposure to two carcinogens, asbestos and benzene. "The sound of the guillotine falling at EPA just rumbled across the Mall to the Labor Department. Thorne was not unmindful of what was happening to his friends." The rule to limit workers' exposure to asbestos was the first emergency standard issued by OSHA in five years: it cost business $30 million. That same year, the NHTSA issued a rule requiring new cars to include a stoplight near the middle of the rear window to reduce rear-end collisions—one of the Carter administration's "midnight" regulations President Reagan had revoked shortly after his inauguration. The agency also recalled twice as many cars in 1983 as it had in 1982. And in 1984, Transportation Secretary Elizabeth Dole issued a rule requiring automakers to phase in some form of "crash protection"—though she did stipulate that if states representing two-thirds of the U.S. population passed laws mandating the use of seat belts by April 1, 1984, the federal regulation would not take effect. Burford's resignation also appeared to have effectively put to rest one of the Reagan administration's most ambitious efforts at deregulation, namely, the easing of controls over cancer-causing substances. Sensitive to charges that it was being "soft on cancer,"[87] the pace of these deregulatory efforts dramatically slowed down after 1983. As the administration official put it, "there's an election coming, and how can we be for cancer or be seen as being in the pocket of big business?"[88]

Less than a year after Burford's resignation, James Watt was forced to resign as well. The immediate cause of his departure had nothing to do with his environmental policies; it was precipitated by remarks at a breakfast meeting with two hundred U.S. Chamber of Commerce lobbyists at which he described the members of his newly appointed coal-leasing commission as including "a black . . . , a woman, two Jews, and a cripple."[89] The furor that his remark created was magnified by the growing public and congressional criticism of his wilderness, oil-drilling, and strip-mining policies. Watt's heavy-handed efforts to open up public land to energy and timber production had a lightning-rod effect, drawing public attention to environmental issues that had been out of the limelight for some time.[90] In 1982, Congress ordered the establishment of a commission to investigate charges that he was virtually giving away federal coal leases by offering them for sale at a time of slack demand. (It was this commission whose composition Watt had been describing). In 1983, Congress prohibited the Department of the Interior from conducting sales of Outer Continental Slope oil leases in southern California, in the Gulf of Mexico next to Florida, and off the Georges Banks fishing grounds of Massachusetts. Following Watt's resignation, Congress voted to set aside more than 8.3 million acres of national forest land in twenty states as federally protected wilderness, thus permanently shielding them from road building, logging, mining, and other development. This was one of the most significant expansions of federal control of land use in more than a decade.

The de facto abandonment of the Reagan administration's commitment to reduce government control of corporate social conduct came in August 1983, when vice-presidential counsel C. Borden Gray announced the abolition of the Task Force on Regulatory Relief. The administration's contention that the task force's goals had been accomplished was greeted with considerable skepticism. The government claimed that the task force had produced savings of $150 billion for business and the public. However, this sum included savings that resulted from deregulatory actions taken by previous administrations and by Congress, as well as savings from the repeal of regulations that had been proposed but not adopted. Moreover, it failed to take into account the fact that in many cases "reforms" that represented a "savings" for a particular industry increased costs in other sectors of the economy. In all, the actual net savings to business from the task force's efforts appeared to add up to about one-third of the sum the task force claimed.

Nonetheless, during its first term in office the Reagan administration did succeed in slowing down the rate of increase in federal controls over corporate social conduct. For the first time in more than two decades, Congress went for three years without passing a single important piece of regulatory legislation, although two pieces of environmental regulation were passed in 1984. In addition, the size of the *Federal Register* (admittedly a crude index of federal regulatory activity) declined each year during the Reagan administration's first term in office—after having increased steadily for nearly two decades. The number of rules proposed by federal regulatory agencies during the first forty-four months of the Reagan administration fell by 25 percent and the number of pages printed in the *Federal Register* declined by 21 percent—relative to the totals from a comparable period during the Carter administration.[91] And virtually every social regulatory agency had a smaller budget—and fewer employees—than when the administration took office. Overall, both the staff and the budget of the nation's social regulatory agencies decreased by 12 percent between 1981 and 1985. Between fiscal year 1980 and fiscal year 1985, the budget of the CPSC declined by 33 percent (in real dollars); the EPA, by 4 percent; the NHTSC, by 22 percent; OSHA, by 10 percent; and the Nuclear Regulatory Commission, by 14 percent.[92]

However, in one area of government regulation, the administration did succeed in bringing about a major change in federal policy: industrial relations.[93] The National Labor Relations Board (NLRB), which was responsible for administering the nation's labor laws, had been relatively uncontroversial for several years: in Democratic administrations, its decisions were somewhat more favorable to organized labor, while in Republican administrations, business enjoyed a slight advantage. Although organized labor was unsuccessful on the legislative front, in 1977 and 1978 the officials appointed to the NLRB during the Carter administration had been generally prolabor. The agency's policies, however, changed dramatically in 1983—as soon as the president's appointees constituted a solid majority. "In only 150 days the new majority has reversed at least eight major precedents. By some estimates, it has already recast nearly 40 percent of the decisions made since the mid-1970s that the conservatives found objectionable." The NLRB's new changes in policy significantly strengthened the rights and prerogatives of management vis-à-vis unions. Compared to those issued during the Carter administration and even to those issued during the Ford administration, its decisions were more consistently probusiness. For example, between 1983 and 1984, 72 percent of its decisions in representation cases favored business—as compared with 46 percent between 1979 and 1980 and 35 percent between 1975 and 1976. At the same time, the board became much more inefficient. There were 800 contested cases awaiting decisions by the full board when Reagan took office; in 1984, its backlog was 1,700. The resulting bottleneck reinforced the board's anti-union "animus," since it effectively made it "much more difficult for unions to organize new workers or effectively represent the members they already had."[94]

The result of the NLRB's policies, along with the 1981–82 recession and increased international competition in manufacturing, was to reduce the number of workers who belonged to unions by 2.7 million during Reagan's first term in office. By 1984, only 15.6 percent of wage and salary workers in the private sector were unionized—a smaller proportion than at any time since the 1930s. And in sharp contrast to the administration's efforts to weaken the enforcement of health and safety regulations, its anti-union policies did not create a political backlash. Indeed, while trade unions have generally done rather poorly in Gallup polls, they did "significantly worse in surveys during the Reagan era, with an almost unchanging rating of 28 percent, than in the previous ones in which their trust scores ranged between 39 percent (1977) and 35 percent (1980). . . . Labor organizations placed at the bottom of a list of twelve institutions evaluated in a March 1985 Roper poll.[95]

The 1984 Election

Although many executives continued to express concern about the size of the budget deficit and frustration with the slow pace of deregulation, on balance they were extremely satisfied with the president's performance during his first term in office. Louis Harris and Associates reported in the summer of 1983 that "business executives have not had a President more to their liking since Dwight Eisenhower." Harris added, "Despite the worst recession since the 1930s business is firmly in the President's corner."[96] By 1984, with the recovery now firmly under way, business support for the president solidified. As the chairman of General Motors, Roger Smith, put it, "You have to admire the tremendous job of restoring the economy that the President has accomplished."[97]

With a handful of exceptions, virtually the entire corporate community preferred President Reagan to his Democratic opponent, Walter Mondale, in 1984. A poll of small-business owners conducted by *Nation's Business* reported that Reagan was favored over Mondale by a nine-to-one margin.[98] Most business people disliked Mondale's proposal to raise taxes and were concerned about his support for domestic-content legislation. They also believed Reagan would be in a better position to cut nondefense spending and thus sustain the economic recovery that had begun in 1983. Mondale's candidacy was, in turn, strongly backed by precisely those political constituencies that had seen their influence erode during the Reagan administration, namely, organized labor—which had backed Mondale's quest for the nomination from the outset—and the public-interest movement. The 1984 election was the first presidential election in which a number of environmental organizations officially endorsed a candidate.

On the other hand, the ties between the Republican party's congressional candidates and business weakened in 1984. Inspired by the considerable successes of Republican challenges to Democratic incumbents in 1980, corporations had distributed an even larger share of their contributions to Republicans in 1982—many of whom were either vulnerable incumbents or high-risk challengers to incumbent Democrats. This strategy, however, did not work as well in 1982 as it had in 1980. Only 45 percent of the candidates endorsed by the U.S. Chamber of Commerce—whose recommendations were followed by many business PACs—were elected, and the Democrats gained twenty-six seats in the House of Representatives. The business community had clearly overestimated the vulnerability of Republican incumbents and the electoral prospects of Republican challengers. As one House Democratic campaign official put it, "We had a message

[for business PACs after 1982], and the message was, 'You got burned.' "
In addition, business's close identification with the Republican party in
both the 1980 and 1982 elections had created strains between various
companies and a number of powerful Democratic members of Congress.
One executive concluded, "When Democrats are going to control the
House, it makes sense for corporate PACs to [support] Democratic candidates who are more pro-business."[99]

The success of Democratic candidates—incumbents as well as challengers—in 1982 persuaded many corporate political strategists that it would
be difficult, if not impossible, to significantly reduce the strength of the
Democratic party in the House of Representatives. At the same time, the
Democratic Campaign Committee, chaired by Representative Tony Coehlo
of California, waged an aggressive campaign to solicit contributions from
business. He urged executives "not to let your ideology get in the way of
your business judgment." The chairman of Tenneco's PAC, one of the
largest corporate PACs, noted that "the political climate has changed
somewhat and is more [supportive of] the private sector." According to
Michael Malbin of the American Enterprise Institute, "congressional Democrats were speaking more about capital formation and other business
issues."[100] As a result, in 1984 the share of business contributions dispersed to Democratic candidates for federal office increased again. For
example, in 1980, 29 percent of the spending of corporate PACs went to
Republican challengers and open-seat races; however, in 1984, only 17
percent went to these candidates. However, as in the late 1970s, corporate
and trade-association support for Democrats was restricted to races in
which a Democratic incumbent was heavily favored. In close races or those
for open seats, business and business-related PAC contributions continued
overwhelmingly to go to Republicans. Ironically, the Republican party did
relatively well in 1984; the Democratic majority was reduced by twelve in
the House of Representatives, although the Democrats did pick up two
seats in the Senate. This led some students of corporate political activity
to argue that business PACs had played it too safe in 1984: 87 percent of
the candidates receiving $50,000 or more from business PACs won their
races.[101]

The pattern of presidential voting in 1984 also revealed an important
shift in the political loyalties of the new class: the majority of young,
college-educated professionals—the very political constituency that had
spearheaded the political challenge to business in the 1970s—voted for
Reagan. For the first time since 1972, business and the new class voted for
the same presidential candidate. The new class did not support Reagan

because of his stance on social regulation, but regulatory policy was not an issue in the 1984 presidential campaign. They supported Reagan because of his tax and spending policies, which benefited them as well as business. Martin Shefter and Benjamin Ginsberg wrote:

> It has been argued that the New Class is inherently liberal, because its members have greater leverage in the public than in the private sector. In point of fact, however, this class has no inherent ideological tendencies. Ronald Reagan has undertaken to divide its members with his tax reductions and domestic budget cuts—expanding opportunities for middle class professionals in the private sector, while restricting opportunities in the public and nonprofit sectors. Those college educated professionals who are in a position to take advantage of these opportunities are being attracted into the Republican party.[102]

In a sense, the new class had come full circle: in the space of twelve years, it had moved from being the primary source of political support of increased restrictions on business to becoming an important component of an electorate that provided a probusiness president with one of this century's most impressive electoral triumphs. In sum, "the Reaganites . . . brought about the political reunification of upper middle-class professionals with business owners and managers."[103]

Equally significant, Ronald Reagan also succeeded in winning the political support of the baby boomers: voters under forty were more likely to vote for Ronald Reagan than voters over forty. What attracted younger voters to Ronald Reagan? As William Schneider wrote:

> Young voters are much better educated than older voters. As a result, they tend to be relatively affluent, upwardly mobile, and optimistic. . . . Since they are higher in status, younger voters tend to be more confident about the future. They have no personal memory of the Great Depression. They do, however, remember the economic decline of the 1970s, and feel that Reagan's policies have reversed many of the negative economic trends.[104]

Fred Siegel observed:

> The baby boomers, part of an enormous demographic clot that entered the job market in the 1970s, were undergoing a major shift in attitude. Faced with an often vicious competition for jobs and dismayed by the temporary prosperity of unionized workers with indexed wages, they were calling for a revival of economic growth by any means possible. Frightened by the prospect of downward mobility, these were the people for whom real estate and investment opportunities were the chief topics of conversation.[105]

The support of yuppies for President Reagan's reelection was only one indication of the rapprochement between the educated middle class and business. College students in the early 1980s were also less hostile to business than their counterparts had been fifteen years earlier. Between 1973 and 1983, the proportion of undergraduates receiving bachelors' degrees in business nearly doubled: by 1983, a quarter of all undergraduates in the United States were majoring in business.[106] Business-school enrollments also increased substantially. Between 1975 and 1985, the number of M.B.A. degrees granted in the United States increased from 36,247 to 67,727. In 1975, 12 percent of all masters' degrees granted were business degrees; a decade later this percentage had doubled.[107]

The nation's social and cultural values, which had been relatively hostile to business during the 1960s, also became more supportive of the private sector. During the first half of the 1980s, a number of business executives became celebrities. Indeed, not since the 1920s were so many business leaders both well known and admired. *Business Week* observed: "Sometime in the late 1970s, America's mood changed. No more radical chic. Instead . . . making money was in. Business, viewed with contempt by some in recent years, is now popular. Making money is an acceptable ambition once again on college campuses. The rise of the executive celebrity reflects these trends."[108] In 1984, the autobiography of Lee Iacocca, who was widely credited with rescuing Chrysler from bankruptcy, led the nonfiction best-seller list; by 1985, it had sold more copies than any other nonfiction book in recent American history. In 1984, Iacocca was ranked among the ten most admired men in the United States—the first business executive to make this list in nearly three decades. One poll reported that he trailed Vice President Bush by only three points in a presidential trial heat. The *National Journal* observed: "Ten years ago in the heyday of the consumer and environmental movements, it would have been as likely to discuss a businessman for president as a general. But times change and heroes reflect their times."[109] Nor was Iaccoca the only business folk hero. T. Boone Pickens, Jr., appeared on the cover of twenty magazines and NBC produced a movie chronicling H. Ross Perot's successful efforts to rescue two employees of Electronic Data Systems from an Iranian jail. Norman Lear wrote in 1987:

Never before has the business of business been such a cultural preoccupation. If media attention is any indication of popular interest—and it is—today there is an unprecedented interest in business affairs. In recent years, a dozen new business programs have burst forth on commercial television, public television and cable. Americans once found their heroes, for the most part, in

Congress or the entertainment world or sports; now more and more people find them in business.[110]

However, this new enthusiasm for business did not result in an endorsement of the position of business on health and safety issues, which was, in part, why the efforts of business and the administration to weaken the regulation of corporate social conduct were so unsuccessful. The sharp decline in the inflation rate in the early 1980s, coupled with the scandals surrounding Burford and Watt, reaffirmed the new class's strong commitment to social regulation in areas that affected its personal health and safety. Ironically, the public-interest movement continued to enjoy substantial political influence precisely because the neoconservative critique of it was valid: support for environmentalism was in large measure based on material self-interest, not altruism.[111] Health and safety requirements imposed on business meant that the upper middle class could go about its business of consuming without having to worry about threats to its physical well-being. At the same time, environmental regulations protected and enhanced property values, in addition to facilitating the consumption of various public goods. In short, for many Americans social regulation had itself become a form of consumption.

It is true that public support for business, as measured by polls, did not increase in the mid-1980s, but this was largely because many Americans remained troubled by the inability of many of the nation's best-known companies to compete successfully in the world economy. (The proportion of those expressing a "highly favorable" opinion of the large business corporation was 18 percent in 1981; by 1984, it had increased only to 21 percent.)[112] But in contrast to the 1970s, "Big business" was now disliked not because it was too powerful but because it was seen as too inefficient. The business heroes of the 1980s tended to be entrepreneurs like Steven Jobs, iconoclasts like Lee Iacocca, or raiders like T. Boone Pickens—none of them typical corporate CEOs.

Although the public may have remained unimpressed by the executives who ran large companies, its opinion of specific industries did improve: attitudes toward the computer and business-machines industry, food processing, airlines, the automobile industry, the telecommunications and information-systems industry, and even the oil industry all became more positive between 1980 and 1984. All but the last were given "highly favorable" marks by more than half of those surveyed.[113] Three years later, when asked to describe their attitude toward business in the United States, 72 percent of those polled characterized it as either "very" or "somewhat favorable" and only 24 percent described it as either "somewhat" or "very unfavorable." When asked whether they would be more likely to vote for a presidential candidate with "strong business backing," 59 percent responded yes.[114]

The Politics of Social Regulation, 1985–88

The politics of social regulation became less salient during the administration's second term, with one notable exception: a bitter fight over the extension of the superfund program, whose five-year authorization of $1.6 billion was due to expire on September 30, 1985. Reversing his earlier position, the president called for the fund's reauthorization in his 1985 State of the Union address. There was little disagreement about whether funding for the program to clean up abandoned toxic waste sites should be increased; rather, the debate was focused on who should pay for it. On this issue, the business community was divided: the oil and chemical industries favored a broad-based business tax while the rest of the business community wanted the fund to be financed by a tax on only those companies.

On the eve of the 1984 elections, the House overwhelmingly passed a strong superfund bill, which provided $10 billion and included a number of provisions to accelerate the cleanup of hazardous wastes. The Senate, however, did not act. The following year, the Sierra Club, concerned that congressional support for the legislation might diminish following the 1984 election, embarked on "the most elaborate membership mobilization in the history of the club." Linda Fowler and Ronald Shaiko wrote: "With the most sophisticated computer system within the environmental movement and some of the most experienced grass roots coordinators within their nationwide membership network, the Sierra Club went to work in Washington and also across the nation."[115]

Both houses of Congress approved legislation extending the superfund program in 1985, but they were unable to reconcile their different versions. In general, the House's version more closely reflected the preferences of the environmental movement. It authorized a total of $10 billion, while the Senate bill authorized only $7.5 billion. The House's bill also included a mandatory cleanup schedule which required the EPA to meet specific deadlines, as well as a section granting citizens the right to sue companies to force them to clean up sites that presented an imminent danger to public health. Both provisions were omitted from the Senate bill. Most important, the House's version funded the cleanup program primarily by taxing the oil and chemical industries, while the Senate's bill included a broad tax on business. The Reagan administration contended that both bills were too expensive—it wanted funding of $5.3 billion over five years—and the president threatened to veto any legislation that included a broad-based tax on business.

In March 1986, both houses approved, by voice vote, an emergency two-month extension of the superfund. A second stopgap measure was approved in August. Finally, on October 3, 1986, the two houses reached an agreement. The authorization level was set at $8.5 billion over a five-year period; approximately half of this sum would come from a tax on petroleum and on chemical feedstocks and about a third would be derived from a broad-based business tax. This compromise was bitterly opposed by the Grocery Manufacturers Association which had organized a coalition of five hundred corporations and trade association to demand that "only the polluters should pay for their cleanup."[116] In a surprising twist, the bill was supported by the politically powerful independent "wildcat drillers," because imported oil was to be taxed at a higher rate than domestically produced oil—a differential that looked very much like a tax on imported oil to officials in the Treasury Department. The bill, reflecting congressional impatience with the slow pace of the cleanup program under Rita Lavelle, also required the EPA to start a minimal number of cleanups in the next five years, but it established no deadlines for their completion.

In three important respects, the bill was stronger than the legislation Congress had approved in 1980. Reflecting the impact of the 1984 explosion of a chemical plant in Bhopal, India, the 1986 reauthorization required that industry provide local communities with information about the chemicals they produce, store, or handle, and the toxic chemicals that they emit into the environment. The 1986 legislation also established a $500 million program to clean up gasoline storage tanks that had corroded and were leaking into the groundwater. Finally, Congress voted to give the victims of toxic dumping additional time to sue those they believed responsible, and it allowed citizens to sue either the EPA or private parties for violation of the provisions of the statute. President Reagan had initially planned to veto the legislation because of its cost and sources of revenue, but he bowed to congressional pressure and, on October 17, 1986, the superfund legislation was signed into law.

That same year, Congress reached an agreement on the reauthorization of another important environmental statute: the 1974 Safe Drinking Water Act. Like the superfund legislation, the new law was stronger in a number of respects than the original statute. The 1974 legislation regulated only about two dozen of the more than six hundred contaminants found in drinking water, but the 1986 statute required that the EPA limit eighty-three contaminants in drinking water and established a deadline of three years for compliance. The 1986 legislation also increased the EPA's authority over state standards for drinking water and increased the maximum civil penalties the courts could impose for violation of drinking-water regulations from $5,000 to $25,000 per day. Its most important and controversial provision required the states to draw up plans for protecting underground drinking water and to submit them to the EPA for approval—although this requirement was not extended to all the nation's groundwater. The administration had opposed the imposition of federal controls on groundwater, believing that this responsibility should remain in the hands of the states. Nonetheless, the president signed the Safe Drinking Water Act into law on June 19, 1985.

President Reagan did refuse to sign one important piece of environmental legislation: on November 6, 1986, he pocket vetoed a water-pollution control bill that had been approved unanimously by both houses in the final days of the 1986 congressional session. He vetoed this bill for the same reason that President Nixon had vetoed a nearly identical piece of legislation fourteen years earlier, namely, its budgetary impact. Congress had authorized $20 billion in federal funds to help local government build sewage treatment plants, a sum, which according to the president, exceeded the government's "intended budgetary commitments."[117] The extent of congressional support for this legislation had little to do with pollution control per se; rather, the bill's political popularity stemmed from the fact that it gave members of Congress a chance to take credit for additional federal spending in their districts. Congress again approved the legislation in January 1987, and the president again vetoed it, describing it as "loaded with waste and larded with pork."[118] Congress then passed the statute for the third time in almost as many months. The House voted 401 to 26 to override the president's veto; the Senate, by 86 to 14.

The relative strength of proregulation forces in Congress throughout the 1980s reflected in part a continued backlash against the administration's earlier deregulatory initiatives. One political analyst noted in 1987 that "the anti-government revolt of the 1970s is over." A public-opinion poll taken in 1987 reported that 61 percent of those surveyed believed that there should be more regulation of the environment and that only 6 percent supported less regulation. In addition, only 38 percent of those surveyed believed there was too much government regulation of the economy—down from 67 percent in 1980.[119] The proportion of those surveyed believing that the United States was spending "too little" on the environment increased from 50 percent in 1980 to 69 percent in 1987. More than three out of five adults surveyed in March 1987 said that there should be more regulation of the environment, and only 6 percent thought that there should be less.[120] In addition, 43 percent of those surveyed in 1987 favored more regulation of automobile safety and only 13 percent favored less.

In response to this evident increase in public support of health and safety regulations, a number of agencies strengthened their enforcement efforts. For example, the Justice Department's environmental crime unit, established at the height of the controversy surrounding the management of the EPA, increased the number of civil suits filed to more than two hundred a year. In 1986, these resulted in consent decrees that required firms to spend a total of $500 million on the cleanup of hazardous waste sites. The Occupational Health and Safety Administration also began to make a more vigorous effort to enforce regulations under its purview. While the agency imposed penalties of only $14,166 on firms for record-keeping violations in 1981, in 1986 it levied nearly $1.5 million in penalties, and in 1987, more than $11 million. Chrysler was fined $1.57 million; Union Carbide Corporation, $1.3 million; and IBP, Inc., $2.6 million—the largest single fine imposed on a firm in the agency's history.[121] And responding to the public's worries about airline safety and complaints about service, Transportation Secretary Elizabeth Dole sped up by four years a requirement that small planes operating at fourteen busy airports have altitude-reporting equipment and issued a regulation designed to reduce the delays on airline flights. Finally, after declining by an average of 4.6 percent a year between 1980 and 1983, the budgets of the agencies responsible for consumer safety and health, job safety, and the environment rose between 1983 and 1988 at an average annual rate of 3.8 percent—only a percentage point lower than their average rate of growth between 1975 and 1980. Their number of employees, which had declined by an average of 0.5 percent between 1980 and 1983, grew by that same percentage between 1983 and 1988.

The Politics of Tax Reform

The politics of business-government relations in 1985 and 1986 was dominated by the issue of tax reform. On October 22, 1986, President Reagan signed into law the Tax Reform Act of 1986. The most far-reaching change in the history of the Internal Revenue Code, this legislation reduced the top individual tax rate from 50 to 28 percent, abolished the special tax treatment for capital gains, and took more than four million low-income families off the federal tax roles. Its impact on corporations was equally sweeping: it reduced the top corporate tax rate from 48 to 42 percent, repealed the tax credit for investment, and abolished or reduced a large number of tax breaks for particular industries. On balance, the legislation transferred approximately $120 billion of taxes from individuals to corporations over the next five years.

The 1986 legislation represented a substantial political setback for a number of segments of the business community, including financial institutions, real estate and construction companies, insurance firms, and capital-intensive manufacturing companies. It also constituted a major political defeat for the capital formation lobby, which had played such an influential role in shaping both the 1978 and 1981 Revenue Acts. If there was an unequivocal winner, it was the Citizens for Tax Justice, a public-interest group formed with the assistance of Ralph Nader, which had been campaigning to make corporations pay their "fair share" of federal taxes since 1969. What made this extraordinary political outcome possible?

Like the consumer protection laws of the 1960s and economic deregulation of the 1970s, tax reform reached the political agenda at the initiative of a handful of politicians. It was a classic case of political entrepreneurship, since, prior to the mid-1980s, there had been little interest in or support for such a radical change in the nation's tax laws. Of these entrepreneurs, undoubtedly the most important was Ronald Reagan, who decided to make tax reform the major domestic political priority of his administration's second term. His effort was supported by a number of other elected officials, including Senator William Bradley (Democrat-New Jersey), Representative Jack Kemp (Republican-New York), and the chairs of the committees responsible for tax legislation in each house, namely, Senator Robert Packwood (Republican-Oregon) and Representative Dan Rostenkowski (Democrat-Illinois). Without the sustained commitment of these individuals, the 1986 legislation would never have been adopted.

Like the deregulation of the airline industry, the tax reform legislation of 1986 appealed to both conservatives and liberals. Supply-siders supported the legislation because it significantly reduced both individual and corporate tax rates, thus eliminating what they viewed as a major disincentive to economic growth. Conservatives also welcomed tax reform because, by eliminating the various incentives and disincentives for particular kinds of investments, it enhanced the role of market forces in the allocation of capital. On the other hand, tax reform appealed to liberals because it abolished many of the tax expenditures that had enabled many wealthy individuals and profitable corporations to pay little or no taxes. At the same time, it reduced the federal income taxes of many low-income individuals. In sum, tax reform appealed to both the left- and right-wing strands of American populism. For different reasons, both wanted to reduce the preferential tax treatment enjoyed by a segment of the nation's wealthy individuals and businesses.

Unlike in 1969, this legislation did not catch the business community off guard. Quite the contrary: the nearly two years of congressional deliberations on the legislation were characterized by intense business lobbying. The members of the House Ways and Means Committee and the Senate Finance Committee were subject to a wide array of efforts to influence their votes, ranging from contributions to their campaigns to personal visits from constituents. (The most unequivocal beneficiaries of the Tax Reform Act of 1986 were the lobbyists, who saw the demand for their services increase exponentially, and the members of the two tax-writing committees, who received a major increase in campaign contributions.) Yet, on balance, business had remarkably little to show for its efforts. While some industries, most notably oil and insurance, were able to retain many of their tax privileges, most had relatively little influence on the final shape of the 1986 statute.

An important factor limiting the overall political influence of business was that, in marked contrast to 1981, the interests of business were divided. Two ad hoc coalitions, the Tax Reform Action Coalition and the CEO Tax Group, strongly supported the bill reported out by the House Ways and Means Committee in December 1985, which reduced the corporate tax rate from 46 to 36 percent while repealing a large number of tax preferences. Their members included trade associations representing apparel manufacturers, electronics firms, supermarkets, wholesalers and distributors, retail merchants, and trucking companies. For the most part, the effective corporate tax rates of these industries were well above the average for all companies because they had not been able to take advantage of the generous depreciation provisions of the 1981 legislation. They thus stood to benefit from a combination of lower tax rates and a broadening of the tax base. In addition, the National Federation of Independent Business strongly supported tax reform because nearly a majority of its members were unincorporated and thus wanted individual tax rates reduced.

The Ways and Means bill was opposed by an equally broad business coalition. In addition to the trade associations representing bankers, insurance companies, mining firms, home builders, and machine-tool builders, a number of general business associations, such as the U.S. Chamber of Commerce, the National Association of Manufacturers, and the Business

Roundtable, also lobbied against the bill. They primarily represented firms in capital-intensive industries that currently paid relatively little in taxes, and thus wanted to preserve the current tax code. The reaction of the business community to the version of the legislation approved by the Senate Finance Committee was equally divided.

An administration official, Richard Darman, subsequently remarked: "I couldn't help thinking that if I were a lobbyist, I would stand in the hallway with a big sign saying: EVERYONE INTERESTED IN KILLING THIS BILL, PLEASE MEET IN THE NEXT CORRIDOR. There would have been an enormous rush, and they would have seen the power of their collective action. . . . They were brought down by the narrowness of their vision. Precisely because they defined themselves as representatives of single special interests, they failed to notice their collective power."[122] The division within the business community increased the power of politicians committed to tax reform, since it meant that they could play off segments of the business community against each other. Moreover, the visibility of many corporate and trade association's lobbying efforts ironically served to strengthen the determination of a number of members of Congress to resist their demands: they felt under pressure to demonstrate to the press and the public that they were not beholden to "special interests." From this perspective, the passage of the 1986 legislation can be seen as a kind of neopopulist backlash to the extraordinary effectiveness of corporate lobbyists in shaping the 1981 Revenue Act.

Yet for all the disappointment of many business lobbyists with the 1986 tax reform legislation, the magnitude of business's defeat must be placed in perspective. First, in sharp contrast to the 1969 tax reform bill, the statute passed in 1986 was revenue-neutral; it did not result in a net transfer of wealth from the private sector to the government. Second, not all segments of the business community were required to pay additional taxes as a result of the legislation: those firms that had not been able to take advantage of the various tax breaks granted by previous tax statutes actually saw their effective tax rates decline. In this sense, the 1986 legislation represented radically redistributed tax burdens *within* the business community. Third, while it is true that, on balance, all corporations would pay substantially more than they had in the past, many individual investors, owners, and managers would in turn pay fewer taxes—thanks to the reduction in individual tax rates. Their companies may have been worse off, but they personally would not be. Finally, the 1986 Revenue Act may have been a reform statute but, in many respects, it also made the tax system less progressive.

Conclusion

What was the impact of the Reagan administration on the political fortunes of business?

While the business community's influence on public policy during the Reagan administration fell substantially below its expectations, in one respect its relative influence did increase: throughout the 1980s, the political and economic influence of organized labor continued to decline. The cumulative effect of the administration's free trade policies, its disbanding of the air traffic controllers' union, its support for economic deregulation, its unwillingness to restrict hostile takeovers and leveraged buyouts, and its tight monetary policies, as well as its appointments to the NLRB, was to weaken the bargaining power of both trade unions and unorganized workers. Real wages declined during the 1980s, and the percentage of workers belonging to unions reached a postwar low of 17.5 percent in 1987—a reduction of 6.5 percent since 1979. There were fewer work stoppages in 1987 than in any year since the Department of Labor started to keep records. Thus the Reagan administration helped business accomplish an objective for which it had been striving since the early 1970s, namely, to reduce labor's claims on its resources. The overall wage share, after increasing by a rate of 0.5 percent between 1966 and 1973, rose by only 0.1 percent between 1973 and 1979. But between 1979 and 1986, it actually declined by 0.4 percent.[123]

The administration also dramatically slowed down the trend toward increased government regulation of corporate social conduct. While it was not able to repeal any of the statutes—or even modify many of the rules—enacted during the previous fifteen years, it certainly affected the rate at which new rules and regulations were promulgated. With a handful of exceptions, the regulatory statutes enacted during the 1980s were virtually all reauthorizations of the laws that had been initially approved during the 1970s: the scope of government controls over corporate social conduct was only marginally greater in 1988 than it had been in 1980. And while enforcement tended to be stricter during Reagan's second term than during his first, in a number of cases it still was less strict than it had been during the 1970s.[124] On balance, the relationship between business and the new social regulatory agencies was much less contentious during the Reagan administration than it had been under its three predecessors.

Third, the 1981 Revenue Act contained the most significant cut in corporate taxes in history. While corporate taxes were increased in 1982, they were significantly lower through 1986 than they had been when Ronald

Reagan took office. At the same time, because of the administration's increases in both defense spending and farm subsidies, the amount of direct government assistance to business was far greater under Reagan than it had been under his four predecessors.

On the other hand, the Reagan administration was clearly unable to fulfill its commitment to roll back the increases in government regulation of corporate social conduct that had occurred during the previous four administrations: the "regulatory time bomb" that David Stockman had committed himself to defuse was ticking as loudly in 1988 as it had in 1980. The administration may have succeeded in making significant segments of the American public more skeptical of the virtues of government intervention in a number of policy areas, but its highly visible failure to provide business with "regulatory relief" ironically helped make the government's responsibility to protect the public's health and safety a part of the national consensus. In addition, the 1986 tax reform legislation represented a major political defeat for significant segments of the business community. Finally, much to the frustration of business, the federal budget deficit continued to expand throughout the 1980s; indeed, by 1987, the national debt was more than twice as large as when President Reagan was inaugurated. Why, then, given the popularity of President Reagan, Republican control of the Senate through 1986, a much more probusiness House of Representatives, and a politically sophisticated and active business community, was business not more politically influential during the Reagan years?

One important part of the explanation has to do with the relationship between the business community and the Reagan administration. While Reagan remained personally popular among corporate executives and owners of small businesses, his election in fact proved to be a mixed blessing for business. After 1976, the political agenda of the public-interest movement and organized labor had become, in a number of critical respects, subordinate to the policies and priorities of the Carter administration, while business, being in "opposition," was able to determine its own political priorities. But after 1980, the reverse occurred. The political fortunes of business now became highly dependent on decisions made by the White House. Significantly, the Business Roundtable, which had functioned as a kind of "central committee" for business during the Carter administration, declined in importance during the 1980s: the interests of business as a whole were now looked after by the White House.

When the priorities of the administration and business were similar, business did well. Thus, both corporate taxes and nondefense spending were significantly cut in 1981, and the federal government was unresponsive to the demands of organized labor and its liberal allies that the government intervene to ameliorate the impact of the 1981–82 recession, either by establishing a jobs program or restricting imports. Both the administration and the business community agreed on the need to reduce the economic power and political influence of organized labor; as a result, trade unions experienced major setbacks in both areas throughout the 1980s. And the president's desire to reduce the size of government helped reduce the rate at which new rules and regulations were enacted, and in many cases made their enforcement less strict. Finally, both placed major priority during the first half of the 1980s on reducing inflation—an objective whose achievement represented one of the administration's most important accomplishments in the area of economic policy.

But business and the Reagan administration were able to work extremely well together only in 1981. Afterward, their priorities and interests diverged. In 1982, the president decided that a tax increase was needed, and after his reelection in 1984 he committed his administration to a sweeping reform of the nation's tax laws. The result of both decisions was to increase the effective corporate tax rate. In the area of social regulation, business depended on the Reagan administration to take the initiative in proposing major statutory changes. But the administration had other priorities: in 1981 and 1982, it was more concerned about the budget and taxes, and in 1983 and 1984, it was preoccupied with preventing the Democrats from making a campaign issue out of its disastrous management of the EPA. In a sense, the administration undermined the position of business twice, initially through its zealotry in attempting to change the direction of regulatory policy and then by moving in the opposite direction to defuse the political fallout that resulted. The business community remained, on the whole, strongly committed to reducing the federal deficit. But this flew in the face of the administration's firm commitment to increase defense spending substantially and to keep individual tax rates low. As a result, the deficit continued to increase.

Many of the president's disagreements with business stemmed from a tension between his own conservative ideology and the economic interests of the private sector. The president was persuaded that a substantial increase in defense spending was necessary if the United States was to reassert its preeminence in world affairs; business, on the other hand, was more interested in reducing the size of the budget deficit. Likewise, it was precisely the president's desire to strengthen the role of the market in allocating capital that led him to support a major reduction in the granting of tax preferences to business in 1986. The administration's resistance to virtually all of the pleas of particular industries for protection from imports as well as its unwillingness to restrict hostile takeovers also stemmed from the president's free-market orientation. In many respects, Reagan was not so much probusiness as he was antigovernment.

A second factor had to do with the performance of the economy. Although Reagan did preside over the worst recession in the postwar period shortly after he took office, the economy recovered strongly after 1982. Between 1983 and 1987, economic growth averaged 3.4 percent and inflation averaged only 3.8 percent. Equally significant, the recovery was a continual one. By the fall of 1988, the economy had begun to approach the previous postwar record for consecutive months of growth set in the 1960s. This performance was not impressive enough to rekindle the economic euphoria of the 1960s or early 1970s. Real family income increased only modestly, and the magnitude of the trade deficit created considerable public anxiety about the long-term competitiveness of American industry. Nonetheless, the success of Reaganomics was sufficient to make politicians less deferential to the demands of business. It is unlikely that Congress would have increased the size of the superfund or raised corporate taxes so significantly in 1986 had the economy not recovered from both the stagflation of the late 1970s and the recession of the early 1980s.

A third factor contributing to the limited political effectiveness of business after 1981 was its own political division. The business community was unable to sustain the degree of unity and political cohesion that had served it so well between 1977 and 1981. With only a handful of exceptions, business lobbying after 1981 was not characterized by the kind of broad coalitions that had proved so effective in the late 1970s. To be sure, corporations and trade associations continued to form alliances; indeed, more than one hundred distinctive business coalitions were established during the 1980s. But more frequently than not, these new coalitions found themselves opposed by coalitions formed by other companies and trade associations. They also frequently sought to enlist nonbusiness constituencies as members in order to enhance their own legitimacy and effectiveness. In addition, 1980 and 1982 marked the high point of business political unity with respect to campaign contributions. In 1984 and 1986, a significant share of corporate spending was directed less at changing either the partisan or ideological composition of Congress than at securing advantages for particular segments of the business community. In 1986, nearly fifty percent of corporate and trade association PAC contributors went to Democrats.

In short, the focus of business political activity changed during the 1980s. Compared to the 1970s, a relatively small share of the political efforts of business was devoted to defending the interests of business as a whole or of particular industries from challenges from either the public-interest movement or organized labor. Rather, more of it was directed at advancing the economic interests of particular segments of the business community—often at the expense of other firms. In effect, the Washington office became another profit center; government relations became an integral component of economic competition. Companies originally came to Washington in the early 1970s primarily to defend themselves. But, once having invested so much in learning how the political process works, many decided to use their political skills to help them gain advantages over their competitors, domestic as well as foreign. As a result, the political agenda became increasingly dominated by the requests of particular firms and industries for changes in public policies that would enhance their competitive positions.

Why was business not able to sustain its internal cohesiveness during the 1980s? One reason, of course, was that after 1980 business was no longer on the defensive: executives may have been disappointed with various of the Reagan administration's policies and priorities, but they certainly felt far less politically vulnerable than they had during the second half of the 1970s. The presence of Reagan in the White House obviated the need for the kinds of sophisticated class-wide coalitions that business had relied on to defend its common interests during the Carter administration. Thus, the improvement in business's political fortunes made both more difficult and less necessary the cooperation that had made the resurgence of business political power possible in the first place.

The politicization of business that had taken place during the 1970s also proved to be a two-edged sword in the 1980s. On the one hand, it meant that a much larger proportion of the nation's businesses were able to be heard in Washington, which in turn had helped make business as a whole more influential. On the other hand, it also made it much more difficult for business to speak with one voice, since there were now so many more voices. These new voices included a new peak organization, namely, the Business Roundtable; a number of organizations that spoke for smaller firms, such as the National Federation of Independent Business; the American Business Conference (which represented rapidly growing companies); a revitalized U.S. Chamber of Commerce; and the Washington offices of hundreds of individual firms and trade associations.

The political effectiveness of business during the 1980s was also limited by changes in the economic balance of power within the business community. The older, larger industrial corporations whose executives had provided leadership for the business community during the mid-1970s—such as Exxon, General Motors, Du Pont, and Continental Can—saw their

relative economic importance decline over the next decade.[125] More generally, the Fortune 500 companies' relative shares of both sales and employment fell significantly between 1977 and 1987. At the same time, firms in
the service sector, in high technology, and some midsize manufacturing
companies experienced relatively rapid growth. The latter group, however,
was unwilling to defer to the former's leadership. The president of the
National Association of Wholesalers commented, "The Fortune 100 don't
own the playing field anymore," while an executive from a small manufacturing firm noted, "The reason the Business Roundtable members are
losing their effectiveness is because of the failure in the economy."[126] Nor
were executives from these more rapidly growing companies either willing
or able to fill the political vacuum created by the retirement of individuals
like Reginald Jones of General Electric or Irving Shapiro of Du Pont,
"respected and politically savvy business statesmen who knew their way
around the Hill."[127] When asked in 1988, "Which individuals speak for big
business today?" 45 percent of the CEOs of the 200 largest companies
replied, "No one in particular" or "Not sure."[128]

Moreover, in sharp contrast to the second half of the 1970s, the issues
that dominated the political agenda during the Reagan administration
tended to be those about which the business community was sharply
divided. These included trade policy, an issue on which the interests of
business have historically differed but which became much more politically salient because of the increase in imports; public policy toward hostile takeovers, which pitted the interests of the financial community and
aggressive investors against the managers of Fortune 500 corporations; and
economic deregulation, whose pace and scope continued to bitterly divide
companies both within and across sectors. Nor was the business community able to agree on a concrete plan for reducing the federal deficit—
although almost all agreed in principle on the importance of this goal.
Significantly, none of the three top business organizations—the Roundtable, the NAM, and the Chamber of Commerce—was able to formulate a
coherent position on either trade policy or tax reform, owing to differences
among their members.

Compounding these differences was an even more fundamental problem. During the second half of the 1970s, there was relatively broad agreement as to what policies were in the interests of business. These included
reducing government taxes and expenditures, curbing the growth of social
regulation, halting inflation, and reducing the power of unions. During the
1980s, however, the interests of business as a whole became less clear. Was
the growing size of the federal deficit good or bad for business? On one
hand, it stimulated the economy, made it more difficult to increase non-

defense expenditures, and enabled both companies and individuals to pay lower taxes. On the other hand, it kept real interest rates higher than they would otherwise have been and helped change the status of the United States from creditor to a debtor nation. Was the Federal Reserve's tight monetary policy good or bad for business? On one hand, it reduced inflation and weakened the bargaining power of labor. At the same time, it substantially increased the value of the dollar, which in turn resulted in major reductions in the domestic and global market shares of many American-based firms. Was free trade good or bad for the American economy? On one hand, it lowered prices to consumers, restrained wage demands, and forced many American firms to become more efficient. On the other hand, it enabled foreign firms, often subsidized by their governments, to undercut domestic producers and at the same time keep out American products, thus severely handicapping a number of industries of strategic importance to the American economy. Likewise, increased defense expenditures increased the budget deficit but were also a boon to substantial segments of American industry, particularly in the areas of high technology. Should the government encourage individuals to save more and spend less? Such a policy might lower the cost of capital and thus increase investment, but it also would adversely affect firms dependent on consumer spending. An important reason why business did not enjoy more influence over a variety of critical public policies during the 1980s is that the business community was uncertain as to what mix of policies was, in fact, in its interest.

X

Conclusion

The Dynamics of Business Political Influence

How powerful is American business? The question itself is miscon-
ceived. There is little point in continuing to debate whether the managers
and owners of American enterprises exercise political influence disproportionate to their share of the American population. Rather than analyzing
the power of business in the abstract, we need to understand its exercise
in dynamic terms: What, in fact, makes business as a whole, or segments
of business, more or less powerful?

One of the most crucial factors that has affected the relative political
influence of business is the public's perception of the long-term strength
of the American economy. The relative political influence of business—
particularly vis-à-vis public-interest groups—declined as a result of the
strong performance of the American economy from the early 1960s
through 1973. The 1974–75 recession did not immediately reverse this
decline. This was due both to the scandals associated with Watergate that
allowed the Democrats to make substantial gains in the 1974 congressional
elections and the depth of public hostility to the oil industry following
OPEC's oil embargo. But by 1978, business had regained the political
initiative. Not only was it able to block the major legislative proposals of
both organized labor and the public-interest movement but it began to
make significant progress in achieving its own legislative goals. The peren-
nial shortage of energy was now attributed in part to price controls, and
in 1978, Congress began to phase them out, while the sluggish growth of
business investment, coupled with stagflation, helped persuade Congress
to reduce the capital-gains tax in 1978 and corporate income taxes three
years later. The continued stagnation of the economy also gave credibility

to the complaints of business about the cost of government regulation. Significantly, the high point of business's political influence during the last two decades coincided with the most severe postwar recession.

In turn, the relatively strong performance of the economy following the 1981–82 recession helped make it more difficult for business to further the political gains it had achieved between 1978 and 1981. It is unlikely that the Tax Reform Act of 1986 would have been enacted had the economy experienced another downturn in the mid-1980s, and a third energy crisis might well have made it more difficult for the environmental movement to continue to occupy the moral high ground following the Gorsuch-Watt scandals. On the other hand, the dramatic growth in foreign competition during the 1980s placed the issue of competitiveness on the political agenda and facilitated the efforts of some sectors of American business to secure government assistance in order to compete more effectively with foreign companies and countries.

A second critical factor that affects the relative political influence of business is the degree of cooperation among different firms and industries. One reason so many industries suffered so many political setbacks between the mid-1960s and early 1970s is that they received no assistance from other sectors of the business community. The automobile industry in 1966 and again in 1970, the textile industry and the meat packers in 1967, the cigarette companies in 1970, and the manufacturers of pesticides in 1972 each fought more or less alone. The only industries that were politically active were those whose members were directly affected by regulatory legislation. Likewise, many of the major political victories experienced by business between 1977 and 1981 can be attributed to the ability of a large number of firms, trade associations, and business organizations to work closely together—an effort that reached its climax with the passage of the Revenue Act of 1981. However, after 1981, the business community was less effective than it otherwise might have been because of divisions both within and among industries.

When business is both mobilized and unified, its political power can be formidable. But while the former is now the norm, the latter occurs relatively infrequently. Large numbers of firms were able to work together effectively only for approximately five years. The class consciousness of American business, like that of the American working class, is limited: companies generally tend to become aware of their common interests only when they are faced with a common enemy. In a number of respects, the 1970s were an unusual decade: a significant proportion of political issues affected the interests of business as a whole. As a result, by the end of the decade, companies and trade associations had learned the importance of cooperating with one another. But during the 1980s, as during the 1960s, relatively few issues united the business community. Instead, companies and industries generally pursued relatively narrow goals: corporate public affairs became another form of economic competition. In short, business is not a monolith: the extent of its political unity, like the extent of its political influence, fluctuates.

The political influence of business is also affected by the dynamics of the American political system. Prior to the mid-1960s, business did not need to become politically active to remain influential in Washington. The centralized structure of congressional decision making, along with the prevailing ideological consensus regarding the appropriate role of the federal government, effectively limited any expansion of government controls over the private sector. Over the next decade, both the institutional and the ideological barriers to increased government intervention were eroded, requiring business to play the game of interest-group politics in order to regain its influence. The political resurgence of business was in turn facilitated by a change in the laws governing campaign spending, the increased fragmentation of decision making in Congress, and an increase in public hostility to government.

However, politicians do not simply react passively to either changing economic conditions or interest-group pressures. They also have their own priorities and preferences, which are in turn shaped by both their ideology and their desire to be reelected. The Democratic senators who played a critical role in enacting consumer and environmental legislation during the 1960s and early 1970s, and who challenged the oil industry in the mid-1970s, were responding less to lobbying by public-interest groups than to their perception of the changing preferences of their constituents. President Johnson viewed consumer and environmental regulation as a way of maintaining the momentum of the Great Society without increasing government expenditures, and President Nixon's support for both occupational safety and health legislation and the strengthening of the Clean Air Act Amendments of 1970 was dictated by electoral considerations. In 1983, Ronald Reagan, motivated by the same considerations as Richard Nixon in 1970, hastily abandoned his effort to provide business with regulatory relief, lest the Democrats use the scandals at EPA to challenge his reelection bid. On occasion, politicians can transform the political agenda on their own. There was virtually no public interest in the issue of tax reform during the mid-1980s. It was placed on the political agenda because Ronald Reagan, supported by a handful of key congressional leaders from both parties, decided to make it the major political priority of his second term.

To paraphrase Karl Marx, business does make its own political history, but it does so in circumstances that are largely beyond its control. Since the mid-1960s, business has tended to be politically effective when its resources have been highly mobilized, when companies share similar objectives, when the public is critical of government, when the economy is performing relatively poorly, and when its preferences coincide with those of powerful politicians. But with the exception of the first, the ability of business to influence each of these contingencies is limited. There are many important issues on which it is simply impossible for substantial numbers of firms and business associations to agree. Business investment decisions are only one of the number of factors that affect the performance of the economy and, in any event, managers and owners are hardly likely to deliberately slow down the economy or reduce their company's profits so that their lobbyists can become more effective. Business certainly can, through both its campaign spending and influence over the climate of public and elite opinion, affect the preferences of politicians. But politicians' calculations are influenced by many considerations other than the desire to placate business. On balance, business is more affected by broad political and economic trends than it is able to affect them.

The Long-term Impact

While the political and economic environment of business has fluctuated considerably since 1960, the last three decades have also witnessed a number of structural changes in the relationship between business and government in the United States. Three are particularly important: the nature of political opposition to business has changed, the scope of government controls over corporate social conduct has increased, and business has become more politically active.

During the 1970s, the public-interest movement replaced organized labor as the central countervailing force to the power and values of American business. Not only has union membership been declining steadily but, even more important, the ties between trade unions and the Democratic party have measurably weakened. The interests and influence of the public-interest movement and organized labor formerly overlapped: during the 1960s, trade unions were the most vocal and effective advocates of consumer-protection legislation, and alliances of public-interest groups and organized labor were instrumental in the growth of regulation during the early 1970s. Yet trade unions have rarely been powerful enough to win on their own: during the last three decades, labor's only important victory on an issue of particular importance to its membership was the enactment of pension reform in 1974. Since the mid-1970s, the interests of labor and the public-interest movement have increasingly diverged. The public-interest movement has been able to maintain much of its political strength while trade unions have increasingly found themselves on the defensive: ironically, unions are now most influential when they are allied with business.

The public-interest movement, of course, encompasses a wide range of organizations with a diversity of causes and interests whose political fortunes, while linked, are not identical. The consumer movement has fared relatively poorly over the last decade. By contrast, environmental organizations have remained extremely influential: they now represent the core constituency of the public-interest movement. The political significance of the environmental movement is not simply measured by the size of its membership, the degree of public support for its objectives, or the number of lobbyists, lawyers, and political organizers it employs—though by all these measures, the resiliency of the environmental organizations over the last two decades has been remarkable. It is rather that, like organized labor during the 1930s and 1940s, the environmental movement has been able to articulate an alternative view of how the quality of life in America ought to be judged and, at the same time, to provide a range of concrete benefits to large numbers of Americans.

Unions have, historically, emphasized the importance of social goals such as full employment and universal access to medical care, housing, and education. Environmentalists, on the other hand, have stressed the need for government, either acting on its own or through the private sector, to supply all Americans with collective goods such as clean air and water, safe products, and undeveloped scenic and wilderness areas. Trade unions have sought to reduce the exposure of Americans to economic risks; environmentalists, to technological ones. Neither vision is particularly radical: both can be accommodated within the framework of democratic capitalism. But their realization does challenge business insofar as it usually involves limiting the prerogatives of property owners and the role of the marketplace. The political appeal of the welfare state has faded, in part owing to budgetary constraints and in part because a substantial portion of it has in fact been realized. But the environmental appeal has increased in importance: the environmental movement has established an alternative standard by which significant numbers of Americans, most of whom do not consider themselves environmentalists, now evaluate the performance of both business and government. Support for environmental regulation is no longer limited to the educated middle class or to liberals; rather, environmental protection has become part of a national, bipartisan consensus.

Each of this country's three reform periods significantly expanded the scope of government intervention in American society. The Progressive Era made government responsible for managing the money supply and for regulating the terms of economic competition among different sectors of the American economy. The New Deal established government controls over financial institutions and markets, involved the federal government in the mediation of labor-management relations, inaugurated a system of old-age pensions and unemployment insurance, and made the federal government responsible for the management of macroeconomic policy. The most recent reform period—upon which political historians have yet to bestow an equally convenient label—has, in addition to expanding the scope of the welfare state, significantly increased the extent of government controls over corporate social conduct. The federal government has now become permanently responsible for ameliorating the impact of corporate decisions that threaten the public's health and safety, as well as for managing the supply and condition of various collective goods. America may continue to be an exception among capitalist democracies in terms of the relative small size of its public sector, but in other respects the American government is highly interventionist: no other capitalist nation has established such extensive controls over business decisions affecting environmental and consumer protection, equal employment opportunity, and occupational health and safety.

The unprecedented increase in the public's expectation of corporate conduct that led to a sudden increase in consumer, environmental-protection, and occupational health and safety legislation during the late 1960s and 1970s was made possible by the equally unprecedented expansion of the American economy during this period. But just as the welfare state established by the New Deal survived the ending of the Great Depression, so have these regulatory laws remained on statute books, even though the "great expansion" of the 1960s has ended. These statutes have now managed to survive two major recessions, double-digit inflation, increasing international competition, and the election and reelection of a president who came into office committed to repealing them. Regulatory issues themselves have become a permanent part of the agenda of American domestic politics, and health and safety regulation has become a central preoccupation of the American middle class. Just as we have spent the half-century since the New Deal debating the scope of the welfare state, so will we spend the next several decades deciding how to respond to the seemingly endless array of risks associated with modern technology. The latter, however, differs from the former in one critical respect: most expenditures will be made by business rather than government.

The last three decades have altered business-government relations in the United States a third way. They have significantly increased the amount of resources that American business firms devote to national politics. In an extensive survey of corporate political activity published in 1969, Edwin Epstein wrote that "political activity commands but a small percentage of the human and material assets of an enterprise and occupies a position of relatively low priority."[1] This is no longer so. Compared to their counterparts in most other capitalist nations, the owners and managers of businesses in the United States remain poorly organized. But compared to the situation less than two decades ago, businesses in the United States have become much more capable of defending and asserting their interests in Washington. Large corporations have become extremely sophisticated at dealing with both the public and government: they closely monitor political and social trends, and for many firms government relations has become an integral part of corporate strategy. In addition, literally millions of small firms have become politically organized as well. Business is unlikely to be caught off guard again.

This is not the first time during this century that business political activity has substantially increased. During both the Progressive Era and the New Deal, business also became more politically active. The United States Chamber of Commerce was established in 1912 at the suggestion of President Taft, and between 1913 and 1919 the number of trade associations grew from 240 to 2,000. The New Deal also stimulated considerable business political activity. The budget of the National Association of Manufacturers increased sixfold, and hundreds of trade associations established offices in Washington, D.C., in order to take part in the National Recovery Administration. In 1933, the Business Council was established in order to strengthen ties between the Department of Commerce and big business. The Liberty League was formed in 1934 to oppose the New Deal.

Business's political activity stabilized during the 1920s and declined after the New Deal. "Of the 800 trade associations formed between 1933 and 1936 only 275 were still active by the time of American entry into the Second World War."[2] By contrast, during the 1980s the overall amount of resources that companies devote to relations with the federal government continued to increase, though more slowly than during the 1970s.[3] There are many reasons for this development. They include the ongoing conflicts over the making and enforcement of government regulation of corporate social conduct, the continual controversy over the pace and scope of economic deregulation, and, most important, the internationalization of the American economy. This last development has forced significant segments of business to turn to the U.S. government to help mediate their relationships with foreign-based firms and governments. It has also led to substantial political activity on the part of foreign-owned businesses in America, many of whose interests conflict with those of American-owned firms. The politicization of business is thus the third important legacy of the 1970s.

While the amount of resources devoted to governmental relations will undoubtedly continue to vary among different companies and industries, depending on both their political and economic circumstances as well as national political and economic developments, it is highly unlikely that the overall resources devoted by business firms to dealing with the federal government will decline in the future. Indeed, the potential increase in business political activity is considerable: nearly half of the Fortune 500 companies have yet to establish a PAC and more than half of the nation's thousand largest firms do not have a Washington office. Nearly two-thirds of the nation's six thousand trade associations are still *not* headquartered in Washington, D.C., and nearly three-quarters of the nation's small businesses are not affiliated with a business organization or trade association.

The Next Round?

In 1939, Arthur Schlesinger wrote an essay in the *Yale Review* entitled "The Tide of National Politics," in which he argued that since the Stamp Act Congress of 1765, American history has gone through eleven alternating periods of liberalism and conservatism—each phase lasting an average of fifteen years. On the basis of this observation, he predicted that the retreat of liberalism, which he dated from 1947, would last until the early 1960s and that "the next conservative epoch will then be due about 1978."[4] In *American Politics: The Promise of Disharmony*, published in 1981, Samuel Huntington wrote that periods of "creedal passion" take place in the United States approximately every sixty years, the most recent having occurred during the 1960s and 1970s—which Huntington labeled the "S and S" years.[5] In an essay published in 1986, Arthur Schlesinger, Jr., restated his father's cyclical theory of American politics, dating the most recent period of liberal ascendancy from 1960 and the contemporary conservative revival from the mid-1970s.[6] He went on to predict a revival of liberalism toward the end of the 1980s.

Each of these depictions of American politics over the last three decades roughly parallels my own analysis; the relative political influence of business is obviously related to other broad trends in American political life. But the dynamics of business-government relations in the United States are more complex than these cyclical interpretations of American politics suggest. Neither periods of relative business dominance nor periods of business political decline follow any particular chronological pattern. The Progressive Era lasted for approximately fifteen years, the New Deal for about eight years, and the most recent wave of challenges to business prerogatives a little more than a decade. On the other hand, the "twenties" lasted a bit less than fifteen years, while the period of business political resurgence after the New Deal endured for more than a quarter-century. Even if one is convinced that the political pendulum will subsequently dramatically shift again, the length of previous "political business cycles" provides us with no basis for predicting when this will occur.

Even more important, the political dynamics of each reform period are quite distinctive. I have sought to explain some of the important changes in the relative political influence of business in Washington since the early 1960s, but I have deliberately refrained from advancing a general theory of the nature of business power in America. While I have drawn some historical parallels, my analysis does not explain the dynamics of either the Progressive Era or the New Deal. There are a number of similarities between the Progressive Era and the most recent reform period. Both occurred during a period of relative prosperity and both reform efforts were supported and led by highly educated members of the middle class. But the Progressive Era was preceded by a decade of economic stagnation and followed by a period of relative economic prosperity. The contrast between the 1930s and the 1960s is even more striking. Business lost considerable political influence during the 1930s, not because the economy was performing well but because it had virtually ceased to function at all. And during the New Deal, the primary political challenges to business came not from the middle class but from the working class. Nor can the politics of business-government relations during the 1980s be usefully compared to either the 1920s or the 1950s: business has not regained the "privileged position" it held during those earlier decades and the U.S. is now more closely integrated in the global economy, thus reducing the options available to policy makers.

Undoubtedly, the political fortunes of business will continue to fluctuate. But, barring either a strong and enduring economic expansion or a sudden and prolonged economic collapse, there is no reason to assume that these fluctuations will be as dramatic in the future as they have often been in the past. Rather, business as a whole, as well as particular firms and industries, may well experience gains in some policy areas and setbacks in others. And the business community is likely to remain highly divided and fragmented. The rate at which new regulations are imposed on business may well increase somewhat. But as long as the ability of American business to compete in the world economy remains problematic, we are unlikely to witness an expansion of demands on or controls over the private sector comparable to that which occurred two decades ago. To the extent that the federal government increasingly intervenes in the American economy, it is as likely to assist business as to restrict it. Business-government relations have historically been more cooperative on the local level because state and local governments must actively compete to attract new investments. Accordingly, to the extent that Americans come to identify their own economic interests with the success of American-based companies, the globalization of the American economy may well encourage more cooperation between business and government at the federal level. However, the adversarial relationship between business and government that has been a defining feature of American politics since the industrial revolution will hardly disappear; it is too deeply rooted in both business and popular culture.[7]

The contemporary resurgence of corporate political power in the United States is thus ironic. Compared to the late 1960s and early 1970s, business faces far fewer challenges to its power and prerogatives from nonbusiness constituencies. Organized labor remains much less influential than it was fifteen years ago, Ralph Nader is much less of a threat than he was in 1975, and, while the environmental movement remains a formidable political adversary, it is not powerful enough to bring about any major changes in federal regulatory policy that business strongly opposes. In this sense, business has won.

But while American business firms may have increased their influence over the American government, the influence of the American government over the American economy has substantially diminished. Indeed, if any business group is now privileged, it is the Japanese, who decide how much and where to invest in the United States. American firms have also become far more vulnerable to threats that emanate not from government but from the market itself—domestic as well as global. The resurgence of corporate political power during the second half of the 1970s was paralleled by increased competition among firms in previously regulated sectors of the economy. The defeat of common situs picketing in 1977 coincided with a tripling of America's merchandise balance of trade deficit, and 1981 witnessed not only an unprecedented reduction in corporate taxes but the beginning of a wave of hostile takeovers that have threatened the power of almost every CEO. In a sense, corporate managers have gone from the frying pan into the fire. Someday GM's management may look back with fondness to the 1960s, when its main worries were Ralph Nader and the United Automobile Workers rather than H. Ross Perot and Toyota.

Notes

Chapter I

1. Samuel Huntington, *American Politics and the Promise of Disharmony* (Cambridge, Mass.: Belknap Press, 1987), p. 38.

2. Henry Demarest Lloyd, *Wealth against Commonwealth* (Englewood Cliffs, N.J.: Prentice-Hall, 1963), pp. 7, 90.

3. Richard Hofstadter, *The Age of Reform* (New York: Vintage Books, 1955), p. 64.

4. Ibid., p. 64.

5. Ibid., p. 231.

6. James Prothro, *Dollar Decade: Business Ideas in the 1920s* (Baton Rouge: Louisiana State University Press, 1954).

7. Quoted in Arthur Schlesinger, Jr., *The Politics of Upheaval* (Boston: Houghton Mifflin, 1960), pp. 638–39.

8. Thomas McCraw, *Prophets of Regulation* (Cambridge, Mass.: Belknap Press, 1984), p. 77.

9. Charles Lindblom, *Politics and Markets* (New York: Basic Books, 1977), p. 356.

10. Michael Pertschuk, *Revolt Against Regulation: The Rise and Pause of the Consumer Movement* (Berkeley: University of California Press, 1982); Thomas Byrne Edsell, *The New Politics of Inequality* (New York: Norton, 1984); Thomas Ferguson and Joel Rogers, *Right Turn: The Decline of the Democrats and the Future of American Politics* (New York: Hill & Wang, 1986).

11. David Truman, *The Governmental Process* (New York: Knopf, 1981); V. O. Key, *Politics, Parties and Pressure Groups* (New York: Crowell, 1942); and Robert Dahl, *Who Governs?* (New Haven: Yale University Press, 1961).

12. See, for example, Peter Bachrach, *The Theory of Democratic Elitism* (Boston: Little, Brown, 1967); G. William Domhoff, *Who Rules America?* (Englewood Cliffs, N.J.: Prentice-Hall, 1967); Ralph Miliband, *The State in Capitalist Society* (New York: Basic Books, 1969); Edward Greenberg, *Serving the Few* (New York: Wiley, 1974); Ira Katznelson and Mark Nadel, *Corporations and Political Accountability* (Lexington, Mass.: Heath, 1977); and David Garson, *Power and Politics in the United States* (Lexington, Mass.: Heath, 1977).

13. Robert Dahl and Charles Lindblom, *Politics, Economics and Welfare* (Chicago: University of Chicago Press, 1976), p. xxxvi.

14. Lindblom, *Politics and Markets*, p. 175.

15. Charles E. Lindblom, "The Market as Prison," *Journal of Politics*, 1982, p. 335.

16. See, for example, David Vogel, "Political Science and the Study of Corporate Power: A Dissent from the New Conventional Wisdom," *British Journal of Political Science* 17 (October 1987): 385–408; and Robert Hessen, ed., *Does Big Business Rule America?* (Washington, D.C.: Ethics and Public Policy Center, 1987).

17. James Q. Wilson, "Democracy and the Corporation," in Hessen, *Does Big Business Rule America?* p. 37.

18. Irving Kristol, *Two Cheers for Capitalism* (New York: Basic Books, 1977).

19. Alan Westin, "Good Marks But Some Areas of Doubt," *Business Week*, 14 May 1979, p. 14.

20. The phrase "mobilization of bias" is from Peter Bachrach and Morton Baratz, "The Two Faces of Power," *American Political Science Review* 56, no. 4 (1962): 952.

21. Paul Taylor, "Will Big Business Become the Next Political Bogeyman?" *Washington Post Weekly Edition*, 16 February 1987, p. 23.

22. See David Vogel, *National Styles of Regulation* (Ithaca, N.Y.: Cornell University Press, 1986).

Chapter II

1. Jim F. Heath, *John F. Kennedy and the Business Community* (Chicago: University of Chicago Press, 1969), p. 4.
2. Kim McQuaid, *Big Business and Presidential Power* (New York: Morrow, 1982), p. 200.
3. Ibid., p. 203.
4. Heath, *John F. Kennedy*, p. 205.
5. "What Business Thinks of the Administration," *Fortune*, January 1962, pp. 59–60.
6. McQuaid, *Big Business*, p. 208.
7. Heath, *John F. Kennedy*, pp. 69, 70.
8. McQuaid, *Big Business*, p. 209.
9. Quoted in Heath, *John F. Kennedy*, p. 72.
10. McQuaid, *Big Business*, p. 208.
11. Heath, *John F. Kennedy*, p. 72.
12. Ibid., p. 71.
13. Quoted in "No Room for Ill Will," *Business Week*, 21 April 1962, p. 25.
14. Heath, *John F. Kennedy*, pp. 43, 46.
15. Bernard Nossiter, *The Mythmakers* (Boston: Beacon Press, 1964), p. 29.
16. Heath, *John F. Kennedy*, pp. 118, 121.
17. "What the Hell Do Those Fellows Want?" *Fortune*, February 1963, p. 81.
18. Harold B. Meyers, "LBJ's Romance with Business," *Fortune*, September 1964, p. 132.
19. *Harvard Business Review* 42, no. 5 (September–October 1964): 23.
20. David Bazelon, "Big Business and the Democrats," *Commentary*, May 1965, p. 39.
21. Theodore Levitt, "The Johnson Treatment," *Harvard Business Review* 45, no. 1 (January–February 1967): 114.
22. Edmund Faltermayer, "The Half Finished Society," *Fortune*, March 1965, p. 219.
23. Levitt, "The Johnson Treatment," p. 116.
24. Richard Barber, "The New Partnership," *The New Republic*, 13 August 1966, p. 22.
25. Quoted in McQuaid, *Big Business*, p. 236.
26. Max Ways, "Creative Federalism and the Great Society," *Fortune*, January 1966, p. 122.
27. "The Public Mandate for Business," Report by Louis Harris presented at the Public Affairs Conference of the National Industrial Conference Board, 21 April 1966, Question 26.
28. Gardiner Means, *The Corporate Revolution in America* (New York: Crowell-Collier, 1962).
29. Quoted in Mark Nadel, *The Politics of Consumer Protection* (New York: Bobbs-Merrill, 1971), p. 123.
30. Quoted in David Aaker and George Day, eds., *Consumerism* (New York: Free Press, 1971), p. 3.
31. Paul Quirk, "Food and Drug Administration," in *The Politics of Regulation*, ed. James Q. Wilson (New York: Basic Books, 1980), p. 198.
32. Nadel, *Politics of Consumer Protection*, pp. 127, 128.
33. Heath, *John F. Kennedy*, p. 54.
34. A. Lee Fritschler, *Smoking and Politics: Policymaking and the Federal Bureaucracy*, 3d ed. (Englewood Cliffs, N.J.: Prentice-Hall, 1983), p. 38.
35. Elizabeth Drew, "The Quiet Victory of the Cigarette Lobby," *Atlantic*, September 1965, p. 79.
36. Ibid., pp. 80, 76.
37. Charles Jones, *Clean Air* (Pittsburgh: University of Pittsburgh Press, 1975), p. 33.
38. Ibid., p. 63.

39. James Hanks and Harold Kube, "Industry Action to Combat Pollution," *Harvard Business Review* 44, no. 5 (September–October 1966): 49.

40. Richard Hofstadter, "What Happened to the Antitrust Movement?" in *The Business Establishment,* ed. Earl Cheit (New York: Wiley, 1964), p. 141.

41. Opinion Research Corporation, "Public Relations: Corporations Face the Worst Attitude Climate in a Decade," *ORC Public Opinion Index,* March 1972, p. 2.

42. Seymour Martin Lipset and William Schneider, *The Confidence Gap* (New York: Free Press, 1983), pp. 29–30, 46–47.

43. Quoted in Edwin M. Epstein, *The Corporation in American Politics* (Englewood Cliffs, N.J.: Prentice-Hall, 1969), p. 178.

44. David Yoffie and Sigrid Bergenstein, "Creating Political Advantage," *California Management Review,* Fall 1985, p. 125.

45. Raymond Bauer, Ithiel de Sola Pool, and Anthony Lewis Dexter, *American Business and Public Policy* (Englewood Cliffs, N.J.: Prentice-Hall, 1964), p. 324.

46. Harold Brayman, *Corporate Management in a World of Politics* (New York: McGraw-Hill, 1967), p. 68.

47. Graham Wilson, *Interest Groups in the United States* (Oxford: Oxford University Press, 1981), p. 59.

48. Ibid., p. 61.

49. "Business and Politics, 1964," *Harvard Business Review,* September–October 1964, pp. 177, 28.

50. James Q. Wilson, "American Politics, Then and Now," *Commentary,* February 1979, p. 40.

Chapter III

1. John Kenneth Galbraith, *The New Industrial State* (London: Hamish Hamilton, 1967).

2. Theodore Levitt, "Why Business Always Loses," *Harvard Business Review,* March–April 1968, p. 83.

3. See James Q. Wilson, "The Politics of Regulation," in *The Politics of Regulation,* ed. James Q. Wilson (New York: Basic Books, 1980), pp. 357–94.

4. See Mancer Olsen, *The Logic of Collective Action* (Cambridge: Harvard University Press, 1965).

5. Wilson, "Politics of Regulation," p. 370.

6. Jack Walker, "Setting the Agenda in the U.S. Senate: A Theory of Problem Selection," *British Journal of Political Science,* October 1977, p. 427.

7. Michael Pertschuk, *Revolt Against Regulation* (Berkeley, Calif.: University of California Press, 1982), p. 25.

8. Ibid., pp. 21, 19.

9. Quoted in ibid., p. 13.

10. "The Public Mandate for Business," Report by Louis Harris, presented at the Public Affairs Conference of the National Industrial Conference Board, 21 April 1969.

11. Pertschuk, *Revolt Against Regulation,* pp. 13–14.

12. Jules Cohn, *The Conscience of the Corporations* (Baltimore: Johns Hopkins Press, 1971), p. 3.

13. "The American Corporation Under Fire," *Newsweek,* 24 May 1971, p. 75.

14. Louis Harris, "The Public Credibility of American Business," *Conference Board Record* 10, no. 3 (March 1973): 36.

15. Elizabeth Drew, "The Politics of Auto Safety," *Atlantic,* October 1966, p. 96.

16. Alan Irwin, *Risk and the Control of Technology* (Manchester: Manchester University Press, 1985), p. 64.

17. Ralph Nader, *Unsafe at Any Speed* (New York: Grossman, 1965).

18. Drew, "Politics of Auto Safety," p. 98.

19. Ibid., pp. 98, 99.

20. David Halberstam, *The Reckoning* (New York: Morrow, 1986), p. 490.

21. Drew, "Politics of Auto Safety," p. 99.

22. Halberstam, *The Reckoning,* p. 496.

23. Drew, "Politics of Auto Safety," p. 99.

24. Irwin, *Risk and the Control of Technology,* p. 63.

25. Dan Cordtz, "Face in the Mirror at GM," *Fortune,* August 1966, p. 210.

26. Irwin, *Risk and the Control of Technology,* p. 66.

27. Drew, "Politics of Auto Safety," p. 101.

28. Ibid., pp. 95, 96.

29. Mark Nadel, *The Politics of Consumer Protection* (New York: Bobbs-Merrill, 1971), p. 142.

30. Walker, "Setting the Agenda," p. 435.

31. Nadel, *Politics of Consumer Protection,* p. 143.

32. Lucy Creighton, *Pretenders to the Throne* (Lexington, Mass.: Lexington Books, 1970), p. 37.

33. *Congressional Quarterly Almanac, 1966* (Washington, D.C.: Congressional Quarterly, 1967), p. 361.

34. Ibid., p. 355.

35. *"Some* Truth-in-Packaging . . . But Not Enough," *Consumer Reports,* February 1967, p. 113.

36. Jeremy Main, "Industry Still Has Something to Learn about Congress," *Fortune,* February 1967, p. 194.

37. Pertschuk, *Revolt Against Regulation,* p. 36.

38. *Congressional Quarterly Almanac, 1967* (Washington, D.C.: Congressional Quarterly, 1968), p. 714.

39. Ibid.

40. Ibid., p. 705.

41. Ibid., p. 712.

42. *Congressional Quarterly Almanac, 1968* (Washington, D.C.: Congressional Quarterly, 1969), p. 205.

43. Nadel, *Politics of Consumer Protection,* p. 131.

44. "Mine Safety," *Science News,* 22 March 1969, p. 279.

45. "Coal's New Prosperity Can't Ease Its Pains," *Business Week,* 23 August 1969, pp. 64–68.

46. "Mine Safety," p. 279.

47. "Coalmen Do Slow Burn," *Business Week,* 10 May 1969, p. 50.

48. Seymour Martin Lipset and William Schneider, *The Confidence Gap* (New York: Free Press, 1983), pp. 48, 33, 39.

49. Robert Fullmer, "Diagnosis: Collegiate Cynicism Syndrome," *Personnel Journal,* February 1968, p. 99.

50. Quoted in Gordon Fish, "Students in Business: What Do They Think About it? Why?" *Vital Issues,* March 1969, p. 1.

51. *Attitudes of College Students Toward Business Careers,* College Placement Council, 1968, p. 1.

52. Ibid., p. 129.

53. Duncan Norton-Taylor, "The Private World of the Class of '66," *Fortune,* February 1966, p. 130.

54. Ibid., p. 132.

55. Edward Bond, Jr., "American Youth: Why They Avoid Involvement with Business," *Public Relations Journal,* May 1966, p. 8.

56. Jeremy Main, "A Special Report on Youth," *Fortune,* June 1969, p. 73.

57. "Why Business Faces Campus Ire," *Business Week,* 9 August 1969, p. 74.

58. "Top Students Sell Business Short," *Business Week,* 9 September 1967, p. 135.

59. Robert Clark, "Bearded Youth and Stereotype Gray Flannel," *Financial Executive,* March 1968, p. 42.

60. V. B. Day, "The Social Relevance of Business," Paper presented at the 1969 Annual College-Business Symposium, 7 December 1969, Providence, R.I., p. 4.

61. Theodore Roszak, *The Making of a Counter Culture* (Garden City, NY: Doubleday, 1969), p. 35.

62. Charles A. Reich, *The Greening of America* (New York: Random House, 1970).

63. Leslie Dawson, "Campus Attitudes Toward Business," *Michigan State University Business Topics,* Summer 1969, p. 36.

64. Quoted in David Vogel, *Lobbying the Corporation* (New York: Basic Books, 1978), pp. 44, 51.

65. Ibid, p. 51.

66. Lewis F. Powell, "Attack on American Free Enterprise System" (Mimeographed), pp. 1, 9.

67. Daniel Yankelovitch, "The Real Meaning of the Student Revolution," *Conference Board Record* 9, no. 3 (March 1972): 13.

68. "Our Future Business Environment and General Electric," April 1968, pp. 23, 38.

Chapter IV

1. Michael Pertschuk, *Revolt Against Regulation* (Berkeley: University of California Press, 1982), p. 29.

2. John F. Witte, *The Politics and Development of the Federal Income Tax* (Madison: University of Wisconsin Press, 1985), pp. 172, 173.

3. Douglas Ross and Harold Wolman, "Congress and Pollution," *Washington Monthly,* September 1970, p. 20.

4. *Congressional Quarterly Almanac, 1969* (Washington, D.C.: Congressional Quarterly, 1970), p. 589.

5. Quoted in *Congressional Quarterly Almanac, 1969*, p. 602.

6. Edwin L. Dale, Jr., "It's Not Perfect, But It's the Best Yet," *The New Republic,* 3 May 1969, p. 10.

7. "Revolt as the Lobbies Dozed," *Business Week,* 26 July 1969, p. 81.

8. Richard Vietor, *Energy Policy in America Since 1945* (Cambridge: Cambridge University Press, 1984), p. 225.

9. Witte, *Politics and Development of the Tax,* pp. 171–72.

10. "Revolt as the Lobbies Dozed," *Business Week,* p. 82.

11. Quoted in Clarence Jones, "Air Pollution and Contemporary Environmental Politics," *Growth and Change,* July 1973, p. 23.

12. Walter Rosenbaum, *Environmental Politics and Policy* (Washington, D.C.: Congressional Quarterly, 1985), pp. 68, 75.

13. "Issue of the Year: The Environment," *Time,* 4 January 1971, p. 21.

14. John Whitaker, *Striking a Balance* (Washington, D.C.: American Enterprise Institute, 1976), p. 264.

15. "A Memento Mori to the Earth," *Time,* 4 May 1970, p. 16.

16. Louis Harris, "The Public Credibility of American Business," *Conference Board Record,* March 1973, p. 35.

17. Richard Liroff, *A National Policy for the Environment* (Bloomington: Indiana University Press, 1976), p. 5.

18. Ibid., p. 12.

19. Frederick R. Anderson, *NEPA in the Courts* (Baltimore: Resources for the Future, 1973), p. 14.

20. Richard Corrigan, "Nixon and Congress Consider Actions to Improve Environment," *National Journal,* 20 December 1969, p. 371.

21. Alfred Marcus, "Environmental Protection Agency," in *The Politics of Regulation,* ed. James Q. Wilson (New York: Basic Books, 1980), p. 267.

22. Robert Diamond, "What Business Thinks," *Fortune,* February 1970, pp. 118, 119.

23. Quoted in Charles O. Jones, *Clean Air: The Policies and Politics of Pollution Control* (Pittsburgh: University of Pittsburgh Press, 1975), p. 201.

24. David Vogel, *National Styles of Regulation* (Ithaca, N.Y.: Cornell University Press, 1986).

25. "Pollution: A Five Year Perspective," *Opinion Research Corporation* pamphlet.

26. Gladwin Hill, "The Politics of Air Pollution: Public Interest and Pressure Groups," *Arizona Law Review* 10 (Summer 1968): 41, 42.

27. Jones, *Clean Air*, pp. 175, 179.

28. "Pollution: Will Man Succeed in Destroying Himself?" *Congressional Quarterly*, January 1970, p. 279.

29. Richard Corrigan, "Tough Local Actions on Air Quality Boost Nation's National Standards Plan," *National Journal*, 9 May 1970, p. 969.

30. Jones, *Clean Air*, p. 182.

31. Richard Corrigan, "Tough Local Actions," p. 968.

32. John Esporito, *Vanishing Air* (New York: Grossman, 1970).

33. Quoted in Jones, *Clean Air*, pp. 191–92.

34. Frank V. Fowlkes, "Washington Pressures: GM Gets Little Mileage from Compact, Low-Powered Lobby," *National Journal*, 14 November 1970, p. 2511.

35. Ibid., p. 2504.

36. *Congressional Quarterly Almanac, 1970* (Washington, D.C.: Congressional Quarterly, 1971), pp. 482, 483, 2511.

37. Corrigan, "Tough Local Actions," pp. 26, 3.

38. Fowlkes, "Washington Pressures," p. 2509.

39. *Congressional Quarterly Almanac, 1970*, p. 485.

40. Mel Horwitch, *Clipped Wings: The American SST Conflict* (Cambridge: MIT Press, 1982), pp. 1–2, 4.

41. Ibid., p. 237.

42. Ibid., p. 272.

43. Ibid., p. 284.

44. Quoted in Horwitch, *Clipped Wings*, p. 288.

45. Ibid., pp. 303, 304.

46. *Congressional Quarterly Almanac, 1971* (Washington, D.C.: Congressional Quarterly, 1972), pp. 713, 714.

47. Robert Durant, *When Government Regulates Itself* (Knoxville: University of Tennessee Press, 1985), p. 22.

48. Rachel L. Carson, *Silent Spring* (Boston: Houghton Mifflin, 1962).

49. *Congressional Quarterly Almanac, 1972* (Washington, D.C.: Congressional Quarterly, 1973), pp. 935, 936.

50. James Heard, "Chemical Industry, Farmers Fear Pending Pesticide Control Shift," *National Journal*, 4 July 1970, p. 1430.

51. Joseph A. Page and Mary Win O'Brien, *Bitter Wages* (New York: Grossman Publishers, 1973), p. 168.

52. Graham Wilson, *The Politics of Safety and Health* (Oxford: Clarendon Press, 1985), p. 36. In fact, the death rate from job-related accidents declined steadily between 1950 and 1970. While occupational injury rates did increase substantially during the 1960s—the injury-frequency rate in manufacturing rose from 11.8 disabling injuries per million hours worked to 15.2 between 1961 and 1970—much of this increase appears to have been due to the upturn in the business cycle.

53. Jack L. Walker, "Setting the Agenda in the U.S. Senate: A Theory of Problem Selection," *British Journal of Political Science* 7, pt. 4 (October 1977): p. 423–45.

54. Charles Noble, *Liberalism at Work* (Philadelphia: Temple University Press, 1986), p. 8.

55. Ibid., pp. 78, 83.

56. Wilson, *Politics of Safety*, pp. 91–92.

57. Quoted in Marcia Silverman, "CPR Report/Occupational Safety Moves Toward New Federal Regulation," *National Journal*, 28 February 1970, p. 452.

58. Dan Cordtz, "Safety on the Job Becomes a Major Job for Management," *Fortune*, November 1972, p. 115.

59. Page and O'Brien, *Bitter Wages*, p. 166.

60. Wilson, *Politics of Safety*, p. 39.

61. Ibid.

62. A. Lee Fritschler, *Smoking and Politics* (New York: Appleton-Century-Crofts, 1969), p. 135.

63. Ibid., p. 139.

64. Elizabeth Drew, "The Cigarette Companies Would Rather Fight Than Switch," *New York Times Magazine*, 4 May 1969, p. 132.

65. Fritschler, *Smoking and Politics*, p. 140.

66. *Congressional Quarterly Almanac, 1970*, p. 146.

67. Riley E. Dunlap and Michael P. Allen, "Partisan Differences on Environmental Issues: A Congressional Roll-Call Analysis," *Western Political Quarterly*, September 1976, pp. 384–97.

68. Kathleen Kemp, "Growth in Federal Economic Regulation: The Nixon Anomaly," Paper presented to the 1985 Annual Meeting of the Midwest Political Science Association, Chicago, April 1985, p. 13. See also James Kau and Paul Rubin, "Public Interest Lobbies: Membership and Influence," *Public Choice*, 1979, pp. 45–54.

Chapter V

1. Quoted in Al Gordon, "Public Interest Lobbies: Nader and Common Cause Become Permanent Fixtures," *Congressional Quarterly Weekly Report*, 15 May 1976, p. 1197.

2. Jeffrey Berry, *Lobbying for the People* (Princeton, N.J.: Princeton University Press, 1977), p. 289.

3. Ibid., p. 13.

4. Joel Handler, Betsy Ginsberg, and Arthur Snow, "The Public Interest Law Industry," in *Public Interest Law*, ed. Burton A. Weisbrod (Berkeley: University of California Press, 1978), p. 50.

5. *Public Interest Perspectives: The Next Four Years* (Washington, D.C.: Public Citizen, 1977).

6. Morton Mintz and Jerry Cohen, *America Inc.* (New York: Dial Press, 1971).

7. "The American Corporation Under Fire," *Newsweek*, May 24, 1971.

8. See Ralph Nader and Mark Green, eds., *Corporate Power in America* (New York: Grossman Publishers, 1973).

9. See David Vogel, *Lobbying the Corporation* (New York: Basic Books, 1978).

10. Mancur Olson, *The Logic of Collective Action* (Cambridge: Harvard University Press, 1965).

11. Andrew S. McFarland, *Public Interest Lobbies* (Washington, D.C.: American Enterprise Institute, 1976), p. 4.

12. Arthur M. Schlesinger, *The American as Reformer* (Cambridge: Harvard University Press, 1950), p. 52.

13. Samuel Huntington, *American Politics: The Promise of Disharmony* (Cambridge: Harvard University Press, 1981), p. 177.

14. Austin Ranney, "The Political Parties: Reform and Decline," in *The New American Political System*, ed. Anthony King (Washington, D.C.: American Enterprise Institute, 1978), pp. 220–22.

15. Everett Carl Ladd, Jr., "Pursuing the New Class," in *The New Class*, ed. B. Bruce-Brigges (New Brunswick, N.J.: Transaction Books, 1979), p. 103.

16. John Kenneth Galbraith, *The New Industrial State* (London: Hamish Hamilton, 1967).

17. Huntington, *American Politics*, p. 146.

18. MacFarland, *Public Interest Lobbies*, p. 6.

19. Seymour Martin Lipset and William Schneider, *The Confidence Gap* (New York: Free Press, 1983), p. 299.

20. Kent D. van Liere and Riley E. Dunlap, "The Social Bases of Environmental Concern: A Review of Hypotheses, Explanations and Empirical Evidence," *Public Opinion Quarterly*, Summer 1980, pp. 181–97. See also James Kau and Paul Rubin, "Public Interest Lobbies: Membership and Influence," *Public Choice*, 1979, pp. 45–54.

21. Irving Kristol, *Two Cheers for Capitalism* (New York: Basic Books, 1978), pp. 27–28.

22. Paul Weaver, "Regulation, Social Policy and Class Conflict," *Public Interest*, Winter 1978, p. 59.

23. Ladd, "Pursuing the New Class," p. 118.

24. Lipset and Schneider, *The Confidence Gap*, p. 24.

25. Ladd, "Pursuing the New Class," p. 114.

26. Everett Ladd, Jr., "The New Lines Are Drawn," *Public Opinion*, July–August 1978, p. 47.

27. Quoted in Michael W. McCann, *Taking Reform Seriously* (Ithaca, N.Y.: Cornell University Press, 1986), p. 51.

28. Quoted in Vogel, *Lobbying the Corporation*, p. 73.

29. Ralph Nader, *Unsafe at Any Speed* (New York: Grossman, 1965).

30. Linda Charlton, "Ralph Nader's Conglomerate Is Big Business," *New York Times*, 29 January 1976, sec. 3, p. 3.

31. James S. Turner, *The Chemical Feast* (New York: Grossman, 1970), p. 98.

32. Mark Green, "The Perils of Public Interest Law," *The New Republic*, 20 September 1975, p. 20.

33. Julius Duscha, "Stop! In the Public Interest," *New York Times Magazine*, 21 March 1971, p. 14.

34. Michael Pertschuk, *Revolt Against Regulation* (Berkeley: University of California Press, 1982), p. 30.

35. Cited in George A. Steiner and John F. Steiner, *Business, Government and Society* (New York: Random House, 1988), p. 93.

36. Burden A. Loomis and Allan Cigler, "Introduction," in *Interest Group Politics*, 2d ed., ed. Allan Cigler and Burden Loomis (Washington, D.C.: Congressional Quarterly, 1986), p. 20.

37. Thomas L. Gais, Mark A. Peterron, and Jack Walker, "Interest Groups, Iron Triangles and Representative Institutions in American National Government," *British Journal of Political Science* 14, no. 2 (April 1984): 169.

38. Berry, *Lobbying for the People*, p. 72.

39. Jack Walker, "The Origins and Maintenance of Interest Groups in America," *American Political Science Review*, June 1983, pp. 399–400.

40. Max Poglin and Edgar Shor, "Regulatory Agency Responses to the Development of Public Participation," *Public Administration Review*, March–April 1977, pp. 142, 144.

41. Quoted in McCann, *Taking Reform Seriously*, p. 44.

42. See Marver H. Bernstein, *Regulating Business by Independent Commission* (Princeton, N.J.: Princeton University Press, 1955); Grant McConnell, *Private Power and American Democracy* (New York: Knopf, 1966); and Theodore Lowi, *The End of Liberalism* (New York: Norton, 1969).

43. Charles Halpern and John Cunningham, "Reflections on the New Public Interest Law," *Georgetown Law Journal* 59 (1971): p. 1097.

44. Quoted in Duscha, "Stop!" p. 16.

45. See Karen Orren, "Standing to Sue Interest Conflict in the Federal Courts," *American Political Science Review* 70 (1976): 723–41.

46. Richard Stewart, "The Reformation of Administrative Law," *Harvard Law Review* 88 (1975): 1670.

47. Quoted in Harold Leventhal, "Environmental Decisionmaking and the Role of the Courts," *University of Pennsylvania Law Review*, January 1974, p. 512.

48. Richard Liroff, "NEPA Litigation in the 1970s: A Deluge or a Dribble?" *Natural Resources Journal* 21, no. 2 (1981): 316.

49. U.S.C.A. §4332(2) (A). *Calvert Cliffs' Coordinating Committee Inc. v. U.S. Atomic Energy Commission*, 449 F.2d 1109, 146 U.S.App.D.C. 33.

50. Liroff, "NEPA Litigation," p. 325.

51. See R. Shep Melnick, *Regulation and the Courts: The Case of the Clean Air Act* (Washington, D.C.: Brookings Institution, 1983).

52. Richard Cohen, "Public Interest Lawyers Start Looking Out for Their Own Interests," *National Journal*, 19 June 1976, p. 861.

53. Hugh Heclo, "The Executive Establishment," *The New American Political System*, ed. Anthony King, p. 88.

54. Gais, Peterron, and Walker, "Interest Groups," p. 164.

Chapter VI

1. Statistics from *The Economic Report of the President* (Washington, D.C.: U.S. Government Printing Office, 1988).

2. Seymour Martin Lipset and William Schneider, *The Confidential Gap* (New York: Free Press, 1983), p. 48.

3. Graham Wilson, *Interest Groups in the United States* (New York: Oxford University Press, 1981), p. 87.

4. Herbert McClosky and John Zallef, *The American Ethos* (Cambridge: Harvard University Press, 1984), p. 184.

5. Quoted in Lester A. Sobel, ed., *Money and Politics* (New York: Facts on File, 1974), p. 16.

6. Ibid., pp. 135, 130.

7. Wilson, *Interest Groups*, p. 66.

8. Sobel, *Money and Politics*, p. 124.

9. Herbert Alexander, *Financing Elections* (Washington, D.C.: Congressional Quarterly, 1976), p. 112.

10. *Interest Groups*, Wilson, p. 63.

11. Quoted in George A. Steiner and John F. Steiner, *Business, Government and Society* (New York: Random House, 1985), p. 106.

12. Quoted in ibid., pp. 64, 70.

13. Sobel, *Money and Politics*, p. 158.

14. Edwin M. Epstein, "The Emergence of Political Action Committees," *Sage Electoral Studies Yearbook*, vol. 5 (Beverly Hills, Calif.: Sage Publications, 1979), p. 165.

15. See Edwin M. Epstein, "Corporations and Labor Unions in Electoral Politics," *Annals of the American Academy of Political and Social Science* 425 (May 1976): 33–58.

16. Congressional Quarterly, *Dollar Politics*, 3d ed. (Washington, D.C.: Congressional Quarterly, 1982), p. 12.

17. Ibid., p. 17.

18. Michael Ruby, "How Clean Is Business?" *Newsweek*, 1 September 1975, p. 50.

19. Rogene Buchholz, *Business Environment and Public Policy* (Englewood Cliffs, N.J.: Prentice-Hall, 1986), p. 561.

20. John J. McCloy et al., *The Great Oil Spill* (New York: Chelsea House, 1976), p. 2.

21. Wyndham Robertson, "The Directors Woke Up Too Late at Gulf," *Fortune*, June 1976, p. 121.

22. David Pauly, "The Great Banana Bribe," *Newsweek*, 21 April 1975, pp. 76–81.

23. See Bruce Ian Oppenheimer, *Oil and the Congressional Process: The Limits of Symbolic Politics* (Lexington, Mass.: Lexington Books, 1974), pp. 30–36.

24. Quoted in Richard Vietor, *Energy Policy in America Since 1945* (New York: Cambridge University Press, 1984), pp. 206, 219.

25. Ibid., p. 244.

26. Ibid., p. 206.

27. Ibid., pp. 206–7.

28. "Oil Profits Under Fire," *Time*, 4 February 1974, p. 32.

29. Vietor, *Energy Policy*, pp. 209–10.

30. Ibid., p. 210.

31. "Oil Profits Under Fire," p. 32.

32. Vietor, *Energy Policy*, p. 207.

33. "Oil Profits Under Fire," p. 32.

34. Vietor, *Energy Policy*, p. 207.

35. Ibid., p. 221.

36. Ibid., p. 222.

37. Ibid.

38. Pietro Nivola, *The Politics of Energy Conservation* (Washington, D.C.: Brookings Institution, 1986), p. 36.

39. Vietor, *Energy Policy*, pp. 249, 250.

40. Ibid., p. 251.

41. *Congressional Quarterly Almanac, 1973* (Washington, D.C.: Congressional Quarterly, 1974), p. 604.

42. Ibid., p. 598.

43. Ibid.

44. Ibid., p. 604.

45. *Congressional Quarterly Almanac,* 1974 (Washington, D.C.: Congressional Quarterly, 1975), p. 739. See also E. W. Kenworthy, "Donald Cook vs. EPA," *New York Times,* 24 November 1974, sec. 3, p. 114, and "Donald Cook Takes on the Environmentalists," *Business Week,* 26 October 1974, pp. 66–77.

46. *Congressional Quarterly Almanac, 1974,* p. 739.

47. Ibid., p. 740.

48. "The Clean Air Act Keeps Its Teeth," *Business Week,* 8 June 1974, p. 23.

49. "The Clean Air Act Will Keep Its Teeth," *Business Week,* 14 July 1975, p. 86.

50. Ibid., p. 90.

51. *Congressional Quarterly Almanac, 1975* (Washington, D.C.: Congressional Quarterly, 1976), p. 177.

52. Ibid., pp. 102, 106.

53. Arthur Applbaum, "Mike Pertschuk and the Federal Trade Commission," Case prepared under the supervision of Stephanie Gould for use in the Senior Managers in Government Program at the John F. Kennedy School of Government, Harvard University, 1981, p. 17.

54. *Congressional Quarterly Almanac, 1974,* p. 327.

55. "Introduction," in *Economic Power Failure: The Current American Crisis,* ed. Summer Rosen (New York: McGraw-Hill, 1975), p. 3; other statistics from *Congressional Quarterly Almanac, 1974* and *1975.*

56. Sar Levitan and Martha Cooper, *Business Lobbies* (Baltimore: Johns Hopkins University Press, 1984), p. 74.

57. *Congressional Quarterly Almanac, 1975,* p. 481.

58. Ibid., p. 482.

59. Ibid., pp. 482, 485, 481.

60. Quoted in Steven Kelman, "Occupational Safety and Health," in *The Politics of Regulation,* ed. John Q. Wilson (New York: Basic Books, 1980), p. 117.

61. Martha Gottron, "Full Employment," *Congressional Quarterly Weekly,* 20 March 1976, p. 641.

62. All quotes from "The Coalition Behind Full Employment," *Business Week,* 12 July 1976, p. 76.

63. Gerald Rosen, "Guaranteed Jobs for All?" *Dun's Review,* May 1976, p. 47.

64. "The Coalition Behind Full Employment," *Business Week,* p. 76.

65. "National Economic Planning," *Social Policy,* July–August 1975, p. 30.

66. Gerald Rosen, "A Plan for the U.S. Economy?" *Dun's Review,* March 1976, p. 36.

67. Quoted in ibid., p. 35.

68. "Straitjacket Planning," *Business Week,* 16 December 1976, p. 92.

69. "The Planners Are Back Again," *Fortune,* July 1976, p. 72.

70. William Martin and George Cabot Lodge, "Our Society in 1985—Business May Not Like It," *Harvard Business Review,* November–December 1985, p. 78.

71. Charles Burck, "A Group Profile of the Fortune 500 Chief Executives," *Fortune,* May 1976, p. 177.

72. Leonard Silk and David Vogel, *Ethics and Profits* (New York: Simon & Schuster, 1976), p. 71.

73. Reginald H. Jones, "Why Business Must Seek Tax Reform," *Harvard Business Review,* September–October 1975, p. 54.

74. William Simon, "Shaping America's Economic Future," *Conference Board Record,* August 1975, p. 21.

75. "The Surprisingly High Cost of a Safer Environment," *Business Week,* 14 September 1974, p. 103.

76. Steven Rattner, "Productivity Lag Causes Worry," *New York Times,* 8 May 1979, p. D.2.

77. Walter Guzzardi, Jr., "Putting the Cuffs on Capitalism," *Fortune,* April 1975, p. 104.

78. Norman Macrae, "America's Third Century," *Economist,* 25 October 1975, p. 7.

Chapter VII

1. Juan Cameron, "Nader's Invaders Are Inside the Gates," *Fortune,* October 1977, p. 253.

2. *Congressional Quarterly Almanac, 1977* (Washington, D.C.: Congressional Quarterly, 1978), p. 122.

3. S. A. Levitan and M. R. Cooper, *Business Lobbies, the Public Good and the Bottom Line* (Baltimore: Johns Hopkins University Press, 1984), p. 121.

4. *Congressional Quarterly Almanac, 1977,* p. 125.

5. Ibid., p. 126.

6. Ibid., p. 124.

7. Ibid., p. 123.

8. Levitan and Cooper, *Business Lobbies,* p. 122.

9. Ibid., p. 129.

10. Thomas Ferguson and Joel Rogers, "Labor Law Reform and Its Enemies," *Nation,* January 6–13, 1979, p. 19.

11. Ibid., p. 19.

12. Robert Merry and Albert Hunt, "Business Lobby Gains More Power as It Rides Antigovernment Tide," *Wall Street Journal,* 17 May 1978, p. 1.

13. *Congressional Quarterly Almanac, 1978* (Washington, D.C.: Congressional Quarterly, 1979), p. 284.

14. Levitan and Cooper, *Business Lobbies,* p. 131.

15. Ibid., p. 135.

16. Seymour Martin Lipset and William Schneider, *The Confidence Gap* (New York: Free Press, 1983), p. 207.

17. Levitan and Cooper, *Business Lobbies,* p. 134.

18. *Congressional Quarterly Almanac, 1978,* p. 284.

19. Quoted in Philip Shabecoff, "Big Business on the Offensive," *New York Times Magazine,* 9 December 1979, p. 90.

20. James W. Singer, "There's Little Joy in Laborville," *National Journal,* 26 August 1978, p. 1368.

21. Quotes from *Congressional Quarterly Almanac, 1978,* p. 272.

22. Charles Noble, *Liberalism at Work: The Rise and Fall of OSHA* (Philadelphia: Temple University Press, 1986), p. 188.

23. Ibid., p. 192.

24. "Storm-Tossed OSHA," *The New Republic,* 17 May 1980, p. 5.

25. Linda Demkovich, "Consumer Groups See End in Sight After Long Fight over Agency," *National Journal,* 29 January 1977, p. 174.

26. Linda Demkovich, "Even a White House Pep Rally May Not Save the Consumer Agency," *National Journal,* 25 June 1977, p. 997.

27. Arthur Applbaum, "Mike Pertschuk and the Federal Trade Commission." Case prepared under the supervision of Stephanie Gould, ed., Case Program, for use in the Senior Managers in Government Program at the John F. Kennedy School of Government, Harvard University, 1981, p. 19.

28. Lipset and Schneider, *The Confidence Gap,* pp. 248–49.

29. *Congressional Quarterly Almanac, 1978,* p. 473.

30. Linda Demkovich, "Where Is the Consuming Public on the Proposed Consumer Agency?" *National Journal,* 10 December 1977, p. 1914.

31. "Consumer Bill Killed by House in 227–189 Vote," *Wall Street Journal,* 9 February 1978, p. 2.

32. Ibid.

33. Philip Shabecoff, "A Dialogue on the Consumer Agenda," *New York Times,* sec. 4, 12 February 1978, p. E2.

34. George Schwartz, "The Successful Fight Against a Federal Consumer Protection Agency," *MSU Business Topics,* Summer 1979, p. 55.

35. Ibid.

36. Applbaum, "Mike Pertschuk," p. 17.

37. Linda Demkovich, "The Nader Nadir?" *National Journal,* 17 December 1977, p. 1968.

38. Applbaum, "Mike Pertschuk," p. 13.

39. Ibid.

40. Ibid., pp. 17, 18.

41. Ibid., p. 30.

42. Ibid.

43. Ibid.

44. Michael Pertschuk, *Revolt Against Regulation* (Berkeley: University of California Press, 1982), pp. 70, 71.

45. Ibid., p. 75.

46. James Singer, "Endangered Species?" *National Journal*, 1 December 1979, p. 2034.

47. James Singer, "The FTC—Business's Government Enemy No. 1," *National Journal*, 13 October 1979, pp. 1680, 1679.

48. Susan Tolchin and Martin Tolchin, *Dismantling America* (New York: Oxford University Press, 1983), p. 153.

49. Pertschuk, *Revolt Against Regulation*, p. 98.

50. Randall Calvert, Mark Moran, and Barry Weingast, "Congressional Influences over Policymaking: The Case of the FTC," in *Congress: Structure and Policy*, ed. Mathew McCubbins and Terry Sullivan (New York: Cambridge University Press, 1987), p. 504.

51. *Congressional Quarterly Almanac, 1980* (Washington, D.C.: Congressional Quarterly, 1981), p. 233.

52. A. O. Sulzberger, Jr., "Will FTC Battle Inhibit Regulation?" *New York Times*, 22 May 1980, p. D 6.

53. Martha Derthick and Paul Quirk, *The Politics of Deregulation* (Washington, D.C.: Brookings Institution, 1985), p. 43.

54. Ibid., pp. 41, 51.

55. Thomas McCraw, *Prophets of Regulation* (Cambridge: Belknap Press of Harvard University Press, 1984), pp. 266, 268.

56. Derthick and Quirk, *Politics of Deregulation*, p. 123.

57. Willard Butcher, "The Stifling Cost of Regulation," *Business Week*, 6 November 1978, p. 22.

58. Michael Jensen, "Federal Paperwork: A Small Businessman's 'Nightmare,' " *New York Times*, 22 March 1978.

59. Timothy Clark, "The Year of Regulation," *National Journal*, 20 January 1979, p. 108.

60. Steven Rattner, "Regulating the Regulators," *New York Times Magazine*, 30 June 1979, pp. 110, 104.

61. Tom Alexander, "It's Roundup Time for the Runaway Regulators," *Fortune*, 3 December 1979, p. 128.

62. Seymour Martin Lipset and William Schneider, "The Public View of Regulation," *Public Opinion*, January–February 1979, pp. 9–10.

63. Ibid., pp. 226, 228.

64. Juan Cameron, "The Tax Education of Jimmy Carter," *Fortune*, 16 January 1978, p. 55.

65. John Witte, *The Politics and Development of the Federal Income Tax* (Madison: University of Wisconsin Press, 1985), p. 207.

66. Robert Kuttner, *The Revolt of the Haves* (New York: Simon & Schuster, 1980), pp. 247, 245–46.

67. See, for example, Charles D. Kuehner, ed., *Capital and Job Formation: Our Nation's 3rd Century Challenge* (Homewood, Ill.: Dow Jones-Irwin, 1978).

68. Charls Walker and Mark Bloomfield, "How the Capital Gains Tax Fight Was Won," *Wharton Magazine* 3, no. 2 (Winter 1979): 38.

69. Witte, *Politics and Development of the Income Tax*, p. 216.

70. Richard Vietor, *Energy Policy in America since 1945* (New York: Cambridge University Press, 1984), p. 308.

71. Ibid., pp. 308, 309.

72. Pietro Nivola, *The Politics of Energy Conservation* (Washington, D.C.: Brookings Institution, 1986), p. 120.

73. Quoted in ibid., p. 35.

74. Edwin McDowell, "Big Oil: A Struggle for Credibility," *New York Times*, 1 July 1979, sec. 3, pp. 1, 4.

75. Ibid.

76. *Congressional Quarterly Almanac, 1979* (Washington, D.C.: Congressional Quarterly, 1980), pp. 609, 610.

77. Ibid., pp. 610, 609.

78. Victor, *Energy Policy,* p. 266.

79. Ibid., pp. 269, 270.

80. Jean Briggs, "Detroit and Congress: Eyeball to Eyeball," *Forbes,* 15 February 1977, p. 34.

81. *Congressional Quarterly Almanac, 1976* (Washington, D.C.: Congressional Quarterly, 1977), p. 137.

82. Bernard Asbell, "The Outlawing of Next Year's Cars," *New York Times Magazine,* 21 November 1976, p. 86.

83. Ibid., p. 83.

84. Norman J. Ornstein and Shirley Elder, *Interest Groups, Lobbying and Policymaking* (Washington, D.C.: Congressional Quarterly, 1978), p. 172.

85. Mercer Cross and Barry Hager, "Auto Workers, Manufacturers and Dealers Unite to Dilute Car Pollution Standards in Clean Air Bill," *Congressional Weekly Report,* 28 May 1977, p. 1024.

86. *Congressional Quarterly Almanac, 1977,* p. 636.

87. Quoted in David Vogel, "A Case Study of Clean Air Legislation 1967–1981," in *The Impact of the Modern Corporation,* ed., Betty Bock et al. (New York: Columbia University Press, 1984), p. 344.

88. Jerry Hultin, "Unions, the Environment and Corporate Social Responsibility," *Yale Review of Law and Social Action* 3 (Fall 1972): 51.

89. Ibid., pp. 181, 182.

90. Peter Domenici, "Clean Air Act Amendments of 1977," *Natural Resources Journal,* July 1979, p. 478.

91. Ornstein and Elder, *Interest Groups,* pp. 170–71.

92. Asbell, "The Outlawing of Next Year's Cars," p. 86.

93. *Congressional Quarterly Almanac, 1979,* p. 603.

94. Dick Kirschten, "Cutting Energy Project Red Tape Raises Legal, Practical Questions," *National Journal,* 1 September 1979, p. 1448.

95. *Congressional Quarterly Almanac, 1980,* p. 483.

96. "Superfund (A): The Early Maneuvering," Case prepared by John F. Mahon, Boston University 741-102, 1982, p. 12.

97. Ibid., p. 30.

98. *Congressional Quarterly Almanac, 1980,* p. 587.

99. Ibid, pp. 587, 575.

100. Lawrence Mosher, "Environmentalists Question Whether to Retreat or Stay on the Offensive," *National Journal,* 13 December 1980, p. 2117.

101. Ibid., pp. 2118–19.

102. Bill Keller, "Environmental Movement Checks Its Pulse and Finds Obituaries Are Premature," *Congressional Quarterly Weekly,* 31 January 1981, p. 212.

103. *Congressional Quarterly Almanac, 1980,* p. 574.

104. Lawrence Mosher, "Talking Clean on the Hustings," *National Journal,* 1 November 1980, p. 1850.

105. Quotes from Martin Tolchin, "Carter's Corporate Brain Trust," *New York Times,* 24 July 1979, p. DI.

106. Cameron, "The Tax Education of Jimmy Carter," p. 58.

107. Robert May, "Business Leaders Heavily Oppose Carter's Economics and Leadership," *Wall Street Journal,* 23 June 1980, p. 25.

Chapter VIII

1. Quoted in Leonard Silk and David Vogel, *Ethics and Profits* (New York: Simon & Schuster, 1976), p. 65.

2. Quoted in Thomas K. McGraw, "Business Roundtable (A)," a case prepared for class discussion at the Harvard Business School, 1979, p. 1.

3. Quoted in Sidney Blumenthal, *The Rise of the Counter Establishment* (New York: Times Books, 1986), p. 77.

4. Quoted in John Saloma III, *Ominous Politics* (New York: Hill & Wang, 1984), p. 67.

5. Quoted in Michael Pertschuk, *Revolt Against Regulation* (Berkeley: University of California Press, 1982), pp. 51–52.

6. Quoted in Thomas Edsell, *The New Politics of Inequality* (New York: Norton, 1984), p. 114.

7. Steven Ratner, "Big Industry Gun Aims at the Hill," *New York Times*, 7 March 1976, sec. 3, p. 3.

8. Quoted in Robert Merry and Albert Hunt, "Business Lobby Gains More Power as It Rides Antigovernment Tide," *Wall Street Journal*, 17 May 1978, p. 1.

9. James Post, Edwin Murray, Jr., Robert Dickie, and John Mahon, "Managing Public Affairs: The Public Affairs Function," *California Management Review* 25, no. 1 (Fall 1983): 135–36.

10. Quoted in Vasil Pappas, "More Firms Upgraded Government-Relations Jobs Because of Sharp Growth in Federal Regulations," *Wall Street Journal*, 11 July 1980, p. 36.

11. Vasil Pappas, "Labor Letter," *Wall Street Journal*, 24 July 1974, p. 1.

12. In Pappas, "More Firms Upgraded Government-Relations Jobs."

13. "New Ways to Lobby a Recalcitrant Congress," *Business Week*, 3 September 1979, p. 148.

14. See, for example, James Brown, *This Business of Issues: Coping with the Company's Environments* (New York: Conference Board, 1979).

15. Phyllis McGrath, *Redefining Corporate-Federal Relations* (New York: Conference Board, 1979), p. 94.

16. Phyllis S. McGrath, *Managing Corporate External Relations: Changing Perspectives and Responses* (New York: Conference Board, 1976). See also Robert L. Fegley, "New Breed of Top Executives Takes Charge," *Los Angeles Times*, 31 December 1976, part 4, p. 6.

17. From a speech by Irving Shapiro quoted in Peter F. Drucker, "Coping with Those Extra Burdens," *Wall Street Journal*, 2 May 1979, p. 22.

18. Quoted in James W. Singer, "Business and Government: A New 'Quasi-Public' Role," *National Journal*, 15 April 1978, p. 596.

19. P. Vanderwicken, "Irving Shapiro Takes Charge at DuPont," *Fortune*, January 1974, pp. 78–81.

20. Louis M. Kohlmier, "The Big Businessmen Who Have Jimmy Carter's Ear," *New York Times*, February 1978, sec. 3, pp. 1, 11.

21. McGraw, "Business Roundtable (A)," p. 2.

22. "New Ways to Lobby," p. 148.

23. David Yoffie and Joseph L. Badaracco, Jr., "A Rational Model of Corporate Political Strategies," Working Paper, Division of Research, Harvard Business School, 1984, p. 2.

24. Robert B. Reich, "Regulation by Confrontation or Negotiation," *Harvard Business Review* 59, no. 3 (May–June 1981), pp. 82–93.

25. Barry Hager, "Business Roundtable: New Lobbying Force," *Congressional Quarterly Weekly Report*, 17 September 1977, pp. 1964–65.

26. See Arthur Levitt, Jr., "Small Business Discovers Its Strength," *Business Week*, 10 March 1980, p. 23, and Richard Cohen, "Small Business Is Getting a Big Reception in Washington," *National Journal*, 11 June 1977, pp. 896–99.

27. Quoted in Brigette Rouson, "Small Business Lobbying: With National Organization More People Are Listening," *Congressional Quarterly Weekly Report*, 1 March 1980, p. 616.

28. Robert Merry, "Small Business, Irked by Taxes and Rules, Develops Political Savvy to Press Its Case," *Wall Street Journal*, 27 July 1979, p. 36.

29. Silk and Vogel, *Ethics and Profits*, p. 178.

30. In Merry and Hunt, "Business Lobby Gains More Power," p. 15.

31. James Singer, "Behind the New Aggressiveness," *National Journal*, 16 August 1980, p. 1367.

32. "A Potent New Business Lobby," *Business Week,* 22 May 1978, p. 64.

33. Arthur Applbaum, "Mike Pertschuk and the Federal Trade Commission," Case prepared under the supervision of Stephanie Gould, ed., Case Program, for use in the Senior Managers in Government Program at the John F. Kennedy School of Government, Harvard University, 1981.

34. Samuel Bowles, David M. Gordon, and Thomas Weisskopf, *Beyond the Wasteland* (Garden City, N.Y.: Doubleday, 1983), p. 49.

35. Quoted in Singer, "Behind the New Aggressiveness," p. 1367.

36. Richard Cohen, "The Business Lobby Discovers That in Unity There Is Strength," *National Journal,* 28 June 1980, p. 1052.

37. A. F. Ehrbar, "Pragmatic Politics Won't Win for Business," *Fortune,* 4 June 1979, p. 77.

38. Merry, "Small Business," p. 36.

39. Quoted in Walter Guzzardi, Jr., "Business Is Learning How to Win in Washington," *Fortune,* 27 March 1978, p. 54.

40. Gary C. Jacobson, "Running Scared: Elections and Congressional Politics in the 1980s," in *Congress: Structure and Policy,* ed. Matthew McCubbins and Terry Sullivan (New York: Cambridge University Press, 1987), p. 40.

41. Guzzardi, "Business Is Learning," p. 56.

42. Merry, "Small Business," p. 15.

43. "Business Lobbying," *Consumer Reports* 43, no. 9 (September 1978): 528, 529.

44. Edsell, *The New Politics,* p. 124.

45. Graham Wilson, *Interest Groups in the United States* (New York: Oxford University Press, 1981), p. 143.

46. McGrath, *Redefining Corporate-Federal Relations,* p. 48.

47. Gerry Keim, "Corporate Grassroots Programs in the 1980s," *California Management Review* 28, no. 1 (Fall 1985): 117.

48. See Neil Ulman, "Companies Organize Employees and Holders into a Political Force," *Wall Street Journal,* 15 August 1978, pp. 1, 15.

49. Quoted in Philip Shabecoff, "Big Business on the Offensive," *New York Times Magazine,* 9 December 1979, p. 91.

50. Larry Sabato, *PAC Power* (New York: Norton, 1985), pp. 11–15.

51. Edwin M. Epstein, "Business and Labor under the Federal Election Campaign Act of 1971," in *Parties, Interest Groups and Campaign Finance Laws* ed. Michael Malbin (Washington, D.C.: American Enterprise Institute, 1980), p. 120.

52. Sabato, *PAC Power,* p. 47.

53. Dan Clawson, Alan Neuwstadtl, and James Bearden, "The Logic of Business Unity: Corporate Contributions to the 1980 Congressional Elections," *American Sociological Review,* December 1986, pp. 801–2.

54. Quoted in Wilson, *Interest Groups in the United States,* pp. 75, 74.

55. Quoted in Maxwell Glen, "At the Wire, Corporate PACs Come Through for the G.O.P.," *National Journal,* 3 February 1979, p. 174.

56. Dick Kirschten, "Corporate PACs—the GOP's Ace in the Hole," *National Journal,* 25 November 1978, p. 1899.

57. This analysis draws upon Edsell, *The New Politics,* pp. 134–36. See also Dennis Farney, "A Liberal Congressman Turns Conservative: Did PAC Gifts Do It?" *Wall Street Journal,* 19 July 1982, pp. 1, 19.

58. Timothy Clark, "Tax Lobbyists Scrambling in the Dark to Fight Taxes That Hit Their Clients," *National Journal,* 22 May 1982, p. 899.

59. Gary C. Jacobson, "Money in the 1980 and 1982 Congressional Elections," in *Money and Politics in the United States,* ed. Michael Malbin (Chatham, N.J.: Chatham House, 1984), p. 45.

60. See Sabato, *PAC Power,* p. 134.

61. Clark MacGregor, "Commentaries," in *Money and Politics,* ed. Malbin, pp. 207–8.

62. Quoted in Edward Handler and John R. Mulkern, *Business in Politics* (Lexington, Mass.: Lexington Books, 1982), p. 105.

63. Gary Andres, "Business Involvement in Campaign Finance: Factors Influencing the Decision to Form a Corporate PAC," *P.S.,* Spring 1985, pp. 213–20.

64. David Liff, *Corporate Advertising: The Business Response to Changing Public Attitudes* (Washington, D.C.: Investor Responsibility Research Center, 1980), p. 13.

65. Quoted in James N. Sites, "Public Policy Communication: The New PR Imperative," *Public Relations Journal* 33, no. 7 (July 1977): 8.

66. See, for example, Louis Banks, "Taking on the Hostile Media," *Harvard Business Review*, March–April 1978, p. 123.

67. John Cooney, "Does Business Want a Sophisticated Press or a Favorable One?" *Wall Street Journal*, 21 July 1977, p. 1.

68. Silk and Vogel, *Ethics and Profits*, p. 109.

69. *ORC Public Opinion Index* (mid-March 1974), p. 2.

70. Michael Unseem, *The Inner Circle* (New York: Oxford University Press, 1984), p. 89.

71. Quoted in S. Prakash Sethi, *Advocacy Advertising and Large Corporations* (Lexington, Mass.: Heath, 1977), pp. 74, 87.

72. See, for example, Stanley Rothman and S. Robert Lichter, "Media and Business Elites: Two Classes in Conflict?" *Public Interest*, Fall 1982, pp. 117–25.

73. Louis Banks, "The Failings of Business and Journalism," *Time*, 9 February 1976, p. 78.

74. Quoted in Sethi, *Advocacy Advertising*, pp. 74, 75.

75. David Mahoney, "On Ending an Adversary Relationship," *New York Times*, 7 July 1977, p. 19.

76. Quoted in McGraw, "Business Roundtable," p. 2.

77. Quoted in "Grooming the Executive for the Spotlight," *Business Week*, 5 October 1974, p. 57.

78. Unseem, *The Inner Circle*, p. 87.

79. Sethi, *Advocacy Advertising*, p. 16.

80. Irwin Ross, "Public Relations Isn't Kid-Glove Stuff at Mobil," *Fortune*, September 1976, p. 109. For another perspective on Mobil's public-relations efforts, see Robert Sherrill, "Mobil's News That's Fit to Print," *Nation*, 17 January 1979, pp. 67, 71–75.

81. Robert Heath and Richard Nelson, *Issues Management* (Beverly Hills, Calif.: Sage Publications, 1986), pp. 87–88.

82. Quoted in ibid., pp. 81, 88, 89.

83. Quoted in Randall Poe, "Masters of the Advertorial," *Across the Board*, September 1980, p. 17.

84. See Stephen Shepard and Daniel Moskowitz, "Why the Networks Reject Mobil's Message," *Business Week*, 20 July 1974, p. 79.

85. Saloma, *Ominous Politics*, p. 117.

86. Seymour Martin Lipset, "The New Class and the Professoriate," in *The New Class?* ed. B. Bruce Briggs (New Brunswick, N.J.: Transaction Books, 1979), p. 76.

87. Silk and Vogel, *Ethics and Profits*, pp. 118, 117.

88. Fred Hechinger, "Survey Finds Business Backs Free Inquiry," *New York Times*, 21 August 1979, p. C4.

89. Quoted in Blumenthal, *The Rise of the Counter-Establishment*, p. 54.

90. Quoted in Robert Bartley, "Business and the New Class," in *The New Class?* ed. Briggs, p. 61.

91. Ibid., pp. 52, 42.

92. Irving Kristol, *Two Cheers for Capitalism* (New York: Basic Books, 1978), p. 145.

93. Ibid., pp. 143, 145.

94. William Simon, *A Time for Truth* (Reader's Digest Press, 1978), p. 233.

95. Quoted in Saloma, *Ominous Politics*, p. 65.

96. See Geoffrey Norman, "The Godfather of Neoconservatism (and His Family)," *Esquire*, 13 February 1979, pp. 36–42.

97. Jude Wanniski, *The Way the World Works* (New York: Simon & Schuster, 1983).

98. Quoted in Blumenthal, *The Rise of the Counter-Establishment*, p. 148.

99. See Bernard Weintraub, "Foundations Assist Conservative Cause," *New York Times*, 20 January 1981, p. 25.

100. For a debate on the wisdom of doing so, see Robert H. Malott, "Corporate Support of Education: Some Strings Attached," *Harvard Business Review*, July–August 1978, pp. 133–138; and Louis Cabot, "Corporate Support for Education: No Strings Attached," *Harvard Business Review*, July–August 1978, pp. 139–44.

101. John Thackray, "How U.S. Business Lobbies," *Management Today*, December 1978, p. 76.

102. Irving Howe, "The Spirit of the Times," *Dissent*, Fall 1986, p. 418.

103. Quoted in Peter Stone, "Not-So-Strange Bed Fellows in Conservative Think Tanks," *Washington Post National Weekly Edition,* 17 June 1985, p. 11.

104. Ann Crittenden, "The Economic Wind's Blowing Toward the Right—For Now," *New York Times,* 16 July 1978, sec. 3, pp. 1, 9.

105. Murray Weidenbaum, "Estimating Regulatory Costs," *Regulation,* May–June 1978, pp. 14–17.

106. Blumenthal, *The Rise of the Counter-Establishment,* p. 48.

107. See, for example, Francis Xavier Sutton et al., *The American Business Creed* (Cambridge: Harvard University Press, 1956).

108. Milton Friedman, *Capitalism and Freedom* (Chicago: University of Chicago Press, 1962).

109. Friedrich von Hayek, *The Road to Serfdom* (Chicago: University of Chicago Press, 1944).

110. George Gilder, *Wealth and Poverty* (New York: Basic Books, 1981); and Michael Novak, *The Spirit of Democratic Capitalism* (New York: Simon & Schuster, 1982).

111. Irving Kristol, "The War of the Words," *Wall Street Journal,* 11 June 1987, p. 24.

112. "Why the Middle Class Supports Reagan," *Business Week,* 18 May 1981, p. 133.

113. Robert Kuttner, *Revolt of the Haves* (New York: Simon & Schuster, 1980), p. 10.

114. Ibid., pp. 20–23.

115. Robert Reich, "The Liberal Promise of Prosperity," *The New Republic,* 21 February 1981, p. 20.

116. The Reindustrialization of America," *Business Week,* 30 June 1980, pp. 58, 57.

117. David Osborne, "Toward a Postindustrial Politics," *Dissent,* Winter 1988, p. 112.

118. Charles Noble, *Liberalism at Work* (Philadelphia: Temple University Press, 1986), p. 111.

119. Seymour Martin Lipset and William Schneider, "The Public View of Regulation," *Public Opinion,* January–February 1979, p. 9.

120. Pat Caddell, quoted in "The Politics of the Baby Boom," in *Left, Right & Baby Boom: America's New Politics,* ed. David Boaz (Washington, D.C.: Cato Institute, 1986), p. 43.

121. Robert Samuelson, "Business's Unlikely Friends," *National Journal,* 25 November 1978, p. 1912.

122. Marjorie Boyd, "The Protection Consumers Don't Want," *Washington Monthly,* September 1977, p. 34.

123. Paul Seabury, ed., *Bureaucrats and Brainpower: Government Regulation of Universities* (San Francisco: Institute for Contemporary Studies, 1979). See also Nathan Glazer, "Regulating Business and the Universities: One Problem or Two?" *The Public Interest* 56 (Summer 1979): 43–65.

124. Seabury, *Bureaucrats and Brainpower,* p. 4.

125. Quoted in Timothy Clark, "After a Decade of Doing Battle, Public Interest Groups Show Their Age," *National Journal,* 12 July 1980, p. 1140.

126. Ross Baker, "Naderism Is Running Amuck with Its Rake," *New York Times,* 8 December 1977, p. 23.

127. Pertschuk, *Revolt Against Regulation,* p. 64.

128. See, for example, Irving Kristol, "The War of the Words"; and Paul Weaver, "Regulation, Social Policy and Class Conflict," *The Public Interest,* Winter 1978.

129. See Edsell, *The New Politics of Inequality;* and Thomas Ferguson and Joel Rogers, *Right Turn* (New York: Hill & Wang, 1986).

Chapter IX

1. Alan Stone, "State and Market," in *The Hidden Election,* ed. Thomas Ferguson and Joel Rogers (New York: Pantheon Books, 1981), p. 236.

2. This paragraph is based on Dan Clawson, Marvin Karson, and Allen Kaufman, "The Corporate Pact for a Conservative America," in *Research in Corporate Social Performance and Policy,* ed. James E. Post, vol. 8 (Greenwich, Conn.: JAI Press, 1986), pp. 223–48.

3. Theodore J. Eismeier and Philip H. Pollock III, *Business Money, and the Rise of Corporate PAC's in American Elections* (New York: Quorum Books, 1988), pp. 85, 52.

4. Theodore Eismeier and Philip H. Pollock III, "The Retreat from Partisanship: Why the Dog Didn't Bark in the 1984 Election," in *Business Strategy and Public Policy*, ed. Alfred Marcus, Allen Kaufman, and David Bean (New York: Quorum Books, 1987), p. 140.

5. Val Burris, "Business Support for the New Right," *Socialist Review* 91 (1988): 32.

6. Dan Clawson, Alan Neustadtl, and James Bearden, "The Logic of Business Unity: Corporate Contributions to the 1980 Congressional Elections," *American Sociological Review*, December 1986, pp. 801–2. See also Dan Clawson, Allen Kaufman, and Alan Neustadtl, "Corporate PACs for a New Pax Americana," *The Insurgent Sociologist* 12 (Summer–Fall 1982): 63–78; and Allen M. Kaufman, Marvin J. Karson, and Jeffrey Sohl, "Business Fragmentation and Solidarity: An Analysis of PAC Donations in the 1980 and 1982 Elections," in *Business Strategy and Public Policy*, ed. Marcus, Kaufman, and Bean, pp. 119–36.

7. Steve Lohr, "Business under Reagan," *New York Times*, 6 November 1980, p. D1.

8. "Ending Washington's Feud with Business," *Business Week*, 24 November 1980, p. 156.

9. Sidney Blumenthal, *The Rise of the Counter-Establishment* (New York: Times Books, 1986), p. 85.

10. William Lanouette, "Business Lobbyists Hope Their Unity on the Tax Bill Wasn't Just a Fluke," *National Journal*, 24 October 1981, p. 1897.

11. Juan Cameron, "The Coming Cuts in Business Taxes," *Fortune*, 3 November 1980, p. 75.

12. Quoted in John Witte, *The Politics and Development of the Federal Income Tax* (Madison: University of Wisconsin Press, 1985), p. 222.

13. Ibid., p. 227.

14. Quoted in Thomas Ferguson and Joel Rogers, *Right Turn* (New York: Hill & Wang, 1986), p. 122.

15. Eismeier and Pollock, *Business Money*, p. 91.

16. Kenneth Bacon, "In Tax-Cut Fight, 'No Name' Group Lobbies Hard for Business Viewpoint," *Wall Street Journal*, 23 June 1981, sec. 2, p. 25.

17. Bill Keller, "Business Tries to Cool Its Back-street Romance with Federal Spending," *Congressional Quarterly Weekly Report*, 27 March 1981, pp. 406–7.

18. Lanouette, "Business Lobbyists," pp. 1896, 1897.

19. Michael Gordon, "Will Reagan 'Turn Business Loose' if Business Wants to Stay Regulated?" *National Journal*, 3 January 1981, p. 10.

20. Larry Gerston, Cynthia Fraleigh, and Robert Schwab, *The Deregulated Society* (Pacific Grove, Calif.: Brooks/Cole Publishing, 1988), p. 47.

21. Lawrence Mosher, "Reagan and Environmental Protection—None of the Laws Will Be Untouchable," *National Journal*, 3 January 1981, p. 17.

22. Gerston, Fraleigh, and Schwab, *Deregulated Society*, p. 50.

23. Ibid., p. 53.

24. Lawrence Mosher, "Regulatory Striptease—Watt Takes Aim at Surface Mining Regulations," *National Journal*, 30 May 1981, p. 972.

25. Quoted in George Eads and Michael Fix, *Relief or Reform?* (Washington, D.C.: Urban Institute, 1984), p. 196.

26. Michael Wines, "Auchter's Record at OSHA Leaves Labor Outraged, Business Satisfied," *National Journal*, 1 October 1983, p. 2008.

27. Michael Wines, "They're Still Telling OSHA Horror Stories But the 'Victims' Are New," *National Journal*, 7 November 1981, p. 1985.

28. "It's Better Under Reagan, but. . . ." *Industry Week*, 20 September 1982, p. 19.

29. Lawrence Mosher, "Despite Setbacks, Watt Is Succeeding in Opening Up Public Lands for Energy," *National Journal*, 11 June 1983, p. 1230.

30. Michael Wines, "Reagan Plan to Relieve Auto Industry of Regulatory Burden Gets Mixed Grades," *National Journal*, 23 July 1983, p. 1532.

31. "Has Reagan Served Business Well?" *U.S. News and World Report*, 6 December 1980, p. 40.

32. Christopher C. DeMuth, "A Strong Beginning on Reform," *Regulation*, January–February 1982, p. 11.

33. Gerston, Fraleigh, and Schwab, *Deregulated Society*, p. 54.

34. Quoted in Mark Green, "The Gang That Couldn't Deregulate," *The New Republic,* 21 March 1983, p. 17.

35. Ibid.

36. Edmund T. Pratt, Jr., "It Has Been an Exciting Beginning," *U.S. News and World Report,* 2 November 1981, pp. 79, 78.

37. A. F. Ehrbar, "The Battle over Taxes," *Fortune,* 19 April 1982, p. 60.

38. *Congressional Quarterly Almanac, 1982* (Washington, D.C.: Congressional Quarterly, 1983), p. 32.

39. Quoted in Bill Keller, "With Tax Hikes in Prospect, Lobbyists Revert to Form: 'Don't Tax Me, Tax Thee,'" *Congressional Quarterly Weekly Report,* 5 June 1982, p. 1328.

40. Ehrbar, "Battle over Taxes," pp. 62, 58.

41. Quoted in Pamela Fessler, "Business Ponders Losses in New Tax Bill," *Congressional Quarterly Weekly Report,* 28 August 1982, p. 2119.

42. Perry Quick, "Reagan's Industrial Policy," in *The Reagan Record,* ed. John Palmer and Isabel Sawhilll (Cambridge, Mass.: Ballinger Publishing, 1984). pp. 297, 300.

43. "How Business Is Getting Through to Washington," *Business Week,* 4 October 1982, p. 16.

44. Richard Corrigan, "United by Deficits," *National Journal,* 29 January 1983, p. 232.

45. Ibid.

46. "Executives Still Support Reaganomics," *Business Week,* 26 April 1982, p. 20.

47. See, for example, "Business Tells Pentagon How to Cut," *U.S. News and World Report,* 11 July 1983, p. 6; and Richard Corrigan, "Business Leaders to Reagan: Trim the Military before Boosting Taxes," *National Journal,* 6 November 1982, pp. 1899–1901.

48. Timothy Schellhardt, "Business Back on Defensive with Congress," *Wall Street Journal,* 11 January 1983, sec. 2, p. 33.

49. "Executives Still Support," p. 20.

50. Richard Corrigan, "Unions Say Labor Board's Hostility Compounds Their Economic Hard Times," *National Journal,* 23 July 1983, p. 1544.

51. "Domestic Content Rolls on," *Fortune,* 9 January 1984, p. 36.

52. See, for example, Robert Reich, "Industrial Policy," *The New Republic,* 31 March 1982, pp. 28–31; Robert Reich, "Making Industrial Policy," *Business Review* 60, no. 1 (1982): 74–80; Robert Reich, "An Industrial Policy of the Right," *The Public Interest* 73 (1983): 3–17; Lester Thurow, "Revitalizing American Industry," *California Management Review* 271 (1984): 9–41; and Lester Thurow, "The Need for Industrial Policies," *Annals of Public and Co-operative Economy* 55, no. 1 (1984): 3–31.

53. Quoted in Timothy Clark, "Digging a Grave," *National Journal,* 29 October 1983, p. 2278.

54. Richard Corrigan, "Democrats Seek an Industrial Policy in Time for the Next Election Campaign," *National Journal,* 11 June 1983, p. 1221.

55. Ibid., p. 1222.

56. Clark, "Digging a Grave," p. 2278.

57. Corrigan, "Democrats Seek an Industrial Policy," p. 1222.

58. Green, "Gang That Couldn't Deregulate," p. 14.

59. Michael Wines, "The Pendulum Swings," *National Journal,* 21 May 1983, p. 1072.

60. Gerston, Fraleigh, and Schwab, *Deregulated Society,* p. 59.

61. Green, "Gang That Couldn't Deregulate," pp. 16–17.

62. See, for example, Lester Lave and Gilbert Omenn, *Clearing the Air: Reforming the Clean Air Act* (Washington, D.C.: Brookings, 1981).

63. Bill Keller, "Environmental Movement Checks Its Pulse and Finds Obituaries Premature," *Congressional Quarterly Weekly,* 31 January 1981, pp. 211–16; and Andy Pasztor, "Reagan Policies Spur Big Revival of the Environmental Movement," *Wall Street Journal,* 9 August 1982, sec. 2, p. 15.

64. Robert Mitchell, "Public Opinion and Environmental Politics in the 1970s and 1980s," in Norman Vig and Michael Kraft, *Environmental Policy in the 1980s* (Washington, D.C.: Congressional Quarterly, 1984), p. 61.

65. William Symonds, "Washington in the Grip of the Green Giant," *Fortune,* 4 October 1982, p. 138.

66. Ibid., p. 140.

67. Everett Carl Ladd, "Clearing the Air," *Public Opinion,* February–March 1982, p. 16.

68. Quoted in Joseph Petulla, *Environmental Protection in the United States* (San Francisco: San Francisco Study Center, 1987), p. 59.

69. Murray Weidenbaum, "Regulatory Reform Under the Reagan Administration," in *The Reagan Regulatory Strategy*, ed. George Eads and Michael Fix (Washington, D.C.: Urban Institute, 1984), p. 23.

70. Symonds, "Washington in the Grip," p. 137.

71. Michael Wines, "Miller's Directive to the FTC—Quit Acting Like a 'Consumer Cop,'" *National Journal*, 5 December 1981, p. 2152.

72. Quoted in Michael Pertschuk, *Giant Killers* (New York: Norton, 1986), p. 92.

73. Ibid., p. 100.

74. Michael Wines, "From Doctors to Dairy Farmers, Critics Gunning for the FTC Again," *National Journal*, 29 January 1983, p. 221.

75. Lawrence Mosher, "Watt's Departure from Interior May Not Mean a Sharp Break with His Policies," *National Journal*, 5 November 1983, p. 2309.

76. Quoted in Eads and Fix, *Relief or Reform?* p. 181.

77. Lawrence Mosher, "EPA, Critics Agree Agency Under Gorsuch Hasn't Changed Its Spots," *National Journal*, 13 November 1982, p. 1941.

78. Robert Crandall, "The Environment," *Regulation*, January–February 1982, p. 29.

79. Lawrence Mosher, "Move Over Jim Watt, Anne Gorsuch Is the Latest Target of Environmentalists," *National Journal*, 24 October 1981, p. 1902.

80. "Business Is Wary on Budget Cuts," *Business Week*, 12 October 1981, p. 179.

81. "Industry's Fear: Regulatory Balkanization," *National Journal*, 31 July 1982, p. 1342. For more on "regulatory vacuums," see Susan Bartlett Foote, "Regulatory Vacuums: Federalism, Deregulation and Judicial Review," *University of California Davis Law Review* (Fall 1985): 113–52.

82. Martha Hamilton, "On Second Thought, We'd Prefer the Feds on Our Back," *Washington Post National Weekly*, 14 December 1987, p. 32.

83. Andy Pasztor, "EPA's Drive to Loosen Some Rules Angers Firms That Have Already Complied," *Wall Street Journal*, 23 September 1982, p. 35.

84. Green, "Gang That Couldn't Deregulate," p. 16.

85. Ann Cooper, "Reagan Has Tamed the Regulatory Beast But Not Permanently Broken Its Grip," *National Journal*, 1 December 1984, p. 2287.

86. "A Bipartisan Swing Back to More Regulation," *Business Week*, 30 May 1983, p. 74.

87. Michael Wines, "Scandals at EPA May Have Done In Reagan's Move to Ease Cancer Controls," *National Journal*, 16 June 1983, p. 1264.

88. Joann S. Lublin and Christopher Conte, "The Rule Slashers," *Wall Street Journal*, 14 December 1983, p. 1.

89. "James Watt's Last Gaffe?" *Newsweek*, 3 October 1983, p. 45.

90. *Congressional Quarterly Almanac*, 1981, p. 504.

91. Robert Litan, "Regulatory Policy in the Second Reagan Term," *Brookings Review*, Spring 1985, p. 23.

92. Rogene Buchholz, *Public Policy Issues for Management* (Englewoods Cliffs, N.J.: Prentice-Hall, 1988), pp. 22–23.

93. This paragraph is based on Ferguson and Rogers, *Right Turn*, pp. 135–37.

94. "NLRB Rulings That Are Inflaming Labor Relations," *Business Week*, 11 June 1984, p. 122. See also Terry Moe, "Interests, Institutions and Positive Theory: The Politics of the NLRB," *Studies in American Political Development*, vol. 2 (New Haven, Conn.: Yale University Press, 1987).

95. Seymour Martin Lipset, "Labor Unions in the Public Mind," in *Unions in Transition: Entering the Second Century*, ed. S. M. Lipset (San Francisco: Institute for Contemporary Studies Press, 1986), p. 289.

96. "Executives Want Reagan to Run Again," *Business Week*, 22 August 1983, p. 14.

97. Monroe W. Karmin, "Behind Business Leaders' Support of the President," *U.S. News and World Report*, 1 October 1984, p. 31.

98. Peter Holmes, "Mondale vs. Reagan," *Nation's Business*, October 1984, p. 21.

99. Maxwell Glen, "Democratic Candidates Got a Larger Share of the Corporate PAC Pie in 1984," *National Journal*, 19 January 1985, pp. 158, 159.

100. Ibid.

101. Ronald Grover, "Did Business PACs Play It Too Safe?" *Business Week*, 26 November 1984, p. 221.

102. Martin Shefter and Benjamin Ginsberg, "Institutionalizing the Reagan Regime," in *Do Elections Matter?* ed. Benjamin Ginsberg and Alan Stone (Armonk, N.Y.: M. E. Sharpe, 1986), p. 193.

103. Martin Shefter and Benjamin Ginsberg, "The Presidency and the Organization of Interests," in *The Presidency and the Political System,* ed. Michael Nelson, 2nd ed. (Washington, D.C.: Congressional Quarterly Press, 1988), p. 322.

104. William Schneider, "Whither the Yuppie Vote?" *Across the Board,* July–August 1984, pp. 10–11.

105. Fred Siegel, "Republicanizing the Democrats," *Dissent,* Summer 1985, p. 304.

106. Andrew Hacker, "The Decline of Higher Learning," *New York Review of Books,* 13 February 1986, p. 36.

107. Earl Cheit, "The Shaping of Business Management Thought," Business and Public Policy Working Paper no. BPP-33, Center for Research in Management, University of California, Berkeley, p. 19.

108. Judith H. Dobrzynski, "Business Celebrities," *Business Week,* 23 June 1986, pp. 101–2.

109. Ronald Brownstein, "Corporate Heroes," *National Journal,* 22 June 1985, p. 1493.

110. Norman Lear, "Our Babylon Is a Tower of Greed and Gratification," *Washington Post National Weekly Edition,* 20 April 1987, p. 23.

111. See, for example, Bernard Frieden, *The Environmental Protection Hustle* (Cambridge, Mass.: MIT Press, 1979.

112. Seymour Martin Lipset and William Schneider, *The Confidence Gap* (Baltimore: Johns Hopkins University Press, 1983), p. 426.

113. "Industry's Improving Image," *Washington Post National Weekly Edition,* 30 April 1984, p. 38.

114. Stephen Wildstrom, "A Risky Tack for Democrats," *Business Week,* 20 July 1987, p. 71.

115. Linda L. Fowler and Ronald G. Shaiko, "The Grass Roots Connection: Environmental Activists and Senate Roll Calls," *American Journal of Political Science* 31, no. 3 (August 1987): 504.

116. *Congressional Quarterly Almanac, 1986* (Washington, D.C.: Congressional Quarterly, 1987), p. 112.

117. *Congressional Quarterly Almanac, 1986,* p. 136.

118. "Reagan Vetoes Clean Water Bill," *Congressional Quarterly Weekly Report,* 31 January 1987, p. 214.

119. Laurie McGinley, "Federal Regulation Rises in Matters That Worry the Public," *Wall Street Journal,* 22 April 1987, p. 1.

120. Richard Marin, "A Cleaner Environment Is Still Part of the American Dream," *Washington Post Weekly Edition,* 22 September 1987, p. 37.

121. Cathy Trost, "Job Agency Is Firing Buckshot Again, and Industry Runs for Cover as Penalties Fly," *Wall Street Journal,* 22 April 1987, p. 70; and Bill McAllister, "Tough Tiger or the Same Old Pussy Cat?" *Washington Post National Weekly Edition,* 17 August 1987, p. 32.

122. Jeffrey H. Birnbaum and Alan S. Murray, *Showdown at Gucci Gulch* (New York: Random House, 1987), p. 287.

123. Samuel Bowles, David Gordon, and Thomas Weisskopf, "The Empire Strikes Back: An Econometric Analysis of Conservative Ascendency and Economic Impasse," Paper prepared for presentation at the annual meetings of the American Economic Association, Chicago, December 1987.

124. See, for example, Dick Russell, "Reagan's EPA: Working on Killer Resumes," *In These Times,* 27 January–2 February 1988, pp. 3, 10, regarding the EPA's systematic overhaul of its toxic-chemicals policy.

125. For a discussion of the critical leadership role these and other firms played in the 1970s, see Michael Unseem, *The Inner Circle* (New York: Oxford University Press, 1984).

126. Alan Murray, "Lobbyists for Business Are Deeply Divided, Reducing Their Clout," *Wall Street Journal,* 25 March 1987, p. 1.

127. William Guzzard, "Big Can Still Be Beautiful," *Fortune,* 25 April 1988, p. 64.

128. Carrie Gottlieb, "And You Thought You Had It Tough," *Fortune,* 25 April 1988, p. 83.

Chapter X

1. Edwin M. Epstein, *The Corporation in American Politics* (Englewood Cliffs, N.J.: Prentice-Hall, 1969), p. 174.

2. G. K. Wilson, "Business Political Strategies," Paper presented at the annual convention of the American Political Science Association, Washington, D.C., 1986, p. 12.

3. See Alfred Marcus and Mark S. Irion, "The Continued Viability of the Corporate Public Affairs Function," in *Business Strategy and Public Policy,* ed. Alfred Marcus, Allen Kaufman, and David Bean (New York: Quorum Books, 1987), pp. 267–82; and Seymour Lusterman, *Managing Federal Government Relations* (New York: Conference Board, 1988).

4. Arthur M. Schlesinger, "The Tide of American Politics," in *Paths to the Present* (New York: Macmillan, 1949), p. 97.

5. Samuel P. Huntington, *American Politics: The Promise of Disharmony* (Cambridge: Belknap Press of the Harvard University Press, 1981).

6. Arthur M. Schlesinger, Jr., "The Cycles of American Politics," in *The Cycles of American History* (Boston: Houghton-Mifflin, 1986), chap. 2, pp. 23–51.

7. David Vogel, "Why Businessmen Mistrust Their State: The Political Consciousness of American Corporate Executives," *British Journal of Political Science* 8, no. 1 (January 1978).

Index

CPSIA information can be obtained at www.ICGtesting.com
Printed in the USA
BVOW072132150112

280521BV00002B/32/A